U0139759

雅思写作高分突破

参考范文 + 解题规律

唐伟胜　编著

商务印书馆
The Commercial Press

图书在版编目（CIP）数据

雅思写作高分突破：参考范文＋解题规律 / 唐伟胜
编著.—北京：商务印书馆，2024
ISBN 978-7-100-22379-9

Ⅰ.①雅… Ⅱ.①唐… Ⅲ.① IELTS—写作—自学参
考资料 Ⅳ.①H319.36

中国国家版本馆CIP数据核字（2023）第075399号

雅思写作高分突破：参考范文＋解题规律
唐伟胜　编著

商 务 印 书 馆 出 版
（北京王府井大街 36 号 邮政编码 100710）
商 务 印 书 馆 发 行
北京新华印刷有限公司印刷
ISBN 978-7-100-22379-9

2024 年 1 月第 1 版　　　开本 710×1000 1/16
2024 年 1 月北京第 1 次印刷　印张 25¾

定价：88.00 元

前　言
写一本"真正有用"的雅思写作指导书

笔者从事雅思写作教学和研究超过 15 年了，一直以来都有一个心愿，那就是写出一本对考生真正有用的雅思写作书。

所谓"真正有用"，是既要提高考生的写作能力，又能提高考生的考试分数。当然，这个理念并不新颖，很多雅思写作书也都是这样宣传的。

然而，做到"真正有用"却非常不容易，现在流行的或不流行的雅思写作书，实现这个目标的，几乎没有，或者干脆可以说，一本都没有。

为什么？

因为，要做到"真正有用"，对写作者的要求太高了！写作者要满足以下几个基本条件，缺一不可：

1. 英文写作理论功底深厚；

2. 英文写作能力出类拔萃；

3. 雅思写作考试得过高分；

4. 全面理解雅思写作规律；

5. 完整掌握雅思写作素材；

6. 充分研究中国学生英文写作问题。

因此，一个完美的雅思写作书作者，首先应该来自英语专业，而且有丰富的教学经验。很多雅思写作书的作者并不是英语专业毕业生，只是凭着自己的摸索和理解，归纳总结了很多所谓的雅思写作规律，或者从其他写作书上把写作规则硬搬过来，乍一看好像是那么回事，但由于未接受过英语专业写作训练，他们往往狭隘地理解和应用这些写作规则，结果反而让读者无所适从。比如，很多雅思写作书都提出，使用高端词汇有利于提高学生的得分，但由于缺乏专业素养，这些书的作者并不知道，究竟什么样的词汇是高端词汇，更不知道如何恰当使用高端词汇，结果造成 I reckon 比 I think 更高端这样令人啼笑皆非的错误认识。

一本优秀的雅思写作书的作者还应全面把握雅思写作规律，这需要他持续跟踪雅思写作真题并对其展开研究。跟踪雅思写作真题，并不限于仅仅对雅思真题进行解析，还要亲自创作范文，只有在不断的创作中，他才能正确总结雅思写作开头、结构和结尾的写作规律，积累雅思写作有用的素材，并把自己的实际写作经验分享给读者。遗憾的是，现在多数雅思写作书的作者，自己并不创作雅思范文，而是坐在电脑前，借用别人的范文，高谈阔论地做空对空的分析。这样写出来的雅思写作指导书，其价值如何可想而知。

面对市面上形形色色的雅思写作书，笔者深感忧虑。雅思考试中，中国学生写作部分的平均分一直徘徊在 5.5 分左右，在全球居于非常靠后的位置，这些质量不高的写作书恐怕难辞其咎。出于这样的忧虑，笔者决心写出一部"真正有用"的雅思写作书，希望改变当前雅思写作图书的混乱局面。

从本科到硕士、博士，笔者一直攻读英语语言文学学位，毕业从事的工作也全部与英语教学相关。更重要的是，近 15 年来笔者潜心雅思写作教学和研究，教过的雅思写作学生数以万计，对学生雅思写作中的问题了如指掌；同时，笔者坚持雅思范文创作，至今已创作雅思范文近 500 篇，这些范文的阅读量超过百万人次，拥有几乎无人能比的雅思写作实践经验。从 2016 年起，笔者在《英语世界》杂志上连续发表雅思写作文章，至今超过 60 篇。基于这些实践和理论方面的资历，笔者有信心写出一部"真正有用"的雅思写作指导书。

一部"真正有用"的雅思写作书应做到内容适切，范文语言质量高，归纳总结全面透彻，讲解清楚，练习设计合理。按照雅思写作考试的任务要求，本书分上、下两篇，其中上篇专门解决 Task 2（即大作文），下篇专门解决 Task 1（即小作文）。对绝大多数考生而言，大作文更具难度，因此本书将重点放在上篇。

上篇共八章。第一章为"概述"，接下来的七章分别从审题、段落写作、词汇、句法、重点题材观点及表达、2010—2022 年雅思复现率最高的 20 篇作文解析及范文、习作评改实例等角度全面透视雅思写作大作文，解决雅思写作中"写什么""怎么写""怎么练"三大关键问题。

笔者认为，审题的重点在于找到题目中的关键词，作文需要紧贴关键词展开讨论。比如 2020 年 11 月 21 日的考题为：Some people think that all young people should be required to have full-time education until they are at least 18 years old. To what extent do you agree or disagree? 本题中有 young people、full-time education、at least 18 years old 三个关键词，需要贴近它们来构思写作观点。本题可以这样写：通常要求 15 岁以下学生在校接受全日制义务教育，将这一年龄延长到 18 岁，虽然有利于年轻人学习到更多知识，但也有很多问题，比如有些孩子家庭情况不允许他们继续上学，有些孩子则是对学校教育根本不感兴趣，因此，可以鼓励 15 岁以上的孩子继续学习，但不宜强制他们接受全日制教育。如果本题仅仅讨论教育的重要性，然后做出年轻人应该全天上学到 18 岁的结论，就没有很好地贴近"至少 18 岁"这个关键词的内涵。

　　虽然有很多固定的开头段写法，但笔者建议考生选择直入主题这一方式。主体段落写作中，最合适的方式是先提出主题句，然后用因果法、列举法、举例法、反证法、对比法等拓展段落内容，行文中需要注意句子与句子之间的连贯。

　　雅思高分写作究竟需要什么样的词汇？笔者认为，雅思写作高分词汇范围大约可以定位在大学英语四级词汇表里的中高段词汇，也就是 4000—5000 那些词汇。大家可以比较一下，就雅思阅读而言，词汇量以 10000 左右为宜，其中 5000—10000 之间的词汇，只要求考生知道其意义，并不要求考生了解其用法，因此不是雅思考试的写作词汇。比如 available、alternative、specific、involve、eventually 这类词汇就属于雅思写作高分词汇，而 tentacle、discrete、legion、populace、beneficiary、demographics、plausible、veneration、ramification、oust、indigenous（笔者在一篇雅思高分范文内发现的词汇）就超出了 5000 个词汇的范围，不宜在写作中使用。词汇是雅思写作的难点所在，本书提供了大量练习让考生掌握写作高分词汇。

　　就雅思写作句法而言，笔者认为，目标为 6 分段的同学不必在意句子的复杂度，仅需要努力写出语法正确的句子即可，但对于目标为 7 分段及以上的同学而言，则需要体现出句子类型的多样性和复杂度。这部分也是很多考生的难点，本书同样提供了大量句子转换练习，训练考生使用多个句型来表达相近的意思。

　　为使读者更好地通过本书备考雅思写作，笔者从 2010—2022 年的所有雅思考试真题中总结出 12 类重点题材，包括教育、社会、生活、政府、媒体、工作、环境与生态、科技、语言文化、旅游、交通、体育，并归纳各类题材下的话题（比如社会类题材下就有"犯罪""性别""城市化与全球化""人口、寿命与健康""幸福社会"等具体话题），按照话题提出核心观点及表达、列出核心词汇并提供精准的句子写作练习。只要读者耐心阅读本书，按照要求完成练习，上了考场就会发现一切尽在掌握，不会感到迷茫。

寻找合适的范文也是雅思备考的一大难点。本书从 2010—2022 年的雅思考试真题中统计出复现频率最高的 20 个题目，并亲自为这 20 个题目撰写解析、高质量范文、范文讲解及参考译文。仔细阅读这 20 篇范文将极大提升读者的雅思作文语感。

上篇的最后一章通过学生习作的评改，直观呈现为什么某篇作文的得分是 6 分，而通过什么样的修改可以将 6 分提升到 7 分，从另外一个角度告诉读者高分作文需要做到什么，同时需要规避哪些问题。

本书下篇解决雅思写作小作文问题，共三章，分别讲解图表题、地图题和流程图的写作，其中重点为图表题。笔者认为，雅思小作文的图表写作的核心在于读懂数据间的关系，抓获图表中有显著意义的数据，然后用恰当的文字加以表达。地图题的核心在于看出不同时段地图的变化情况并用适当的语言表达，而流程图则需要考生具有描写某个事物发展变化过程的语言表达能力。基于这个认识，本部分重点在于通过范文告诉读者如何从题目中提取掌握重要数据、地图变化情况和发展过程，另外还归纳总结了常用表达法。

最后，笔者还想利用这个机会强调本书的几大特色。第一，本书所有词汇、所有句子、所有段落均来自雅思写作真题原创范文，因此，相比于市面上同类书籍，本书具有最为真实的原创特色；第二，本书是迄今为止最为系统的雅思写作指导书，涉及雅思写作的构思、段落、词汇、句子、题材、范文、评改；第三，本书强调讲练结合，每一处讲解都配备了适量的练习，让读者实现举一反三的学习效果。

《雅思写作高分突破：参考范文 + 解题规律》付梓之际，笔者想对商务印书馆出版本书表示最衷心的感谢！商务印书馆是中国一流的学术著作出版机构，选择出版这本雅思写作书，本身就是对本书质量的认可。

愿所有读者能够在《雅思写作高分突破：参考范文 + 解题规律》中找到通向雅思写作高分的钥匙，勇敢筑梦，实现自己的人生梦想！

唐伟胜

2024 年 1 月

目　　录

下篇　雅思写作 Task 1

上 篇
雅思写作
Task 2

第一章　概述

　　在雅思考试的听、说、读、写四项中，写作可能是多数同学的梦魇。据雅思官方发布的最新统计数据，2021 年参加雅思考试的中国学生，写作平均分为 5.5 分，在全球所有国家中排名非常靠后。造成这个现象的原因很多，笔者认为最根本的原因是中国学生的英语输入严重不足。很多学生希望提升写作水平，但并不试图解决根本性的输入问题，而是寄希望于背写作模板和押题，很多英语老师（尤其是某些培训机构的老师）则顺势而为，迎合学生这种投机取巧的心态，前赴后继地开发各种雅思写作模板。这样，学生并没有真正学到写作思维逻辑，也没有学到如何用恰当的语言表达思想，而是利用宝贵的学习时间去背一堆模板，考试时不分场合地生搬硬套，根本无法形成连贯的思维与表达。

　　如果说用这种模板法对付国内英语考试尚有一定成功的可能（为什么有成功的可能，原因是多方面的，有试题因素，也有阅卷老师的因素），那么在雅思考试中，则几乎不可能取得成功。经过这么多年，雅思已经形成了一套完整的测试学生英语应用能力的体系，在全球英语测试界享有很高的认可度，几个所谓金牌写作老师开发的模板根本不可能打败它。

　　学术雅思写作分两项写作任务，分别为 Task 1 和 Task 2，写作时间共 1 小时。上篇先谈 Task 2，俗称"大作文"，一般要求在 40 分钟内完成，字数要求最低 250 词。大作文对雅思写作部分的得分有举足轻重的地位，相对于 Task 1 来说，也是更难对付的。

　　大作文的命题方式通常有三种：

　　第一，给出一个观点／现象，要求考生讨论该观点／现象的利弊；

　　第二，给出两个观点，要求考生讨论这两个观点的优劣；

　　第三，给出一种现象／问题，要求考生解释其原因，并提出解决办法／分析利弊。

作文涉及的题材非常广泛，比如教育、社会、工作、生活、环境、政府、媒体、体育、文化、旅游、交通等，无所不包，没有人能真正预测某一次考试的题材，更无法预测这次考试会考到什么具体问题。

那么，怎样的作文才算是一篇好的雅思作文呢？笔者认为，雅思作文也和其他作文一样，最重要的是写的文章要让人能读懂。这要求作文文字清晰，观点明确。只要能按照题目要求，用英语清晰地表达出自己的思想，雅思作文得分就不是问题。至于语言是否优美，思想是否高深，那不是雅思写作考试考查的重点。我们不妨先来看看雅思官方给出的作文评分标准。

① 对写作任务的反应：是否切题；

② 连贯性和结构层次：观点是否连贯且有逻辑性地呈现；

③ 词汇资源：用词能否准确表达自己的思想；

④ 句法多样性及准确性：句子能否准确表达思想。

再次提醒大家，在这个官方评分依据中，没有看到思维深度方面的要求。在第一条中，切题就可以了，也就是围绕题目要求组织内容。其实所有雅思题目，内容都可深可浅。笔者的建议是应避免写艰深的内容，因为多数考生的语言水平很难说清楚艰深的内容。如果说不清楚，思维深度不仅不能加分，反而会减分，这就是很多同学考完之后，很得意地认为自己写出了新意，结果对得分却大失所望的原因。第二条要求把想出来的几个分论点，按照一定逻辑顺序进行安排，一般由浅入深，由低到高，由物质到精神 / 情感，由个人到社会 / 群体等。第三条和第四条强调的是语言层面，写出的词汇和句子要正确表达思想。

这个官方标准仅仅给出了评价的角度，也就是说，考官阅读学生作文后，会从这四个角度打分，然后加起来除以 4，就是这篇作文的得分了。在每个角度上，考官的打分原则上可以在 0—9 分浮动。那么，考官凭借什么做出给分决定呢？事实上，没有任何考官能 100% 客观准确地说出其评分依据，他们依据的多半是读后的感受，或"读感"。笔者多年从事英语写作教学，改过的学生作文成千上万，基于经验，笔者尝试将"读感"分为如下类型，并配以不同分数，或许可以给各位读者提供一种有价值的参考。

雾里看花型：能围绕题目写点别人模模糊糊能看懂的东西 = 4 分。比如：Without a healthy body, other factors are needn't to consider.

Because it is impossible to every citizens have right to deprive others in this civil society.

In conclusion, depends on different situation, laws can be introduce to ban join in some machine work.

半梦半醒型：能围绕题目写别人勉强能看懂的东西，有些正确的句子，有些正确的单词，词能达意 = 5 分。比如：

Today, as the world population keeps boosting, unemployment is a severe and hard solving problem.

In my perspective, whether they should be arrested really depends on how serious the law that they broke are.

Instead, he can be educated in the police office and pay a fine, to warn him not do it anymore.

平平淡淡就是真型：有点想法，有点逻辑，多数能看懂，有点复杂句，有几个好词 = 6 分。比如：

We can draw a conclusion that the students may adapt to the society earlier if they go to work immediately. However, they are not skillful enough. It is a better choice to study in depth.

Therefore, although there are advantages for students to go to work, they had better study before working, unless they are going to study art subjects in the future.

明明白白我的心型：有些想法，相当清晰，有些好词，有些好句子，几乎没错 = 7 分。比如：

In recent years, whether the students who graduate from high school should go to college or go to job market becomes a heated topic among people. It is believed by some that college helps them prepare for future career while others think job market can increase their work experience.

Basically, law-breakers are sent to jail with the purpose of preventing them from being against the law and protecting interest of other citizens.

我的心思你最懂型：有思想，清晰，不少好词，不少好句子，没有错误 = 8 分。比如：

Undoubtedly, those who do not obey the laws should be put into prison so that they would no longer be able to harm other citizens. Once being put into jail, the law-breakers are almost isolated from the outside world and they would be watched all day long. In addition, since there are few things to do in the prison, the criminals can reflect what they have done wrong, change their attitude towards life or society and think about how they can help to offset the impact of their mistake in order to be forgiven.

"平平淡淡就是真"是目前很多考生的状态，要做到"明明白白我的心"，背模板就是南辕北辙。有些同学本来有 6 分的写作水平，但听到某些所谓雅思写作大师的高招后，一味使用大词和长句子，结果造成文理不通，让人无法理解，结果得分回到 5 分段。这样的大师，实在是很害人的。

那么，怎么样才能提高写作水平，或者提升雅思考试得分？笔者认为，提升写作水平，可分长远计划和短期计划。

所谓长远计划，就是注重语言输入，通过大量阅读和记忆，在脑海中积累大量的语言材料及各种说理方法和素材。其实，这才是提升写作的根本大法，但很多学生（甚至他们的家长）并不明白这个道理。笔者曾遇到这样一位家长。他的孩子刚读初中，计划大学去英国念书，需要雅思成绩。该家长马上把孩子送到一家著名的雅思培训机构"学雅思"。该机构用真题给孩子当教学材料。两个月下来，钱花了不少，孩子却对英语完全失去了信心。雅思真题材料的语言难度，远远超过了孩子当前的接受水平，因此每一堂课都等于是在消磨孩子对英语的兴趣。其实，对这样的学生，他还有三年时间才需要考雅思，他应该做的是"学英语"，而不是"学雅思"。世界上根本就没有所谓"雅思英语"。雅思英语也是英语，是某个级别的英语，要达到这个级别，必须一步步地来。每天读和听适合自己水平的英语，日积月累，慢慢进步，自然而然会达到雅思考试这个级别的水平，这就是最好的长远计划。只要输入足够，听、说、读、写这些基本语言技能水到渠成，就可从容应对雅思考试。

那么，什么是短期计划？这针对的是那些马上就需要雅思成绩的学生。英语水平就是这样了，考试前不可能实质性地提高，在这种情况下，如何提升写作得分？遇到这样的学生，笔者通常建议他们丢掉幻想，不要制订不切实际的计划。比如，只有 6 分的水平，就不要盼望得到 7 分，老师能做的，就是最大限度地帮学生得到 6 分，或者稍微超水平，最多得到 6.5 分。要做到这一点，其实并不容易，笔者认为可以从思维和语言应用两个方面给学生制定符合实际的短期备考策略。

首先，在**思维方面**，也就是写什么内容的方面，可把学生的高阶思维降到低阶思维。这里有一个基本前提：6 分的语言水平，就应该去写适应于 6 分的内容，这才是最佳的配合。乘 6 分的车，赶往 6 分的目的地，悠然自得，轻轻松松，何乐而不为？相反，如果只有 6 分水平，非要按照 7 分标准去写，结果一定是错误百出。那么，6 分的思维内容到底是什么？笔者的答案是：大致相当于小学五年级的思维水平。回想一下，小学五年级的思维水平是什么？不知道政治，不知道哲学，不知道人类，虽然可能略略知道要保护环境，要热爱父母，要喜欢动物，要做好人好事，但一定不知道保护环境是要让空气中的氧气多一些，树木会通过光合作用吸收二氧化碳并释放氧气，人类演化的原理是优胜劣汰、适者生存，等等。对于多数雅思考生来说，悲剧恰恰在于，考雅思的时候，思维已经很深了，但其英语语言水平还在小学五年级阶段，于是不和谐的一幕就出现了：用 10 岁的英语水平去表达 20 岁甚至 30 岁的思想，能说清楚、说流畅了才怪！因此，对于基础不够好的学生，老师无法短期提高其英语实力，但可以短期内"降低"学生的思维水平，这样学生就更容易写出能让人读懂的作文来了。比如，这里有两段文字，都是赞美老师的：

① 迎新晚会的歌舞仍在进行着，而我的思绪却似一叶小舟飘荡在深情的小河上，两岸一一闪过的是我小学、中学、大学老师的可敬可爱的面容……是的，人如舟，情似水。你投身于教育事业，满怀真情地辛勤耕耘，你就会被一种美好的情愫滋润着。于是，你的人生便总展现着斑斓的色彩……

② 期末考试，许老师领着我们很仔细地复习，又很耐心地解答我们各种各样的问题。期末考试，我考得很好，这都得感谢许老师！许老师让我感到教师职业是很伟大的。我将来也想当许老师那样的老师。许老师，您是我的榜样！

第一段相当于大学思维，第二段大约是小学五年级思维。如果用英语来翻译，相信学生翻译第一段时会出现很多错误，很多地方无法表达，如果非要用自己五年级的英文水平去表达，就会出现很多匪夷所思的结果，别人根本无法读懂。如果识时务，主动放弃第一段，去翻译第二段，学生会轻松自如，错误一定少很多，写出来的东西也一定清楚很多，明晰很多，得到的分数自然也会理想很多！

其次，**在语言使用方面**，要求学生把词汇控制在 3000 以内，务求正确，同时把句子长度控制在 15—20 个词内，力求把每个句子的语法和意义都交代清楚。总之，不求复杂，但求清楚。遗憾的是，雅思考生往往不会使用直截了当的表达方法，而是去选择很大的词汇或很长的句子，结果造成语义模糊不清，读者无法理解，得分惨不忍睹。请看以下学生的写作：

It is hard to deny that the transmission of specific information in diverse aspects should be strictly restricted due to the fact that such propagation may spread the privacy and lead to a consequence of economic downturn, and such a fact leads impressionable people to generate the idea that much information in specialized field like business should not be transferred freely. However, such a statement suffers from both logical and factual fallacies, and it should be examined meticulously. As far as globalisation, technology and feasibility are concerned, I strongly hold that messages that matter to the entire world should be shared as much as possible.

本段第一句长达 4 行，61 词，这在雅思作文中是不鼓励的，尤其是不鼓励语言驾驭能力还较弱的学生尝试写这样的句子。本句虽然很长，但表达的内容其实很简单。这种用虚张声势的语言来表达很简单的内容，在雅思写作中是不可取的。in diverse aspects 后面接的又是 economic downturn 这样具体的领域，显得很突兀，造成前后不连贯。propagation 是用词不当，雅思写作一般不用这样的词汇，矫揉造作，且很不准确，只能造成意义的模糊。spread the privacy？没有这样的搭配。impressionable people 是什么？这样用词只能拉低得分。

第二句：However, such a statement suffers from both logical and factual fallacies, and it should be examined meticulously. 本句纯属废话，因为本文后面既没有围绕 logical fallacy 也没有围绕 factual fallacy 来谈。fallacy 用词太大，meticulously 是用词错误。

第三句：As far as globalisation, technology and feasibility are concerned, I strongly hold that messages that matter to the entire world should be shared as much as possible. 本句中，matter 用法错误（后面不跟 to）。此句一出，文章后面应该谈 globalisation、technology、feasibility 三个方面，但后面又没有完全谈这三个方面。

总之，本段非常失败，语言矫揉，表达奇怪。看起来是很严肃地写，其实写出来的是很奇怪的东西。建议是，好好地写作，好好地说话，有什么就直接说，不要用模糊不清的语言绕圈子。笔者试修改如下：

Many people believe the important information in some fields should be restricted on the ground that the publicity of these information may result in serious consequences. While being generally supportive of this belief, I insist that people in scientific research, business, and academic world should share as much information as possible.

改文极大压缩了词汇幅度，精简了表达方式，使整个句子读起来清楚且轻松。这就是笔者希望学生在短期计划中达到的目标。

在确定长远计划和短期计划后，考生也就确定了雅思写作的备考策略和基本方法。现在考生需要对雅思考试写作的 Task 1 和 Task 2 做更深入的了解，首先是审题，然后是写段落、锤炼词汇和句子、了解各题材的基本解题思路等。因此，笔者强烈建议学生继续向下阅读。

第二章 雅思写作审题

在雅思官方给出的四条写作评分标准中，第一条是 Task response，大家把这个叫"任务反应"，其实就是我们常说的"审题"。你写的东西必须符合题目的要求，这当然是写作中首要的环节，否则，你再如何完美地满足了其他三条标准，即内容连贯、语法正确多样、词汇使用准确有幅度，也都是白搭。笔者这些年多次参加各种写作阅卷，包括高考、英语四级和六级、考研等，发现个别不会写作的考生不知从哪里学到了一个"绝招"，即在写作答题纸上将阅读题中的段落照抄下来。这样的段落内容绝对连贯、语法绝对正确多样、词汇使用绝对准确有幅度，但是与题目要求完全不相关。笔者见到这样的作文，肯定直接给 0 分；笔者甚至给相关部门建议，对这样做的考生，应该给予严重警告处分，因为这是赤裸裸的作弊行为，公然挑衅考试的公正度和诚信度，理应受到比 0 分更加严厉的惩罚。

为了准确地完成题目的任务要求，考生有必要搞清楚雅思题目的组成部分。雅思大作文题目中，首先必须有个"话题"（topic），即这个题目要求讨论的是什么，然后必须有一个或两个观点（viewpoint），即关于"话题"的立场和态度。"话题"和"观点"是所有作文题目都必须有的，但有些作文题目更复杂，除了基本的"话题"和"观点"外，可能还提供原因（reason）、结果（result）、手段（means）等。作文既可能要求考生比较对某个话题的不同观点，也可能要求考生讨论某个观点（或某个现象）的原因、结果或手段。这样，考生在审题的时候，必须识别出题目中的这些成分，并确定题目要求论证的重点是什么，之后才谈得上谋篇布局和语法词汇等具体问题。

笔者的经验表明，**在雅思写作大作文的 40 分钟里，审题应该占 3—5 分钟**。一定要先想好再开始写，否则，写到中间才来构思，那就基本意味着这次交的 2000 大洋考试费全部白费了！

那么，审题的这 3—5 分钟，考生应该做什么？笔者觉得，至少可以做以下三件事情：

① 搞清楚题目要求写什么；

② 选择自己的立场；

③ 确定作文采取什么结构。

首先是第一条：题目到底要求写什么？这个问题看似很简单，但其实有时候也不那么简单，可能在简单而熟悉的外表下暗含杀机，随时准备偷去你交纳的那 2000 大洋考试费！

考生需要牢记：题目中的每一个单词，每一个意思都是重要的，都需要加以讨论，漏掉其中任何一个关键点，都可能导致答偏，或者答题不完整，而只要出现答偏或答不完整，语言再好，都不会上 7 分了！有时候考生认为自己写得很顺，或者碰到了自己写过的类似作文，最后成绩却不理想，也许愤愤不平，但现在我们知道，问题可能出在审题那里！

2.1 查找题目中的关键词

为了正确理解题目要求，考生在拿到一个题目后，首先要找到关键词，对其进行分析，然后贴近关键词去组织观点进行讨论。

题目中的关键词通常以名词的面目出现，有时候是表示时间或地点的状语成分。关键词相当于限定了题目的讨论范围，如果无视关键词，那么讨论就很容易走偏。写作偏题，往往是没有找到或者没有正确理解题目中的关键词。以下以雅思考试真题为例进行说明。

例 1 It is difficult for people in cities to get enough physical exercise. What are the causes and what solutions could be taken to solve the problem? （220709）

第一步：找到关键词。本题中有 people in cities 和 physical exercise 两个关键词。

第二步：找到题目观点。城市居民身体锻炼不够，要求讨论原因及解决办法。

第三步：分析关键词。需要贴近"城市居民"（people in cities）的特点，比如工作忙、城市缺少锻炼身体的空间、城市人越来越多自己开车上班。这些都可能影响城市居民锻炼身体的热情。如果本题写人们越来越懒惰，因此不愿意从事体育锻炼，则没有贴近"城市居民"，因为越来越懒惰不能用来概括"城市居民"的特点。

例 2　It is suggested that everyone in the world should have a car, a TV and a fridge. Do you think the advantages outweigh the disadvantages?（220521）

第一步：找到关键词。本题中有 everyone in the world、car 和 TV and fridge 这些关键词。

第二步：找到题目观点。人人都该拥有汽车、电视和冰箱，要求分析利弊。

第三步：分析关键词。需要贴近"世界上每个人"（everyone in the world）。每个人都拥有汽车、电视和冰箱，会造成自然资源的枯竭，城市的拥挤和污染。如果本题仅仅讨论汽车、电视和冰箱可以给人们带来很多好处，因此值得人们拥有，就没有贴近"世界上每个人"这个关键词。

例 3　Some people think that all young people should be required to have full-time education until they are at least 18 years old. To what extent do you agree or disagree?（201121）

第一步：找到关键词。本题中有 young people、full-time education、at least 18 years old 三个关键词。

第二步：找到题目观点。应该要求年轻人全日制上学，至少上到 18 岁，你在何种程度上同意这个说法？

第三步：分析关键词。需要贴近"全日制上学"（full-time education）和"至少上到 18 岁"（until they are at least 18 years old）。通常要求 15 岁以下学生在校接受全日制义务教育，将这一年龄延长到 18 岁，虽然有利于年轻人学习到更多知识，但也有很多问题，比如有些孩子的家庭情况不允许他们继续上学，有些孩子则对学校教育根本不感兴趣，因此，可以鼓励 15 岁以上的孩子继续学习，但不宜强制他们接受全日制教育。如果本题仅仅讨论教育的重要性，然后做出年轻人应该全日制上学到 18 岁的结论，就没有很好地贴近"至少上到 18 岁"这个关键词的内涵。

2.2 审题中的几个陷阱

2.2.1 遗漏关键词

例 1 Nowadays both scientists and tourists can go to remote natural environments such as the South Pole. Do you think the advantages of this development outweigh the disadvantages? （150129）

本题关键词是 scientists and tourists 和 remote natural environments，其中 scientists and tourists 提及的是两类不同的人群，即科学家和游客，而 remote natural environments 涉及的是偏远自然环境，其特点是生态保护完好，但同时具有一定危险性。如果贴近关键词来写作，则不难写出这样的内容：游客去偏远自然环境虽然能欣赏到原始风景，但可能会破坏其生态，而且有风险，因此弊大于利，但科学家去这样的地方则是利大于弊，因为科学家都经过专门训练，知道如何保护生态和规避风险，更重要的是，科学家可以对偏远地区进行研究，从而丰富人类对世界的知识。

如果考生完全不考虑游客和科学家这两类人的差异，把他们处理成普遍意义上的 people，然后讨论"人们去偏远自然环境的好处和坏处"，这就属于审题不到位。

注意：当题目中出现 and 连接两个名词的时候，是否应该如本题一样分别进行讨论，取决于这两个名词的性质：如果两个名词有分别讨论的价值，则需要分别讨论；如果没有分别讨论的价值，则不需要分别讨论。以下几个题目中 and 连接的名词就不需要分别讨论。

（1）With the increasing demand for energy sources of <u>oil and gas</u>, people should look for sources of oil and gas in remote and untouched places. Do the advantages outweigh the disadvantages of damaging such areas? （220625）

本题中，oil and gas 都是能源，对于去偏远无人的地方寻找能源来说，oil 和 gas 并无区别，因此，不需要分别讨论。

（2）Some people claim that <u>public museums and art galleries</u> will not be needed because people can see historical objects and works of art by using a computer. Do you agree or disagree with this opinion? （190831）

public museums 和 art galleries 虽然不同，但本题讨论的话题为"是否因为电脑科技的存在就不再需要 public museums 和 art galleries"。就此而言，两者是没有区别的，也就是说，我们无法在两者间进行区分。如果需要，两者都需要；如果不需要，两者都不需要。因此，本题无须将两者分开讨论。

（3）Human activities have negative effects on <u>plant and animal species</u>. Some people think it is too late to do anything about this problem. Others believe effective measures can be taken to improve this situation. Discuss both views and give your opinion.（190601）

同样，本题也不需要区分 plant 和 animal，因为就人类活动造成的负面影响而言，plant 和 animal 没有区别。

例 2　An increasing number of developing countries are expanding tourist industries. Why is the case? Is it a positive or negative development?（210814）

本题关键词是 developing countries 和 tourist industries，要求讨论的问题是为什么发展中国家（developing countries）要大力发展旅游业。一般说来，发展旅游业的原因无非是增加收入，创造就业机会，此外，发展旅游业能促使改善环境，提高各种服务水平，也能让本地人的生活条件得到改善。当然，发展旅游业还有助于宣传国家或地区的独特文化，促进不同国家和地区之间的交流和沟通，消除各种误解。但是如果这样写，则仅仅回答了"为什么要发展旅游业"，而没有回答"为什么发展中国家要发展旅游业"。所谓发展中国家，就是经济、技术、教育、人民生活水平程度相对落后的国家。提高人民生活水平的终极路径肯定是提高教育水平和科技水平，但这绝非一朝一夕之功，相比而言，开发旅游资源，更容易给发展中国家带来可观的收入，创造就业机会，从而改善人民生活水平。这才是发展中国家（而不是发达国家）要大力推进旅游业的关键原因。因此，在写作本题的时候，应该先贴近发展中国家的特点，根据这些特点讨论发展中国家为什么要发展旅游业，这样才是充分切题的。

例 3　Education of young people is highly prioritized in many countries today. However, some believe that educating the adults who cannot read and write is also important, so more public money should be spent on this. To what extent do you agree or disagree?（210710）

本题关键词是 adults who cannot read and write 及 public money，需要讨论的问题是"政府是否应该花钱来提高那些不识字的成年人的教育水平"。我们当然可以认为，政府 100% 应该做这件事，因为成年人如果学会读书写字，他们找工作就会变得更加容易，此外，有了阅读能力，他们也可以更加深入理解自己和世界，从而更有可能成为对社会有用的人。从这个角度去论证并不难。但这么论证，回答的是"教育为什么重要"，而不是"政府是否应该给不识字的成年人投入"的问题，相当于遗漏了 adults who cannot read and write 以及 public money 这两个关键词。事实上，任何一项政府投入都会产生某些好处，但公共资金的投入不可能是无限的，某方面投入多了，就意味着必须要减少其他方面的投入。因此，对于这类政府投入的话题，我们应该思考政府投入的成本（cost）和收益（return）的问题。

　　因此，可以这样构思：政府投入教成年人学会读写，这有很多好处（比如帮助他们更容易找工作等），但随着学习者年龄的增加，这项投入产生的效应会越来越小（经济学上叫作"边际效用递减"）；对此，我的建议是，政府应该给 50 岁以下的人投入，而对 50 岁以上的人群，政府宜采用鼓励他们自学的方式，而不宜过多投入，因为这样的投入产生的效益非常小，不值得投入过多的 public money。

例 4　During holidays and weekends, young people spend less time on outdoor activities in natural environment, such as hiking and mountain climbing. Why? What can be done to encourage them to go out?（210417）

　　本题的两个关键词是 young people 和 outdoor activities in natural environment，需要讨论的问题是"为什么年轻人不愿在自然环境中从事户外活动"。如果笼统说人们太忙，没时间从事户外活动，或者在自然环境中从事户外活动有风险，就很难说是切题的，因为这样的答案没有贴近关键词 young people。换句话说，本题的问题不是"人们为什么不从事户外活动"，而是"年轻人为什么不从事户外活动"。如果贴近 young people 和 natural environment，就能想到如下内容：现在电子产品提供的娱乐方式实在太多，很多年轻人被吸引，宁愿有空就上网打游戏、看电影或者和朋友聊天；年轻人，尤其是中学生，学习任务很重，很难找出 3—4 个（或更多）小时去徒步行走或爬山；现在能提供户外活动的地方太少了，总是很拥挤，而且没有任何娱乐和运动设施，年轻人不喜欢拥挤，而且觉得单调，因此会完全放弃户外活动。

例 5　Students in some countries leave school without good understanding of how to manage their money. What do you think are the reasons? What are the solutions to this problem?（210116）

本题的关键词是 students、school 和 manage their money，需要讨论的问题是"为什么学生毕业时不懂理财"。如果笼统说学生没有理财意识，就漏掉了关键词 school。如果考虑到这个关键词，就能找到如下理由：学校没有教这些课程；学生在校期间由父母支持，因此他们觉得没有必要学习如何管理财务；学校生活相对简单，学生没有机会来实践财务管理。这三个理由均与学生在学校的经历有关，从而扣住了题目关键词。

2.2.2 遗漏重要观点

例 1 The restoration of old buildings in major cities in the world costs numerous governments' expenditure. This money should be used in new housing and road development. To what extent do you agree or disagree?（180203）

有的同学一看到这个题目非常高兴，因为以前写过类似于"该不该重修老建筑"的题目，于是大笔一挥，开始讨论应该重修老建筑的三大理由，比如可作为旅游景点给城市带来收入，重修老建筑可以让城市变得更为美丽，重修老建筑可以让人们记住城市的历史，然后总结表明自己支持重修老建筑的观点。这样写，高分基本没戏了，因为完全忽略了题目中另一个重要观点：This money should be used in new housing and road development. 如果完全不涉及这个观点，丢分在所难免，非常可惜。所以说，考试的时候不要得意忘形，碰到熟悉的题目也要认真斟酌。就本题而言，讨论完应该重修老建筑的观点后，可以在结论段增加以下内容：当然，如果一个城市的居民居住条件还很紧张，交通状况还很糟糕，重修老建筑的工作应该暂缓进行，首先将有限的政府资金用于解决人们的基本生活问题。这样就对题目中所有观点进行了回应，作文就完整了。

例 2 Some people believe there are intelligent life forms existing on other planets and it is better to send messages to them, but others think it is a bad idea because it is very dangerous to do this. Discuss both views and give your opinion.（161013）

很多同学看到这个题目心里又是一喜，这不是写过的题目吗？当即写下完全赞同应该和外星人联系！理由如下：首先，可以学习外星人的科技来改善我们自己的生活；其次，外星人可以和地球人做伴，从而我们不会孤独；最后，当地球毁灭的时候，外星人还可拯救我们。由此得出结论：我们必须和外星人联系。这样写就是典型的"作死"节奏，因为根本没有回应题目的另外一个观点：it is a bad idea because it is very dangerous to do this！就本题而言，讨论完应该和外星人联系之后，需要（简要）讨论为什么和外星人联系并不危险。比如，比我们文明的外星人不会危害我们，不如我们文明的外星人又威胁不到我们，或者即使有危险，我们也可以控制这种危险，又或者这种危险与收获的益处相比根本算不上什么，因此值得去冒险。不管用哪种方式，都需要对题目中的观点给予回应。

2.2.3 遗漏隐含的观点

例 1 Music has always been and continues to be <u>the universal language of mankind</u>. To what extent do you agree or disagree?（210313）

本题关键词为 music 和 the universal language of mankind，要求对"音乐是人类共同语言"这个说法进行评论。如果仅仅从正面展开论述，则忽略了该题目隐含的对立观点，即"音乐有时候并不是人类共同语言"。值得一提的是，虽然雅思考试中不是都需要讨论题目隐含的对立观点（当题目没有给对立观点留下讨论空间时就不需要讨论），但在多数情况下，都需要对其进行讨论，这样讨论后得出的结论才是有说服力的。就本题而言，如果考虑隐含的对立观点，可以按如下思路写。的确，全世界的音乐都具有相同的基本元素，很多时候能被所有人理解，如贝多芬的《第五交响曲》（Beethoven's *Fifth Symphony*），全世界任何角落的听众都喜爱，并受到它的激励。尽管如此，在很多情况下，对音乐的理解还是取决于听众所处的文化语境，比如中国人喜欢的音乐在很大程度上就与欧洲人喜欢的音乐不同。此外，即使是面对同一音乐作品，不同国家的人的理解也不一样，比如面对任何一个国家的国歌，本国人和外国人的感受会完全不同。由此可知，虽然音乐的基本元素是普遍的，而且很多音乐也为全球所共享，但很多情况下，因文化不同，听众对音乐的感受很不一样。因此，"音乐是人类的共同语言"这个说法并不完全准确。这样的审题和构思，充分考虑了题目中给出的正面观点和隐含的反面观点，结论就显得更让人信服。

例 2 The spread of multinational companies and the resulting increase in globalisation produce positive effects to everyone. Do you agree or disagree with this statement?（210109）

本题关键词有 multinational companies、globalisation、everyone，要求对"全球化对所有人都产生积极影响"这个说法进行评论。很显然，如果本题仅从正面进行讨论，就忽略了题目中隐含的对立观点，即"全球化对某些人产生了消极影响"。考虑到这个对立观点，可以这样构思：首先讨论全球化带来的积极影响，比如用户能够享受到更好的产品和服务，刺激本地企业增强竞争力，增进不同文化的相互了解；然后讨论全球化带来的问题，比如剥夺本地工作机会，耗费更多能源，消灭本体文化；最后的结论是，虽然全球化有利有弊，但其弊端可以被克服，而其带来的益处更大，因此赞同全球化。

例 3 Whether or not a person achieves his aims in life is mostly a question of luck?（201031）

本题关键词为 achieves his aims in life、luck，问题是"实现生活目标是否主要取决于运气好要坏"。这个题目在审题上似乎不会构成任何困难，因为其隐含的对立观点显而易见：实现生活目标，主要不是靠运气，而是靠努力。但恰恰因为这个隐含观点太过明显，很多同学反而忽略了题目观点也具有一定合理性，即有些情况下，成功的确是需要一些运气的。如果考虑双方观点，可以这样构思：首先讨论生活中运气的确扮演重要角色，然后讨论成功主要依靠努力，最后得出结论，虽然运气有助于我们成功，但成功主要来自努力工作，而且运气也常光顾那些努力工作的人。

2.3 两类常见题型

2.3.1 因果关系类

我们来看下面一组雅思考试真题：

（1）Some people think that technology makes life complex, so we should make our life simpler without using the technology. To what extent do you agree or disagree?（170208）

（2）Most of the world's problems are caused by over-population. To what extent do you agree or disagree?（190511）

（3）The increasing use of technology in the workplace has made it easier for young people to find jobs and harder for older people to do so. To what extent do you agree or disagree?（190504）

（4）Art classes like painting and drawing are important to students' development and should be made compulsory in high school. To what extent do you agree or disagree? （170107）

（5）Some people believe that children can learn effectively by watching TV and they should be encouraged to watch TV at home and school. To what extent do you agree or disagree? （170318）

（6）Some people think everyone should be a vegetarian, because they do not have to eat meat to stay healthy. To what extent do you agree or disagree? （150919）

（7）The use of mobile phone in certain places is just as antisocial as smoking. Do you think mobile phone should be banned like smoking? （150214）

仔细阅读这些题目，我们会发现它们有一个共同特点，那就是这些题目中都蕴含了因果关系，详细分析请看下表。

题号	因	果
（1）	技术让我们的生活变得复杂	我们应该抛弃科技，让生活更简单
（2）	人口过多	引发世界上多数问题
（3）	工作场所新技术使用越来越多	年轻人更容易找工作，年纪大的更难找工作
（4）	艺术课程对学生发展很重要	艺术课程应该在高中成为必修课
（5）	孩子可以通过电视有效学习	应该鼓励孩子在家和学校多看电视
（6）	人不需要吃肉就可以保持健康	每个人都应该成为素食主义者
（7）	有时候用手机和抽烟一样对他人有害	手机应该和香烟一样被禁止

可以看到，这些题目中的因果关系，有些是很清楚地表达出来，比如题（1）使用 so 这个连接词直接表明前后的因果关系，题（6）使用 because 来提示原因；有些题目的因果关系则是间接隐含的，比如题目（3）使用 "... has made it..." 这个句型来表达前后的因果关系，题目（4）和（5）则是通过 and 来暗含前后的因果关系。但无论哪种方式，我们在阅读题目的时候，都需要看出题目中的因果关系。

面对这种因果关系的题目时，我们不外乎有以下四种思维方式：

第一，承认原因的合理性，也承认结果的合理性；

第二，承认原因的合理性，但否认结果，论证原因不一定导致结果；

第三，否认原因，承认结果，论证导致这个结果的另有其他原因；

第四，否认原因，否认结果。

拿到这类因果关系的题目时，考生容易出现两种倾向：一是不讨论因果之间的关系，仅片面论证原因或者结果，导致审题不完整；二是不加分析地承认原因和结果，使作文缺乏批判性。正确做法是：先分析原因，再分析这个原因与结果之间是否存在必然的因果关系，是否还存在其他（或许更重要的）原因。笔者在雅思教学和写作实践中发现，面对因果关系类题目，一般的做法都是先承认原因，然后批判论证这个原因与结果之间的逻辑关系。当然，这只是一般情况，各位"烤鸭"应该根据题目具体情况具体分析。结合以上分析，笔者尝试给出以上七个题目的审题思路，供大家参考。

（1）技术让我们的生活变得复杂，因此我们应该抛弃科技，让生活更简单。

思路：承认技术有时候让生活变得复杂，比如我们得记住很多密码，最严重的是很多时候只能依赖技术，而一旦技术停止工作，我们的生活就会陷入困境。但这并不意味着抛弃科技生活就会更简单，因为新技术在给我们带来困惑的同时，也为我们提供了很多便利。结论是，我们应该拥抱新科技，同时也努力不成为科技的奴隶。

（2）人口过多引发世界上多数问题。

思路：承认人口过多给世界带来了很多问题，比如环境和社会问题。但是，人口过多并不是世界多数问题的根源，因为当今人口爆炸并没有降低人们的生活水平，而且人口过多问题正在得到改善。结论是，我们应该关注人口过多带来的问题，但不宜过分夸大其影响。

（3）工作场所新技术使用越来越多，因此，年轻人更容易找工作，而年纪大的更难找工作。

思路：承认工作场所新技术使用越来越多，并在很多情况下有利于年轻求职者。但是这不意味着新技术对年纪大的求职者不利，因为一方面年纪大的求职者也可以学习新技术，另一方面新技术并不是求职的最重要因素，年纪大的求职者的经验和忠诚度往往让他们在求职中更有优势。结论是，新技术的广泛使用让年轻人在求职中占据一定优势，但这并不意味着年纪大的求职者找工作更难。

（4）艺术课程对学生发展很重要，因此艺术课程应该在高中成为必修课。

思路：承认艺术课程对学生知识、情感、美学的发展很重要。但是，艺术课程成为必修课值得商榷，因为每个学生的实际兴趣和未来发展规划不同，应该由学生自己选择。结论是，艺术课程的确很重要，但是否投入很多时间去学习，选择权应该留给学生自己。

（5）孩子可以通过电视有效学习，因此应该鼓励孩子在家和学校多看电视。

思路：承认孩子可以通过电视有效学习。但是这并不意味着要鼓励孩子尽量多看电视，因为看电视过多影响孩子的身体健康，更重要的是，通过看电视学习有局限性，孩子们无法通过电视学习合作精神和领导才能。结论是，看电视有利于孩子学习，但学习方式应该多样化，不宜过多鼓励孩子看电视。

（6）人不需要吃肉就可以保持健康，因此每个人都应该成为素食主义者。

思路：不承认人类健康不需要吃肉，论证人类需要肉类食品来维持身体需要，因此不能要求每个人都成为素食主义者。即使人类不需肉类食品就可保持健康，也不能要求所有人都避免食肉，因为这是个人自由选择问题。结论是，只要不破坏动物多样性，人类有理由食肉，要求每个人都成为素食主义者是不合理的。

（7）有时候用手机和抽烟一样对他人有害，因此手机应该和香烟一样被禁止。

思路：承认有时候用手机和抽烟一样对周围的人有害，抽烟让周围的人被动吸烟，影响他们的身体；用手机产生辐射，制造噪音，同样影响别人健康。但这并不意味着手机和香烟一样该被禁止，手机除了给周围的人带去轻微的伤害外，还有很多重要的功能，而香烟除了伤害还是伤害。结论是，手机不应该被禁止，但手机使用者应该尽量避免给他人带来不利影响。

下面是一篇范文，读者可以结合实例看看这种因果关系类的题目一般是怎样来写的。

【题目】

Some people believe that children can learn effectively by watching TV and they should be encouraged to watch TV at home and school. To what extent do you agree or disagree?（170318）

【范文】

Children sitting in front of TV and enjoying their favourite programmes is certainly an attractive scenario, yet TV is an even more attractive tool for the education of children. ［引出话题］

Travel channels take children to many different places around the globe, thus opening their eyes to the vast outside world. History programmes give children a sense of the past by telling them about historical events and figures. And, if children watch such programmes as "animal world", they may cultivate an awareness of the environment around them and then they may understand the importance of maintaining good relationships with animals. ［孩子们可以通过电视学到什么］

Furthermore, TV often presents knowledge in far more vivid ways than books and teachers, which makes learning from TV very enjoyable and efficient. ［通过电视学习效率高，有趣味］

However, it does not follow that children should be encouraged to watch TV as much as they want at home and in school. ［质疑题目中的结果部分，提出不应该鼓励孩子看那么多电视］ In the first place, watching too much TV is harmful to the eyes of the children. As a matter of fact, many children become short-sighted at an early age simply because they spend too much time staring at the TV screen. ［原因 1：看太多电视对孩子的视力有害］ Then, watching too much TV means that children have to sacrifice their time for reading and other creative activities. As many experts suggest, though children can learn a great deal from watching TV, yet their imagination and language skills can be better developed by reading. ［原因 2：看电视学习不利于培养孩子想象力和语言能力］ Even worse, if children sit in front of TV for too long, they will have little time for other children, which may put their interpersonal skills at stake. ［原因 3：看太多电视不利于孩子培养人际交往能力］

To conclude, when we consider the positive role TV plays in children's development, we need to take into account its possible consequences. We should allow children to watch TV because it is a good way for them to learn about the world, but we should also set a limit on their TV-watching time so that our children can find time for other activities that may help improve their personalities, imagination and interpersonal skills. [结论：应该控制孩子看电视的时间，使孩子们有时间培养其他能力]

2.3.2 手段-目的类

我们来看下面一组雅思考试真题：

（1）Some people think the best way to improve road safety is to increase the minimum legal age for driving cars and motorcycles. To what extent do you agree or disagree?（150212）

（2）Some people who have been in prison become good citizens later. Many think that they are the best people to talk to school students about the danger of committing a crime. Do you agree or disagree?（150808）

（3）The best way to teach children to cooperate is through team sports at school. To what extent do you agree or disagree?（151114）

（4）The best way for the government to solve the traffic congestion is to provide free public transport 24 hours a day, 7 days a week. To what extent do you agree or disagree?（140109，170121）

（5）Some people believe that the best way to produce a happier society is to ensure that there are only small differences between the richest and the poorest members. To what extent do you agree or disagree?（140201）

（6）Increasing the price of cars and petrol is one of the best ways to solve growing traffic and pollution problems. To what extent do you agree or disagree?（180310）

（7）Some people think that the best way to reduce time spent in travelling to work is to replace parks and gardens close to the city centre with apartment buildings for commuters, but others disagree. Discuss both views and give your opinion.（190406）

仔细阅读这些真题，我们会发现题目中都蕴含了"手段-目的"的逻辑关系，通常表述为"做……的最好办法是……，你是否同意"。详细分析请看下表。

题号	目的	（最佳）手段
（1）	改善道路安全	提高机动车最小驾驶年龄
（2）	让学生知道犯罪的危害性	请改造好的前犯人现身说法
（3）	教会孩子合作精神	让孩子在学校参加团体型体育运动
（4）	解决交通阻塞问题	政府免费提供全天候公交服务
（5）	创建幸福社会	最大限度消除贫富差距
（6）	解决交通和污染问题	提高汽车和燃油的价格
（7）	减少上下班所花费的时间	将城市中心附近的花园改建为公寓大楼

　　面对这种蕴含"手段–目的"关系的题目时，我们要尽量避免一边倒的思维方式，也就是不宜绝对认可手段与目的之间的逻辑关联，也不宜绝对否认。通常的做法是：

　　第一步，承认某个手段对实现特定目的会起到积极作用；

　　第二步，分析这个手段可能引发的副作用；

　　第三步，提出其他更好的手段。

　　当然，这只是一般情况，各位"烤鸭"应该根据题目具体情况具体分析。结合以上分析，现尝试给出上面七题的审题思路，供大家参考。

　　（1）为了改善道路安全，最好办法是提高机动车最小驾驶年龄。

　　思路：承认提高机动车最小驾驶年龄有助于改善道路安全，因为年龄越大，通常越具有责任心，而且也越有经验来正确处理驾驶中遇到的某些紧急情况。然而，提高机动车最小驾驶年龄，意味着以往有资格开车的人不能再开车，这会大大降低这些人的工作效率乃至生活幸福感。牺牲很多人的工作效率和幸福感来换取道路安全的一点点改善，似乎得不偿失。改善道路安全的更有效做法是通过教育或加大惩罚力度，从根本上提高大家的道路安全意识。

　　（2）为了让学生知道犯罪的危害性，最好办法是请改造好的前犯人现身说法。

　　思路：承认请改造好的前犯人现身说法可以帮助学生了解犯罪的危害，因为前犯人有直接经验，因此可能比老师或书本讲得更生动，更吸引学生。但是，"前犯人"这个身份可能让学生在心理上与之保持距离，从而大大降低教育的效果。让学生了解犯罪危害性的更有效办法也许是让他们观看合适的影视作品，既生动，同时又不至于让学生产生心理距离。

（3）为了教会孩子合作精神，最好办法是让孩子在学校参加团体型体育运动。

思路：承认参加团体型体育运动可以帮助培养孩子的合作精神，因为团体型体育运动（比如篮球、足球等）往往需要队员们共同努力才能取胜。然而，只有部分同学对体育运动感兴趣，而且很多体育运动（比如羽毛球、乒乓球等）更强调个人表现，并不能培养孩子的合作精神。培养孩子们的合作精神，应该通过其学习和生活中的点点滴滴，而不仅仅是通过参加团体型体育运动。

（4）为了解决交通堵塞问题，最好办法是政府免费提供全天候公交服务。

思路：承认免费提供全天候公交服务有助于解决交通堵塞问题，因为有了免费公交，比如公交汽车、地铁等，开私家车出行的人会大大减少。然而，有了免费公交服务，很多原本不计划出门的人也会出门，从而引起公共交通的拥挤，甚至瘫痪；另外，政府免费提供公交服务会给政府预算带来巨大压力，迫使政府减少在其他领域（比如教育、医疗）的投资，从而影响城市居民的整体生活质量。解决交通堵塞问题，政府应该大力倡导绿色出行，同时修建更多设计合理的道路。

（5）为了创建幸福社会，最好办法是最大限度消除贫富差距。

思路：承认贫富差距太大会影响社会的整体幸福感，因为贫富差距很可能导致社会不公正，并引发诸如犯罪等社会问题。然而，贫富差距是任何社会都不可避免的，贫富差距的存在往往也是社会发展的动力所在，如果最大限度消除贫富差距，社会发展速度有可能大大减缓。创建幸福社会的关键在于倡导人人平等，保障公平公正，不管他是否有钱。政府应致力于给所有人，尤其是贫困家庭的孩子提供上升通道。

（6）为了解决交通和污染问题，最好办法是提高汽车和燃油的价格。

思路：承认提高汽车和燃油价格有助于解决交通和污染问题，因为汽车和燃油价格的提升将降低私家车的使用，这样交通和污染问题都有望得到缓解。然而，提高汽车和燃油价格可能引发其他诸多问题，比如汽车销量下滑会导致国家经济受损；燃油价格高了，其他很多行业（尤其是制造业）的成本都会增加，导致很多产品价格上升，最终影响人们的日常生活。此外，提高汽车和燃油的价格，可以让中产阶级及以下人群减少开车，却无法阻止那些富有阶层的人开车，因此这个措施最终会扩大阶层之间的差异。为了解决交通和污染问题，政府应该倡导绿色出行，并大力投资道路建设。

（7）为了减少上下班所花费的时间，最好办法是将城市中心附近的花园改建为公寓大楼。

思路： 将城市中心的花园改建为公寓大楼，上下班的人就不用再花很多时间在路上了，因为住在工作单位附近，人们可以步行上下班。然而，如果城市中心被公寓大楼挤满，必将变得拥挤不堪；而且，如果城市中心没有花园，那么，一方面城市中心的空气将变得很糟糕，另一方面人们下班后将不再有地方可以休闲，他们不得不花很多时间到城市中心外寻找休闲的地方，这在很大程度上抵消了在城市中心建公寓而为他们节约的时间。为了减少上下班所花费的时间，政府应该改善交通状况，各公司可以修改上下班时间，错开交通高峰，甚至可以让员工在家工作（互联网时代，在家工作已经完全可以实现）。

下面是一篇范文，读者可以结合实例看看这种"手段–目的"类的题目一般是怎样来写的。

【题目】

Some people think that the best way to reduce time spent in travelling to work is to replace parks and gardens close to the city centre with apartment buildings for commuters, but others disagree. Discuss both views and give your opinion.（190406）

【范文】

With the expansion of cities, people have to spend more and more time travelling to and from work.［引出话题］As one solution to this problem, it is suggested that apartment buildings should be planted near the city centre in place of parks and gardens.［重述拟讨论的观点］

This idea, if well carried out, can be rather effective in reducing the commuting time for many workers.［段落主题句，承认题目中方法的有效性］Living in the apartment buildings close to work can help save a lot of time because the commuters do not have to travel that much. They can even walk to their offices.［分析原因］This is actually a beautiful dream for many who have been troubled by the heavy traffic in big cities on their way to and from work.［相当于换种方式做段落总结］

On second thoughts, however, the dream may not be that beautiful at all. 〔段落主题句，对上一段观点转折，承接上文的 dream 一词，使文章显得连贯〕We can hardly imagine what the city centre would look like when millions of people moved into the numerous apartment buildings there. 〔用虚拟语气结构，从总体上提出假设：人们都搬到城市中心公寓里是不可想象的〕It would become a great deal more crowded and polluted than before. 〔具体解释前句总体性假设的论据之一：拥挤和污染〕To make it worse, when they need to find a park or garden so that they can take a little rest, people would have to spend a few hours travelling out of town. 〔具体解释前句总体性假设的论据之二：人们得外出才能找到可以休息的公园〕Working and living in such a busy and noisy environment, people would not be able to find the pleasure that is so important for their work and life, and the benefits they have gained from the shortened travelling time would be undone to a large extent. 〔段落小结：住在这样的城市中心没有快乐，同时节约上下班时间的目的也大打折扣〕

In fact, in order to reduce the commuting time, there are better measures than having more apartment buildings in the city centre. 〔段落主题句：提出新方法〕One such measure is to take advantage of the advanced telecommunication technologies which enable people to work from home. 〔在家办公〕This will save them from travelling a long way to work and at the same time maintain their positive feeling towards life and work. 〔提出在家办公的好处〕

2.4 审题中的辩证思维

总体来说，雅思写作有三种命题方式：

第一，给出一个观点，要求考生讨论是否同意（或在何种程度上同意）这个观点。比如：If a country is already rich, any additional economic wealth does not make its citizens happier. To what extent do you agree or disagree? （210918）

第二，给出两个观点，要求考生讨论同意哪个观点（或哪个观点更合理）。比如：Some people think that it is more beneficial to take part in sports which are played in teams, like football. But other people think that taking part in individual sports is better, like swimming. Discuss both views and give your own opinion.（211009）

第三，给出一种现象，或提出一个问题，要求考生讨论产生这种现象 / 问题的原因，并给出问题的解决办法（或分析现象的利弊）。比如：Nowadays, some parents put a lot of pressure on their children to succeed. Why? Is this a positive or negative development for the children?（211030）

在这三种命题方式中，无论是 to what extent do you agree or disagree、discuss both views and give your own opinion，还是 is this a positive or negative development，都要求考生在对题目观点 / 现象（以下为论述方便，统称为"观点"）进行分析的基础上，明确提出自己的观点。因此，在雅思写作四项评分标准中的 Task response 这里，考官评分的依据应该是两条：其一，是否对题目观点进行了分析；其二，是否有自己明确的观点（即，是否明确回答了题目的问题）。在 6 分段或以下的作文中，考生要么没有对题目观点进行恰当分析，要么没有在分析基础上明确回答题目问题。如果希望在写作中得到 7 分甚至更高分数，考生必须掌握题目观点分析方法以及明确提出自己观点的方法，两者缺一不可。

分析题目观点的原则是完整性和说服力。完整性指充分考虑题目中的问题，选准关键词，贴近关键词进行讨论，不能遗漏关键词和题目中的主要观点，甚至还要考虑题目隐含的观点，相关内容已经在前面充分讨论，本节主要谈说服力这个问题。那么，怎样才能让作文具有说服力？笔者认为，只有充分考虑题目观点中的各个方面，我们得出的结论才会显得有说服力；反之，如果仅讨论题目观点中的某一面，而不顾及其他方面，那么无论观点多么明确，都会给人一种强词夺理的感觉，也就是缺乏说服力，从而影响在 Task response 这个评分标准上的得分。这种多方面考虑题目观点的方式称为"辩证思维"。为实现"辩证思维"，笔者提出分层讨论、双边讨论和分类讨论三种具体写作策略。

2.4.1 分层讨论策略

分层讨论策略尤其适用于"一边倒"作文结构中。

所谓一边倒，就是完全同意题目中所给的观点（或者同意两个观点中的某一个而反对另一个）。举例来说，"父母是否应该给孩子很多压力"这个题目中，考生可以选择一边倒的论述结构，如"父母完全不应该给孩子很多压力"，接下来就此展开论证。再比如，"高中生是否应该免费去做社区服务工作"这个题目，考生可以一边倒地论述"高中生应该免费去参加社区服务工作"。再比如，"在家吃饭还是在餐馆吃饭更好"，考生可以一边倒地选择论证"在家吃饭更好"。值得注意的是，雅思考试中，需要谨慎采取一边倒论述结构，因为绝大多数考题给出的观点中都隐含了"既合理又不合理"的成分，因此需要考生做更细致的思考。**只有在那些没有给考生留下多少反向思考余地的题目中，才适合使用一边倒的结构。如果题目中直接提出的或隐含的对立观点也明显有道理，则不适合用一边倒的结构。**笔者收集了《剑桥雅思官方真题集》（后文简称《剑桥雅思》）第 4 至 16 册中的所有 7 分以上作文范文共 22 篇，发现用一边倒结构的仅有 3 篇。

确定使用一边倒结构后，如何让作文显得更加辩证？笔者提出"三层次"策略，即从物质（physical）、心理（psychological）和社会（societal）三个层次全面论证观点，从而让自己的讨论显得更加全面，也更加有逻辑性，从而增加说服力。具体来说：

物质层次指的是与身体、时间、空间、金钱／成本等相关的层次，这是一种比较浅显的层次。比如看电视，从物质层次上讲，坏处就是浪费时间、电费（金钱），还可能伤害眼睛（身体），但它的好处就是让我们了解各种信息，等等。

心理层次指的是与心理、情感、精神等相关的层次，这是一种涉及感情和思想的层次，比物质层次要深入一些。比如看电视，从心理层次上讲，坏处就是让我们养成被动接受信息不再自主思考的习惯，好处就是能陪伴我们度过空虚的时光，等等。

社会层次指的是与环境、社会、文化、道德等相关的层次，这个层次相当于脱离了与个人的关联，而进入到更宏大的社会之中，因此比心理层次显得更高。比如看电视，从社会层次上讲，坏处可能包括暴力节目引发犯罪、虚假广告可能误导消费者等，好处就是电视生产和消费有利于促进国家的经济发展，等等。

以下用真题为例说明三层次策略。

例 1 In some countries, more people choose to live by themselves in recent years. Why is the case? Is it a positive or negative development for society? （161109）

本题问的是"独居现象是好还是坏"。如果选择一边倒论证"独居现象不好"，则可以从以下三个层次来进行。首先，**从物质层次**，独居可以给我们自由的空间和时间，我们想干吗就干吗，比如不扫地，不洗碗，房间乱糟糟都不用担心，但这种自由的代价是可能养成一些不好的生活习惯；其次，**从心理层次**，独居能让我们心里很放松，但是如果长期一个人住，就可能失去社交的能力；最后，**从社会层次**，独自居住虽然减少了人与人之间的冲突，但也给社会资源增加了负担和压力。从这三个层次展开，可以较好地确保作文的逻辑性和说服力。

例 2　The government should control the amount of violence in films and on television in order to decrease the level of violent crime in society. To what extent do you agree or disagree?（180520）

本题涉及"政府应该控制影视中的暴力呈现"，比较适合选择一边倒地同意这个观点。我们可以提出以下三个层次的理由：首先，**从物质层次看**，影视中的暴力可能让人模仿伤害其他人的方式；其次，**从心理层次上**，影视中暴力太多，容易让人觉得这个世界不安全，于是用极端的方式来保护自己；最后，**从社会层次看**，影视中的暴力经常被呈现为英雄行为，这会让很多观众认为暴力是合理合法的。这三个层次可以有效地帮助我们论证"控制影视中的暴力呈现可以降低社会中的犯罪率"这个观点。

例 3　It is a good thing for those in the senior management position to have much higher salaries than other workers in the same company or organisation. To what extent do you agree or disagree?（161029）

本题的问题是"高管的工资应该比普通员工高很多"，可以用一边倒的方式来回答，即完全同意题目的这个观点。首先，公司企业高管承担的责任更大，要管理的事务更多，与只需做好本职工作的普通员工相比，高管需要投入更多时间和精力，这无疑是他们应该得到更高收入的第一条原因，即**物质原因**。其次，高管要对公司企业的业绩负责，在激烈的市场竞争中确保公司企业的良性运作，他们要承担的心理压力要大得多，这当然就是他们理应获得更高收入的第二条原因，即**心理原因**。最后，千军易得，一将难求，普通员工容易找到，而优秀的高管却是稀缺人才，按照供求关系决定价格的基本理论，这就是高管收入理应大大高于普通员工的第三条原因，即**社会原因**。

三层次分析法不仅可用于一边倒作文中，还可用于更为辩证的双边讨论作文中，体现"题目观点在这个层次合理，但在另外一个层次不合理"的思路。

比如：

例4 An increasing number of people are choosing cosmetic surgery in order to improve their appearance. Why? Is it a positive or negative development?（200927）

本题的问题是"整容是好还是坏"。很明显，整容有好有坏，因此不适合用一边倒结构来写。但整容好在哪里，坏在哪里？我们可以用三层次分析法来讨论这个问题。**从物质层次看**，整容能让人变得好看，更好地被他人接纳，从而带来各种工作机会；**从心理层次看**，整容帮助人们提升自信心和自尊心，从而带来更大的生活幸福感。但是，**从社会层次看**，整容不一定是件好事。如果整容成为风尚，那么人们将不再关注内心和性格的发展。而且，整容往往需要花很多钱，因此整容主要是让有钱人获益，结果导致社会不公平。

本书提出的三层次分析法可以帮助同学们迅速想出要写的内容，在"一寸光阴一寸金"的考场，能节约很多时间。在具体操作过程中，笔者认为应注意以下几点：

① 一般的顺序是由低到高层次写作，这样可以确保内容的逻辑性。也就是说，先写物质层次，然后写心理层次，最后写社会层次。

② 不同话题，可能需要考虑不同层次的详略。比如，某些话题可能在物质层次上多写，在社会层次略写；其他话题可能考虑社会层次更多，物质层次一带而过。在表达自己的观点时，可能在某个层次上同意题目中的观点，而在另外一个层次上反对题目中的观点。这些都需要在谋篇布局阶段考虑清楚。

③ 究竟写到哪个层次，或者在哪个层次多用力，取决于英语水平高低。如果你对自己的英语水平比较自信，那就尽量考虑写完三个层次，而且在社会层次上不露怯；但如果你的英语水平还不够好，那就尽量在物质层次上多找几个点写下去，然后适当写点心理层次的内容，社会层次就不要去写，否则错误多，得分低。具体建议是：争取5分的同学，只写物质层次，内容简单，语言错误也有望减少很多；争取6分的同学，主要写物质层次，适当简写心理层次；争取7分或以上的同学，物质层次一笔带过，以心理层次和社会层次为主。

④ 很多学生一拿到题目，首先想到的就是心理和社会层次的内容，反而忘记了物质层次的内容，结果很难有逻辑地写下去。笔者建议，拿到任何题目，

首先想物质层次。即使你想在心理和社会层次上用力，也需要先简要论述物质层次，然后以此为跳板，过渡到另外两个层次上，这样的写作才会显得自然，有望获得高分。

分层讨论作文一例

【题目】

It is a good thing for those in the senior management position to have much higher salaries than other workers in the same company or organisation. To what extent do you agree or disagree?（161029）

【解析】

公司或机构的高级管理人员的收入是否应该比一般工人或工作人员高很多？可能多数人的答案是肯定的。那么，到底哪些因素决定高管收入要大大超过普通员工呢？很多同学对这个问题没有什么头绪，甚至想不出什么内容来，更不要说讲出一些有逻辑、有条理的道理来。但是，如果我们用分层讨论策略，本题则可迎刃而解。

首先，公司企业高管承担的责任更大，要管理的事务更多，与只需做好本职工作的普通员工相比，需要投入更多时间和精力，这无疑是高管应该得到更高收入的第一条原因，即物质原因。其次，高管要对公司企业的业绩负责，在激烈的市场竞争中确保公司企业的良性运作，他们要承担的心理压力要大得多，这当然是他们理应获得更高收入的第二条原因，即心理原因。最后，千军易得，一将难求，普通员工容易找到，而优秀的高管却是稀缺人才，按照供求关系决定价格的基本理论，这是高管收入理应大大高于普通员工的第三条原因，即社会原因。当然，并非所有时候、所有高管的收入都应大大高于普通员工，比如一位工作不投入、管理没水平、业绩不突出的高管当然不配高收入；另外，当经济下行，社会对普通技术工人的需求甚至高于对高管的需求时，高管的收入也不会比普通员工高很多。

【范文】

Those who hold a senior management position are paid much higher than other workers and technicians in the same company or organisation.［引出现象］I believe this is reasonable because the top executives usually work longer hours and under greater pressure, and more importantly, they are harder to find in the job market. [提出自己的整体观点]

Compared with other workers or technicians whose main task it is to perform their own responsibilities, a top manager has to fully grasp the market dynamics before making suitable business plans and then coordinates various resources available to him/her to achieve the targets and objectives. This means the top executive has to work with people of all levels in the company such as HR, financial officers, technology people, technicians, and so on, and not surprisingly, he/she has to work many extra hours. [讨论第一个理由：高管工作时间长]

Besides longer work hours, the high-level manager has to work under tremendous load of stress because he/she is probably the only one to be responsible for the survival, development and profitability of the company. If he or she fails in managing a company, his/her whole professional career may be at stake. We have had numerous examples of top managers who can no longer find a job after their failure in the previous positions. [讨论第二个理由：高管工作压力大]

Just because the top management positions are highly demanding, people suitable for these positions are hard to come by. As a matter of fact, there are always more excellent technicians than managers in the job market, which is an important reason why top managers can often earn much higher salaries than technicians. [讨论第三个理由：高管人才难求]

Of course, there are always managers out there who are paid highly yet should not be. They are not efficient or effective, nor cooperative enough to lead their team. At the same time, we can also always find the most excellent technicians or workers who receive the same salaries as their managers. This most likely happens when the economy is suffering from recession, where the demand for the technicians is even higher than the managers. [讨论高管不应获得高收入的特殊情况]

2.4.2 双边讨论策略

三层次写作策略非常有用，但并不是所有题目均适合使用这个策略，尤其是那些用一边倒结构不具说服力的题目。在题目中两个观点（或一个观点的正反面）明显都具有一定合理性的情况下，为了 Task response 部分得到理想分数，我们可以采用双边讨论策略，即对双方观点的优势 / 理由分别进行讨论，最后提出自己的观点。双边讨论的写作结构如下：

首先，同意观点 A 的理由（1—2 条）；

其次，同意观点 B 的理由（1—2 条）；

最后，自己的观点。

采用这种结构的好处是对题目中的双方观点都进行了讨论，难度在于最后必须给出自己的观点，因为我们不能在讨论双方观点的合理性后，简单粗暴地得出"双方都合理"的结论。那么，在双边讨论后，如何鲜明表明自己的立场呢？笔者提出三种方法。

方法一：讨论双方后，指出其中某一方更合理，更值得支持。

例 1 Some students take one year off between finishing school and going to university in order to travel or to work. Do you think advantages outweigh disadvantages?（200806）

本题提出：一些学生高中毕业后，不立刻去大学学习，而是用一年时间去旅游或工作，对此进行利弊讨论。很明显，这种"间隔年"（gap year）的做法有好处，但也有坏处，考生需要分别讨论好处和坏处，最后给出自己的结论。比如，间隔年的好处是学生能开阔视野，了解自己的真实兴趣，以后回来上大学就会更有动力，坏处则是年龄增大一岁，可能间隔年后不再想回来上大学了。双边讨论完毕之后，可以这样提出自己的观点：虽然间隔年有一定风险，但还是应该得到鼓励，因为年轻人应该扩大视野，了解自己，以便未来有更好的学习动力。这种写法相当于肯定了间隔年的合理性，从而显示了考生自己的立场和选择。

方法二：讨论双方后，指出其中一方会带来明显问题，因此应该支持另一方。

例 1 Some people think that it is good for a country's culture to show imported film and TV programmes. Other people think that a country should develop their own film and TV programmes instead. Discuss both views and give your own opinion.（201017）

本题要求考生讨论的问题是：应该引进国外影视，还是发展自己的影视？很显然，这两者不是非此即彼的关系，都有合理性，因此适合双边讨论。可以首先讨论引进国外影视作品的理由：有利于我们了解国外的风土人情，开阔眼界，促进本国文化兼收并蓄，一些创新的节目形式也可以启发本国影视，从而开发出更好的本国节目来。然后讨论发展本国影视节目的好处：在物质层次上，影视业可以创造经济价值，提供就业机会；在精神和社会层次上，只有本国影视才能更好地反映本国文化，从而娱乐和教育本国观众，同时帮助本国文化在全球推广。双边讨论后，可以这样给出自己的观点：虽然外国影视节目可以为我们所借鉴，但其中暗含的文化价值观可能影响我们，尤其是青少年，从而造成本国文化的扭曲，甚至丢失，因此我们更应该重视发展本国影视。这种写法相当于通过指出一方的消极面来否定它，从而肯定另一方，也显示出考生的明确立场。

　　方法三：讨论双方后，指出双方合理性依据的不同情况或条件。

　　例 1　It is more important for school children to learn about their local history than the world history. Do you agree or disagree?（220604）

　　本题问：学校的孩子学习本地历史比学世界历史更重要吗？很明显，我们很难一边倒地在本地历史和世界历史之间进行选择，因此，本题适合双边讨论。我们可以先讨论孩子学习本地历史的重要性，然后讨论孩子学习世界历史的重要性，最后得出自己的结论：本地历史更重要还是世界历史更重要，这是很难判断的，应当取决于孩子的未来规划；如果孩子的未来规划着眼于解决本土问题，那么学习本地历史就比世界历史更为重要，但有世界历史的知识会是很好的帮助。这种写法相当于指出本地历史更为重要的条件，从而显示了考生自己的观点。

　　例 2　Team/group activities can teach more important skills for life than those activities which are played alone. To what extent do you agree or disagree?（211009）

　　本题问：集体活动比单人活动能教会更多生活技能，你在何种程度上同意或反对这个观点？很明显，无论集体活动，还是单人活动，都能教会我们一些技能，因此，本题适合用双边讨论。可以先讨论集体活动教会我们的技能（比如合作、领导能力），然后讨论单人活动教会我们的技能（如独立解决问题、独立承担责任的能力），最后得出结论：两类活动能分别教会我们一些不同的能力，但我们无法确定哪些能力更重要，因此无法确定是集体活动还是单人活动更重要。

双边讨论作文一例

【题目】

Some people think that the Olympic Games is an exciting event and can bring nations together. Others, however, think that it is a waste of money. Discuss both views and give your own opinion. (220716)

【解析】

本题提出的两个观点是：有人认为奥运会可以团结世界各国各民族，但也有人认为奥运会就是浪费金钱。显然，这两个观点都是有一定道理的，因此适合双边讨论。可以首先讨论奥运会团结世界人民的功能，然后讨论举办奥运会的确非常耗钱，最后得出结论：奥运会虽然很烧钱，但奥运会的价值非常巨大，因此值得花这些钱（还可以顺便提一句，举办奥运会不是为了展示主办国实力，因此需要尽量节约）。这样的解题思路为：讨论双边观点后，选择支持一方。

【范文】

As the most prestigious and most influential sports meet in the world, the Olympic Games has sparked a lot of controversies in recent years. [引出话题]

On the one hand, the Olympic Games is considered by many as an opportunity for all nations across the world to get together and achieve a better understanding of each other. [段落观点] This is indeed true. In the Olympic Games, which usually lasts about 20 days, the sportsmen from all countries, regardless of race and nationality, not only compete on the same stage, but also communicate and make friends with each other. [说理] That is why the Olympic Games has been so popular with people, especially young people, who love to see all sportsmen coming together and competing in a friendly manner. [结果]

On the other hand, we often hear a different voice complaining that the Olympic Games is way too costly. [段落观点] It is exactly the case. According to a report issued by the Olympic Organization Committee, the 2016 Olympic Games held in Brazil cost as much as 200 billion RMB (roughly $ 40 billion), which is equivalent to the annual income of a medium-sized country. [举例论证] As a matter of fact, it is precisely because of the immense cost that many countries have to give up the opportunity to host this event. [结果]

In my view, the Olympic Games is well worth the money spent on it. [自己的观点] No other sports events can be so influential as the Games. The grand party thrown every four years is a golden chance for all people to get to know each other better. It is, therefore, the responsibility of all countries to support, and if possible, to host this event. [说理论证] That said, I would be quick to add that, far from an opportunity to flaunt the economic strength of the host country, the Olympic Games should not waste a dollar more than is necessary. [让步论证，使自己的观点显得更为温和全面]

2.4.3 分类讨论策略

当面对用一边倒结构明显不具说服力的题目时，除了使用双边讨论策略外，还可以采用分类讨论策略。当题目中的关键词含义比较笼统，很难进行整体讨论时，我们可以对题目关键词进行分类，也就是分几种情况就题目中的观点进行讨论，然后指出题目观点在哪些情况下合理，在哪些情况下不合理。这种辩证思维方式能更加全面地讨论题目中隐含的观点，因此容易得到考官的青睐。我们来看几个例子。

例 1 Some people believe that nowadays we have too many choices. To what extent do you agree or disagree with this statement? （《剑桥雅思 13》，Test 2）

这个题目要求考生讨论在何种程度上同意"现在我们的选择太多了"这个观点。稍微想一想就能发现，在生活中的很多方面，我们的确面临太多选择（比如电视频道），而在其他方面（比如工作、好书等），我们的选择并不多，甚至不够。如果用一边倒的结构来写这个题目，无论是同意题目观点，还是不同意题目观点，都显得片面而难以让人信服。因此，可以采用分类讨论策略：在某些方面，我们的选择太多，甚至让我们困扰；在另外一些方面，给我们的选择远远不够。这样，作文的思路就显得全面、合理得多了。

例 2 Some people think that climate change could have a negative effect on business. Other people think that climate change could create more business opportunities. Discuss both views and give your own opinion. （200111）

这个题目问：气候变化对企业来说是消极影响还是机遇？很显然，气候变化对不同企业的影响是不同的。因此，本题可以用分类法进行双边讨论，即气候变化会给某些企业带来不利，同时会给另外一些企业创造商机，最后得出结论：作为企业而言，面对气候变化，应该迅速反应，这样才能获得发展的机会。

例 3　In modern world, it is no longer necessary to use animals for food or use animal products, for instance, clothing and medicines. To what extent do you agree or disagree?（160312）

本题需要讨论：现在我们是不是不需要食用动物，或者不需要使用动物产品了？动物保护者当然会同意，理由很简单。当今的科技已经可以制造食品来替代动物食品，人类也不再需要用动物的皮毛制品来保暖。同时，杀死动物可能破坏环境平衡，从而使人类自身遭殃。但是，如果完全拒绝动物食品，人类的营养又会成问题。因此，这个题目不适合一边倒。不妨这样解题：将动物分成野生动物和家养动物，对于野生动物，我们不能过度猎杀以保护环境平衡，但将家养动物作为食品或者药品则是可以的，这样才能保证人类有充足营养。这里使用的解题技巧就是将题目中的关键词 animal 分成不同类别，然后分别进行讨论。

例 4　Some people think young people are not suitable for important positions in the government, while other people think it is a good idea for young people to take on these positions. Discuss both views and give your own opinion.（181121）

本题问：年轻人是否适合担任政府重要职务？关键词是 young people 和 important positions in the government。贴近关键词进行分析，我们认为年轻人的特点是精力充沛，善于创新。很显然，这些特点适合政府中某些领域的职位，比如教育、商业、安全领域等，但不适合另外一些更依赖工作经验的职位，比如外交等。因此，可以这样解题：将政府职位分为两类，一类是基于创新的，一类是基于经验的；年轻人适合基于创新的政府职位，而年纪大的人更适合基于经验的政府职位。如此解题，就避免了一边倒思路造成的尴尬，使论证更有说服力。

例 5　Some people think that children nowadays have too much freedom. To what extent do you agree or disagree?（200118）

本题与本节第一个例题有异曲同工之妙：例 1 中的观点是我们现在的选择太多了，而本题的观点是孩子们现在的自由太多了。与例 1 一样，本题也可以分类讨论：**就有些自由而言（比如自由使用电脑等）**，现在给孩子的自由的确太多，会影响孩子的学习和性格发展，**但就另外一些自由而言（比如自由思考、自由做负责任的决定），就不存在过多的问题，而是越多越好**。因此，本题的基本写作思路依然是分类讨论，即对题目中的关键词进行分类，然后分别进行讨论，最后得出自己的观点。

分类讨论作文一例

【题目】

People living in the 21st century have a better life quality than the people who lived in the previous centuries. To what extent do you agree or disagree?（220312）

【解析】

本题问：生活在 21 世纪的人们，其生活质量是不是比之前提高了？本题关键词为 the 21st century 和 life quality。很多同学会毫不迟疑地写道：我 100% 同意，生活在当今世纪，生活质量比以往世纪要高。然后列出诸多理由，比如：现在有飞机、高铁，想去哪里旅游就去哪里旅游；有电脑、网络，信息获取和发送就在指尖；有高级的医疗技术和医疗条件，身体越来越健康；有全球化，可以享受世界各地的食物和产品，生活越来越丰富……

事实上，即使你列出 100 条 21 世纪的好处，也无法合理地直接导出绝对的结论：今天的生活质量比以前好。因为，很明显，21 世纪的确在某些方面提高了我们的生活，但在其他方面，我们的生活质量其实下降了。比如：21 世纪生活节奏加快了，我们生活在更大的竞争压力之下，其结果是，即使物质生活质量提高了，但付出的代价是心理健康和幸福感下降；21 世纪城市化进程在全球的深化，让我们享受城市里的各种便利，但由此带来的城市拥挤、环境污染问题也让我们苦不堪言。

因此，面对本题考生需要考虑其中的隐藏观点，使用分类讨论策略，并得出结论：和生活在以往世纪的人们相比，生活在 21 世纪，我们的确在物质生活的方方面面都得到了极大提高，但与此同时，我们也得承受心理压力加大、环境日渐恶化的代价。因此，现在我们的生活质量是不是提高了，答案因人而异。

【范文】

Many claim that people living in this century are most fortunate because they enjoy a better life than those living in any previous ages. [重述题目观点] To my mind, this is only partly true. [给出自己的观点]

It is certainly right to say that our material life quality today is much higher than those living in preceding centuries. [段落观点] With the development of cheap flights and fast train, we can now travel to any places in the world in one single day, and with computing technologies and the Internet so readily available, all the information we need and friends we want to contact are just a click away from us. [举例论证] Besides, we are now enjoying a much longer life than ever before, due to the advanced medicine and medical services. [再举一例]

Yet this is not to say that all these benefits have come without a price. [段落观点] As the pace of modern life becomes increasingly quick, many people find themselves living under greater pressure. [代价之一：压力大] Unlike their predecessors in old times who lived in the same places and did the same jobs all through their lives, they keep shifting from one job to another, or moving from one city to another so that they are living with the perpetual anxiety to learn new things, thus greatly affecting their psychological well-being. [比较论证现在压力大及所致后果]

One more price contemporary people have to pay is the environment. [代价之二：环境问题] The 21st century has witnessed the deepening of urbanisation throughout the world, which has brought people benefits such as the convenient supermarkets, the improved education and transport, but also urban problems unheard of in previous centuries, such as crowds, filthiness, noises, and above all, the deteriorating environment. [说理论证]

To conclude, living today is indeed a lucky thing, yet it is quite an overstatement to say that we enjoy a 100% better life quality than those living before this century. [结论]

2.5 审题练习

找出并分析以下题目中的关键词，结合题目给出的问题，确定作文的写作思路。

（1）Many people believe that scientific research should be carried out and controlled by the governments rather than private companies. To what extent do you agree or disagree with this opinion?（210821）

找出关键词：

分析关键词：

写作思路：

（2）When you learn a foreign language, all four skills (listening, reading, speaking, writing) are equally important. To what extent do you agree or disagree?（210123）

找出关键词：

分析关键词：

写作思路：

（3）The government should control the amount of violence in films and on television in order to decrease the level of violent crime in society. To what extent do you agree or disagree?（170520）

找出关键词：

分析关键词：

写作思路：

（4）Some people believe that unpaid community service should be a compulsory part of high school programmes (for example working for a charity, improving the neighbourhood or teaching sports to younger children). To what extent do you agree or disagree?（《剑桥雅思 9》，Test 2）

找出关键词：

分析关键词：

写作思路：

（5）Some people think that it is government's responsibility to transport children to school, while others think parents should get their children to school.

Discuss both views and give your own opinion.（211127）

  找出关键词：

  分析关键词：

  写作思路：

  （6）Some people think visual images (like photograph or video) can tell information more accurately in a news story, while others think they are not reliable sources. Discuss both views and give your opinion.（220806）

  找出关键词：

  分析关键词：

  写作思路：

  （7）More and more people move from the countryside to big cities. Does this development bring more advantages or disadvantages to the environment? （220723）

  找出关键词：

  分析关键词：

  写作思路：

  （8）The world of work is changing rapidly and people cannot depend on the same jobs or same conditions of work for life. Discuss the possible causes for this rapid change and give your suggestions on how people should prepare for work in the future.（191102）

  找出关键词：

  分析关键词：

  写作思路：

  （9）In many countries today, women as well as men work full-time, so it is logical for women and men to share household tasks equally. To what extent do you agree or disagree?（180915）

  找出关键词：

分析关键词：

写作思路：

（10）Some people think that technology makes life complex, so we should make our life simpler without using the technology. To what extent do you agree or disagree?（170218）

找出关键词：

分析关键词：

写作思路：

第三章 雅思段落写作

英语作文段落的基本要求是：每段有且仅有一个主题，段落所有句子都要为这个主题服务，段落的句子之间要有连贯性。雅思作文的段落也不例外，只有同时满足这三个条件，才算得上好的段落。本章拟从雅思作文的段落结构、段落发展方法、句子连贯手段等几个方面详细讲解。

3.1 段落结构

从结构上讲，雅思作文通常由 4—6 段构成，包括：开头段、主体段（2—4段）和结尾段。

3.1.1 开头段

雅思作文开头段一般 30—60 词，2—3 句话，包括 3 项任务：引出现象/问题，重述题目的观点，给出自己的观点。部分同学喜欢花很多笔墨去写背景（比如"随着社会和经济的发展"这类背景），这是完全没有必要的，因为这类大背景往往与作文要讨论的话题并无直接关联。笔者建议，无论遇到什么题目，都应直入主题，即直接写现象/问题，然后重述题目观点，最后给出自己的观点。

例 1 Some experts believe that it is better for children to begin learning a foreign language at primary school rather than secondary school. Do the advantages of this outweigh the disadvantages? （《剑桥雅思 9》，Test 1）

下面是该书给出的高分范文开头段：

Traditionally, children have begun studying foreign languages at secondary school, but introducing them earlier is recommended by some educationalists. This policy has been adopted by some educational authorities or individual schools, with both positive and negative outcomes.

本段共 37 词，分为 2 句。第一句重述题目中的观点：有些专家让孩子从小学开始学习外语。第二句提出自己的观点：这样做产生的结果有好也有坏。第二句表明，本文即将采取双边讨论策略，即分析从小学开始学外语的好处和坏处。

例 2 Some people believe that unpaid community service should be a compulsory part of high school programmes (for example working for a charity, improving the neighbourhood or teaching sports to younger children). To what extent do you agree or disagree? (《剑桥雅思 9》, Test 2)

下面是该书给出的高分范文开头段：

It has been suggested that high school students should be involved in unpaid community services as a compulsory part of high school programmes. Most of the colleges are already providing opportunities to give work experience, however these are not compulsory. In my opinion, sending students to work in community services is a good idea as it can provide them with many sorts of valuable skills.

本段共 65 词，分为 3 句。第一句重述题目观点，第二句指出现象，第三句给出自己的观点。第三句表明，本文即将采取一边倒策略，即讨论孩子从事免费社会服务工作到底能给他们带来哪些技能。

重述题目内容时，建议考生不要照搬原文，而是要对原文进行改写。改写的方法通常有：同义词替换、主动句和被动句转换、改变主语（因此改变句型）、适当提供细节。来看几个例子。

例 1

题目句：Some people believe that unpaid community service should be a compulsory part of high school programmes... (《剑桥雅思 9》, Test 2)

改写句：<u>It has been suggested</u> that <u>high school students should be involved in</u> unpaid community services as a compulsory part of high school programmes...

这里的改写有：

（1）将题目中的主动句 "some people believe that..." 改成了被动句 "it has been suggested that..."。

（2）将题目从句中的主语 unpaid community service 改成了 high school students，由此导致后面的谓语动词及句型调整。

例2

题目句：Countries are becoming more and more similar because people are able to buy the same products anywhere in the world.（《剑桥雅思10》，Test 3）

改写句：It is said that countries are becoming similar to each other because of the global spread of the same products, which are now available for purchase almost anywhere.

这里的改写有：

（1）套加了"it is said that..."句型。

（2）将题目 because 引导的从句变成了 because of + 名词 + which 引导的非限定性定语从句。

例3

题目句：In some countries young people are encouraged to work or travel for a year between finishing high school and starting university studies.（200806）

改写句：It is quite common these days for young people in many countries to have a break from studying after graduating from high school. The trend is not restricted to rich students who have the money to travel, but is also evident among poorer students who choose to work and become economically independent for a period of time.

这里的改写有：

（1）套加了"it is quite common for... to do..."句型。

（2）提供了 young people 的两种类型：rich students and poor students，指出两类学生都在做 have a break from studying 的事情。

例4

题目句：In some countries, there has been an increase in the number of parents who educate their children themselves at home instead of sending them to school.（160213）

改写句：Contrary to the conventional practice of sending their kids to school, more and more parents today choose to educate their children themselves at home.

这里的改写有：

（1）将题目中的 instead of sending them to school 改为 contrary to the conventional practice of sending their kids to school。

（2）将题目中的 there be（存在）句型 "there has been an increase in the number of parents who educate their children themselves..."，改为主动句型 more and more parents choose to educate their children themselves at home。

例5

题目句：More and more people are using mobile phones and computers to communicate. Therefore, they are losing the ability to communicate with each other face to face. To what extent do you agree or disagree?（161126）

改写句：We live in a world where communication through modern technologies such as the smartphone and computer is so prevalent that it's hard to go anywhere without seeing someone texting, emailing, writing blogs, and tweeting.

这里的改写有：

（1）将题目中 "more and more people are using mobile phones and computers..." 这一句型置换为 "we live in a world where communication through modern technologies such as the smartphone and computer is so prevalent..."。

（2）将题目中 to communicate 细节化为 "someone texting, emailing, writing blogs, and tweeting"。

3.1.2 主体段

雅思作文主体段通常分 2—4 段，共 200 词左右。每段 4—7 句，有且仅有一个主题。一般包含 4 项任务：

首先，写出段落主题句，揭示本段主题（1 句）；

其次，对主题句做进一步解释（1—2 句）；

再次，对主题句进行论证（2—3 句）；

最后，对段落进行小结（1 句，可选）。

例1　Some people say that the best way to improve public health is by increasing the number of sports facilities. Others, however, say that this would have little effect on public health and that other measures are required.（《剑桥雅思 9》，Test 3）

范文第三段：① However, there may be better ways of tackling this problem. ② Interest in sport is not universal, and additional facilities might simply attract the already fit, not those who most need them. ③ Physical activity could be encouraged relatively cheaply, for example by installing exercise equipment in parks, as my local council has done. ④ This has the added benefit that parents and children often use them together just for fun, which develops a positive attitude to exercise at an early age.

　　本段共 79 词，4 个句子。主题在句①中出现：还有更好的办法来解决公众健康状况下降问题。句②解释为什么题目中提及的办法（即增加运动设施数量）有缺陷：不是所有人都对运动感兴趣，因此增加运动设施，获益的只有那些爱运动、身体已经很好的人。句③提出一个更好的办法：在公园里安装运动设备。句④进一步说明这个方法的好处：父母和孩子可以开心地在一起使用它们，因此可以从小就培养孩子对运动的积极态度。至此本段句②至句④的顺序就是：原来的办法为什么不好—有更好的办法—这个办法为什么更好。很明显，这几句是紧紧围绕主题句在展开。

　　例2　Today, many tasks at home or work have been done by robots. Is this a positive or negative development?（201010）

　　范文第三段：① For all these real or potential problems, robots can provide us with so many benefits to our life and work that we think they are truly useful. ② As robots can keep working for long hours and will not feel tired, they help to save a lot of our time which we can put to more enjoyable or creative activities. ③ Robots can achieve high efficiency and quality since they seldom make mistakes in their work. ④ Furthermore, robots can work in situations that are considered to be impossibly dangerous for humans, such as cleaning up radioactive waste, so they can reduce safety hazards in workplaces.

　　本段共 103 词，4 个句子。句①给出了段落主题：机器人给我们的工作和生活都带来了很多好处。句②至句④用列举的方法来论证这些好处，其中句②说明机器人给我们节约了时间，句③说明机器人工作效率和工作质量很高，句④说明机器人可以帮助我们完成高危险性的工作。这样，本段的结构是"主题句 + 列举论证"，句②至句④紧紧围绕主题句展开。

　　例3　The restoration of old buildings in major cities in the world costs numerous governments' expenditure. This money should be used in new housing and road development. To what extent do you agree or disagree?（190718）

范文第三段：① Yet old buildings—at least some of them—are significant historically and culturally, and hence should be restored for that reason. ② They carry some important messages about the city or even the whole nation. ③ The Summer Palace, for instance, is a perfect reminder of how the imperial family in the Qing Dynasty in feudal China were living and so has great cultural significance. ④ Such old buildings, if well preserved, can become tourist spots and attract thousands of visitors from all around the globe.

本段共 85 词，4 个句子。句①给出段落主题：有些老建筑有历史和文化意义，因此应该得到重修。句②对主题句进行具体说明：这些老建筑带有城市甚至国家的重要信息。句③用举例的方法证明主题句：颐和园能让我们想起清王朝的帝王之家如何生活，因此有重要的文化意义。句④则指出保留这些老建筑的价值所在：变成景点，吸引全世界游客。本段的结构是"主题句＋解释＋举例论证＋结果"，句②至句④紧紧围绕主题展开。

3.1.3 结尾段

按照雅思写作三大写作思路，笔者归纳了三种结尾方式。

第一，一边倒型：完全同意／反对题目中的一方观点。这种作文的结尾一般是再次重述观点，并总结前文给出的理由，篇幅通常是 30—50 词。

例 1 Many people say that cooking and eating at home is better for the individual and the family than eating out in restaurants and canteens. Do you agree or disagree?（《剑桥雅思》4，Test 2）

结尾段：① In brief, I believe that eating at home is healthy and clean. ② If people want to save money, eating at home is also a good choice. ③ In addition, people can cook what they like as well. ④ So I personally prefer eating at home.

本范文一边倒地支持应该在家里吃饭，并给出了三个理由：省钱、做自己想吃的味道、干净卫生。结尾段共四句，前三句对前面讨论的三个理由分别进行总结，最后一句再次表明全文观点：更愿意在家吃饭。

例 2 Countries are becoming more and more similar because people are able to buy the same products anywhere in the world. Do you think this is a positive or negative development?（《剑桥雅思 10》，Test 3）

结尾段：Some may argue that all people are entitled to have access to the same products, but I say that local objects suit local conditions best, and that faceless uniformity worldwide is an unwelcome and dreary prospect.

本范文一边倒地认为，国家之间越来越趋同是一个不好的现象。前文从文化多样性、工作机会、旅游三个方面论证国家趋同产生的不良影响。结尾段先扬后抑，首先承认所有人都有权利使用相同的产品，然后用 but 转折，进而总结全文观点：地方产品最适合地方的条件，全球统一化是不受欢迎的（unwelcome），而且会让世界变得无聊透顶（dreary）。

第二，**双边讨论型**：先对双方观点的优劣分别进行讨论，然后给出自己的观点或看法。这种作文的结尾比一边倒型作文要困难一些，因为考生需要在结尾段总结双方观点，更重要的是，必须提出自己的观点，并简单给出理由。自己的观点要么倾向于更赞同某一方，要么认为双方都有道理，但其合理性适应于不同条件或情况。篇幅通常是 50—80 词。

例1 In some countries young people are encouraged to work or travel for a year between finishing high school and starting university studies. Discuss the advantages and disadvantages for young people who decide to do this.（200806）

结尾段：My view is that young people should be encouraged to broaden their horizons. That is the best way for them to get a clear perspective of what they are hoping to do with their lives and why. Students with such a perspective are usually the most effective and motivated ones and taking a year off may be the best way to gain this.

本范文首先分别讨论高中毕业后去旅游或工作一年的好处和坏处，最后得出自己的结论：赞同年轻人去旅游或工作一年，因为这样做可以开阔他们的视野，更好地理解自己未来想做什么，从而会更有效率（effective），也更有动力（motivated）。

例2 In some countries, the criminal trials are shown on the TV and the general public can watch them. Do the advantages outweigh the disadvantages?（161022）

结尾段：However, I personally do like the idea of putting criminal trials on TV. Besides telling us right from wrong in a more vivid way and preempting us from committing crimes, TV trials will let us know how the punishment is meted out and how justice is done. This, I believe, is what our basic civil right is all about.

本范文首先分别讨论电视直播罪犯审判的好处和坏处，最后得出自己的结论：赞同电视直播罪犯审判，因为这不仅能教会人们是非观念，而且能够让我们知道如何量刑，以及如何实现公正，这是我们的公民权利（civil right）所在。

第三，**报告型：**先分析问题 / 现象产生的原因，最后提出解决办法 / 分析利弊。因此，该题型的结尾可以提出解决方案或者分析利弊。篇幅通常是 100 词左右。

例 1 Increasing the price of petrol is the best way to solve growing traffic and pollution problems. To what extent do you agree or disagree? What other measures do you think might be effective? （《剑桥雅思 8》，Test 3）

结尾段：However, traffic congestion will not be solved by changing the type of private vehicle people can use. To do this, we **need** to improve the choice of public transport services available to travellers. For example, if sufficient sky train and underground train system **were** built and effectively maintained in our major society, then traffic on the roads **would** be dramatically reduced. Long-distance train and coach services **should** be made attractive and affordable alternatives to driving your own cars for long journeys.

本范文首先讨论提高油价不是解决交通和污染问题的最好办法，然后在结尾段提出其他更好的办法，即增加公共交通服务的种类，比如空中列车（sky train）、地下铁路系统（underground train system）、长途火车和汽车服务（long-distance train and coach services）。需要注意的是，报告型题目往往要求学生提出解决方法，因此学生需要掌握提建议的多种方法。通过此例，笔者介绍三种提建议的表达方法：

方法一：need 引导的建议

To do this, **we need to** improve the choice of public transport services available to travellers.

方法二：if 引导的虚拟语气表达委婉建议

... **if** sufficient sky train and underground train system **were** built and effectively maintained in our major society, then traffic on the roads **would** be dramatically reduced.

方法三：should 引导的建议

Long-distance train and coach services **should** be made attractive and affordable alternatives to driving your own cars for long journeys.

例 2 In many countries, people are wearing more western-style clothes (suits and jeans) rather than their traditional clothes. Why? Is this a positive or negative development?（201226）

结尾段：Generally, I think wearing more western-style clothes is a positive development. In addition to the conveniences they afford in the work situations, western-style clothes can also help people to better assimilate into the world. The clothes people wear are pretty much like the language they speak, and they certainly feel more at ease with those wearing the similar kind of clothes, just like they feel more comfortable with those speaking the same language.

Yet going too far in this direction of westernization is certainly negative. Anything that is traditional, clothes included, carries the unique cultural code that should be preserved. In this sense, traditional clothes should never be discarded altogether, even when we do not wear them in everyday life.

本范文首先分析了人们喜欢西式服装的原因：西方文化的影响以及西装的实用性。利弊分析分两段进行，前一段从总体上承认穿西式服装是积极的，后一段则认为服装过于西化可能导致传统服装的消失。

3.2 段落拓展方式

如前所述，雅思作文每段一般包含 4—7 个句子，只能有一个观点，所有句子都要为这个观点服务。那么，我们可以用哪些方式来展开讨论段落的主要观点呢？笔者提出六种办法，即结果分析法、原因分析法、列举法、举例法、反证法和对比法。

3.2.1 结果分析法

所谓结果分析法，就是揭示主题句观点可能产生的结果，通过结果来支持或反对主题句中的观点。该方法应用比较广泛，尤其适用于讨论段落内某个观点／做法带来的好处或坏处。

例 1 Some people believe that unpaid community service should be a compulsory part of high school programmes (for example, working for a charity, improving the neighbourhood or teaching sports to younger children). (《剑桥雅思 9》，Test 2）

第三段：① By giving them compulsory work activities with charitable or community organisations, they will be encouraged to do something more creative. ② Skills gained through compulsory work will not only be an asset on their CV but also increase their employability. ③ Students will also gain more respect towards work and money as they will realise that it is not that easy to earn them and hopefully will learn to spend them in a more practical way.

本段共 3 句，给出支持高中生做免费义工的两个理由。本段没有主题句。句①提出一个理由，即学生由做免费义工而得到鼓励，去做一些创新性（creative）工作。句②紧跟着分析做创新性工作带来的结果，即增加简历的厚度（an asset on their CV），同时增加找到工作的机会（increase their employability）。句③用 also 引出另外一个理由，即学生通过做义工会更加尊重劳动和金钱；该句后半部分通过 and 引出尊重劳动和金钱产生的结果，即学生可以学会如何更合理地花钱（spend them in a more practical way）。不难看出，本段的拓展方式是分析前一句观点产生的结果。

例 2 Some experts believe that it is better for children to begin learning a foreign language at primary school rather than secondary school. Do the advantages of this outweigh the disadvantages? (《剑桥雅思 9》，Test 1）

第四段：① There are, however, some disadvantages. ② Primary school teachers are generalists, and may not have the necessary language skills themselves. ③ If specialists have to be brought in to deliver these sessions, the flexibility referred to above is diminished. ④ If primary language teaching is not standardised, secondary schools could be faced with a great variety of levels in different languages within their intake, resulting in a classroom experience which undoes the earlier gains. ⑤ There is no advantage if enthusiastic primary pupils become demotivated as soon as they change schools. ⑥ However, these issues can be addressed strategically within the policy adopted.

本段共 6 句，论证的是"从小学开始学外语的劣势"。句①表达段落主题。

句②指出小学外语教师的问题，即这些老师自身可能缺乏足够的语言技能。句③分析这个问题带来的后果之一，即需要从外面请老师来给小学生上外语课。句④和句⑤则论证另外一个后果，即小学外语教学若不均衡，中学生的语言技能就会有不同层次，从而让那些积极性很高的小学生进入中学后对语言学习不再有动力。可见，本段的拓展方式是，首先提出一个论证的起点，即小学老师自身可能缺乏必要的语言技能，从这个起点开始分析其产生的几个后果。

表示"结果"的常用英文表达有：consequently、as a result、result in、lead to 等。比如：

（1）However, while pursuing excellence is a good thing, it may also be harmful to the development of students. Often, in order to win over others, many students may choose not to help their peer classmates. **Consequently**, those best students are often the most isolated ones.（160604，孩子应该学会相互合作还是相互竞争？）

（2）Additionally, if universities are open to more high school students, they will face less intense academic pressure. **As a result**, these students can enjoy more freedom to learn things that really interest them and so they can learn them better as interest is always the best teacher.（160616，更多年轻人上大学是好还是坏？）

（3）In addition, many people like to use animal products, so they never hesitate to kill wild animals, **resulting in** the loss of species diversity and destruction of the ecological system.（200822，让一代人放弃舒适生活是解决环境问题的关键吗？）

3.2.2 原因分析法

所谓原因分析法，就是为段落主题观点提供原因。该方法应用也比较广泛，尤其常用于当主题句的观点需要进一步解释的时候。

例1 Some people prefer to spend their lives doing the same things and avoiding change. Others, however, think that change is always a good thing. Discuss both these views and give your own opinion.（《剑桥雅思6》，Test 4）

第二段：① Those people who believe they have achieved some security by doing the same, familiar things are living in denial. ② Even when people believe they are resisting change themselves, they cannot stop the world around them from changing. ③ Sooner or later they will find that the familiar jobs no longer exist, or that the safe patterns of behaviour are no longer appropriate.

本段共 3 句。先提出一个观点，即那些认为可以永远做同一份工作而实现稳定的人是在自我欺骗（... are living in denial），然后对这个观点进行解释：虽然人们认为自己在拒绝变化，却无法阻止周围的世界变化，他们早晚会发现自己熟悉的工作不存在了，或者安全的行动模式也不再适宜了。很显然，句②和句③是在为主题句提供原因。

例 2　Most of the government funding should be invested in teaching science rather than any other subjects in order for a country to develop and make progress. To what extent do you agree or disagree?（201205）

第二段：① The most obvious sign of a country's development and progress is of course its economic prosperity and material wealth. ② In this sense, arguing that the government should mainly support science-related subjects makes a lot of sense. ③ Only with enough talents working in various scientific fields can a country become strong economically. ④ The more scientific and technological breakthroughs a country makes, the more developed it is. ⑤ His has been proved true by the 19th-century U.K. and 20th-century U.S.A., who largely depended on, respectively, industrial revolution and automobile industry for their prosperity.

本段共 5 句，其中，句①和句②引出段落观点，即政府应该主要支持与科学相关的课程。句③和句④给出原因：只有科技领域里有足够多的人才，国家在经济上才会强大。句⑤用举例的方法来证明段落观点。

表示"原因"的常用英文表达有：because、for、since、as、for the reason that、on the ground that 等。比如：

（1）Today, boat-racing has nothing to do with our daily living; we don't even need boats for fishing, but Chinese people are still celebrating this event every year **for the reason that** it reminds them of the cruelty of politics in that period of time.（160910，传统习俗应该被抛弃吗？）

（2）As is known to all, the only solution to poverty and hunger is economic growth. However, many people raise objections to economic progress **on the ground that** it will cause huge damage to the environment.（190907，经济

发展与环境保护的关系）

（3）Print has been facing a steady decrease in readership, **as** nowadays people are accustomed to getting information at the touch of a key or screen.（191012，我们不需要印刷版书籍和报刊了吗？）

3.2.3 列举法

所谓列举法（enumeration），指列举几个方面，共同论证主题句，尤其适用于在一个段落内列举几个原因来说明某个观点。

例 1　As most people spend a major part of their adult life at work, job satisfaction is an important element of individual wellbeing. What factors contribute to job satisfaction? How realistic is the expectation of job satisfaction for all workers?（《剑桥雅思 8》，Test 1）

第二段：① Employees get job satisfaction in a number of ways. ② Firstly, a person needs to feel that they are doing valued and valuable work, so positive feedback from superiors is very important in this respect. ③ A sense of fulfillment is also encouraged if a worker feels the job is worth doing because it contributes to society or the economy as a whole. ④ Secondly, when someone feels they are improving or developing their skills through training opportunities, for example, then there is a sense of progression and purpose that rewards a worker. ⑤ The sense of belonging to a team or a working community also contributes to job satisfaction because colleagues help each other to enjoy their working lives. ⑥ Satisfaction is also increased by a sense of responsibility for and loyalty to a team.

本段共 6 句。句①给出主题句：员工可以从多方面获得工作满足感。句②和句③由 firstly 引出，讨论第一个方面，即员工感觉到自己正在从事有价值的、受重视的工作（老板的正面评价，以及对社会和经济的贡献）。句④由 secondly 引出，讨论第二个方面，即员工通过培训改进或培养新技能。句⑤由 also 引出，讨论第三个方面，即员工有归属感。句⑥同样由 also 引出，讨论第四个方面，即员工有责任感或团队忠诚感。很显然，本段列举了四个方面，共同说明主题句。

例 2　In some countries the number of people who use bicycles as their main form of transport is decreasing even though riding bicycles has many benefits. What are the reasons? What could be done to encourage the use of bicycles? （210410）

第二段：① I think three factors are responsible for this problem. ② In the first place, as more and more families own their own cars, they choose to live further and further away from where they work, making it unrealistic for them to ride bicycles to and from work. ③ Another reason is that, with more and more fantastic TV programmes and games available on TV and computers, some people now prefer to stay at home and sit in front of the screen rather than ride bicycles in the open air. ④ Finally, riding bicycles is now considered to be out of joint with society as a whole as the great majority of other people are trying to get ahead with the precept in mind that "time is money".

本段共 4 句。句①给出主题句：造成人们不再骑自行车的原因有三个。句②到句④则分别列举这三个原因。句②由 in the first place 引出，讨论第一个原因，即人们住的离工作地方越来越远。句③由 another reason is that 引出，讨论第二个原因，即各种娱乐方式太多。句④由 finally 引出，讨论第三个原因，即自行车的速度赶不上"时间就是金钱"的心理。可见，本段的拓展方式也是列举法。

表示"列举"的常用英文表达有：firstly..., secondly..., finally...；to start with；in the first place；more importantly；at the most basic level 等。比如：

（1）**More importantly**, in big cities, people enjoy better medical services because the best hospitals and medical professionals are often found in big cities rather than rural countryside.（180603，生活在大城市不利于身体健康吗？）

（2）There are a host of reasons why the urban old buildings should be pulled down. **To start with**, the old buildings are no longer suitable for people to live in, therefore they should be destroyed and give way to new buildings so that people, especially young people in the cities have more living spaces. （181202，老建筑应该被拆除吗？）

（3）In my view, there mainly are three reasons why young people are doing so. **At the most basic level**, young people find that frequent job changing can often bring them the pay rise they expect. （180607，年轻人频繁更换工作的原因及利弊）

3.2.4 举例法

所谓举例法，是指用恰当的例子来证明自己的观点。尤其当不容易直接说理的时候，我们可以考虑使用生动的例子来讨论。由于举例法使用非常广泛，本书将专辟一节讨论雅思写作中的举例问题（见本章 3.3）。

例 1　In the past, the main role of the teacher was to provide information. Today, however, students can get access to a wide range of information. Therefore, some people think there is no role for the teacher in the modern education. To what extent do you agree or disagree?（170325）

第二段：① In the first place, the Internet, along with other similar non-human sources, is far from perfect as a source of information and knowledge. ② For one thing, information on the Internet may be unreliable, or even incorrect. ③ A friend of mine recently got into serious trouble because she obtained an article from the Internet and submitted it to her supervisor, only to find later that the article was about Australia, rather than Austria as she had originally expected.

本段共 3 句。句①和句②提出段落论点，即网上的信息不可靠，甚至是错误的。句③举例说明这个论点：一个学生从网上直接下载文章交给老师，结果发现弄错了，从而遇到麻烦。

例 2　The restoration of old buildings in major cities in the world costs numerous governments' expenditure. This money should be used in new housing and road development. To what extent do you agree or disagree?（190718）

第三段：① Yet old buildings—at least some of them—are significant historically and culturally, and hence should be restored for that reason. ② They carry some important messages about the city or even the whole nation. ③ The Summer Palace, for instance, is a perfect reminder of how the imperial family in the Qing Dynasty in feudal China were living and so has great cultural significance. ④ Such old buildings, if well preserved, can become tourist spots and attract thousands of visitors from all around the globe.

本段共 4 句。句①提出段落主题，即有些老建筑有历史和文化意义，应该重修。句②对主题句提供具体解释。句③用中国的颐和园为例证明老建筑具有历史和文化意义。句④进一步指出这些老建筑如果保护得好可能成为景点。

表示"举例"的常用英文表达有：for example、for instance、take sth as an example (illustration)、to illustrate、a case in point is that、the latest survey shows that 等。比如：

（1）Sports stars, if they do not behave properly, may also negatively influence young people. Maradona, who died not long ago, **is just a case in point**. Arguably the best football player in the world, he did not set a good example to young people by taking drugs and shooting journalists, giving his young admirers a false impression that a star can do anything regardless of the law and moral standards.（201219，年轻人崇拜负面明星是好还是坏？）

（2）When online shopping gradually comes into our life, older people are far less enthusiastic about it than the young. **A survey shows that** almost 95% of young people are doing their shopping online, while only less than 30% of people above 40 are doing the same.（160430，购物习惯取决于年龄吗？）

3.2.5 反证法

所谓反证法，是讨论某个观点的反面带来的后果，从而证明该观点的合理性，尤其适用于正面说理比较困难的时候。

例 1　It is generally believed that some people are born with certain talents, for instance for sport or music, and others are not. However, it is sometimes claimed that any child can be taught to become a good sports person or musician.（《剑桥雅思 7》，Test 1）

第四段：① I personally think that some people do have talents that are probably inherited via their genes. ② Such talents can give individuals a facility for certain skills that allow them to excel, while more hard-working students never manage to reach a comparable level. ③ But, as with all questions of nature versus nurture, they are not mutually exclusive. ④ Good musicians or artists and exceptional sports stars have probably succeeded because of both good training and natural talent. ⑤ Without the natural talent, continuous training would be neither attractive nor productive, and without the training, children would not learn how to exploit and develop their talent.

本段共 5 句。句①和句②表达作者的个人观点，即天赋的确是很重要的。句③和句④由 but 引出转折，表达作者的另一个观点，即天赋和努力并非互相排斥的（mutually exclusive），音乐家、艺术家和体育明星的成功既需要天赋，也需要努力。为了证明这个观点，句⑤使用了反证法：没有天赋，持续的训练不会有结果；没有训练，天赋得不到利用和开发。

例 2　Competitiveness is considered to be an important quality for people in many societies. How do you think it affects individuals? Is it a positive or negative trend?（201112）

第四段：① In my opinion, competition is needed for human progress, without which we would probably still be living in the primitive world, as every important invention and discovery may have resulted from competition of one kind or another. ② On the other hand, people ought to understand that besides competition, cooperation is also needed to keep the world going.

本段共 2 句。句①的观点是人类进步需要竞争，句②则认为合作也是必要的。在论证句①观点时，作者使用了反证法：如果没有竞争，人类可能还生活在原始世界，因为人类所有的发明和发现可能都是源于竞争。

表示"反证"的常用英文表达有：without、if not 等。比如：

（1）Undoubtedly, experience is of utmost importance for many government positions. These positions have to deal with a great number of people every day and crisis may emerge any time. For example, a foreign affairs minister has to make quick responses to the problems that may come from all over the world every minute. **Without** the rich experience collected from his long-time service in this field, it would be unlikely for him to fulfill his duties. Young people, therefore, are not really suitable for this type of government positions.（181021，年轻人适合在政府担任要职吗？）

（2）The family activities that young people can engage in include eating meals together, talking about the events of the day, sharing joys and defeats, doing household chores together and spending evenings watching TV. All these things can send a strong message of family love, which is the overall positive side about juveniles staying more at home. To some, these activities may seem not always necessary, but **without** them, it is impossible for young people to learn to love the family. （181027，年轻人应该多在家还是在外面娱乐？）

（3）Then, apart from enforcing regulations and using penalties or fines as a means to hold individuals accountable for their damage to the environment, the government should do more to alert people to the way the environment is going, then people would be more likely to do their bit. **If** people are **not** reminded of the risks that affect their own local environment, they will often forget.（190414，政府应该让人们负责保护本地环境吗？）

3.2.6 对比法

所谓对比法，是将某个观点与其他观点进行比较，通过比较来证明该观点的合理性，尤其适用于有过去与现在对比、不同措施相比较之类的情况。

例1 Children today find it difficult to concentrate on or pay attention to school. What are the reasons? How can we solve this problem?（160429）

第二段：① Students today are surrounded by so many distractions that they gradually find that learning is boring and uninteresting. ② While students two decades ago had nearly no choice but sit in the classroom and read books, students today have easy and fast access to Internet, on which they can do almost all things. ③ For instance, they can play computer games, watch videos, search for any information they need, and chat with their friends, to mention just a few. ④ So, having been used to this kind of "easy" online life, many young people simply cannot put their heart into the more serious and consuming school work.

本段共4句。句①提出段落主题，即今天的学生受到很多干扰，发现学习是无聊的。句②通过比较20年前的学生和现在的学生来说明后者受到的干扰。句③通过举例具体说明学生受到的干扰。句④对全段进行总结。

例2 In many parts of the world, children have more freedom than they used to have. Is this a positive or negative development?（170708）

第二段：① It may turn out to be a bad thing that children have much free time at their disposal. ② Without the supervision of their parents and teachers, many children end up being addicted to computer games or other unhealthy habits. ③ This is detrimental to both their academic development and character formation. ④ In contrast, children three decades ago had to help their parents do the housework and they did not have calculators or computers to help them with their maths, so they would have to spend much time on all these tasks during which they learned the value of hard work and cooperation.

本段共 4 句。句①是段落主题句：孩子的自由时间多可能是坏事。句②和句③将"坏事"具体化：沉迷电脑游戏或其他不健康的习惯。句④则比较现在的孩子和 30 年前的孩子，通过比较，说明现在的孩子因自由时间多而产生的坏处。

表示"对比"的常用英文表达有：in/by contrast、on the contrary、conversely、while 等。比如：

（1）Admittedly, home-education can bring about a bunch of benefits. With only one kid to teach, the parents will be able to know completely about the problems the kid has. **In contrast**, the teachers in school cannot spend that much time on the same kid because they have dozens of others to take care of.（160213，孩子在家接受教育的利弊）

（2）A parenting course is one designed to help parents understand how to bring up their children in a better way. **While** many people think such a course is extremely useful, I think it is of very little use, if not at all, to parents who wish to give their children a better future.（160528，新父母应该参加育儿课程吗？）

（3）Furthermore, older people are generally more sensitive to the price, so they tend to buy those less flashy and cheaper stuff. **On the contrary**, young people are always attracted by the famous brands.（160430，购物习惯取决于年龄吗？）

3.3 如何举例

雅思作文经常需要举例，一是字数的需要，二是论证的需要，三是让作文显得生动活泼的需要。因此，几乎所有雅思作文都需要举例。那么，雅思写作到底该如何举例呢？

首要问题就是：举什么作为例子？其实，例子很多，名人经历，个人经历，同学朋友经历，小说里读到的，电影里看到的，报纸上刊登的……，都可以作为例子来证明你的观点！但是，笔者认为，对多数"烤鸭"来说，首先考虑写个人经历或周围熟悉的人或物，因为熟悉，所以可以降低犯错的概率。

那么，我们应该怎么举例？笔者提供两类举例方法：有形的举例和无形的举例。有形的举例就是用 for instance、for example、a case in point is that 这样的连接词来举例，通常显得生硬，但很明晰；无形的举例就是把例子自然地融入上下文中，虽然没有连接词，却胜似有连接词，这样的举例就像武功高手，收放自如，举重若轻，显得优雅，有格调。本节先讲有形的举例供 6—7 分段同学参考，然后再总结高分段的举例策略。

3.3.1 有形的举例

常用来引导举例的连接词有：

（1）Take... for example. 以……为例。

（2）To see this more clearly, let's take... as an illustration. 为看得更清楚，我们举……为证。

（3）A (good) case in point is... 一个（恰当的）例子是……

（4）Perhaps the most well-known/important/convincing/interesting example is... 也许最为人所知 / 重要 / 有说服力 / 有趣的例子是……

（5）... is frequently quoted/cited/taken as an illustration of... 人们经常举……来证明……

（6）There is abundant evidence to support... 有足够的证据支持……

（7）The latest survey/poll/study conducted by... indicates/reveals/shows that... 最近由……进行的调查 / 民意测验 / 研究表明……

例 1　Hard work is more important than the innate talent. For example, my friend John is a great piano player though he is not really gifted, because he practices playing the piano almost every day.（《剑桥雅思 7》，Test 2，努力与天赋的重要性）

本段的主题为：努力工作比天赋更重要。怎么来论证这个道理？最好的办法就是举例。举什么？举作者的朋友约翰。虽然他天分不怎么样，但他依然弹得好，因为他基本上天天练习弹钢琴。这个例子很直接地说明了努力比天分更重要。

例 2　Sports stars, if they do not behave properly, may also negatively influence young people. Maradona, who died not long ago, is just a case in point. Arguably the best football player in the world, he set a bad example to young people by taking drugs and shooting journalists, giving his young admirers a false impression that a star can do anything regardless of the law and moral standards.（201219，年轻人崇拜负面明星的利弊）

本段的主题为：负面明星会给年轻人带来消极影响。怎么说明这个道理？仍然是举例。马拉多纳是足球明星，但他吸毒，甚至枪杀记者，从而让年轻人觉得明星可以无法无天。这个例子很有力地说明了论点。

例 3　More significantly, living with people of different ethnic groups will enable us to become more understanding and tolerant, which is, of course, very important to a peaceful world. In my neighbourhood, for example, there are people from China, India and African countries. During Chinese New Year holidays, we invite our Indian and African friends to our house and show them how Chinese people celebrate their Spring Festival. Our Indian neighbours teach us how to play cricket, which is their national sports and African friends show us the beautiful dances particular to their culture. In this way, we share what we have and learn what we do not, and our neighbourhood is always happy and full of joy.（20160402，多种族社会的利弊）

本段主题为：不同种族的人住在一起，会让我们变得更为通情达理和宽容。为了说明这个道理，作者用自己居住的小区为例，说明住在同一小区的中国人、印度人和非洲人怎样相互分享和相互学习。

例 4　Obviously, photographs and videos enjoy some advantages over written words in communicating news. They present news in a vivid and direct way as if their audiences were looking at what is happening with their own eyes, making them feel that the news is real and accurate. The audiences of videos, for instance, can not only see what is going on there, but also such factual details as the facial expressions and gestures, and can distinguish the attitude of people through their voices. With all these information available, the audiences believe that they are in a good position to make their own judgments, in a way that is not possible when they are reading verbal form of news.（220806，视频新闻更准确吗？）

本段主题为：视频呈现新闻的方式直接和生动。为了论证这个观点，作者通过举例，具体说明观众可以从视频中看到的内容：不仅可以看到发生了什么，还可以看到人们脸上的表情和动作，从声音中分辨出人们的态度。

3.3.2 举例高分策略

笔者在多年雅思写作教学中，总结出三条举例高分策略：第一，高度浓缩，直指需要论证问题的核心；第二，多用复杂句，包含比较丰富、具体的内容；第三，举例一般用一句，也可用一个短句＋一个长句的组合。

例 1　Some students use websites which offer ready-made assignments. This is not a good idea, even if you ignore the fact that it is cheating, because such websites may contain factual errors or biased views. In a recent case, a student found herself in serious trouble when she submitted an essay from one of these sites only to discover that it was about Austria, not Australia, but had an error in the title.（170325，网络时代不需要老师了吗？）

本段需要论证网络上获取的信息可能不准确。怎么论证？举例。怎么举例？一位同学惹上了麻烦，为什么呢？因为她从网站上找了一篇文章，然后提交给了老师，却发现这篇文章标题有错，不是澳大利亚，而是奥地利。这个例子内容既丰富又具体。原文用 in a recent case（＝ for example）引导出一个长例子。如果我们这样来改写这个例子，看看差距在哪里？

For example, a student got an essay from one website and then submitted it to the professor. Then she discovered that it had an error in the title. It was about Austria, not Australia. The student found herself in serious trouble.

改写段的信息与原文完全一致，但原文的一个句子在这里被分散成了四个句子。众多分散的短句给人感觉不是在举例说明前面的论点，而是在讲述这个例子本身了。改写段虽然语法没错，但就举例本身而言，这样写仅能得到 6 分。

例 2　Sometimes the most talented person can make for（走向；成为）one of the most ineffective managers. You can see this in sports, for example, where retired superstars often find it difficult to coach or manage successfully because they are now supervising lesser mortals that weren't blessed with the same degree of innate talent.（BBC, May 28, 2014）

本段来自英语知名媒体，要论证的是：最有才华的人可能成为最糟糕的经理。然后举运动员为例：那些退役的超级球星往往很难成功地当教练或经营管理，因为他们现在管理的这些人的天赋远不及他们。我们现在不妨来仿写一段，话题是"就带团队而言，年轻人比年纪大的人可能做得更好"：

Sometimes young people can do a better job than their older counterparts in leading a team forward. You can see this in IT sector, for example, where the old people often find it impossible to head a team because their past experience and expertise fall out too soon to be useful any more.

3.3.3 学生举例习作一例

我们来看学生习作中的一个段落：

The situation would be better if people really tried their best to save the creature. Panda is a good example. Panda is a typical endangered animal which only lives in China. The number of Panda used to be less than 200. Nevertheless, the lovely appearance of panda attracts the world's attention. It is favoured by people all over the world. Finally, though it is still endangered, the number of panda grows to 1000. According to these, it is obvious that the situation can be changed.

本段主题是，如果我们尽力挽救动物，动物灭绝的情形就会改变。怎么论证？该同学举了熊猫的例子。她的思路是这样的：熊猫是一种濒危动物，只有中国才有。熊猫以前的数量不足 200。然而，熊猫的可爱模样吸引了世界的注意力。全世界的人都喜欢熊猫。最后，虽然还是濒危动物，但其数量增长到了 1000。这就说明，情况显然是可以改变的。这个举例内容很合适，完全说明了观点，举例的语言大体也清楚，这样的作文可得 6 分，若要更上一层楼就必须加以改进。按照前文所述的高分举例标准，举例最多两句话，重点内容用主句，细节用从句。笔者这样修改：

The situation would be better if people really tried their best to save the creatures. Panda is a good example. As an endangered species found only in China, the panda has grown in number from 200 a decade ago to 1,000 today, thanks to the protection from people all over the world attracted by their lovely appearance.

修改段落中，原文用来举例的 6 个句子被压缩成为两句，后面一句是结构相对复杂的长句，其中"熊猫的数量从 10 年前的 200 增长到现在的 1000"被安排成了主句，而其他相关信息被处理为附属成分围绕在主句周围。

3.4 句间连贯及其实现方式

段落中，句子与句子之间需要保持内容和形式上的连贯，也就是说，句子之间要存在某种关系，这样作文读起来才能顺畅。有时候，学生习作段落中的单句看起来问题不大，把这些句子放在一起，却在形式和内容上缺乏关联，让人有断裂之感，从而造成不连贯而丢分。

增强句间连贯的方式有很多，比如**使用连接词 and、so、but、since 等**，这些连接词很明确地显示句子之间的关联，因此能让句子之间保持连贯。在使用连接词方面，我们需要注意汉英的区别，即汉语中连接词使用相对英语而言要少得多，这导致学生在写英语句子时，往往按照汉语习惯，该用连接词的地方不用连接词，从而导致句子之间缺乏连贯性。除了使用连接词，**还可以使用代词、名词重复等方式来实现句子之间的连贯**。这些方法，只要多加注意，学生是比较容易掌握的。

3.4.1 使用连接词

使用连接词是最方便的连贯手段，因为连接词可以明确表示句子之间的关系。句子间的关系有很多种，相关连接词如下：

（1）表示原因：for this reason、due to、thanks to、because、because of、as、since、owing to 等。

例 1 Some people believe that it is beneficial to have a dress code in the workplace, if only for image reasons. Workers may be asked to wear a uniform to communicate a corporate image and ensure that people easily identify them. This is particularly true to a workplace where employees have regular face-to-face contact with customers and clients. **For this reason**, nowadays an increasing number of workplaces prefer to set up a dress code and subtly promote the visual uniformity.（180113，员工着装和工作品质的关系）

例 2 Independence means more freedom and less restrictions. Following this definition, we can easily find we have become much more independent than ever before. For instance, **thanks to** the Internet, we can now sit at home and send letters to our friends without bothering to go to the post office. We can also use our smartphones as a tool for shopping and reading so that we are freed from driving to the supermarket or carrying heavy books with us.（161105，我们现在更加独立了吗？）

（2）表示结果：as a result、thus、hence、so、therefore、accordingly、consequently、as a consequence 等。

例 1 More importantly, as cosmetic surgery is often very costly, only the rich people can afford the operation, which means only the rich people can benefit from the surgery. **Consequently**, cosmetic surgery has contributed to the ever-widening gap between the rich and the poor.（200927，整容的利弊）

例 2 Most important of all, people, especially those commuters, will be able to make it to where they work on time and in good mood, and **accordingly**, their work efficiency will improve.（160130，收取拥堵税的利弊）

（3）表示强调：still、indeed、apparently、of course、after all、significantly、interestingly、surely、certainly、undoubtedly、in any case、above all、actually、in fact、especially、obviously、clearly、as a matter of fact 等。

例 1 Today, we can **apparently** accomplish a lot of things without the help of others, which leads to the popular belief that we are becoming more and more independent. However, while we enjoy this independence in some ways, we are **actually** becoming more dependent on each other in others.（161105，我们现在更加独立了吗？）

例 2 Needless to say, university students should devote most of the time to their academic work rather than these club activities. **After all**, to become expert in one specialized field and get prepared for future life should become the major concerns for all university students, and these are also what the students pay their tuition for.（170826，大学生应该从事学习之外的活动吗？）

（4）表示对比：by/in contrast、on the contrary、while、unlike、instead、 conversely、different from、nevertheless 等。

例 1　**Unlike** many worried parents who prefer to educate their kids at home, I believe school is the best place for kids' education. While there may be some bad influences outside home, there are also many excellent people who could be role models for kids. Most important of all, it is just in not so pure a place as school that kids can learn to tell right from wrong, good from bad and eventually become physically and psychologically healthy when they grow up.（180426，孩子在家接受教育的利弊）

例 2　Happiness is very difficult to define, because it means so many different things to different people. **While** some people link happiness to wealth and material success, others think it lies in emotions and loving personal relationships. Yet others think that spiritual paths, rather than either the material world or relationships with people, are the only way to true happiness.（《剑桥雅思 4》，Test 2，实现幸福的因素）

（5）表示比较：like、similarly、likewise、in the same way、in the same manner、equally 等。

例 1　Lured by the promises of advertising, some people may choose to commit crimes, which then causes a lot of social problems. A student, for instance, may rob his classmate of an iPhone 8, for he saw in advertisements that iPhone 8 is superior to its previous versions. **Likewise**, an official may take bribery to buy an expensive house by the lake because the advertising says the luxury of living there is superb.（180422，广告对经济和个人的影响）

例 2　Reading or telling stories, besides providing an opportunity for the parents to stay together with their children, is also often considered as a wonderful occasion for parents to share their life's lesson or wisdom with their children. So the fairy tale about a fox is often not just an interesting story, but one that tells the kids about the risks of greed, and **similarly**, the story of George Washington cutting a cherry tree makes the kids realize the importance of honesty.（170715，父母应该给孩子读书讲故事吗？）

（6）表示列举 / 举例：for example、for instance、such as、take... for example、to illustrate 等。

例 1 One of the most amazing things about the university is that it always has a great variety of clubs that students can join **such as** yoga club, international chess club, literature club, to name only a few. (170826, 大学生应该从事学习之外的活动吗？)

例 2 Nowadays, the general trend seems to be that more and more young people go to college and receive higher education. In China alone, **for example**, about 7 million out of 9.4 million high school students were accepted by universities in 2014, while 35 years ago, only 5% high school students went to college. (180930, 大学生增加会导致毕业生高失业率吗？)

（7）表示时间：finally、at last、eventually、meanwhile、at the same time、immediately、recently、nowadays、since、as soon as、afterwards、after a while 等。

例 1 Admittedly, the kids in early-start mode may excel their peers in school grades, but this mode can also result in negative consequences. Forcing a kid to sit at home and learn things in which he/she does not have any interest at all when he/she is supposed to play with other kids outside might **eventually** kill the kid's passion for learning. That is exactly why many kids who did really well in primary school end up nowhere when they get to the university level. (170819, 学生从小就得努力学习的利弊)

例 2 Another factor has much to do with our habit or psychology of being a tourist. When we get to a new place, our natural inclination is to bring something back home as some sort of souvenir, even if it is just a flower, a plant, or a small piece of soil. **Meanwhile**, we also wish to leave our footprints in the new place we visit, like some graffiti on the walls and trees. All these seem rather trivial and harmless, yet when a million people are doing the same thing, an irrevocable destruction to the local environment and culture will surely occur. (180720, 做负责任的游客很难吗？)

（8）表示顺序：first、second、third、then、finally、to begin with、first of all、in the first place、above all、last but not least、first and foremost 等。

例 1 To prevent criminals from committing crimes again, the **first and foremost** thing that ought to be done is improving the quality and effectiveness of prison education which should be carried out with the aim to turning the prisoners into good people rather than victims of physical punishment.（201107，被惩罚后罪犯继续犯罪的原因及解决办法）

例 2　Yet I do not think dangerous sports should be banned. **In the first place**, these sports actually result in very few deaths each year, though every death will cause enormous amount of media sensation. Thousands of bungee jumpers, for instance, return home safe and sound with no injury whatsoever involved. To ban these sports would definitely disappoint the sports fans who are willing to draw excitement and even inspirations from these sports.（220827，危险运动应该被禁止吗？）

（9）表示换一种方式来解释：in other words、in fact、as a matter of fact、that is、namely 等。

例 1　However, some people believe that innate talent is what differentiates a person who has been trained to play a sport or an instrument, from those who become good players. **In other words**, there is more to the skill than a learned technique, and this extra talent cannot be taught, no matter how good the teacher or how frequently a child practises.（《剑桥雅思 7》，Test 1，天赋和努力哪个更重要？）

例 2　Admittedly, TV trials, particularly the live shows, may bring about negative effects as well. Often the TV trials will present a lot of details of the criminal offenses such as killing, embezzling, cheating, so much so that they become a promotion of these crimes. **As a matter of fact**, many juvenile offenders admit they have been under great influences of TV criminal shows.（161022，直播罪犯审判现场的利弊）

（10）表示递进：what is more、in addition、besides、also、furthermore、moreover、additionally 等。

例 1　In the first place, schools should shoulder their share of responsibility. **Besides** imparting knowledge, schools ought to improve their students' ethical and legal awareness by showing them how to tell right from wrong. Many schools, for example, pay much attention to the artistic education of their students for the reason that art can help a child become a better person. **What is more**, the government should play an active role in educating the future generation. One recommendable policy the government has made recently is to ban the entry of young people under 15 to the bars and the Internet cafe. This policy makes it possible for children to spend more time with their parents and teachers, thus reducing the likelihood of their misconducts. （191010，如何解决青少年犯罪上升问题？）

例 2　Keeping knowledge in the Internet, however, will make us excessively dependent on electronic devices. Simply put, in case of power-off or computer break-down, we would be thrown into a terribly helpless situation. But this is not a problem for people who learn things from books. **Additionally**, many people simply prefer reading real books for knowledge to online sources, because they believe books are more reliable and they find themselves emotionally and intellectually more attached to knowledge in books. （170303，知识存储在网络上的利弊）

（11）表示让步：although、while、for all、in spite of、despite、even if/though、admittedly、whatever may happen 等。

例 1　On balance, the development of having useful appliances at your home is more positive than negative. **Despite** some bad effects typical of modern consumerism, life has become so much more full of pleasure due to these devices available from the kitchen to the bedroom. Now, ask yourself if you would rather live in today's society or yesterday's. （180106，家用电器越来越多的利弊）

例 2　**For all** the advantages that online socializing has to offer, it can never really replace human contact. The basic reason behind is that humans are social animals and they love getting around with people, particularly with friends. Nothing can beat the feelings of walking together, playing games, doing sports, going for picnics and excursions or short trips. （180602，网络社交的利弊）

（12）表示转折：however、rather than、instead of、but、yet、on the other hand、unfortunately、whereas、while 等。

例 1　The new graduates themselves are partly to blame for this problem, for many of them spend their university time mostly on their smartphones and computer games, **rather than** social activities. Yet the most important reason is that interpersonal skills are "soft skills" that are not likely to be taught in the classroom in the same way "hard skills" (school subjects) are taught. （180721，刚毕业的员工缺乏人际交往能力的原因及解决办法）

例2　If by "the most important invention" we mean one that is not only ground-breaking but also completely necessary for human beings to exist, the Internet is perhaps not a suitable candidate for "the most important invention", since, without the Internet, the human world would still be there just as it was in the pre-Internet age. So, **instead of** the Internet, I would label language as "the most important invention", because it was the invention of language that ultimately distinguished humans from animals and made possible everything we have now in the human world. （201025，互联网是人类最重要的发明吗？）

（13）表示总结：on the whole、in conclusion、in a word、to sum up、in brief、in summary、to conclude、to summarize、in short 等。

例1　**To sum up**, in order for our food to be healthy, both individuals and the government have their share of, though different, responsibilities. A healthy diet would only be possible with the efforts made by both individuals and the government. （180921，饮食健康该由政府还是个人负责？）

例2　**In conclusion**, even when people can pay a virtual visit to museums and art galleries, they still need to go to the real ones in order to obtain the valuable personal experience and avoid being misled by the information online. （190831，网络时代，我们还需要博物馆和艺术馆吗？）

（14）其他：mostly、occasionally、currently、naturally、mainly、exactly、evidently、for this purpose、to a large extent、in many cases、in this case 等。

例1　To my mind, it is certainly a good thing to have more people receive university education since this can upgrade the overall quality of the workforce in a country. Meanwhile, more university graduates do not **naturally** lead to more people losing their job.（180930，大学生增加会导致毕业生高失业率吗？）

例2　Working and living in such a busy and noisy environment, people would not be able to find the pleasure that is so important for their work and life, and the benefits they have gained from the shortened travelling time would be undone **to a large extent**. （190406，在城市中心建公寓楼可减少通勤时间

吗？）

例 3　**In this case**, it would be impossible to ask all parents to send their children to high school because many families are so poor that they simply cannot afford the expensive tuition. Even if the government helps to waver the tuition fee, some young adults still cannot continue their education because they are old enough to work and help support their family.（201121，18 岁以下年轻人必须全日制上学吗？）

3.4.2 避免流水句

在雅思写作考官给定的评分细则里，经常出现"本作文的标点符号使用有不少问题"的评语。很多同学不太明白这个标点符号问题究竟指的是什么。其实，对中国学生而言，标点符号问题往往出现在该用句号的时候却用逗号，从而造成所谓的流水句（run-on sentence）。流水句写得多了，分数也会无可奈何随之流走，非常可惜。

中国学生容易被流水句困扰的原因是英语和汉语的区别。汉语中，两个独立句子只要有关系，就可以用逗号连接，且不需要任何表示两句关系的连接词，而在英语中，这两个句子若用逗号连接，就必须有表示两句关系的连接词，否则必须用句号。若既无连接词，又用逗号连接，就构成了不符合英语语法规范的流水句。中国学生由于受到汉语影响，流水句问题屡见不鲜，屡教不改，是英语教师比较头痛的难题。比如中国学生作文中常见的一句：We should work together to fight air pollution, this is very important.（我们必须团结起来与空气污染做斗争，这一点非常重要。）这样的英语就是受到了汉语的影响，两个独立的句子用逗号相连，而且没有连接词。为了消除这里的流水句，我们可以把它们分开成两句，或者把其中一句变成从属句：

修改方法一：We should work together to fight air pollution. This is very important.

修改方法二：We should work together to fight air pollution, which is very important.

修改方法三：It is very important that we work together to fight air pollution.

为了消除流水句，考生需要记住：英语写作中，一个句子写完之后，应该直接加句号；如果用逗号，就要用连接词使之和下一句连接起来。**不能用**

逗号连接两个完整的句子。

我们来看看以下段落中的流水句现象。

Students in schools are suffering under large pressure of competition, from this, teachers and parents are all encouraging students to develop their sense of competition. As a result, children could realize that they have to study very well in order to get to a famous university and finally be employed by a well paid company. And this realization might encourage teenagers to be diligent and work hard on study. Besides, developing children's competition sense provides a "warm up" for their future job, when they get to work, competitions are more intense and unavoidable. The earlier children develop the sense of competition the better they can fit in the working environment.

画线部分是典型的流水句。先看这句：Students in schools are suffering under large pressure of competition, from this, teachers and parents are all encouraging students to develop their sense of competition. 本句前半部分 students in schools are suffering under large pressure of competition 是一个完整的独立句子，后半部分 "from this, teachers and parents are all encouraging students to develop their sense of competition" 也是一个完整的独立句子，学生将这两个句子并列起来，且无任何连接词，因此构成流水句。按照前面提出的修改办法，修改如下：

修改方法一：Students in the school are suffering from huge pressure. Therefore, teachers and parents are all encouraging students to develop their sense of competition.（用句号隔开）

修改方法二：As students in the school are suffering from huge pressure, teachers and parents are all encouraging students to develop their sense of competition.（把前面一句变成原因状语从句）

修改方法三：Students in the school are suffering from huge pressure, which is why teachers and parents are all encouraging students to develop their sense of competition.（把后面一句变成非限定性定语从句）

再看这句：Besides, developing children's competition sense provides a "warm up" for their future job, when they get to work, competitions are more intense and unavoidable. 本句前半部分是一个独立句子，后半部分又是一个独立句子，两者用逗号连接，而且没有任何连接词，因此也是典型的流水句。修改为：

Besides, developing children's sense of competition provides a "warm up" for their future job, since competitions will become more intense when they get to the job market. （把后面一句变成原因状语从句）

3.4.3 句式选择与连贯

同样一个意思，我们可以选择不同的句式来表达，比如主动语态 / 被动语态；用什么词作主语，往往也决定了后面需要用什么句式；此外，还有倒装句、强调句、复合句（包括主语从句、状语从句、定语从句、宾语从句等）等。比如"他今天上午说的话让我们大吃一惊"可以用很多不同的英语句式来表达：

He said something this morning that startled us.

He said something this morning, and we were startled by it.

What he said this morning startled us.

What he said this morning was startling to us.

The words he said this morning startled us.

The words he said this morning were startling to us.

Something he said this morning startled us.

Something he said this morning was startling to us.

We were startled by what he said this morning.

We were startled by the words he said this morning.

这些句子语法上都是正确的，主语不同导致句型发生变化，但到底使用哪个句型才最合适，这需要考虑上下文的制约。通常可以用"新信息 + 旧信息"和"同一主语 + 新信息"两个模式。

我们先讨论**"新信息 + 旧信息"模式**，看以下这个段落：

例 1　It will be a long time before any landing on Mars can be attempted. This will only be possible when scientists have learnt a lot more about the atmosphere that surrounds the planet. If a satellite can one day be put into orbit round Mars, scientists will be able to find out a great deal. An interesting suggestion for measuring the atmosphere around Mars has been put forward.（《新概念英语》第三册第 9 课）

画线部分的句子可以改写成：Only when scientists have learnt a lot more

about the atmosphere that surrounds the planet will this be possible. 从语法上看，改写句毫无问题，但原文为什么不使用这个句子呢？同学们在阅读中可能很少会问这样的问题，但其实思考这样的问题对大家提高写作太重要了。可以看到，原文句中的 this 指代的是前面 landing on Mars，后面部分则引出科学家如何去了解火星周围的大气层。这样，本句在该段中就扮演了承上启下的功能，this 放在句首承上句，"when scientists have learnt more about..." 放在后面接下句。这样的句式安排完美地实现了句间的连贯。如果用改写的句式，这种严密的连贯性就会遭到破坏。不妨再看一例：

例 2　Pumas are large, cat-like animals which are found in America. When reports came into London Zoo that a wild puma had been spotted forty-five miles south of London, they were not taken seriously.（《新概念英语》第三册第 1 课）

当有人向伦敦动物园报告说当地看见了一只 puma，为什么人们不以为意？这需要在上文寻找答案。puma 是"体型大、形状似猫的动物"与本问题无关，只有"生长在美洲"与问题相关；正因为 puma 是生长在美洲的动物，因此当有人向伦敦动物园报告看到了一只 puma，人们便不以为意。这样，which 从句所表达的内容就解释了后面一句的内容，把这个从句安排在句末，显然更有利于句子之间的连贯。如果更换句式，将原句改写成：Pumas are animals found in America, which are large, cat-like. 这个句子语法没有错误，但放在这个语境中，句间连贯性就大为减弱了，因为改写句强调的信息是"体型大、形状似猫"，而这个信息与后面人们为什么不以为意没有关系。

如果从以上两个例子归纳出一个规则来，我们似乎可以这样说：段落中的句子，其前半部分的内容最好是旧信息，承接前面句子中的内容，后半部分最好提出新信息，预告后面句子中的内容，即"旧信息 + 新信息"模式，下一句的旧信息就是上一句中的新信息。这样的句式安排有利于实现句间连贯。

下面，笔者拟从雅思高分范文中提取几个实际例子，从句间连贯的要求来解释这些范文中的句式选择。

例 3　① However, learning to understand and share the value system of a whole society cannot be achieved just in home. ② Once a child goes to school, they are entering a wider community where teachers and peers will have just as much influence as her parents do at home. ③ At school, children will experience working and living with people from a whole variety of backgrounds from the wider society. ④ This experience should teach them how to cooperate with each other and how to contribute to the life of their community. (《剑桥雅思 8》，Test 3，学校和家庭对孩子的影响哪个更大？)

本段共四句。句①接上段，说"学习社会价值体系不只在家里实现"，这句的重心在后面，"不只在家里实现"是新信息，引出句②中的 once a child goes to school。如果把第一句写成 "However, home is not the only place for children to learn to understand and share the value system of a whole society."，那它就很难自然地接第二句。句②的重心在后面，即"教师和同伴对孩子的影响很大"，引出句③中的 "children will experience working and living with people..."。句④则很自然地以 this experience 开头，承接上句，然后提出新信息，即"这种经历教会孩子们互相合作"。如果把最后一句改为 "They can learn how to cooperate with each other... from this experience."，语法虽然正确，但连贯性就差很多。不难看出，本段中的每个句子都是按照"旧信息＋新信息"的模式来安排的，其中旧信息承接上句，新信息启动下句。

例 4 ① In many countries, the birth rate is decreasing so that families are smaller with fewer children. ② These children are often spoilt, not in terms of love and attention because working parents do not have the time for this, but in more material ways. ③ They are allowed to have whatever they want, regardless of price, and to behave as they please. ④ This means that the children grow up without consideration for others and without any understanding of where their standard of living comes from. (《剑桥雅思 4》，Test 2，溺爱孩子的后果)

本段也由四句构成。句①提出许多家庭的孩子数量减少了，把 with fewer children 放在句末以引出后面的 these children。如果将第一句改写为 "In many countries, families are smaller with fewer children because the birth rate is decreasing."，那么句子的重心就落在 birth rate，也就很难引出下面的 these children are often spoilt 了。句②和句③是并列的，采取的句式都是被动句，共同说明现在社会孩子的问题（这是句子间连贯的另外一种方式，请看后文讲解）。句④则由 this means 承前，并引出下面的内容。这个段落中的句子模式也基本是"旧信息＋新信息"，前一个句子后半部分的新信息成为后一个句子前半部分的旧信息，并由这个旧信息再引出新信息，以此类推。

例5　① However, there are certainly dangers in taking time off at that important age. ② Young adults may end up never returning to their studies or finding it difficult to readapt to an academic environment. ③ They may think that it is better to continue in a particular job or to do something completely different from a university course. ④ But overall I think this is less likely today, when academic qualifications are essential for getting a reasonable career.（200806，高中毕业后旅游或工作一年的利弊）

本段依然由四句构成（的确，常规的雅思写作段落都在四至五句之间）。其中句①是主题句；句②和句③是并列的，共同说明间隔年（gap year）可能对 young adults 产生的影响；句④则表明作者自己的立场。句②和句③采用的都是主动句，主语是 young adults。句④为了承接前面，将 this is 置于句首，而将 when 引导的状语从句置于句末。如果按照正常语序，将 when academic qualifications are essential for getting a reasonable career 置于 this is less likely today 之前，则会影响到②③两句与句④之间的连贯性。

归纳起来，这种"新信息 + 旧信息"模式是这样运作的：

A + B（第一句）

B + C（第二句）

C + D（第三句）

D + E（第四句）

…………

当然，第二句中的 B 可能是第一句中 B 的替换形式，如代词（this、they）等。这样的段落行文比较容易保持句子之间的紧密关联，从而实现连贯效果。

另外一个句间连贯模式是"**同一主语 + 新信息**"，即几个句子连续用同一个主语，而每句都提供该主语的不同信息。

例1　① These children are often spoilt, not in terms of love and attention because working parents do not have the time for this, but in more material ways. ② They are allowed to have whatever they want, regardless of price, and to behave as they please.（《剑桥雅思4》，Test 2，溺爱孩子的后果）

这个段落中的两句，主语分别是 these children 和 they，它们指的是一个实体，因此，这两句谈论的是这些孩子的两个方面：他们被溺爱，他们被允许做自己想做的任何事情。这样行文，读者会发现这两句是很连贯的。

例 2　① Young adults may end up never returning to their studies or finding it difficult to readapt to an academic environment. ② They may think that it is better to continue in a particular job or to do something completely different from a university course.（200806，高中毕业后旅游或工作一年的利弊）

同样，这个段落里的两句也具有相同的主语，分别讨论高中毕业生去旅游或工作的两个角度：他们可能再也无法适应学习环境了，他们也许会认为继续工作更好，而不再上大学了。

归纳起来，这种"同一主语＋新信息"模式是这样运作的：

A＋B（第一句）

A＋C（第二句）

A＋D（第三句）

…………

同样，第二句及以后句子中的 A 有可能是代词或名词改写等替换形式。

3.5 段落写作练习

I. 看以下题目，写出第一段，注意对题目进行改写。

（1）In many countries women are allowed to take maternity leave from their jobs during the first months after the birth of their baby. Does advantages outweigh disadvantages?（181013）

第一段：

（2）Some people think that instead of preventing climate change, we need to find a way to live with it. To what extent do you agree or disagree?（160716）

第一段：

（3）With the increasing demand for energy sources of oil and gas, people should look for sources of oil and gas in remote and untouched places. Do the advantages outweigh the disadvantages of damaging such areas?（220625）

第一段：

（4）Many people believe that scientific research should be carried out and controlled by the governments rather than private companies. To what extent do you agree or disagree with this opinion?（210821）

第一段：

（5）Some people think adults should give children freedom to make mistakes. Others think adults should prevent children from making mistakes. Discuss both views and give your own opinion.（210807）

第一段：

II. 阅读如下段落，分析段落主题及段落拓展方法。

（1）Earlier scientists thought that during a man's lifetime the power of his brain decreased. But it is now thought that this is not so. As long as the brain is given plenty of exercise it keeps its power. It has been found that an old person who has always been mentally active has a quicker mind than a young person who has done only physical work. It is now thought that the more work we give our brains, the more work they are able to do.（《大学英语精读 1》, Unit 9）

主题：

拓展方法：

（2）Several factors contribute to food waste from the food-service industry outlets. Firstly, consumers seem to be willingly responsible for wasting a lot of food because they can afford to buy more than they can consume and throw away whatever food they do not need. Secondly, speaking of health risks, many well-to-do people would rather be safe than sorry, so they choose to discard food, thinking that older food and food that is past its expiry date would make them sick. Finally, even if the majority of consumers know that food waste is a problem, they are too stubborn to change the habit. As a result, nearly all excess food on the plate would go to the waste.（190117, 人们为什么浪费食物？）

主题：

拓展方法：

（3）With mobile phones, we can get the first-hand information about our family and friends as well as our work in a fast and convenient way that was unimaginable in the past. Before we had mobile phones, we had to spend hours writing a letter and then travelling a few miles to the post office to send it to our friends, and then waited many days for the reply. But now it is a matter of just a few clicks. Yet the increased use of mobile phones has greatly reduced the opportunities for people to engage in face-to-face communication. Without the help of body language and facial expression, the communication over mobile phones may easily end in misunderstanding. Of course, the excessive dependence upon mobile phones for information may also contribute to the estrangement among their users.（200926，手机交流对个人和社会的影响）

主题：

拓展方法：

（4）To reverse the climate change is never an easy undertaking. The widely acknowledged causes of climate change include the automobile gas emissions, factory pollution, deforestation, among others. If we wish to prevent the climate change, we will have to significantly reduce the use of cars and airplanes, close most of the factories and stop people from cutting trees. This means that, in order to make the Earth become cooler by one or two centigrade degree, our normal life will have to sacrifice. This is a cost most of us would never want to pay, although we have been repeatedly told of the benefits of doing so to the future generation.（160716，避免气候变化还是想办法适应气候变化？）

主题：

拓展方法：

（5）Many researchers have found that age, among other things, is the most differentiating factor in many activities people do, including shopping. For instance, people under 35 prefer to shop in huge supermarkets while older people would like to buy things in traditional off-road stores. This is probably because younger people like the greater variety of goods the supermarkets offer and the older shoppers like the familiar environment of the small stores. In addition, when older people may spend hours and hours looking around and comparing different goods, young people are more likely to buy the goods they like and immediately get back home and watch their favourite NBA games. (160430, 购物习惯取决于年龄吗？)

主题：

拓展方法：

(6) The reasons for this trend may involve the recognition that a young adult who passes directly from school to university is rather restricted in terms of general knowledge and experience of the world. By contrast, those who have spent some time earning a living or travelling to other places, have a broader view of life and better personal resources to draw on. They tend to be more independent, which is a very important factor in academic study and research, as well as giving them an advantage in terms of coping with the challenges of student life. (200806, 高中毕业后旅游或工作一年的利弊)

主题：

拓展方法：

(7) Another important factor that affects the students' attitude towards learning is that a good education seems not as important as before. For quite a long time, receiving a good education was the only way for young people to get a decent job and earn a high salary. But now, this is apparently not the case any more. Influenced by business stars like Bill Gates and Steve Jobs, many young people now begin to believe that one's success is not in proportion to the education she/he receives. The students, therefore, are not motivated enough to focus on their learning. (170304, 年轻人不喜欢学习的原因及解决办法)

主题：

拓展方法：

III. 阅读以下段落，观察句间连贯方式的使用。

（1）Obviously, the influx of people from the countryside will impose immense pressure on the urban environment. To accommodate their new comers, the cities have to build more houses, and make more public transportation service available. As a result, the cities will become a great deal more crowded and noisier. That is actually why a lot of city dwellers begin to think of their "good old days" when there were not as many people as today.（220723，人口朝城市流动对环境的影响）

本段用了哪些连贯手段：

各句句型使用是否合适：

（2）Looking for new energy in uninhabited areas is a very attractive idea. Such places always abound with energy desperately needed by human race, thus attracting generations of people to take their chances. Besides, the exploration of energy in these areas has little immediate impact on the everyday life of people since it happens far away from where they live.（220625，应该去偏远地区开发能源吗？）

本段用了哪些连贯手段：

各句句型使用是否合适：

（3）On the other hand, we often hear a different voice complaining that the Olympic Games is way too costly. It is exactly the case. According to a report issued by the Olympic Organization Committee, the 2016 Olympic Games held in Brazil cost as much as 200 billion RMB (roughly $ 40 billion), which is equivalent to the annual income of a medium-sized country. As a matter of fact, it is precisely because of the immense cost that many countries have to give up the opportunity to host this event.（220716，奥运会是浪费金钱吗？）

本段用了哪些连贯手段：

各句句型使用是否合适：

（4）Another important factor is that the sports facilities in many cities are not readily available to all who need them. The trouble to find a place for physical exercise discourages a lot of city dwellers from participating in physical activities.（220709，城市居民身体锻炼不够的原因及解决办法）

本段用了哪些连贯手段：

各句句型使用是否合适：

（5）Activities that are played alone can develop our sense of self-reliance and responsibility. This is because in such activities, success is entirely a matter of personal efforts, and we will have to learn to rely on ourselves and face the consequences of our own decisions and action. Furthermore, playing alone means that we must motivate ourselves as there is no team pressure and there is nobody else to blame for our failure. Further still, we can perhaps derive more happiness and satisfaction from our success in individual sports, and this sense of self-recognition is essential in our work and life.（211009，参加团体活动比单人活动更有益吗？）

本段用了哪些连贯手段：

各句句型使用是否合适：

（6）In addition, news media are more educational than evil. There is little doubt that some news media are so irresponsible that they often carry negative messages like violence, sex and other forms of crimes. However, most news media are sensible enough to present the news for educational purposes. In the newspaper coverage of a violent killing I read a few days ago, the focus was not on the crime itself, but on the lessons to be drawn from the crime. This kind of news media tell their readers what is right and what is wrong and thus are very important as an educational tool.（160123，新闻媒体影响越来越大的利弊）

本段用了哪些连贯手段：

各句句型使用是否合适：

（7）Living longer than before after retirement is a good thing, as it enables people to see more of the world and take greater part in the life of their children, or even grandchildren, sharing their happiness and sadness, and giving advice when necessary. But a longer life may sometimes be bad as well. Many people, for instance, shudder at the thought that they will no longer be needed in the boring twenty or even thirty years of their retirement life. Worse still, many others may have to spend their long retirement years in hospital, which is not only painful to themselves, but also burdensome to their children.（220611，长寿对个人和社会的影响）

本段用了哪些连贯手段：

各句句型使用是否合适：

第四章　雅思写作词汇

4.1 雅思写作需要什么样的词汇

笔者注意到，很多"烤鸭"对写作中应该使用什么词汇有一个很大的误区，认为写作中使用的词汇应该越高级越好。事实上，很多雅思写作老师也持同样观点，因此在写作教学过程中让学生用所谓高级词汇替换低级词汇（比如用 I reckon 来代替 I think），并认为这样可以获得阅卷老师赞赏，从而获得更好的分数。

笔者并不一味反对使用高级词汇，但无论什么词汇，都要在表意上准确，在风格上适切。如果用"准确"和"适切"作为衡量标准，那么对很多"烤鸭"来说，使用所谓高级词汇可能带来三种风险：一是拼写错误（如果由于拼写错误导致句子意思让人无法读懂，那就会导致更大的错误）；二是用法错误（词汇越高级，使用的场合越受限制）；三是文体错误（在一篇多数都是一般词汇的文章里，突然插入几个很高级的词汇，其结果是破坏整个文体统一性，读起来极不协调）。

那么，雅思高分写作中，体现水平的词汇到底长什么样？我们先来看看《剑桥雅思 13》中，考官对一篇 7 分作文使用的词汇所做的评价：

词汇丰富，显示出一定的准确性和灵活度，有不太常见的用词，文体正式，搭配正确。比如：complex、list of favourites、fits... my ability、specific area、many available channels。

从这个评价中，我们可以看到，雅思 7 分作文词汇需要一定的幅度，同时需要正式的文体和正确的搭配，不能有过于口语或方言式的表达。这里顺便说一句，被很多雅思老师推崇的 I reckon，在表达 I suppose/think 这个意义时，其实只是一种特定群体才用的方言，不适合用于雅思作文中。那么，"一定幅度的词汇"指哪些词汇呢？看看考官举出的例子：complex、favourite、specific、available 等。可以发现，所谓高分词汇，其实不是那些吓人的词汇，而是一些相对不常用的普通词汇而已。按照笔者的估算，**雅思写作高分词汇幅度大约可以定位在大学英语四级词汇表里的中高段词汇，也就是 4000—5000那些词汇**。在这里，笔者想特别解释一下雅思阅读词汇和写作词汇的差异。英语的基础词汇大约为 6000，这些词汇是需要考生知道其意义和用法的，因此也是雅思写作的词汇，但就雅思阅读而言，词汇量应该在 10000 左右为宜，其中 6000—10000 之间的词汇，只要求考生知道其意义，并不要求考生了解其用法，因此不是雅思考试的写作词汇。

现在，我们一起看一篇《剑桥雅思 9》中考官提供的雅思高分范文，其中黑体部分是高分词 / 词组。

题目：Some people believe that unpaid community service should be a compulsory part of high school programmes (for example working for a charity, improving the neighbourhood or teaching sports to younger children). To what extent do you agree or disagree? (《剑桥雅思 9》，Test 2)

高分范文：

It has been suggested that high school students should **be involved in** unpaid community services as a compulsory part of high school programmes. Most of the colleges are already **providing** opportunities to give work experience, however these are not **compulsory**. In my opinion, sending students to work in community services is a good idea as it can provide them with many sorts of **valuable skills**.

Life skills are very important and by doing **voluntary work**, students can learn how to communicate with others and work in a team but also how to manage their time and improve their **organisational skills**. Nowadays, unfortunately, teenagers do not have many after-school activities. After-school clubs are no longer that popular and students mostly go home and sit in front of the TV, **browse the Internet** or play video games.

By giving them compulsory work activities with **charitable** or community organisations, they will be encouraged to do something more **creative**. Skills gained through compulsory work will not only be **an asset on their CV** but also increase their **employability**. Students will also gain more respect towards work and money as they will realise that it is not that easy to earn them and hopefully will learn to spend them **in a more practical way**.

Healthy life balance and exercise are strongly **promoted** by the NHS, and therefore any kind of spare time charity work will prevent them from sitting and doing nothing. It could also possibly reduce the crime level in the high school age group. If students have activities to do, they will not be bored and **come up with** silly ideas which can be dangerous for them or their surroundings.

In conclusion, I think this is a very good idea, and I hope this programme will be **put into action** for high schools and colleges **shortly**.

大家不妨看看黑体字标示出来的高分词和词组，其中，involve、provide、compulsory、valuable、organisational、browse、creative、asset、practical、promote、shortly 等词即使在大学英语四级词汇表里，也算不上最难的。而且，这还是所谓的"9分作文"，如果"烤鸭"的目标仅仅是 7 分，还可以进一步将其中某些词汇简单化。比如这句：Skills gained through compulsory work will not only be an asset on their CV but also increase their employability. 如果考生对 an asset on sth 和 employability 的用法不熟悉，可以将本句改为：Skills gained through compulsory work will not only be an attractive part of their CV but also help them find a job.

此外，笔者还想评论本范文最后一段中的 I think this is a very good idea。很多所谓金牌雅思老师或雅思书籍上的金牌规则都告诉学生，不要用 I think，不要用 good，不要用 a very good idea，因为这些太低级，太口语化。但事实上，在高分范文中，类似表达并不少见。其实，笔者反对的是通篇使用这样简单的表达法（因为没有幅度），但这并不意味着这些表达法本身不能用在雅思写作中。**在一篇 250 词左右的作文中，如果有 10 个左右词／词组属于上文笔者定义的高分词汇（即四级词汇表中的中高段词汇）就够了，其余 240 个词就用 2000 左右的一般词汇就可以了。**

接下来，笔者举一个反面例子，看频繁使用"高级词汇"如何损害了作文的质量。其中，黑体部分是不合适的高级词汇，画线部分是语法失误之处。

题目：The spread of multinational companies and the resulting increase in globalisation produce positive effects to everyone. Do you agree or disagree with this statement?（210109）

某机构提供的范文：

The world is moving in a direction where the **tentacles** of cross-national corporations are **reaching to** all corners of the world. While this trend has been **applauded** by the **devotees** of globalisation as a blessing for everyone, I will say it is a generalized opinion ignoring the **discrete interests** of individuals.

There seems to be reasons why the **prosperity of multinational companies** and the ensuing globalisation is assumed beneficial to all. Those who think in this way may point to **legions of advantages** in daily life, whether these be job opportunities, equal accessibility to the same product from any corners of the world, or **the easy to reach after sales service** wherever they go. Examples regarding these including the international brands such as Dell, Apple and MacDonald, all of which play a key role in employment and their products are becoming an imperative part in lives of various demographics. Given this, **here comes the assumption** that the **populace** is the whole **beneficiary** of a globalised economy.

Plausible though it seems, it is difficult for me to see the **veneration** of a globalised business world as a blessing to all. Those who focus on its positive side of this trend are oblivious to the fact that the **ramifications of any social episodes** should be domain specific and context dependent. Based on this, the discussion can then move on to hand questions as to which social impacts are more desirable in the local context or what local stakeholders value more. From the perspective of local industries in developing countries, the relentless invasion of international brands may **oust** them from local market. To complicate matters even more, the disappearance of **indigenous** artefacts may jeopardize the national identity and cultural diversity in the world.

From what has been discussed above, it is my opinion therefore, the benefits of a globalised economy dominated by multinational companies do not apply to everyone.

本文看起来高大上，高级词汇满天飞，实际上用词和语法错误不断，造成语义模糊，甚至有几处让人无法读懂。整个作文读起来装腔作势（pompous），极不顺畅，根本不是现代英语的风格，倒有些接近 19 世纪维多利亚时代的扭捏文风（awkward style），只是语言表达错误百出。笔者强烈建议大家远离这样的"范文"。

从用词的角度，本文使用了不少超纲词，比如 tentacle、discrete、legion、demographics、populace、beneficiary、plausible、veneration、ramification、oust、indigenous，其中很多词都是误用，或让本来明确的意思变得很朦胧。令人匪夷所思的是，在一篇看起来正规得拿腔拿调的作文中，突然出现一句非常口语化的"here comes the assumption that..."，读起来实在让人忍俊不禁。

4.2 20 个万能词汇

以下介绍的 20 个词汇，是基于笔者多年研究和创作雅思真题范文的经验。需要说明的是，所谓"万能"，是指这些词汇在多数题材中都可用到，因此考生既可以为了意思表达需要使用这些词汇，也可以为了用出这些词汇而调整需要表达的意思。

万能词汇 1：available

available 是一个非常有用的高端写作词，其基本意思是"可以获得的；可以使用的；有效的"。比如：

Do you have a room available? 你们有空房间吗？

You will be informed when the book becomes available. 那本书一到就通知你。

There were no tickets available for Friday's performance. 周五的演出已经没有票卖了。

The goal is to make higher education available to everyone who is willing and capable regardless of his financial situation. 目标是让每个有意愿、有能力的人都可获得高等教育，无论他的经济状况如何。

在《剑桥雅思 8》的一篇关于交通类题材的官方范文中有这么一句：

However, traffic congestion will not be solved by changing the type of private vehicle people can use. To do this, we need to improve the choice of public transport services **available to** travellers.（《剑桥雅思 8》，Test 3）然而，改变人们能够使用的私人交通工具并不能解决交通堵塞问题。为了解决这个

问题，我们需要提高可供人们选乘的公共交通服务。

在这个句子中，we need to improve the choice of public transport services available to travellers 完全可以改写为 we need to improve the choice of public transport services that can be used by travellers，但这样一来，词汇的幅度就显得不足了。以下再看笔者原创的雅思真题高分范文中的两个句子。

例 1　Meanwhile, cities and towns built centuries ago do not have enough entertainment and sports facilities **available to** contemporary city dwellers who, relieved of the manual labour by the technological advances, suddenly find they have a great amount of free time.（161103，旧城市带来的问题）同时，由于技术的发展，当代城市居民已经从手工劳作中解脱出来，他们突然发现自己有大量空闲时间，但是数世纪前修建的城镇没有足够的娱乐和体育设施供他们使用。

例 2　We live in an age of electronic communication, and the Internet helps us in a lot of ways. Yet the fact that we have computers and smartphones **readily available** does not mean that we do not need face-to-face communication any more.（180421，网络交流取代面对面交流是好还是坏？）我们生活在电子通信时代，互联网在很多方面帮助我们。然而，我们可以随时使用电脑和智能手机这一事实并不意味着我们不再需要面对面的交流。

万能词汇 2：specific

specific 使用也比较广泛，其基本含义是"特定的；具体的"，经常用作 to be more specific，意思为"说得更具体点"。比如：

There are several specific problems to be dealt with. 有几个具体问题需要解决。

She declined to give more specific reasons for the separation. 她拒绝给出导致分手的更确切的原因。

He is a teenager. To be more specific, he is fifteen now. 他有 10 多岁，说得更具体点，他现在 15 岁。

以下我们看 specific 在雅思范文中是如何使用的。

例 1　Undoubtedly, many people may benefit from the practice. **To be more specific**, in a country where the government pays the tuition, all people, especially those from poverty-stricken areas, are entitled to the equal access to higher education regardless of their background.（130817，政府支付学费的好坏）毫无疑问，这个做法会让很多人获益。说得更具体些，在由政府支付学费的国家，所有人，尤其是那些来自贫困地区的人，都能获得相同的高等教育机会，无论其背景如何。

例2 Yet one issue is still in debate: to whom should the money of charity organisations go, exclusively to people who live in the same country as the organisations, or to all people regardless of where they live? To my mind, the answer to this question depends largely on the mission of **specific** charity organisations.（160820，慈善机构应该只帮助本国人吗？）然而，有一个问题仍在争论中：慈善组织的钱该用在谁身上，只用于与机构同一国家的人，还是用于所有人，不管他们居住在哪？在我看来，这个问题的答案在很大程度上取决于特定慈善组织的使命。

例3 A city designed on the basis of clearly-defined functional areas can make our life a lot easier and more efficient. When we want to buy a **specific** model of computer, for example, we can simply visit the city's hi-tech market without having to rummage every corner of the city.（180727，城市功能分区好吗？）基于明确功能划分的城市能使我们的生活更轻松、更有效。比如，当我们想买一台特定型号的计算机，我们可以访问城市的高科技市场，而不必搜寻城市的每个角落。

万能词汇3：alternative

alternative 绝对是一个万能词，可作形容词，表示"另外的；其他的；可用来替换的"，也可以作名词，表示"另一个选择"。比如：

I'm awfully sorry, there's no alternative but to sell the car. 真的很抱歉，我没有其他办法只能卖汽车了。

Every one will accept computers, because there is no alternative. 我们都会接受电脑，因为别无选择。

Competitive success is commonly seen as the American alternative to social rank based on family background. 在美国，在竞争中胜出常被看作基于家庭背景而提升社会地位的另一选择。

在《剑桥雅思8》一篇关于"开车利弊"的高分范文中有这么一句：

Long-distance train and coach services should be made attractive and affordable

alternatives to driving your own cars for long journeys. (《剑桥雅思 8》，Test 3）本句中的 alternative 用作名词，全句的意思为：应该让长途火车和汽车既有吸引力，价格又便宜，在长距离旅行中来替代自驾。以下是其他范文中的 alternative。

例 1 In conclusion, there are reasons why countries should reduce their consumption of fossil fuels such as oil, coal and natural gas, but more realistically, they should find ways of generating and storing **alternative sources** such as solar and wind energy. (191019，我们必须少使用化石燃料吗？)总之，各国应该减少石油、煤炭和天然气等化石燃料的消耗是有原因的，但更现实的是，它们应该找到方法来产生和储存替代能源，如太阳能和风能。

例 2 Environmentally-friendly **alternative energy** such as solar energy ought to be widely used so that people may continue their present lifestyle but with little environmental impact. (200822，让一代人放弃舒适生活是解决环境问题的关键吗？)环境友好的替代能源，如太阳能，应该被广泛使用，以便人们可以继续他们目前的生活方式，而不会对环境产生什么影响。

万能词汇 4：afford

afford 这个词也比较灵活，其基本意思是"提供；承担得起"。比如：

These trees afford a pleasant shade. 这些树提供了阴凉，很舒服。

I can't afford a holiday this summer. 今年夏天我没钱度假。

以下看 afford 在范文中是如何使用的。

例 1 I still remember a few days ago when walking in front of a supermarket, I saw how a little girl, with her eyes glued to an advertising board, pestered her mother for the expensive toy on it that her mother evidently could not **afford**. (180422，广告对经济和个人的影响)我仍记得几天前路过一家超市时，看见一个小女孩眼巴巴地盯着一个广告牌，缠着她母亲买上面宣传的一个昂贵的玩具，但很显然，她妈妈买不起这个玩具。

例 2 If people have to pay for their own health care, I think many problems may arise. The most serious one is that those poor people cannot enjoy health care because they are not able to **afford** the costs. (160319，应该全民免费医疗吗？)如果人们必须自己支付医疗费用，我认为会有许多问题。最严重的就是穷人将无法享受医疗，因为他们负担不起费用。

例 3　The money squandered on developing technology to find other life forms, for instance, should be used to help children who cannot **afford** to go to college and those who cannot enjoy decent medical services.（181201，应该投资太空技术吗？）比如，为了寻找其他生命形式而开发技术从而浪费的钱，应该用来帮助那些上不起大学的孩子和那些不能享受较好医疗服务的人。

例 4　Drug companies in the developed world are under the moral obligation to make their medicinal products available and **affordable** in the underdeveloped world so that the poorer people do not die unnecessarily.（190810，医药公司的主要职责是挣钱还是为贫穷国家研究新药？）发达国家的制药公司有道德上的义务，使其药品在欠发达的世界中买得到，也买得起，从而避免贫穷的人不必要地死去。

万能词汇 5：primarily

primarily 来自于 primary，意思为"主要地；根本地"，相当于 mainly、initially 等。比如：

Laziness is the primary cause of our failure. 懒惰是我们失败的主要原因。

Steel is an alloy composed primarily of iron and carbon. 钢是一种合金，主要由铁和碳构成。

It's very interesting to note where the debate about diversity is taking place. It is taking place primarily in political circles. 观察关于多样性的争论发生在何处是很有趣的。这些争论主要发生在政治圈子里。

以下句子摘自雅思真题高分范文。

例 1　We all know different people have different shopping habits. Now the question is: are these differences in shopping habits caused **primarily** by the age differences of the shoppers? My personal answer to this question is a definite "yes".（160413，购物习惯取决于年龄吗？）我们都知道不同的人有不同的购物习惯。现在问题是：导致购物习惯不同的主要原因是购物者年龄吗？我个人对这个问题持肯定回答。

万能词汇 6：involve

involve 这个词的常用意思为"使卷入……"，但其转义"包含；需要"在雅思写作中用处更大。比如：

I seem to have involved myself in something I don't understand. 我似乎已

经卷入了我不了解的事情当中。

I don't want to do anything that would involve me in a long-term commitment. 我不想做任何会使自己卷入长期承诺的事情。

Running a kitchen involves lots of discipline and speed. 管理厨房需要讲究方法和速度。

在《剑桥雅思 9》的一篇关于"中学生是否应该参加社区服务工作"的官方范文中有这么一句：

It has been suggested that high school students should **be involved in** unpaid community services as a compulsory part of high school programmes.（《剑桥雅思 9》，Test 2）有人建议，作为高中课程必不可少的组成部分，高中生应参与无偿的社区服务。

在这个句子中，be involved in 的意思是"参加，加入"，相当于 do 或者 take part in。再如：

例 1   The reasons for this trend may **involve** the recognition that a young adult who passes directly from school to university is rather restricted in terms of general knowledge and experience of the world.（200806，高中毕业后旅游或工作一年的利弊）造成这一趋势的原因可能是人们认识到，直接从中学转到大学的年轻人在一般知识和世界经验方面非常有限。

本句的话题是"中学生毕业后是否应该去旅游或工作一年后再上大学"，其中的 involve 一词使用非常地道。如果不用这个词，我们可以用"The reasons for this trend may have something to do with the recognition that..."，意思虽然相同，但词汇的幅度下降了不少。以下再看笔者原创的雅思真题高分范文中的两个句子。

例 2   In my opinion, modern digital means of communication are certainly a positive development because they can help to solve many of our problems. What remains to be done is that we make the best use of them and reduce the risks they may **involve**.（170812，现代通信科技对我们有好处吗？）我认为，现代数字化通信方式无疑是积极的进步，因为它们可以帮助我们解决很多问题。剩下要做的是充分利用它们，同时降低它们可能带来的风险。

例 3   We need to take good care of these buildings and keep them as long as possible, however much money it may **involve**, so that they can tell the stories of the city or the nation to our future generations.（190718，用于修缮老建筑的钱应该用于新住房和道路建设吗？）我们需要照顾好这些建筑物，并尽可能长时间地保存它们，不管这会需要多少金钱，这样它们就可以向我们的后代讲述城市或国家的故事。

万能词汇 7：justify

justify 的意思是"证明……有理；为……找理由"，这个词在以议论为主的雅思作文中使用非常频繁。比如：

No argument can justify a war. 没有什么理由能证明战争有理。

How do you justify your failure in the final exam? 你怎么解释期末考试不及格？

In my opinion, the decision was wholly justified. 在我看来，这个决定完全合理。

The robber tried to justify his crime by saying that he needed money to pay his debts. 抢劫犯说他需要钱来还债，企图以此为他的罪行辩护。

以下看 justify 在雅思真题范文中的使用情况。

例1　Undoubtedly, such pressing problems as housing, education, and medicare ought to be taken care of by the government, but it is also the responsibility of the government to prepare for the future of the Earth. Seen in this light, a reasonable investment on the life on other planets is perfectly **justifiable**.（181201，应该投资太空技术吗？）毫无疑问，诸如住房、教育和医疗保险等紧迫的问题应该由政府来解决，但政府也有责任为地球的未来做好准备。从这个角度来看，对探索其他行星上的生命进行合理投资是完全合理的。

例2　To make things worse, entertainment producers these days tend to present, quite misleadingly, violent acts as an expression of heroism and have them well **justified**, giving the viewers, especially those young viewers, a false impression that violence is a cool and always right thing to do.（180520，控制影视中的暴力可以降低犯罪率吗？）更糟糕的是，今天的娱乐节目制片人往往将暴力行为表达为一种英雄行为，而且为其辩护，这是很有误导性的，给观众，尤其是年轻观众，一种错误的印象，即暴力是一件很酷也总是正确的事情。

万能词汇 8：excessive

excessive 绝对是一个万能词，使用非常广泛，表示"过多的；过分的"。

比如：

Excessive dosage of this drug can result in injury to the liver. 这种药使用过量会损害肝脏。

Excessive rainfall had made the harvest impossible. 雨量过多，丰收已经不可能了。

Excessive speed plays a major role in as much as one fifth of all fatal traffic accidents, according to the foundation. 据该基金会称，在多达五分之一的致命交通事故中，超速是重要原因。

以下看 excessive 在雅思真题范文中是如何使用的。

例 1　Generally, more and more employees are experiencing conflicts between their career and personal roles. On the one hand, they are having **excessive** work responsibilities; while on the other hand, they are having responsibilities for other aspects of their lives. （190720，工作与生活难以平衡的原因及解决办法）一般来说，越来越多的员工正经历着职业生涯和个人角色之间的冲突。一方面，他们有过多的工作责任；另一方面，他们有对其生活其他方面的责任。

例 2　Besides, as many secondary school students are not yet mature intellectually and mentally, the **excessive** exposure to international news may actually have negative influence on their ways of looking at their own country. （200816，中学生应该学习国际新闻课吗？）此外，许多中学生在智力和心理上都还没有成熟，过度接触国际新闻实际上可能会对他们如何看待自己的国家产生消极影响。

例 3　There seems to be more and more detailed criminal description on media these days, such as beating, murdering, gun fighting, blood shedding, among others. As I see it, the **excessive** exposure to these criminal scenes will negatively influence newspaper readers and TV viewers, thus increasing the likelihood of their committing the same crimes in real life, but to restrict them on media is quite another story. （201024，是否应该限制报纸电视中的犯罪描写？）现在，媒体上似乎有越来越多的详细犯罪描述，如殴打、谋杀、枪战、流血等。在我看来，看到太多类似犯罪场景将对报纸读者和电视观众产生负面影响，从而增加他们在现实生活中犯下同样罪行的可能性，但在媒体上限制这些描写则完全是另一回事。

万能词汇 9：eventually

eventually 比较常见，其基本意思是"最后；终于"，与 at last 和 finally 经常可以互换使用。比如：

He worked so hard that eventually he made himself ill. 他工作太卖力，最后自己病倒了。

It was a long journey, but we eventually arrived. 旅程很长，但我们最后还是到达了。

Many in the credit industry expect that credit cards will eventually replace paper money for almost every purchase. 信贷业中许多人认为，信用卡最终将取代纸币来完成所有购买。

以下我们看 eventually 在雅思真题范文中是如何使用的。

例 1 Such is human nature that we always ask for more than is necessary for us, which, if not brought well under control, will make us greedy and **eventually** lead us all the way to prison.（200815，犯罪是天性使然吗？）我们总是想得到比自己需要的更多，这就是人类的天性。如果不能很好地控制，这个天性会让我们变得贪婪，最终把我们卷进监狱。

例 2 If the government and individuals alike tried their best to help the criminals by creating job opportunities for them and showing enough respect, I believe they would **eventually** come back to normal life and would not commit more crimes.（201107，被惩罚后罪犯继续犯罪的原因及解决办法）如果政府和个人都尽力帮助罪犯，为他们创造就业机会，并表现出足够的尊重，我相信他们最终会恢复正常生活，不会犯下更多的罪行。

例 3 Most important of all, it is just in not so pure a place as school that kids can learn to tell right from wrong, good from bad and **eventually** become physically and psychologically healthy individuals when they grow up.（160213，在家教育还是去学校？）最重要的是，正是在像学校这样不那么纯的地方，孩子才能够学会分辨正误和好坏，待他们长大之后，最终成为身心健康的人。

万能词汇 10：apparently

apparently 来自于 apparent，意思为"显而易见地；表面上地"。比如：

It was apparent to all that he was guilty. 大家都清楚，他是有罪的。

She heard the news of his death with apparent unconcern. 她听到他的死讯，看起来无动于衷。

His proposal is apparent to all of us and you do not need to tell us more about it. 我们都明白他的计划，因此你无须多说。

In 1914, an apparently insignificant event in a remote part of Eastern Europe plunged Europe into a great war. 1914 年，在东欧一个偏远地区发生的一件看起来不起眼的事件，将欧洲拖入到一场大战中。

以下句子摘自雅思真题高分范文。

例 1　Today, we can **apparently** accomplish a lot of things without the help of others, which leads to the popular belief that we are becoming more and more independent. （161105，我们现在是更独立还是更相互依赖？）今天，我们看似没有别人的帮助也能够做成很多事情，这让大家都相信，我们正变得越来越独立。

例 2　For quite a long time, receiving a good education was the only way for young people to get a decent job and earn a high salary. But now, this is **apparently** not the case any more.（170304，年轻人不喜欢学习的原因及解决办法）在很长一段时间内，接受好的教育是年轻人获好工作、挣高工资的唯一路径，但是现在看起来不再是那样了。

万能词汇 11：confine

confine 的意思为"将……控制 / 限制在……范围内"，通常用作词组"confine... to..."（把……限定在……）。比如：

Health officials have successfully confined the epidemic to the area. 卫生官员们已经成功地将该传染病控制在这个地区。

They decided not to let their new dog run loose, confining it to a fenced enclosure during the day. 他们决定不让他们新养的狗到处乱跑，白天把它关在围栏里。

以下看雅思真题高分范文如何使用这个词。

例 1　An organisation aiming at solving local issues should spend its money helping people who live in the same country, but it should not **confine itself to** a single country if an organisation sets its eyes on global issues.（160820，慈善机构应该只帮助本国人吗？）致力于解决区域问题的机构应该将善款用

于帮助生活在同一国家的人，但是如果一个机构关注全球问题，那它就不应该局限在一个国家了。

例2　But we all know that **confinement to oneself** is no good, no matter how many friends or fans you may have online. As part of the solution to the problem, I would suggest everybody have an "Internet-free moment". （160924，城市居民不再互相交往的原因及解决办法）但是我们都知道封闭自我不好，无论你在网上有多少朋友或者粉丝。为了解决这个问题，我提出一个方案，建议每个人都有一个"无网时刻"。

例3　However, it does not follow that university students must **confine themselves to** the library and the classroom. Quite the opposite, they ought to engage in as many extracurricular activities as possible, for if the academic study makes them prepared intellectually, these club activities may be helpful to their future career in many different ways. （170826，大学生应该参加课外活动吗？）然而，这并不意味着大学生必须局限于图书馆和教室。恰恰相反，他们应该尽可能多地从事课外活动。如果学业学习为他们做好知识上的准备，这些俱乐部的活动可能在多方面有助于他们未来的职业生涯。

例4　With dwindled outdoor areas, people will **find themselves confined to** the limited number of indoor activities. If in the past they were able to engage in such activities as walking, gardening, weeding, and planting in their back-yard, when they got back home from work, now what people can do is sitting in the sofa and watching TV. （200116，室外空间越来越少是好还是坏？）随着室外区域的减少，人们会发现自己局限于有限的室内活动。如果过去下班回家后，他们能在后院从事散步、园艺、除草、种植等活动，现在人们能做的就是坐在沙发上看电视。

万能词汇12：derive

derive 的基本意思为"获得，得到；衍生"，相当于 get、obtain，通常用于词组"derive... from..."（从……获得；从……衍生而来）。比如：

Mr. Ying is one of those happy people who derive pleasure from helping others. 英先生是那种助人为乐的快活人。

This word is derived from a Greek word. 这个词是从一个希腊词衍生而来的。

以下看 derive 在雅思真题高分范文中的使用情况。

例 1 Further still, people can perhaps **derive** more happiness and satisfaction **from** their success in individual sports, and this sense of self-recognition is an essential skill in their work and life.（180929，团队活动比个人活动能教我们更多生活技能吗？）*此外，人们可能从个人运动的成功中获得更多的幸福和满足，这种自我认同感是他们工作和生活中必不可少的技能。*

万能词汇 13：compel

compel 算得上是一个万能词，使用非常广泛，表示"强迫；迫使"，意思相当于 force、make，搭配是 compel sb to do sth（强迫某人做某事）。比如：

The heavy rain compelled us to stay indoors. *大雨迫使我们留在家里。*

以下看 compel 在雅思真题范文中是如何使用的。

例 1 Except for the very few who may take art as their lifelong career, the great majority of students will not get a job in relation to art when they finish their high school. Besides, what is the point of **compelling** a student who has no interest in art to spend many hours restlessly in the art classes?（170107，艺术课程应该成为高中必修课吗？）*除了极少数学生会将艺术作为终身事业，绝大多数学生高中毕业后都不会从事与艺术相关的工作。此外，一个对艺术不感兴趣的学生在艺术课上心神不宁地耗费时间有什么意义？*

例 2 However, I believe the intensified competition resulting from the arrival of the foreign food is beneficial to the long-term development of the local food industry, because it will **compel** the local food companies to improve the quality of their products, which in turn will make them more competitive in the global market.（180513，食用进口食品利大于弊吗？）*然而，我相信，随着外国食品到来而引起的激烈竞争对本地食品业的长远发展是有好处的，因为这会迫使本地食品公司改进产品质量，反过来会让它们在国际市场上更具竞争力。*

例 3 For example, a paper-making factory will be more careful with its wastes if it is **compelled** to pay a tremendous amount of money for the water it pollutes, and a car owner may choose to use public transport if he is made to pay an extra pollution fee for driving.（191026，该谁来负责清理环境？）*例如，如果强迫造纸厂为其污染的水支付巨额费用，它就会更加注意排污；如果让*

车主为驾驶而支付额外的污染费，他就可能选择使用公共交通工具。

万能词汇 14：expose

expose 本义为"揭穿；暴露"，但常用于表达"把……置于（某种不利情况）"的意思，用于词组"expose... to..."，其名词形式为 exposure。比如：

It's very foolish of the commander to expose his men to unnecessary risks. 这个指挥官让士兵们冒不必要的危险真是太愚蠢了。

Don't expose your skin to the sun for too long at noon, or it will easily get burnt. 正午的时候不要让皮肤在阳光下曝晒太久，否则很容易晒伤。

以下我们看 expose/exposure 在雅思真题范文中是如何使用的。

例 1　Besides, as many secondary school students are not yet mature intellectually and mentally, the excessive **exposure to** international news may actually have negative influence on their ways of looking at their own country.（200816，中学生应该学习国际新闻课吗？）此外，许多中学生在智力和心理上都还没有成熟，过度接触国际新闻实际上可能会对他们如何看待自己的国家产生消极影响。

例 2　As I see it, the excessive **exposure to** these criminal scenes will negatively influence newspaper readers and TV viewers, thus increasing the likelihood of their committing the same crimes in real life, but to restrict them on media is quite another story.（201024，是否应该限制报纸电视中的犯罪描写？）在我看来，看到太多类似犯罪场景将对报纸读者和电视观众产生负面影响，从而增加他们在现实生活中犯下同样罪行的可能性，但在媒体上限制这些描写则完全是另一回事。

例 3　Catering to the psychological needs of children, many advertisements describe the world in highly imaginative and unrealistic manners. For instance, when they want to promote their doll weapons, they will describe the world as a place full of bad guys. A child **exposed to** such advertising may develop a deep sense of hostility to the world.（160220，儿童广告应该被禁止吗？）为了迎合孩子的心理需求，很多广告用极其富于想象力和不现实的方式描述这个世界。比如说，当要推广玩具武器时，广告会把世界描述为坏人横行之处。孩子处于这样的广告环境下可能会对世界有很深的敌意。

万能词汇 15：exclusively

exclusively 来自于 exclude（把……排除在外），意思为"排他地；唯一地"，相当于 only。比如：

Today he was able to focus his message exclusively on the economy. 今天他做到了将重点全部聚焦在经济方面。

Up till that time, his interest had focused almost exclusively on fully mastering the skills and techniques of his craft. 在那之前，他的兴趣几乎全部聚焦在全面掌握工艺技能和技术上。

以下句子摘自雅思真题范文。

例 1 The government in any country provides funding for the development of its higher education, but there are divided opinions about where this government funding should go. Should it go **exclusively** to those "top students" or indiscriminately to all students?（170624，政府应该只资助优秀学生吗？）任何国家的政府都为本国高等教育的发展提供资助，但关于政府资助该用在哪里有不同观点。它是应该只用于"优秀学生"还是不加区分地用于所有学生？

例 2 Charity organisations are supposed to offer help to people in great need, such as those suffering from incurable diseases, natural disasters and unexpected accidents. Yet one issue is still in debate: to whom should the money of charity organisations go, **exclusively** to people who live in the same country as the organisations, or to all people regardless of where they live?（160820，慈善机构应该只帮助本国人吗？）慈善组织应为急需帮助的人提供帮助，比如身患不治之症的人，遭受自然灾害的人和遭遇意外事故的人。然而，有一个问题仍在争论中：慈善组织的钱该用在谁身上，只用于与机构同一国家的人，还是用于所有人，不管他们住在哪？

万能词汇 16：determine

determine 的意思为"查明；确定；决定；决心"，词组"be determined to do..."的意思是"决心做……"。比如：

The size of the chicken pieces will determine the cooking time. 鸡块的大小决定烹饪时间。

Experts say testing needs to be done on each contaminant to determine the long-term effects on humans. 专家说需要对每种污染物进行检测，以查明对人

类的长期影响。

His enemies are determined to ruin him. 他的敌人决意要毁了他。

以下看雅思真题范文如何使用这个词。

例 1 To conclude, where the charity money should go is mainly **determined** by the chief concerns and missions of different charity organisations. （160820，慈善机构应该只帮助本国人吗？）总之，慈善款应用于何处，主要取决于不同慈善组织的首要关注点和使命。

例 2 In my view, both ways are effective to address the traffic problem in cities, but it is the city conditions that will **determine** which way is better. （180707，建更多铁路和地铁好，还是修更多道路好？）在我看来，这两种方法都能有效地解决城市的交通问题，但哪种方法更好取决于城市的条件。

例 3 While it is hard to **determine** how the visual uniformity is related to quality at work, having a dress code in place may help the way a corporation wants to be perceived.（180113，员工着装和工作品质有何关系？）虽然很难确定视觉统一性与工作质量有何关系，但设置着装规范可能会帮助公司确立希望被人感知的方式。

万能词汇 17：relieve

relieve 的基本意思为"缓解；减轻；使解脱"，相当于 lessen，通常用于词组 "relieve... of..."（把某人从……中解脱出来）。比如：

Drugs can relieve much of the pain. 药物可以大大缓解疼痛。

A housekeeper can relieve you of the house chores. 一位管家可使你从家务中解脱出来。

I felt much relieved when I heard the good news. 听说这个好消息后，我感觉轻松了很多。

以下看 relieve 在雅思真题范文中的使用情况。

例 1 Meanwhile, cities and towns built centuries ago do not have enough entertainment and sports facilities available to contemporary city dwellers who, **relieved of** the manual labour by the technological advances, suddenly find they have a great amount of free time.（161103，旧城市带来的问题）同时，由于技术的发展，当代城市居民已经从手工劳作中解脱出来，他们突然发现自己有大量空闲时间，但是数世纪前修建的城镇没有足够的娱乐和体育设施供他

们使用。

例 2 Children today are apparently enjoying more freedom than ever before. This is so because the technological advances have **relieved** children **of** much of their manual labour and because the parents and schools these days are far less controlling than in the past.（170708，孩子们自由更多了是好还是坏？）今天的孩子显然享受着比以前更多的自由。之所以如此，是因为技术进步解放了孩子们很多手工劳动，也因为现在家长和学校远不如以前那样控制孩子了。

例 3 Even those more leisurely activities such as guitar playing or singing can **relieve** the students of their heavy load of academic work and make them more resilient to physical and emotional stresses in life.（170826，大学生应该从事学习之外的活动吗？）即使那些较为悠闲的活动，如吉他演奏或唱歌，也可以缓解他们沉重的学习负荷，让他们更具韧性，来对付生活中的身心压力。

万能词汇 18：assume

写作中，assume 这个词若用得恰当，在词汇方面可以占得先机。该词有三个常见的意思：一是"假设，假定，认为"，相当于 think；二是"承担（责任）"；三是"呈现（外观或特征）"。比如：

Scientists assume that there is no animal life on Mars. 科学家们猜测，在火星上没有动物生命。

The reality that has blocked my path to become the typical successful student is that engineering and the liberal arts simply don't mix as easily as I assumed in high school. 现实情况阻碍了我成为一名典型的成功学生，那就是工程学和文科根本不像我在高中时想象的那样容易融合。

以下看 assume 在雅思真题范文中是如何使用的。

例 1 As we can see on television, the important positions in the government are often held by gray-haired men and women. While it is **assumed** by many that the elderly people are more experienced and capable, I would say that some important government positions should also be open to young people.（181021，年轻人适合在政府担任要职吗？）我们可以在电视上看到，政府重要职位通常是由头发花白的人担任。虽然很多人认为，老年人更富有经验和能力，但我想说，政府的一些重要职位也应开放给年轻人。

例 2　Although new forms of classroom technology like digital textbooks are more accessible and portable, it would be wrong to **assume** that students are automatically better served by digital reading just because they prefer it.（180818，学生学习不需要书籍了吗？）尽管像数字教材这样的新形式课堂技术更容易获取，更便于携带，但仅仅因为学生喜欢就认为电子阅读必然对学生更有益，那就错了。

例 3　Luck may **assume** different forms and help people in various ways. A man luckily born into a wealthy family will stand a better chance of becoming a successful businessman than one with poor family background.（201031，实现生活目标主要是运气使然吗？）运气可以用不同的形式，以各种方式帮助人们。一个幸运地出生在富裕家庭的人比一个家庭背景不好的人更有可能成为成功的商人。

万能词汇 19：emerge

emerge 的意思是"出现"，尤其是指从隐蔽处突然出现。其名词形式是emergence，注意要将它与 emergency（紧急情况）区别开来。比如：

The sun emerged from behind the clouds. 太阳从云层后面露出来了。

It has emerged that he stole the money. 现在终于发现，是他偷了那笔钱。

A new idea began to emerge from his mind when he was on his way back home. 在回家的路上，一个新主意出现在他的脑海中。

以下我们看 emerge/emergence 在雅思真题范文中是如何使用的。

例 1　Undoubtedly, experience is of utmost importance for many government positions. These positions have to deal with a great number of people every day and crisis may **emerge** any time.（181021，年轻人适合在政府担任要职吗？）毫无疑问，对许多政府职位来说，经验是最重要的。这些职位每天必须与大量的人打交道，危机随时可能出现。

例 2　As a great variety of employment opportunities **emerge** in big cities, people flood into the urban areas to realize their self-value and obtain more materially abundant life.（130727，大城市应该重修老建筑还是建设新楼房和新道路？）随着大城市就业机会的大量出现，人们涌入城市，实现自我价值，获得更丰富的物质生活。

例 3　Furthermore, with the **emergence** of new technologies, the work efficiency has been improved greatly. The invention and application of machines have replaced labour and saved much time for workers. （140920, 发展中国家应该引进新技术，还是发展免费教育？）此外，随着新技术的出现，工作的效率得到了大大提高。机器的发明和应用已经取代了劳力，为工人节省了很多时间。

万能词汇 20：restrict

restrict 的意思是"限制"，相当于 limit，其名词形式是 restriction。比如：

There is talk of raising the admission requirements to restrict the number of students on campus. 有提高录取条件来限制校园里学生数量的说法。

I try to restrict my smoking to five cigarettes a day. 我力图限制自己每天只抽 5 支烟。

以下我们看 restrict 在雅思真题范文中是如何使用的。

例 1 It is quite common these days for young people in many countries to have a break from studying after graduating from high school. The trend is not **restricted to** rich students who have the money to travel, but is also evident among poorer students who choose to work and become economically independent for a period of time. （200806, 高中毕业后旅游或工作一年的利弊）如今，许多国家的年轻人在高中毕业后暂时中断学习是很常见的。这一趋势不仅局限于有钱旅行的富裕学生，在选择工作并在一段时间内实现经济独立的贫困学生中也很明显。

例 2 There seems to be more and more detailed criminal description on media these days, such as beating, murdering, gun fighting, blood shedding, among others. As I see it, the excessive exposure to these criminal scenes will negatively influence newspaper readers and TV viewers, thus increasing the likelihood of their committing the same crimes in real life, but to **restrict** them on media is quite another story. （201024, 是否应该限制报纸电视中的犯罪描写？）现在，媒体上似乎有越来越详细的犯罪描述，如殴打、谋杀、枪战、流血等。在我看来，看到太多类似犯罪场景将对报纸读者和电视观众产生负面影响，从而增加他们在现实生活中犯下同样罪行的可能性，但在媒体上限制这些描写则完全是另一回事。

例 3 Independence means more freedom and less **restrictions**. Following this definition, we can easily find we have become much more independent than ever before. (161105，我们现在是更独立还是更相互依赖？)独立意味着更多自由和更少的限制。按照这一定义，我们很容易发现我们比以往任何时候都更独立。

4.3 高分词汇

（1）**available** *a.* 可以获得的；有空闲的

（2）**absorb** *v.* 吸收；招收；使专注

（3）**accomplish** *v.* 完成，做成

（4）**accuse** *v.* 指控

（5）**achieve** *v.* 实现；达成

（6）**adapt (to)** *v.* 适应 / 改编（以适应于……）

（7）**adopt** *v.* 采纳，采用；收养（孩子）

（8）**afford** *v.* 支付得起（affordable *a.* 支付得起的，便宜的）

（9）**alternative** *a.* 替换的 *n.* （二选一的）选择

（10）**anticipate** *v.* 预期；期待（= predict, foresee）

（11）**apparent** *a.* 表面的；显然的

（12）**approach** *n.* 方法，措施 *v.* 靠近

（13）**arouse** *v.* 引起；激发起

（14）**artificial** *a.* 人工的

（15）**assemble** *v.* 集合；组装

（16）**assume** *v.* 假定，假设（assumption *n.* 前提；假设）

（17）**attach** *v.* 把……附上（贴上）；重视（attach importance to... 重视……）

（18）**compel** *v.* 迫使（= force）

（19）**competent** *a.* 胜任的；有能力的

（20）**complex** *a.* 复杂的

（21）**complicated** *a.* 复杂的

（22）**concentrate on...** *v.* 集中注意力于……

（23）**confine (to)** *v.* 将……控制 / 限制在……范围内

（24）**considerable** *a.* 相当多的；相当大的

（25）**consistent** *a.* 前后一致的，一贯的

（26）**continuous** *a.* 连续不断的

（27）**content** *n.* 内容；目录 *a.* 满足的（be content with... = be satisfied with...）

（28）**contribute (to)** *v.* 为……做贡献；投稿

（29）**dependent (on) / independent (from)** *a.* 依赖的 / 独立的

（30）**depress** *v.* 使压抑（depression *n.* 压抑；抑郁）

（31）**derive** *v.* 获得；衍生（derive satisfaction from... 从……获得满足感）

（32）**determine** *v.* 查明；确定；决定；决心

（33）**distinguish** *v.* 分辨（distinguish the good from the bad 分辨好坏）

（34）**distract** *v.* 分散（注意力），使分心

（35）**eliminate** *v.* 消灭；消除（eliminate mistakes 消除错误）

（36）**emerge** *v.* （突然）出现

（37）**eventually** *adv.* 最后；终于

（38）**exceed** *v.* 超过

（39）**excessive** *a.* 过多的

（40）**exclusively** *adv.* 排他地，唯一地（= only）

（41）**expose (to)** *v.* 使暴露于……（之下）；置于……（之下）

（42）**extend** *v.* 延伸

（43）**forbid** *v.* 禁止（forbid sb to do... 禁止某人做……）

（44）**fraction** *n.* 分数；小部分（a small fraction of... ……很小的一个部分）

（45）**identify** *v.* 识别

（46）**inspire** *v.* 激励；给灵感

（47）**instruct** *v.* 指示，吩咐；教（= teach）

（48）**interrupt** *v.* 打断

（49）**involve** *v.* 使卷入；包含，包括

（50）**isolate** *v.* 使孤立

（51）**justify** *v.* 为……辩护；证明……有道理（justifiable *a.* 可以辩护的，有道理的）

（52）**maximum** *n.* 最大值 *a.* 最大的

（53）**mutual**　*a.* 相互的（mutual understanding 相互理解；mutual respect 相互尊重）

（54）**object**　*n.* 物体；对象　*v.* (to) 反对……（objection *n.* 反对）

（55）**oblige**　*v.* 迫使（be obliged to sb 感激某人）

（56）**occasion**　*n.* 场合

（57）**optional**　*a.* 可以选择的；选修的（required/mandatory *a.* 必修的）

（58）**particular**　*a.* 特指的；特别的

（59）**primarily**　*adv.* 首要地；根本地

（60）**prohibit**　*v.* 禁止（prohibit sb from doing... 禁止某人做……）

（61）**prospect**　*n.* 前景，前途

（62）**reveal**　*v.* 透露；显示

（63）**recognize**　*v.* 认出；承认

（64）**regardless (of)**　*prep.* 无论……；不管……

（65）**relieve**　*v.* 减轻，解除

（66）**remove**　*v.* 移走，搬走

（67）**represent**　*v.* 代表；展现

（68）**restrict**　*v.* 限制

（69）**routine**　*n.* 常规，例行程序　*a.* 日常的

（70）**secondary**　*a.* 第二位的

（71）**shrink**　*v.* 收缩，缩水

（72）**specific**　*a.* 具体的；明确的

（73）**stimulate**　*v.* 刺激；鼓励

（74）**stress**　*v.* 强调　*n.* 压力（stressful *a.* 有压力的）

（75）**subsequent**　*a.* 后来的

（76）**substitute**　*v.* 替换，代替　*n.* 替换的人或物

（77）**sufficient**　*a.* 足够的

（78）**superior**　*a.* 更高级的　*n.* 上司

（79）**survive**　*v.* 幸存，存活

（80）**transform**　*v.* 改变

（81）**ultimate**　*a.* 最后的，终极的

（82）**urgent**　*a.* 紧急的；急迫的

（83）**vague** *a.* 模糊的，不清楚的

（84）**variety** *n.* 种类（diversity *n.* 多样性）

（85）**virtually** *adv.* 几乎（= almost, practically）

（86）**widespread** *a.* 广泛的，普及的

4.4 常用功能词汇

所谓功能词汇，指那些可以帮助考生表达某种特定动作的词汇，比如"增加""发展""促进"等。这些词汇在雅思写作中使用非常广泛，值得考生关注。以下是笔者收集到的常用功能词汇。

（1）**导致 / 带来 / 引起**：*v.* cause, bring about, give rise to, lead to, generate, create

（2）**认为**：*v.* point out, argue, claim, suggest, think, consider

（3）**解决**：*v.* combat, address, tackle, resolve, solve

（4）**承认**：*v.* concede, admit, acknowledge, accept, allow

（5）**支持**：*v.* support, advocate, agree with

（6）**改善 / 提升**：*v.* improve, enhance, upgrade, boost

（7）**扩张 / 扩大**：*v.* expand, enlarge, extend, widen, broaden

（8）**提高**：*v.* increase, develop

（9）**发展**：*v.* develop, advance, grow, evolve

（10）**获得**：*v.* acquire, gain, get, obtain, attain

（11）**执行 / 实施**：*v.* implement, execute, put into effect, perform

（12）**实现**：*v.* achieve, fulfill, gain, accomplish, attain

（13）**促进**：*v.* promote, further, advance, encourage

（14）**鼓励**：*v.* stimulate, encourage, motivate

（15）**唤起 / 激发起**：*v.* arouse, cause, trigger, spark off

（16）**需要**：*v.* call for, demand, require

（17）**取代**：*v.* replace, take the place of, substitute for

（18）**加快**：*v.* accelerate, speed up, quicken

（19）**减轻 / 降低**：*v.* lessen, reduce, alleviate

（20）**保护**：*v.* protect, preserve

（21）保卫：*v.* safeguard, defend

（22）建立：*v.* establish, set up, found, construct

（23）遵守（规则、法律）：*v.* abide by, comply with, follow, respect

（24）允许：*v.* allow, permit

（25）反对：*v.* object, oppose

（25）减少：*v.* decrease, lower, reduce, cut down

（27）阻碍：*v.* hinder, impede, hamper

（28）限制：*v.* limit, restrict, place a limit on

（29）危及：*v.* endanger, imperil, jeopardize

（30）恶化：*v.* deteriorate, worsen

（31）加剧：*v.* intensify, sharpen

（32）破坏：*v.* damage, destroy, ruin

（33）污染：*v.* pollute, contaminate

（34）削弱：*v.* weaken, undermine, impair

（35）干涉：*v.* interfere in/with

（36）与……相违背／相矛盾：*v.* contradict (each other) = conflict with

（37）误解：*v.* misunderstand

（38）逃避：*v.* escape, evade

（39）遭受：*v.* suffer from, be afflicted with, be subjected to

（40）违反：*v.* violate, disobey

（41）忽视：*v.* ignore, neglect

（42）怀疑：*v.* doubt, suspect

4.5 10 个增分副词

我们先来看看《剑桥雅思 9》里给出的一篇高分范文（黑体字为笔者所加）：

It has been suggested that high school students should be involved in un-paid community services as a compulsory part of high school programmes. Most of the colleges are **already** providing opportunities to give work experience, **however** these are not compulsory. In my opinion, sending students to work in community services is a good idea as it can provide them with many sorts of valuable skills.

Life skills are very important and by doing voluntary work, students can learn how to communicate with others and work in a team but also how to manage their time and improve their organisational skills. Nowadays, **unfortunately**, teenagers do not have many after-school activities. After-school clubs are no longer **that** popular and students **mostly** go home and sit in front of the TV, browse the Internet or play video games.

By giving them compulsory work activities with charitable or community organisations, they will be encouraged to do something more creative. Skills gained through compulsory work will not only be an asset on their CV but also increase their employability. Students will **also** gain more respect towards work and money as they will realise that it is not **that** easy to earn them and **hopefully** will learn to spend them in a more practical way.

Healthy life balance and exercise are **strongly** promoted by the NHS, and **therefore** any kind of spare time charity work will prevent them from sitting and doing nothing. It could also **possibly** reduce the crime level in the high school age group. If students have activities to do, they will not be bored and come up with silly ideas which can be dangerous for them or their surroundings.

In conclusion, I think this is a very good idea, and I hope this programme will be put into action for high schools and colleges **shortly**.

粗略统计，本范文共使用了 11 个副词。其中有程度副词 that、mostly、strongly、possibly、shortly，关联副词 however、therefore、also，时间副词 already，方式副词 unfortunately、hopefully 等。

限于篇幅，笔者无意对英汉副词的用法差异进行详细阐述，但相关研究表明，英语副词的语法功能较多，接近实词，而汉语副词语法功能相对较少，介于实词和虚词之间。因此，总的来说，英语副词的词类地位高于汉语副词，这导致英语中副词可以灵活地出现在句子的不同位置，使用频率也远高于汉语。英语写作中恰当使用副词，可使文章读起来更接近英语表达习惯，从而有助于在考试中得到更加理想的分数。

以下是笔者总结的十大增分副词。同学们可以在平时写作练习中尝试使用它们。

（1）**specifically** 具体地说

（2）**virtually** 几乎（＝almost, practically）

（3）**obviously** 很明显

（4）**increasingly** 越来越……

（5）**accordingly** 相应地

（6）**eventually** 终于，最后（＝ultimately）

（7）**consequently** 结果，因此

（8）**undoubtedly** 毫无疑问

（9）**largely** 在很大程度上

（10）**partly** 部分地

现在，我们来研习几个句子，看这些副词是如何具体使用的。

例 1　The first problem that faces the young people in big cities is that a good job will become **increasingly** difficult to come by since the competition in the job market will **surely** intensify as young people, most of whom are well educated, decide to pursue their dreams in the big cities.（181125，城市扩张给年轻人带来的问题及解决方法）大城市的年轻人面临的第一个问题是，好工作将变得越来越难以获得，因为随着年轻人（多数都受过良好的教育）决定在大城市里追求自己的梦想，就业市场上的竞争必将加剧。

例 2　Instead of the Internet, I would label language as "the most important invention", because it was the invention of language that **ultimately** distinguished humans from animals and made possible everything we have now in the human world.（211225，互联网是不是人类最重要的发明？）我愿意把"最重要的发明"这个标签送给语言文字，而不是互联网，因为正是语言的发明才最终将人类与动物区分开来，使现在人类世界中拥有的一切成为可能。

例 3　Far from being just a personal matter, our health is something that **largely** guarantees the health of the community, as has been **repeatedly** evidenced in the Covid-19 pandemic that is still troubling the world today.（210515，照顾好自己的身体是我们对社会应尽的义务吗？）我们的健康远不仅仅是个人问题，它在很大程度上保证了社区的健康，这被今天仍困扰世界的新冠大流行一再证明。

例 4　At the same time, advertising aimed at children is **partly** responsible for children being kept away from the reality.（160220，儿童广告的弊端）同时，儿童广告某种程度上导致了儿童远离现实。

例 5 To begin with, advances across **virtually** all fields of science show promise for solving puzzles about the nature of the world—from diseases and climate-change to the origin of the universe.（180913，科学研究是浪费时间和金钱吗？）首先，几乎所有科学领域的进展都显示出有希望解决有关世界本质——从疾病和气候变化到宇宙的起源——的疑惑。

4.6 10 个增分连接词（组）

多用连接词可使文章显得紧凑。由于汉语更注重意义上的连接，因此经常省略连词，这导致部分同学在用英语写作文的时候，也经常在该使用连接词的地方没有使用连接词，从而造成语法错误或者意义表达不清晰。以下是笔者推荐的十大增分连接词（组）。

（1）**for the sake of** 因为……的缘故

（2）**in terms of** 在……方面

（3）**likewise / similarly / by the same token** 同理

（4）**for all / in spite of** 虽然，尽管

（5）**as well as** 以及（= and）

（6）**regardless of** 不管

（7）**as a result** 结果

（8）**in addition (to)** 除……之外

（9）**like/unlike** 像 / 不像……一样

（10）**in regards to** 就……来说

例 1 These children are often spoilt, not **in terms of** love and attention because working parents do not have time for this, but in more material ways.（《剑桥雅思 4》，Test 3，孩子行为问题产生的原因及解决方法）这些孩子经常被惯坏，但不是在爱和关注上，而是在物质上，因为在职父母没有时间给孩子爱和关注。

例 2 **For the sake of** traffic and environment, the government, rather than providing funds for free public transport, should construct more roads and introduce stricter rules of car ownership and use.（181101，政府应该资助公共交通免费吗？）为了交通和环境，政府不应该为免费公共交通提供资金，而应该建设更多的道路，并引入更严格的汽车拥有和使用的规则。

例3 Yet, rather than a simply personal issue, food is always also a social issue **in terms of** its production, distribution and consumption.（180921，饮食健康该由政府还是个人负责？）然而，食品不仅仅是一个简单的个人问题，它在生产、分配和消费方面也往往是一个社会问题。

例4 Yet one issue is still in debate: to whom should the money of charity organisations go, exclusively to people who live in the same country as the organisations, or to all people **regardless of** where they live?（160820，慈善机构只该帮助本国人吗？）然而，有一个问题仍在争论中：慈善组织的钱该用在谁身上，应该用于与机构同一国家的人，还是用于所有人，不管他们生活在哪？

例5 **Unlike** many worried parents who prefer to educate their kids at home, I believe school is the best place for kids' education.（170426，孩子该在家接受教育还是去学校？）与许多忧心忡忡而宁愿在家教育孩子的父母不同，我相信学校才是教育孩子的最佳地方。

4.7 10个增分语气词

语气是英语写作中的一个重要方面。表达观点时，我们可以非常坚决，但通常情况下需要留一些余地，让自己的观点显得更加缓和，也更容易被别人接受。英语写作尤其如此，即使作者想表达一个肯定的观点，他往往也会通过增加语气词来让自己的观点显得更为客观。笔者归纳了以下10个语气词。

（1）**perhaps/probably** 也许，或许

（2）**yet** 仍然，还

（3）**hardly** 几乎不

（4）**certainly** 当然

（5）**even** 甚至

（6）**just** 仅仅，只是（= merely）

（7）**also** 也

（8）**quite** 相当（= rather）

（9）**around** 大约（= about）

（10）**necessarily** 必然地

例1 In my opinion, university is **probably** not the place for people to learn such qualities as ambition, courage, resilience and self-confidence. （181117，成功者的素质在大学里学不到吗？）在我看来，大学可能不是人们学习雄心、勇气、韧性和自信等素质的地方。

例2 To sum up, while legally employers should give their staff a paid annual leave in the hope of making them better at their jobs, it does not **necessarily** mean that by so doing there will be as many benefits as expected. （190302，每年四周假期能让员工更好地工作吗？）总而言之，虽然雇主应依法给予员工带薪年假，指望他们能更好地工作，但这并不一定意味着这样做会带来预期中的那么多好处。

例3 We can **hardly** imagine what the city centre would look like when millions of people moved into the numerous apartment buildings there. It would become a great deal more crowded and polluted than before.（190406，在城市中心建公寓楼可减少通勤时间吗？）我们很难想象当数以百万计的人搬进市中心无数公寓楼时，那里会是什么样子。它将变得比以前更加拥挤和污染。

例4 As the government of any country is mainly responsible for protecting its own citizens from harm of any kind, it seems **quite** absurd to give money to people in other countries when the citizens at home are suffering from poverty.（210725，本国还有人不富裕时，政府是否应该进行国际援助？）由于任何国家的政府都主要负责保护本国公民免受任何形式的伤害，因此当本国公民遭受贫困的时候却把钱给外国人似乎是相当荒谬的。

4.8 常用词组

（1）**stand up for** 赞同；支持

（2）**except for** 除了……之外

（3）**in relation to** 与……相关

（4）**to my mind** 在我看来

（5）**survival skills** 求生技能；生活技能

（6）**in the long run** 从长远看

（7）**to name just a few** 如此等等；诸如此类

（8）**in proportion to...** 与……成正比

（9）**set limits on...** 给……设限

（10）**devote... to...** 投入……到……

（11）**it does not follow that...** 这不意味着……

（12）**as a matter of fact** 事实上

（13）**mix up with...** 与……混在一起

（14）**at stake** 处于危险中（= in danger）

（15）**take into account** 把……考虑进去

（16）**sth is not uncommon** ……不罕见

（17）**at hand** 在附件的；在手边的

（18）**rely on** 依赖

（19）**far from** 绝非

（20）**for one thing... for another...** 其一，……；其二，……

（21）**only to find...** 却发现……

（22）**end up** 最终变成……

（23）**after all** 无论如何；毕竟

（24）**in terms of** 在……方面

（25）**when it comes to...** 当谈到……

（26）**put one's heart to...** 集中精力做……

（27）**as I see it** 在我看来；我认为

（28）**excel in...** 在……方面很优秀

（29）**be deprived of...** ……被剥夺

（30）**relieve sb of...** 把……从……中解脱出来

（31）**at one's disposal** 供某人支配

（32）**on the part of...** 对……来说

（33）**figure out** 弄明白

（34）**focus on** 聚焦于……

（35）**concentrate on** 集中精力于……

（36）**be open to...** 不排斥……；接纳……

（37）**result in** 导致

（38）**needless to say** 不必说

（39）**confine oneself to...** 把自己关闭在……

（40）**engage in** 从事

（41）**in light of** 根据

（42）**make... into...** 使……变成……

（43）**in some cases** 在某些情况下

（44）**it may turn out to be...** 它可能变成……

（45）**take trouble to do...** 不辞辛劳做……

（46）**break down** 崩溃

（47）**get rid of...** 抛弃……

（48）**on the contrary** 相反

（49）**it is just a matter of...** 它只不过是……（简单的）事情

（50）**depend on...** 取决于……

（51）**stay away from...** 远离……

（52）**keep abreast of...** 紧跟……

（53）**sth is a huge waste of money** ……是巨大的金钱浪费

（54）**at the tip of fingers** 近在咫尺；在指尖

（55）**brick-and-mortar** 实体的（相对于虚拟的）

（56）**time-consuming** 耗时的

（57）**be dependent on...** 依赖于……

（58）**prefer... to...** 更喜欢……而不喜欢……

（59）**find its way to...** 走进……

（60）**show up** 出现，露面

（61）**commuting time** 通勤时间

（62）**not without** 不是没有……

（63）**come by** 获得（＝obtain）

（64）**people with pessimistic bend of mind** 有悲观心态的人

（65）**scenic spot** 景点

（66）**cater to the needs of...** 满足……的需求

（67）**seen in this light** 从这个角度看来

（68）**a matter of personal preference** 个人喜好问题

（69）**make headline news** 成为头条

（70）**more often than not** 经常

（71）**make (both) ends meet** 量入为出；收支相抵

（72）**free from...** 没有……；免于……（= without...）

（73）**get ahead** 出人头地

（74）**on top of...** 除……之外

（75）**maternity leave** 产假

（76）**be content with...** 满足于……

（77）**crave for...** 渴望

（78）**glue one's eyes to...** 紧盯着……

（79）**be superior to...** 比……好

（80）**keep... in check** 控制……

（81）**among others** 等等

（82）**a host of** 众多的

（83）**give way to** 让位于……

（84）**give rise to** 引发

（85）**get accustomed to...** 习惯于……

（86）**set aside** （特别地）留出……

（87）**at the most basic level** 在最基本的层面

（88）**dawn on** 让某人明白

（89）**take... for granted** 把……视为想当然

（90）**subject to...** （使）遭受

（91）**set about doing...** 开始着手做……

（92）**social ladder** 社会阶梯

（93）**catch up with the Joneses** 与邻居攀比

（94）**work extra hours** 加班工作

（95）**stay healthy** 保持健康

（96）**on a daily basis** 每天

（97）**on the part of...** 就……而言

（98）**not to mention...** 更不用提……

（99）**soar up** 飙升

（100）**impose... on...** 强加……在……身上

（101）**in vain** 徒劳地

（102）**abide by** 遵守

（103）**call for** 要求

（104）**for my part** 我认为（= in my view, in my opinion）

4.9 词汇练习

I. 阅读下列雅思真题范文中的句子，按照汉语提示，在空格处填写功能词汇（注意正确的语法形式）。

（1）In many parts of the world, people who have _____（违法）are put into prison, which is a very effective way of preventing them committing more crimes.（180303，解决犯罪问题，教育比监狱更有效吗？）

（2）If big companies and factories, together with their huge number of employees, move to the countryside, there will be fewer people living in the city, then with the housing pressure _____（降低），the housing prices will surely go down.（180505，企业迁往农村可解决大城市交通和住房问题吗？）

（3）By contrast, I believe the traditional culture should be _____（保存下来），for it plays a pivotal role in our understanding of history and formation of identity even if it is irrelevant to our daily life.（160910，传统习俗应该保留吗？）

（4）On the one hand, we should protect wild animals, especially the _____（濒临灭绝的）species of animals and recognize their importance to the entire ecosystem.（191130，当今时代不需要动物食品或动物产品了吗？）

（5）In fact, one of the most important reasons why people participate in extreme sports is that these sports can refresh their feeling of life and _____（鼓励）them to meet the challenges in life.（201128，极限运动应该被禁止吗？）

（6）In my view, both ways are effective to _____（解决）the traffic problem in cities, but it is the city conditions that will determine which way is better.（180707，建更多铁路和地铁好，还是修更多道路好？）

（7）In my view, it is unrealistic for the government to put a ban on the car ownership or use since cars have been so important in our daily life, yet we cannot _____（忽视）the negative effects they have on the environment.（190622，私家车对个人的好处及对环境的坏处）

（8）Today, we can apparently _____（完成）a lot of things without the help of others, which leads to the popular belief that we are becoming more and more independent.（161105，我们现在是更独立还是更相互依赖？）

（9）It is one thing to say that one has the legal right to enjoy a paid annual leave, but it is quite another to conclude that vacations can always _____（提高）productivity.（190302，每年四周假期能让员工更好地工作吗？）

（10）Undoubtedly, the "vehicle-free day" may also cause problems. The most immediate one is that, when people do not drive their cars, the public transportation system may _____（遭受）tremendous pressure.（180102，无车日是好还是坏？）

参考答案

（1）violated the law

（2）reduced

（3）preserved

（4）endangered

（5）encourage

（6）solve/address

（7）ignore

（8）accomplish

（9）boost

（10）be subjected to

II. 根据汉语提示，将恰当的副词填入空格处。

（1）First, a great many countries have been now undertaking the exploration of new energies in some remote rural areas. Indeed, numerous benefits could be gained. _____（具体说来），it will enrich our knowledge about the energy exploration.（140628，我们应该去偏远地区寻找能源吗？）

（2）To whom should the money of charity organisations go, _____（仅仅）to people who live in the same country as the organisations, or to all people regardless of where they live? To my mind, the answer to this question depends _____（在很大程度上）on the mission of specific charity organisations.（160820, 慈善机构应该帮助别国人民吗？）

（3）The entire United States, for example, was paralysed right after the 9/11 terrorist attack, but it quickly recovered from that paralysis, _____（在很大程度上）because American people were inspired by the artistic works which encouraged them to face the reality and move on.（180909, 政府不应该给艺术家投资吗？）

（4）In order to catch up with the Joneses, we often have to make more money by working extra hours which will _____（最终）affect our health.（180603, 生活在大城市不利于身体健康吗？）

（5）Besides, as many scientists have speculated, the Earth will _____（最终）die and disappear into the black hole. We therefore need to find other planets suitable for living so that when that day does come, our future grand, grand children will not perish from the Earth.（181201, 应该投资太空技术吗？）

（6）While hard skills can be learned through proper training, soft skills are harder to develop. And this _____（部分地）explains why soft skills are extremely valuable these days.（181110, 应聘者的社交能力和资历同等重要吗？）

（7）To achieve the greatest success in sports, first it requires physical ability. However, strength and fitness being equal, it is _____（最终）the right mental attitude that makes a big difference.（200105, 体育运动中身体和心态哪个更重要？）

（8）Owing to its _____（几乎是）unlimited capacity, the Internet can store all knowledge in the world. This makes it quite unnecessary for us to spend that much money constructing the brick-and-mortar libraries.（170330, 知识存储在网络上是好是坏？）

（9）At the same time, advertising aimed at children is _____（部分地）responsible for children being kept away from the reality.（160220, 儿童广告

的弊端）

（10）If a considerable number of jobs are occupied by those who are unwilling to retire when getting old, there will be fewer opportunities left to the young, which may _____（因此）lead to a more competitive employment market.（181102，老年人应该继续工作吗？）

参考答案

（1）Specifically

（2）exclusively; largely

（3）largely

（4）eventually/ultimately

（5）eventually/ultimately

（6）partly

（7）ultimately

（8）virtually

（9）partly

（10）consequently

III. 阅读下列雅思真题范文中的句子，按照汉语提示，在空格处填写高频词汇（注意正确的语法形式）。

（1）However, many people are gradually losing their interest in news, for they have every reason to doubt the truthfulness of news. They often _____（指责）journalists of presenting the truth or reality in a wrong way so as to mislead the readers.（160305，我们是否应该相信新闻记者？）

（2）Just 100 years ago, women serving in the armed forces was basically unheard of, yet now in many countries, women are able to join the armed forces as easily as men. Not afraid of the _____（指责）of being prejudiced or even male chauvinistic, I strongly believe that men and only men should be members of the army, navy and air forces.（160519，女性该参军吗？）

（3）Compared with other workers or technicians whose main task is to perform their own responsibilities, a top manager has to fully grasp the market dynamics before making suitable business plans and then coordinates various resources _____（可以得到的）to him/her to achieve the targets and objectives.（161029，高管应该获得高收入吗？）

（4）Around us there are many people who are ambitious and always work hard to _____（得到，实现）what they want, but there are also many who seem to have nothing to squeeze out of life.（180211，我们应该有抱负吗？）

（5）In conclusion, I believe that anything which could enable young people to become economically and academically active and able members of society should be _____（采纳）.（140318，18 岁以下的年轻人都应该全日制上学吗？）

（6）Besides, some irresponsible celebrities could even _____（激发）negative attitudes of the public. What effect can it bring about when a celebrity asks people to give aid to the poverty-stricken children while he lives a luxurious life without giving away a dollar himself?（190413，名人参加国际救援活动是好是坏？）

（7）So, far from a waste of time, sharing stories with kids can be an occasion with both emotional and instructional value. Parents should not stop reading and telling stories to their kids until they become old enough to read _____（独立地）.（170715，父母应该给孩子读故事吗？）

（8）As long as the language instructors are excellent enough, students do stand the chances of mastering perfect language skills. Hence, there is no _____（显著的）difference between teaching a small class or organising a large one.（141204，语言学习应该小班教学吗？）

（9）The same survey has also _____（揭示）that many employed older people are able to combine what they have learned in technology with seasoned communication skills in real life. Therefore, it should come as no surprise that the average age of an outstanding entrepreneur is 45, not 25, and there are more top-ranking managers over 50 than 35.（190504，广泛使用新技术让年轻人更容易找到工作吗？）

（10）Today, we can apparently _____（完成）a lot of things without the help of others, which leads to the popular belief that we are becoming more and more independent.（161105，人们现在越来越独立了吗？）

（11）Therefore, to _____（解决）the traffic problem, providing free public transport alone is not enough. Instead, we should assemble efforts from various sides such the government, the drivers as well as the pedestrians.（180121，提供免费公交可以解决交通问题吗？）

（12）On the other hand, businesses moving to a rural area will _____（刺激）the consumption and facilitate infrastructure in this area apart from offering employment opportunities to the local people.（180505，企业迁往农村可以解决城市交通和住房问题吗？）

（13）First of all, as we all know, green plants can carry out photosynthesis, which not only _____（吸收）carbon dioxide, but also release oxygen.（150312，城市空地应该种树还是建楼？）

（14）This, according to these people, will help university students to _____（聚焦于）the subject they are studying without being _____（分散精力）by having to spend time and energy on other subjects.（170803，大学生应该只学一门课程吗？）

（15）As the work might easily _____（分散精力）by house chores, therefore staff working from home might prove not as efficient as they are expected to be.（140426，在家工作学习的利弊）

（16）On the contrary, if they receive more general education, they will surely have a better time _____（适应）to the fast-changing world.（190912，普通教育还是职业教育？）

（17）To conclude, where the charity money should go is mainly _____（决定）by the chief concerns and missions of different charity organisations.（160820，慈善机构应该只帮助本国人吗？）

（18）However, there are certainly dangers in taking time off at that important age. Young adults may end up never returning to their studies or finding it difficult to _____（适应）to an academic environment.（200806，高中毕业后旅游或工作一年的利弊）

（19）First, today the students are surrounded by so many _____（干扰）that they gradually find that learning is too boring and uninteresting. While students two decades ago had nearly no choice but sit in the classroom and read books, students today have easy and fast access to the Internet, on which they can do almost all things.（170305，年轻人不喜欢学习的原因）

（20）While it is hard to ＿＿＿＿＿（确定）how the visual uniformity is related to quality at work, having a dress code in place may help the way a corporation wants to be perceived.（180113，员工是否应该统一着装？）

（21）An organisation aiming at solving local issues should spend its money helping people who live in the same country, but if an organisation sets its eyes on global issues, it should not ＿＿＿＿＿（局限）itself to a single country.（160820，慈善机构只能帮助本国人吗？）

（22）Some people hunt after endangered animals just to make beautiful clothes. This kind of behaviour should be ＿＿＿＿＿（禁止）. Hunting rare animals will lead to their extinction and affect animal diversity, which is detrimental to the balance between nature and animal.（191130，当今时代不需要动物食品或产品吗？）

（23）Further still, people can perhaps ＿＿＿＿＿（获得）more happiness and satisfaction from their success in individual sports, and this sense of self-recognition is essential in their work and life.（180929，团队活动更有利于提高我们的生活技能吗？）

（24）Except for the very few who may take art as their lifelong career, the great majority of students will not get a job in relation to art when they finish their high school. Besides, what is the point of ＿＿＿＿＿（强迫）a student who has no interest in art to spend many hours restlessly in the art classes?（170107，艺术课应该成为高中必修课吗？）

（25）We have seen many local food brands become obsolete when their foreign replacements are introduced to the market. However, I believe the intensified competition resulting from the arrival of the foreign food is beneficial to the long-term development of the local food industry, because it will ＿＿＿＿＿（迫使）the local food companies to improve the quality of their products, which in turn will make them more competitive in the global market.（180513，进口食品的利弊）

（26）Finally, the cities and towns constructed long time ago cannot possibly have _____（预期）the negative effects of environmental issues brought over by our modern life, so they usually have residence area, industrial area and business area all mixed up without separating them.（161103，旧城市带来的问题）

（27）For one thing, advertising may make us less _____（满足）with what we have and what we are now and leave us craving hopelessly for those unattainable commodities. I still remember a few days ago when walking in front of a supermarket, I saw how a little girl, with her eyes glued to an advertising board, pestered her mother for the expensive toy on it that her mother apparently could not afford.（180422，广告对经济和个人的影响）

（28）Meanwhile, the complete dependence on the Internet for communication may result in the sense of alienation and _____（沮丧）which will keep us apart from the rest of the real world.（180421，网络交流取代面对面交流的利弊）

（29）At the same time, opening-to-tourism can also bring about profits which can effectively _____（减轻）the government of the financial burden.（151219，文化传统是否应该对旅游开放？）

（30）Meanwhile, cities and towns built centuries ago do not have enough entertainment and sports facilities available to contemporary city dwellers who, _____（摆脱）of the manual labor by the technological advances, suddenly find they have a great amount of free time.（161103，旧城市带来的问题）

（31）Besides, taking a few months off her work after the baby is born is also a good way to release the anxiety and _____（压力）the mother must have experienced during her pregnancy, so she will more likely behave normal after going back to work.（160227，女性应该休产假吗？）

（32）Even those more leisurely activities such as guitar playing or singing can _____（减轻）the students of their heavy load of academic work and make them more resilient to physical and emotional _____（压力）in life.（170826，大学生应该从事课外活动吗？）

（33）The greater flexibility of the primary timetable allows for more frequent, shorter sessions and for a play-centred _____（方法），thus maintaining learners' enthusiasm and progress. （《剑桥雅思 9》，Test 3，应该从小学开始学习外语吗？）

（34）Many people simply prefer reading real books for knowledge to online sources, because they believe books are more reliable and they find themselves emotionally and intellectually more _____（连接的）to knowledge in books.（170330，知识存储在网络上是好是坏？）

（35）Undoubtedly, the increased price of cars and petrol will _____（阻止）people from owning and using their own cars, which will surely contribute to the solution of traffic congestion and make big cities cleaner.（180310，提高车价和油价是解决交通和污染问题的最好办法吗？）

（36）For instance, when they want to promote their doll weapons, they will describe the world as a place full of bad guys. A child _____（置身于）such advertisements may develop a deep sense of hostility to the world.（180811，儿童广告应该被禁止吗？）

（37）The excessive _____（接触）to the violent scenes on TV will greatly affect the theatre-goers and TV viewers, thus increasing the likelihood of their committing the same violent crimes in real life.（180520，控制影视中的暴力可以降低犯罪率吗？）

（38）Employees get job satisfaction in a number of ways. Firstly, a person needs to feel that they are doing valued and valuable work, so positive feedback from _____（领导／上司）is very important in this respect.（《剑桥雅思 10》，Test 2，员工获得满足感的方式）

（39）A student, for instance, may rob his classmate of an iPhone 8, for he was told by advertising that claims iPhone 8 is _____（更好）to its previous versions.（180422，广告对经济和个人的影响）

（40）Nowadays, some people think it unnecessary for us to use animals for food, clothing or medicines any longer because modern technology has found the _____（替代品）for them.（160312，我们还需要使用动物产品吗？）

（41）Most museums and art galleries now have an online presence, but it can be argued that the virtual reproduction will never _____（替代）the physical historical objects and works of art featured on exhibition.（190831，我们还

需要博物馆和美术馆吗？）

（42）While it is _____（假设）by many that the elderly people are more experienced and capable, I would say that some important government positions should also be open to young people.（181021，年轻人适合担任政府要职吗？）

（43）We live in an age of electronic communication, and the Internet does help us in a lot of ways. Yet the fact that we have computers and smartphones readily _____（可以获得的）does not mean that we do not need face-to-face communication any more.（180421，网络交流取代面对面交流是好还是坏？）

（44）As future leaders of the world, kids should learn how to work out a problem in cooperation with others. No matter how smart a person might be, he could not possibly succeed in solving a highly _____（复杂的）problem all by himself.（160604，孩子教育中，合作和竞争哪个更重要？）

（45）For example, compared with houses made of mud and bricks in the past, apartments made of concrete and steel have sounder foundations and therefore are more likely to _____（幸存）the natural disasters like hurricanes or earthquakes.（130314，建筑物最重要的是实用，而非外观好看，你是否同意？）

（46）Undoubtedly, such pressing problems as housing, education, and medicare ought to be taken care of by the government, but it is also the responsibility of the government to prepare for the future of the Earth. Seen in this light, a reasonable investment in the life on other planets is perfectly _____（有理由的）.（170225，应该投资寻找外星生命吗？）

（47）To make things worse, entertainment producers these days tend to present, quite misleadingly, violent acts as an expression of heroism and have them well _____（辩护）, giving the viewers, especially those young viewers, a false impression that violence is a cool and always right thing to do.（180520，控制影视暴力可以减少犯罪吗？）

（48）This may be true, but modern medical technology has significantly reduced the risks _____（涉及，包含）in birth-giving and equally significantly prolonged our life span so that the older parents, like their younger counterparts, can just as well accompany their kids in their life's journey.（180408，晚育的

原因及利弊）

（49）(Undoubtedly, experience is of utmost importance for many government positions.) These positions have to deal with a great number of people every day and crisis may _____（突然出现）at any time. For example, a foreign affairs minister has to make quick responses to the problems that may come from all over the world every minute.（181021，年轻人适合担任政府要职吗？）

（50）In a world of consumerism, home electrical and electronic appliances have become so integral to modern life that, in many ways, they are what _____（区分）today's society from yesterday's.（180106，家用电器越来越多的利弊）

（51）Needless to say, staying at one job is beneficial to the mutual confidence and sense of security on the part of both employers and employees. Doing the same occupation also allows people to accumulate valuable working experience. Therefore, they are more _____（胜任的，有能努力的）to deal with the cases of emergency.（180916，经常换工作是好还是坏？）

（52）Likewise, most parents see computer games as a negative influence or simply as an evil temptation harmful to children's mental abilities. Overdoing computer games, for example, might affect children's ability to understand the real world. Taken together, both watching TV and playing computer games _____（过多地）are believed to be bad for children's mental development.（190216，电脑游戏会影响孩子智力发展吗？）

（53）Some people believe that it is beneficial to have a dress code in the workplace, if only for image reasons. Workers may be asked to wear a uniform to communicate a corporate image and ensure that people easily _____（认出，识别）them.（180113，员工统一着装有好处吗？）

（54）In my view, it is unrealistic for the government to put a ban on the car ownership or use since the cars have been so important in our daily life, yet we cannot overlook the negative effects they have on the environment. To get out of this dilemma, to my mind, there are two _____（选择），the first being to develop car technology and produce cars that burn less fuel and the second, encourage the car owners to use public transportation whenever possible.

（190224，私家车的影响）

（55）I still remember a few days ago when walking in front of a super-market, I saw how a little girl, with her eyes glued to an advertising board, pestered her mother for the expensive toy on it that her mother apparently could not _____（买得起）.（180422，广告对经济和个人的影响）

（56）By listening to the personal stories of former prisoners, youngsters may be touched and become more conscious of the consequences of committing crimes, yet _____（其他的，替代的）measures should be found when this does not work out.（180728，改造好的犯人是给学生宣讲犯罪危害的最佳人选吗？）

（57）In conclusion, there are reasons why countries should reduce their consumption of fossil fuels such as oil, coal and natural gas, but more realistically, they should find ways of generating and storing _____（替代的）sources such as solar and wind energy.（191019，我们必须少使用化石燃料吗？）

（58）Actually, the government has tried numerous ways to bring down the traffic, but mostly in vain. Recently, it is proposed that anyone who drives in rush hours pay a _____（相当大的）amount of tax. I believe this proposal will effectively solve the traffic problem in the city.（160130，拥堵税可以解决交通堵塞问题吗？）

（59）The technology connects us to our online suppliers, colleagues in the workplace, families and friends from all over the globe for just a small _____（部分）of the cost required of an offline meeting.（180421，网络交流取代面对面交流是好还是坏？）

（60）The world of work is in transition due mainly to automation enabled by technologies including robotics and _____（人工的）intelligence. Automation is replacing human tasks, changing the occupational skills that employers are looking for in their employees.（191103，工作变化快的原因及应对措施）

（61）Often, in order to win over others, many students may choose not to help their peer classmates. Consequently, those best students are often the most _____（孤立的）ones.（160604，竞争还是合作？）

（62）Therefore, whereas digital games have their share of cognitive benefits ranging from improved problem solving skills to spatial navigation abilities, they nevertheless tend to _____（隔离）children from the real world and real people.（180802，现在的游戏不及传统游戏有助于孩子发展技能吗？）

（63）To begin with, as TV has taught us once and again, the single-occupant home can be a breeding ground for eccentricities. In a sense, living alone _____（表示）the self let loose. In the absence of anybody else and his/her watchful eyes, the solo dweller is free to indulge his or her odd habits: no dish washing after dinner, standing naked in your kitchen at 2 a.m., eating peanut butter from the jar, and so on. You may do these things again and again until it is too late for you to make a change.（161109，独居是好还是坏？）

（64）Today, boat-racing has nothing to do with our daily living; we don't even need boats for fishing, but Chinese people are still celebrating this event every year for the reason that it reminds them of the cruelty of politics in that period of time. If boat-racing were no longer celebrated, Qu Yuan and the history he _____（代表）might have disappeared into the dust of time.（160910，应该保留传统习俗吗？）

（65）It is a well-known fact that rural areas lack economic and academic opportunities compared with urban areas. Usually, a _____（种类）of serious issues confront young people in villages such as the high unemployment rate and low educational level. So, it is only logical that young people are being pushed away from rural areas and being pulled to urban areas in search of better-paid jobs or better-managed schools.（190425，乡村年轻人进城读书和工作）

（66）Rich countries like the United States and the Great Britain often give money to some poorest countries in Africa as a kind of financial relief. Many people hold that this is not the best way to solve the poverty problem. I strongly support this idea and think rich countries should deliver other types of aid (intellectual and technological, for instance) so as to _____（消除）the poverty in poor countries.（200801，富裕国家应该给贫穷国家经济援助吗？）

（67）Admittedly, the kids in early-start mode may excel their peers in school grades, but this mode can also result in negative consequences. Forcing a

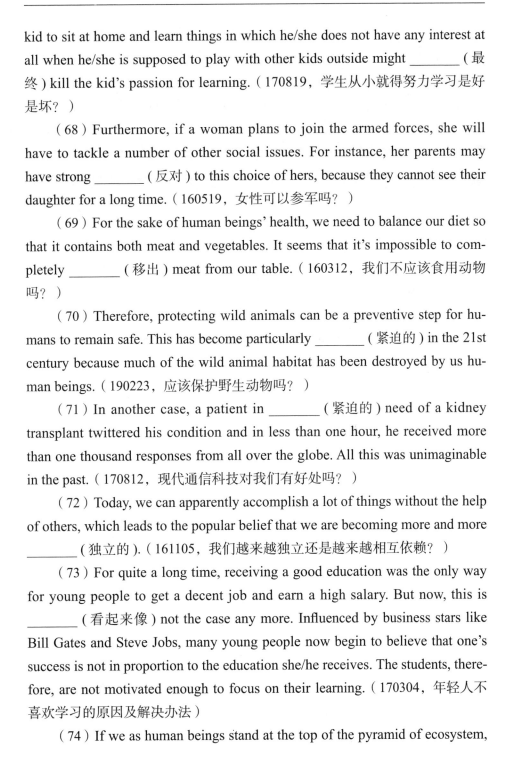

kid to sit at home and learn things in which he/she does not have any interest at all when he/she is supposed to play with other kids outside might _____（最终）kill the kid's passion for learning.（170819，学生从小就得努力学习是好是坏？）

（68）Furthermore, if a woman plans to join the armed forces, she will have to tackle a number of other social issues. For instance, her parents may have strong _____（反对）to this choice of hers, because they cannot see their daughter for a long time.（160519，女性可以参军吗？）

（69）For the sake of human beings' health, we need to balance our diet so that it contains both meat and vegetables. It seems that it's impossible to completely _____（移出）meat from our table.（160312，我们不应该食用动物吗？）

（70）Therefore, protecting wild animals can be a preventive step for humans to remain safe. This has become particularly _____（紧迫的）in the 21st century because much of the wild animal habitat has been destroyed by us human beings.（190223，应该保护野生动物吗？）

（71）In another case, a patient in _____（紧迫的）need of a kidney transplant twittered his condition and in less than one hour, he received more than one thousand responses from all over the globe. All this was unimaginable in the past.（170812，现代通信科技对我们有好处吗？）

（72）Today, we can apparently accomplish a lot of things without the help of others, which leads to the popular belief that we are becoming more and more _____（独立的）.（161105，我们越来越独立还是越来越相互依赖？）

（73）For quite a long time, receiving a good education was the only way for young people to get a decent job and earn a high salary. But now, this is _____（看起来像）not the case any more. Influenced by business stars like Bill Gates and Steve Jobs, many young people now begin to believe that one's success is not in proportion to the education she/he receives. The students, therefore, are not motivated enough to focus on their learning.（170304，年轻人不喜欢学习的原因及解决办法）

（74）If we as human beings stand at the top of the pyramid of ecosystem, our _____（生存）is totally dependent on the existence of other "lower" animals.（190223，是否应该保护野生动物？）

（75）Yet for such organisations as Bill Gates Charity Foundation whose money comes from the entire world, it is far from enough only to help Americans, although it is headquartered in the U.S. As a matter of fact, Bill Gates Charity Foundation, along with other "global" charity groups, has _____（提供）its help to all people in all countries and regions throughout the world.（160620，慈善机构应该帮助其他国家需要帮助的人吗？）

（76）In conclusion, the golden days of print news are gone forever, but nothing is like the feeling of physically holding a newspaper in hands. After all, the different ways of learning about news are not _____（互相排斥的）. Each news media outlet is effective in its own way.（180324，报纸是获取新闻的最佳途径吗？）

（77）Reading or telling stories, besides providing an opportunity for the parents to stay together with their children, is also often considered as a wonderful occasion for parents to share their life's lesson or wisdom with their children. So the fairy tale about a fox is often not just an interesting story, but one that tells the kids about the risks of greed, and _____（同样地）, the story of George Washington cutting a cherry tree makes the kids realize the importance of honesty.（170715，父母应该给孩子读书讲故事吗？）

（78）To begin with, the concept of "top students" is rather _____（含义模糊的）or sometimes downright mistaken. As I see it, all university students are "top" in one way or another. Some of them may be good at their academic subjects, while others may excel in music, sports, designing, to mention only a few. As each student is unique in his/her own way, to sort out a few and label them as "top students" is senseless and misleading.（170624，政府应该只资助优秀学生吗？）

（79）On the other hand, the younger generation may want their fun time outside and get away from the boring daily _____（常规，例行程序）. This is also important because young people are full of energy which needs to be channeled in positive forms.（181027，年轻人应该多在家还是在外面娱乐？）

（80）Obviously, international charity groups can take advantage of the publicity of those famous people. They can draw more media attention and make more people _____（认识到）the importance of a certain issue.（190413，名人支持国际救助组织是好还是坏？）

（81）Mentally speaking, children who have more screen time are likely to have difficulty forming friendships and productive social networking. In their imagination, the world is _____（缩小）as they begin to stop engaging in real-life, preferring the fantasy world offered by technology instead.（190817，父母应该允许孩子使用电子设备吗？）

（82）Today individuals are surrounded by all kinds of advertising, some of which is directly aimed at children and significantly influences them. It has been suggested that such advertisements ought to be _____（限制）due to their detrimental impacts on youngsters. I am however not convinced by that.（140424，儿童广告是否应该禁止？）

（83）Thirdly, consumers develop loyalty to particular brands that provide a _____（一贯的）, high-quality experience, and that loyalty is essentially an emotional attachment to a brand.（180623，人们喜欢购买名牌的原因及利弊）

（84）Many people think that luck plays the most significant role in a successful life, but in my view, to achieve success in life, one needs _____（持续不断的）hard work, though luck does help in some cases.（201030，实现生活目标主要是运气使然吗？）

（85）The government in any country provides funding for the development of its higher education, but there are divided opinions about where this government funding should go. Should it go _____（仅仅）to those "top students" or indiscriminately to all students? My personal view is, however, quite definitive: the government money should be provided for all students.（170624，政府应该只资助优秀学生吗？）

（86）What is more, since traditional games are usually played with minimal technology and _____（最大的）freedom, children can learn by example from other children without any pre-programmed rules. Children need to play traditional games as a physical and mental necessity in the open air, instead of just playing computer games like a little nerd in front of the screen. (180802, 现在的游戏不及传统游戏有助于孩子发展技能吗？)

(87) Unless there is a _____ (特别的) crisis going on, it is always the case that the public will become immune to shocking statistics or terrible photos, for they have seen too many of them and tend to neglect them. It is, therefore, the job of the government to keep informing the public (through television or other media) of the current environmental issues. (190414, 政府应该让人们负责保护本地环境吗？)

(88) A key responsibility of the world's rich countries is to increase the amount of aid provided to the poorer countries, _____ (尤其是) in the field of health. The question is: should drug companies be responsible for finding new medicine for these countries or should they mainly focus on making money? (190810, 医药公司的主要职责是挣钱，还是为贫穷国家研究新药？)

(89) Surrounded by advertisements, we can easily be led to a belief that our life is all about buying things. This _____ (广泛的) consumerism can persuade us into buying many things we do not really need on the one hand, and make us less content with what we have on the other, and crave hopelessly for those un-attainable commodities. (180201, 广告对我们生活的影响)

(90) In conclusion, to achieve development and progress, the government ought to invest in both sciences and humanities. The effect of the investment in sciences may be immediately visible, while it may take a long time for that in humanities to be felt, which means that the government must have the foresight to give _____ (足够的) support to humanities before it is too late. (201205, 大多数政府资金应该投入理科教育吗？)

(91) Sports stars, if they do not behave properly, may also negatively in-fluence young people. Maradona, who died not long ago, is just a case in point. Arguably the best football player in the world, he did not set a good example to young people by taking drugs and shooting journalists, giving his young admirers a false impression that a star can do anything _____ (不管) the law and moral standards. (201219, 年轻人崇拜负面明星，是好还是坏？)

(92) Advertising is, of course, very useful, informing us about what to

buy, where to buy and how to buy, but it also has negative effects, especially by
_____（改变）what we regard as important in our life.（180201，广告对我
们生活的影响）

参考答案

（1）accuse

（2）accusation

（3）available

（4）achieve

（5）adopted

（6）arouse

（7）independently

（8）striking

（9）revealed

（10）accomplish

（11）solve/address/combat

（12）stimulate

（13）absorb

（14）concentrate on; distracted

（15）distracted

（16）adapting

（17）determined

（18）adapt

（19）distractions

（20）determine

（21）confine

（22）prohibited

（23）derive

（24）compelling/forcing

（25）compel/force

（26）anticipated

（27）content

（28）frustration

（29）relieve

（30）relieved

（31）stress

（32）relieve; stress

（33）approach

（34）attached

（35）discourage/prevent

（36）exposed to

（37）exposure

（38）superiors

（39）superior

（40）substitutes

（41）substitute/replace

（42）assumed

（43）available

（44）complex

（45）survive

（46）justifiable

（47）justified

（48）involved

（49）emerge

（50）distinguishes

（51）competent

（52）excessively

（53）identify

（54）options/choices

（55）afford

（56）alternative

（57）alternative

（58）considerable

（59）fraction

（60）artificial

（61）isolated

（62）isolate

（63）represents

（64）represents

（65）variety

（66）eliminate

（67）eventually

（68）objections

（69）remove

（70）urgent

（71）urgent

（72）independent

（73）apparently

（74）survival

（75）provided/extended

（76）mutually exclusive

（77）similarly

（78）vague

（79）routine

（80）recognize

（81）shrinking

（82）restricted

（83）consistent

（84）continuous

（85）exclusively

（86）maximum

（87）particular

（88）particularly

（89）widespread

（90）sufficient

（91）regardless of

（92）transforming

第五章　雅思写作句法

　　雅思写作在句子方面的要求对各分数段来说是不同的。句子质量包括三个维度，即语法正确与否、类型多样与否、地道与否。

　　4分段的作文，多数句子语法不正确，且很多句子语义模糊，让人难以理解；5分段的作文，很多句子语法都有瑕疵，但总体上能让人看懂；6分段的作文，多数句子语法都是正确的，即使有瑕疵也不影响理解，但句子类型不够多样，比较简单或单调；7分段的作文，句子语法基本没有错误，而且做到类型多样；8分段的句子，除了正确、多样，还要确保地道。从这个意义上说，雅思写作要达到7分，通过恰当的训练，在句子层面上是可以实现的，但要达到8分，也就是要地道表达，则只有通过大量阅读和积累才能实现，非一般短期培训所能及。

　　本章先讨论句子正确性和多样性问题，然后讨论句子写作中容易出现的几个典型错误，最后讨论如何在写作中做到长短句配合以及如何增强句子的语义密度等问题。

5.1 句子正确性

5.1.1 句子写作概述

　　"句子是表达完整意义的最小单位。"句子也是文章构成的基本单位。句子写得好不好基本可以反映一个外语学习者的语言知识和语言能力。用英语写文章关键要把握英语句子的内部特征，让句子为作者所要传达的信息服务，而语言的纯正也都体现在句子之内。

　　写作在句子方面的要求：写结构完整的句子；句子以大写字母开头，以句末标点结束；每个句子只能表达一个完整的意思。

1. 句子结构的完整性

英语句子的基本结构可以表示为：

主语（S）+ 谓语（VP）

一致关系

其中 S 由 NE（名词性成分）充当，VE（动词性成分）充当谓语，于是上述基本句子结构还可以表示为：

NE + VE

所有的英语句子都是在此基础上发展而来的。无论多么复杂，其结构都是有章可循的。如以下句子在结构上就是完整的：

She came.（主语 + 谓语）

John is a good teacher.（主语 + 系动词 + 表语）

The students use these dictionaries every day.（主语 + 谓语 + 宾语 + 状语）

He didn't know what had happened and was going to ask Mr. Smith, who was usually well informed.（主语 + 谓语 + 宾语从句 + 并列谓语 + 定语从句）

结构不完整的句子严格地讲就不算句子，如：

How to operate this computer.（缺主语和谓语）

Have lost my key.（缺主语）

He continued working in the classroom. Because he hadn't finished his assignment.（because 连接从句，不能单独成句）

The old man returning home after eight years' absence, only to find that all the neighbours he had known were no longer there.（returning 是分词，不能作谓语）

Mark Twain whose experience as a sailor on the Mississippi provided him with abundant material for the novels he was to write.（只有主语和修饰主语的定语从句，缺少谓语动词）

Mr. Wang, a man trusted by his leaders and all his fellow workers, known as an expert in computer programming.（只有主语，缺少谓语动词）

The old man who had taught at the school for 40 years and was given a medal of honour for his devotion to the cause of education before he retired.（只有主语及修饰主语的定语从句，缺谓语）

To tell my friend the good news that the letter was posted at once.（缺主语）

2. 句子内容的统一性

一个句子表达一个完整的意思。一个句子的内容要围绕一个主题；句子内部各个部分都必须与这个主题有直接或去之不远的间接关系。句子的主题应该在主句中得到体现。凡是从句都是对主句的修饰、说明或补充；其内容从属于主句内容，并与之一道形成对句子主题的完整表述。句子内的各个部分可以有层次高低之分但一定是彼此呼应形成一个主题鲜明的整体。不能归属于同一主题的句子即便是写在一个句法结构单位内也不是好的句子。相反，把本该在一句话内交代的内容强行写成两句话也会破坏句子的统一性。此外，句法结构的完整并不等于句子内容的统一。例如：

Born in a small town in South China in the early 50s, he grew up to be a famous musician.

这句话在句法结构上无可挑剔。但是如果从内容上着眼，不难发现，born in 与 grew up to be a famous musician 之间没有必然的因果关系。作者想在本句中表达的主题由于各个层次内容之间的不相关性而无法得到体现。试改写如下：

He was born in a small town in South China in the early 50s. He liked singing in his childhood. As he dreamed, he grew up to be as famous musician later.

这样一来，不同的主题放在不同的句子中表达，各个句子围绕着 he 的成长经历形成了一段话。

3. 句子内容的连贯性

结构完整且内容统一的句子算是基本合格的句子。但想让句子真正能准确清楚地传递信息，完整和统一还不够，还需要句子内容的连贯性。句子内容的连贯性既是结构问题也是内容问题。连贯性可以定义为句子内各个部分在内容和结构两方面都要清晰合理地相互联系。

连贯性大致体现在四个方面：

第一，修饰语与被修饰语的关系要有明确体现，不能造成歧义。

第二，不存在悬垂的成分，即无法判断与其他部分关系的部分。

第三，没有含混不清的指称成分。

第四，没有人称、数、时态、语态和情态等方面混乱的跳动。

下面几个句子都因各种理由存在连贯性差的问题。

A man is judged not only by what he says but also by his deeds.（结构不对称）

We have great faith and hope for her.（faith 后应接 in）

She told my sister that she was wrong.（代词指代不清楚）

He was knocked down by a bicycle, but it was not serious.（it 指代不明）

Looking out of the window, the square expands in all directions.（悬垂修饰语）

To get ready for the trip, all the things she needed were put into a suitcase.（悬垂修饰语）

I read an interesting story in a magazine about sportsman.（歧义）

The idea he mentioned at first sounded good.（歧义）

An important thing for the student to remember is that when writing a paper, you should not plagiarize.（人称转移）

What one knows is more important than the wealth one has.（第二个 one 应用 he/she）

4. 句子重点突出的手段

既然句子中的内容有主次之分，那就存在将什么信息置于主要地位，什么信息置于次要地位的问题。一般情况下，主句的内容是主要信息。此外，还有几种句子内部突出重点的手段：

（1）强调句结构

<u>It is</u> **just at the beginning of the new millenium** <u>that</u> the only superpower breaks the international law, launching Iraqi War.

上面例子中画线部分是强调结构，而黑体部分则是强调的内容（下文同）。这是大家都比较熟悉的一种手段。

（2）置于头尾

句子的头尾是天然的强调位置，这两个位置最容易引起读者的注意。如果必要且可能，要突出的内容应该放在这两个位置之一。

In the temple, there is a big tree, which is said to be 300 years old.

In the 20th century, scientists have made many great discoveries.

Jonathan is a good student, **modest and hardworking**.

（3）重复内容

只在必要的时候才重复，无谓重复会破坏句子的简洁性。

Bright, very bright, were the stars over the wild, dark Yenan Hills.

（4）从属关系

从属关系不仅仅是结构上的从属，更是意义上的从属。主句的内容在重要性上要比从属成分的内容高些。所以在安排句内各个层次的意思时可以把次要的内容置于从属成分当中从而达到突出主要内容的目的。试比较：

① The professor walked into the classroom and he carried a bag of books with him.

② **The professor walked into the classroom**, carrying a bag of books with him / with a bag of books under his arm / a bag of books under his arm.

5.1.2 常见句子语法错误类型

1. 时态误用

〔误〕 I had a look at my watch and I knew what <u>will</u> happen.

〔改〕 I had a look at my watch and I knew what **would** happen.

〔误〕 Riding bicycles <u>had</u> more advantages than taking a bus.

〔改〕 Riding bicycles **has** more advantages than taking a bus.

常见错误：用现在时叙述过去的事；用过去时谈论经常发生的事；现在完成时与明确表示过去的时间范畴合用。

2. 主谓不一致

〔误〕 Every one of us <u>have</u> the right to be happy.

〔改〕 Every one of us **has** the right to be happy.

〔误〕 The eating habit of Chinese people <u>have</u> changed dramatically in the past decade.

〔改〕 The eating habit of Chinese people **has** changed dramatically in the past decade.

〔误〕 There <u>is</u> so many countries using English that it had been regarded as an international language.

〔改〕 There **are** so many countries using English that it has been regarded as an international language.

常见错误：主语为单数，谓语用复数；主语为从句或动名词，谓语用复数。

3. 代词误用

［误］If the humans want to live well, <u>we</u> must keep nature in balance.

［改］If the humans want to live well, **they** must keep nature in balance.

［误］I always told myself that I shouldn't cry when the time to leave was coming because <u>it was not mature</u>.

［改］I had always told myself that I wouldn't cry when the time arrived for me to leave home, **for that was a sign of my immaturity.**

［误］So long as you have the Internet access and some necessary rights, <u>anyone</u> can receive education wherever you lives in.

［改］So long as you have the Internet access and some necessary licenses, **you** can receive education wherever you live in.

［误］Whether one enjoys or resents <u>advertisements</u>, <u>we are</u> actually bombarded with <u>it</u> every hour of the day.

［改］Whether one enjoys or resents **them**, **he is** actually bombarded with **advertisements** every hour of the day.

常见错误：代词在性、数、格上与指称部分不一致；代词频繁变化；代词指代不明。

4. 比较级错误

［误］With the advancement of science and technology, I believe that people's life will be <u>more and more happier</u>.

［改］With the advancement of science and technology, I believe that people's life will become **happier and happier**.

［误］The world is getting <u>more smaller and smaller</u>.

［改］The world is getting **smaller and smaller**.

常见错误：more and more + 形容词比较级；形容词原形 + than。

5. 悬垂修饰语

［误］In order to get a good mark, <u>it took me</u> much time, when I didn't have classes this weekdays, to get ready for this exam.

［改］In order to get a good mark, **I spend** much of my spare time getting ready for this exam.

〔误〕There are many ways to improve city traffic, <u>for example widening the streets, building subways and so on</u>.

〔改〕There are many ways to improve city traffic. **For example, we can widen the streets, build subways and so on.**

〔误〕My friends told me one of my old classmates had been killed in a sudden accident. <u>Heard</u> of that, I couldn't think anything for a long time.

〔改〕My friend told me one of my old classmates had been killed in a sudden accident. **Hearing** of that, I couldn't think of anything for a long time.

常见错误：主句主语和非谓语动词的逻辑主语不匹配。

6. 从句使用错误

〔误〕If someone wanted to go back to ancient society, <u>which</u> had no electricity, cloth and room, almost every people would say he was crazy.

〔改〕If anyone wants to go back to ancient times, **in which** there was no electricity, cloth or room, almost every people will say he is crazy.

〔误〕It is said that we'd better live in a small town instead of the big city if we want better health and longer life, and it is analyzed that the reason is the different life styles between the cities and towns <u>which</u> people have a relaxation life in town but a nervous life in city.

〔改〕It is said that we'd better live in a small town instead of the big city if we want a better health and a longer life. This is because, they say, the life style in the city is nervous while that in the town is relaxed.

常见错误：关系代 / 副词漏用或误用。

7. 错误搭配

〔误〕When TV came into the world, the people's life <u>had a large changes</u>.

〔改〕After TV came to the world, people's life **changed a great deal**. (Or: The arrival of TV greatly changed people's life.)

〔误〕But <u>in another aspect</u>, some disaster were brought from the same science and technology.

〔改〕**On the other hand**, science and technology can also bring about some disasters.

〔误〕By contrast, other people don't <u>agree above viewpoint</u>. They like change jobs from time to time.

〔改〕By contrast, other people don't **agree to that viewpoint**. They like to change jobs from time to time.

〔误〕Everyone, <u>no matter what age</u>, needs exercise every day.

〔改〕Everyone, **regardless of his age**, needs exercise every day.

〔误〕In a lonely cabin, there are several <u>children with bad wearing</u>.

〔改〕In a lonely cabin, there are several **children in rags**.

〔误〕She completed all courses in <u>primitive school</u>, in high school.

〔改〕She completed all the courses in **primary** and high **school**.

常见错误：介词错误搭配；不符合习惯搭配；中文式搭配。

8. 句型错误

〔误〕With the Chinese economy developing, <u>cars entering families in China is more and more usualness</u>.

〔改〕As China's economy develops, **there will be more and more cars entering families in China**. (Or: As China's economy develops, **it will become more and more common for cars to enter families in China**.)

〔误〕It made me <u>can not forget</u> my grandmother…

〔改〕It made me **unable to forget** my grandmother…

〔误〕In a word, <u>as a scholar</u>, <u>college teachers</u> will become <u>more wise</u> and more practical <u>instead of losing their time and energy</u>.

〔改〕In a word, **working as a scholar**, **a college teacher** will become **wiser** and more experienced in practice. **By no means is it a waste of time and energy.**

〔误〕China develops very fast which could supply so many chances of jobs for people that a few of people have several jobs at the same time, and they must improve their efficiency including walking in the road.

〔改〕As China develops rapidly, so many new job opportunities are opened up that some people can take several jobs at the same time, which makes it necessary for them to minimize their travel hours.

常见错误：中文式句型。

9. 重复表达

〔误〕One reason is that the people may have more money than ever before, which makes it possible for them to buy cars for their families. Another is the development of automobile industry brings down the price of cars, <u>which</u> <u>makes it possible for them to buy cars</u>.

〔改〕One reason is that the people have more money than ever before, which makes it possible for them to buy private cars. Another reason is the development of automobile industry brings down the price of cars, thus **paving their way into the households in China**.

常见错误：使用几乎相同的单词或句型表达同样的意思。

10. 结构不平衡

〔误〕No matter what choice you made, the final goal should be <u>to do bet-</u> <u>ter work and further development</u>.

〔改〕No matter what choice you make, the final goal should be **for a better job and further development**.

〔误〕<u>Psychological health</u> let us have good <u>individual character</u> including steady feeling, gentle disposition, and strong will, easy to get along with <u>other</u> <u>person, can adapt oneself to complicated circumstances as well as have good re-</u> <u>lation with other people</u>.

〔改〕**Mental health** gives us desirable **personalities** such as stable feeling, gentle disposition and strong will, which make it easy for us to get along with others, **to adapt ourselves to the complicated circumstances as well as maintain favourable interpersonal relationships.**

常见错误：并列成分采用不同类型的表达方式。

11. 情态误用

〔误〕In a word, if we <u>have</u> no TV, we <u>may</u> lose something which bring us happy.

〔改〕In a word, if we **had** no TV, we **might** lose something which brings us happiness.

常见错误：陈述与事实相反的观点时，不采用虚拟语气形式。

12. 破碎句

［误］ Will, like a light tower in the sea, <u>which can</u> conduct us to advance on a right track.

［改］ Will, like a light tower in the sea, **can** conduct us to advance on a right track.

［误］ They object to changing job frequently. <u>Because frequent job-hopping will result to nothing can done.</u>

［改］ They object to changing jobs frequently, **because that might result in their getting nowhere at all** (or: **because that might lead to failure in every job they do**).

［误］ But the science and technology also is a two-edge sword, <u>if uses unsuitably will bring the suffering of destruction to people.</u>

［改］ But science and technology is also a double-edged sword, which might be destructive to human beings if used improperly.

［误］ The most funny thing is that <u>there were five of my classmates were born in November, 1983.</u>

［改］ The most funny thing is that there were five of my classmates **who** were born in November, 1983.

常见错误：句子缺乏主语或谓语；because 引导独立句子；there be 句型后直接跟动词原形。

13. 流水句

［误］ A chairman was having lunch, a soldier <u>stood</u> by him.

［改］ A chairman was having lunch, a soldier **standing** by him.

［误］ I was born in a small town, in the town there was only one school, I studied there for six years.

［改］ I was born in a small town. In it there was only one school. I studied there for six years. (Or: I studied for six years at the only school in the small town where I was born.)

［误］ In former times, elephants hadn't long noses. They only had a black nose which was like shoe. <u>Then, a little elephant was born, he was curious, he always asked others: "why?"</u>

〔改〕In former times, elephants did not have long noses. They only had black noses like shoes. **Then, a little elephant was born who was curious and always asked others "why".**

〔误〕As China entered WTO, the cost of a car is decreasing in these years, many families could buy and use a family car.

〔改〕As China has become a member of WTO, the cost of a car is keeping lowering down in recent years **so that many families could afford a private car**.

〔误〕There are many bad books that are poisonous to our mind, we should not read them.

〔改〕There are many bad books that are poisonous to our mind. We should not read them.

〔误〕Health is the most important factor in our lives, we can lose money and authority, but we can't lose health.

〔改〕**Health is the most important factor in our life. We can lose money and power, but we cannot lose health.**

常见错误：两个或以上的独立句子用逗号相连。

5.2 避免代词误用

英语和汉语在代词使用方面存在较大差异。首先，英语使用代词的频率明显高于汉语，而汉语中省略代词和名词重复的频率则远远超过英语。汉语主张少用代词，对待代词的原则是：为了明白，就重复名词；为了简洁，名词代词都不用。英语则要求避免同一名词在相近的语言环境中重复使用。汉英的这一差异，加之英语代词系统的独特性，使中国学生在英语代词使用中容易出现偏误。以下笔者将使用例句一一分析，各位同学看看自己的写作中是否存在相似的问题。

5.2.1 名词重复过多

如前所述，汉语倾向于重复名词以使上下文连贯，而英语则倾向于使用代词。这种差异往往造成中国学生在英语作文中大量重复名词，而不喜欢用代词，使作文读起来既不流畅也不精练。

例1 The man is not a young man, but <u>the man</u> is not old. He is about forty-four or forty-five years old. <u>The man</u> is a good-looking man, tall, handsome, rather thin, with dark-brown hair just beginning to go gray. <u>The man</u> is always well-dressed, but quiet in good taste.

例2 Turkey had the highest proportion of national consumer expenditure in food, drinks and tobacco, at 32.14%, which was approximately twice as much as that of Italy. Ireland had the second <u>highest proportion of national consumer expenditure in food, drinks, and tobacco</u>. It was 28.91%.

例3 Self-confidence is very important for us. With <u>self-confidence</u> we can do whatever we want to; without <u>self-confidence</u>, we can achieve nothing.

例1中，the man 毫无必要地重复了四次，虽然在汉语中这样重复并无违和感。我们可将后面出现的所有 the man 改为 he。例2中出现的重复更是极端，在描写土耳其和爱尔兰两个国家在食物、饮料和香烟方面的花销时，文字上居然完全重复，全然没有使用代词的概念。可做如下修改：Ireland had the second highest proportion in this sector/field/expenditure, at 28.91%. 例3没有明显语法错误，但读起来颇似汉语表达。"自信对我们很重要。有了自信我们百事可为，没有自信则一事无成。"很明显，学生受到了汉语结构的影响。这句可改为：Self-confidence is very important for us. With it we can do whatever we want to, or else we can achieve nothing.

5.2.2 该用代词的时候不用代词

例1 People should not spend too much time on hobbies in order to avoid disturbing <u>normal work and study</u>.

例2 Many international meetings on environment protection are held, at which scientists from different countries can <u>exchange ideas</u> and learn from each other.

例1义为"人们不应该在业余爱好上花太多时间，以免影响正常工作和学习"。例2义为"在许多有关环境保护的国际会议上，世界各地的科学家可以交流思想和互相学习"。汉语中不使用物主代词不会引起误解，读起来也非常自然，然而，在英语中则应该加上物主代词，所以两句中画线部分最好分别改为 their normal work and study 及 exchange their ideas。

5.2.3 代词前后不一致

例 1 So long as <u>you</u> have the Internet access, <u>anyone</u> can receive distance education.

例 2 Before leaving for foreign countries, it is necessary for <u>us</u> to know about the local culture and language since this can help <u>you</u> avoid some cultural misunderstanding.

代词使用时要保持前后一致，一般不随意转换，否则就会造成所指不明的错误。这种错误在中国学生的英语作文中相当普遍，尤其是在不定代词的使用方面，其根源在于，汉语不定代词的使用是可以随意转换的（比如"我们大家都要努力工作，要不然你就会丢工作"），而英语一般情况下需要保持一致（We must work hard, or we will lose our job.）。例 1 中，从句中用 you，主句中用 anyone，明显不一致，可将 anyone 改为 you。例 2 中，前面用 us，后面用 you，将 you 改为 us 即可实现一致性。

5.2.4 代词的性、数、格与所代成分不一致

例 1 We all know that everyone is forever a child in <u>their</u> parents' eyes.

例 2 If a friend of <u>you</u> asks you to do a wrong thing for him, your best answer is of course "No!"

例 3 The old have their lifetime knowledge, but many young people regard it as a long-term burden and consider <u>they</u> are of little value to <u>our</u> life.

人称代词、反身代词以及相应的限定代词必须和它们指代的对象保持性、数、格上的一致。以第三人称单数为例，若指代对象为阳性名词，代词通常用 he、him、himself、his；若指代对象为阴性名词，代词通常用 she、her、herself、hers；若指代对象是表示无生命事物的名词，代词常用 it、its、itself。代词的格分为三种，分别是主格、宾格和所有格，各有其相应的形式，都不能出错。例 1 中，everyone 是单数，后面用 their 来指代就违反了数的一致性，应为 his/her。例 2 中，a friend of you 应该是 a friend of yours。例 3 "many young people regard it... and consider they... to our life" 中，it 明显指代前文中的 knowledge，是不可数名词，但后面又用了复数形式 they，这也违反了数的一致性，可改为 it；此外，本句主语是 young people，后面却用 our life 来指代，这就是上文说到的"代词前后不一致"，改为 their life 就一致了。

5.2.5 代词使用引发流水句

例 1　Students are always faced with great pressure from examination, some of them even choose suicide.

例 2　Students with a part-time job have chances to contact different people, this will make them more experienced to deal with interpersonal relationships in future.

例 3　Students spend too much time preparing for examination, they always ignore outdoor activities and exercises.

　　流水句是中国学生最容易犯的句法错误之一，代词使用往往引发这一错误，其根源依然是汉语的负迁移。在汉语句子中，代词引导的句子和主句无缝衔接，直接用逗号相连，但英语语法并不允许这种用法。例 1 中，前句主语为 students，后句主语为 some of them，这是两个不同主语引起的句子，无法直接用逗号连接，可在两个句子中间加连接词 and，或者将第二句变为从属句，比如将 them 改为 whom。与此相同，例 2 两句也可用 and 连接，或将后句 this 改为 which。例 3 两句可加 and 或 so 来连接。

5.3 避免并列结构错误

　　在概念上，汉英并列结构都是一样的，指的是句子中那些意思不同，但功能相同的成分。但是，在表达形式上，汉英有一个重大区别，那就是英语的并列结构要求语法形式一致，汉语的并列结构则没有这个要求。在汉语的并列结构中，只要求意义平行，形式则可以相当随意。在很多方面，汉语的确是一门非常"任性"的语言，它"无招胜有招，灵活飘逸"，与严谨的英语语法形成了对比。难怪很多人说，汉语是一门诗性的语言，英语则更偏重逻辑和形式。

　　我们来看几个例子。

例 1　研究表明，有兼职工作的学生与没有兼职工作的学生相比更加自信，且能更好地管理时间。

　　这里，"更加自信"和"能更好地管理时间"是并列成分，都是用来说明"有兼职工作"和"没有兼职工作"的学生的区别。语法形式上，"更加自信"是形容词（有语法学家认为，"自信"不是形容词，形容词也是西方语法的概念，这个问题我们暂且不论），"管理时间"则是动宾结构。如果要表达成英语，"更加自信"和"能更好地管理时间"就应该处理成同样的语法结构。请看以下两句：

① According to the study, students who do part-time jobs are more confident and can manage their time better than those who do not.

② According to the study, students who do part-time jobs are more confident and better in time-management than those who do not.

句①中 are more confident（形容词结构）和 can manage their time better（动宾结构）语法结构不一致，显然是受到汉语思维的影响；句②则把它们统一为形容词短语，更符合英语表达习惯。

例 2　教小孩子如何挣钱以及正确理财十分关键，这能够让他们成功地处理人生中的各种关系。

这里，"如何挣钱"和"正确理财"是并列成分，但汉语里使用了不同结构，若直接按照这种结构写成英语，则不符合英语表达习惯。请看以下两句：

① It is very important to teach children how to earn money and the correct way of using money, so they can successfully deal with different kinds of relationship in their life.

② It is very important to teach children how to earn money and how to use money, so they can successfully deal with different kinds of relationship in their life.

句①中 how to earn money 和 the correct way of using money 语法形式差异太大，虽然意思可以读懂，但明显不是规范的英语。句②则将"正确理财"转化为 how to use money，与前面的 how to earn money 不仅意义上并列，语法形式上也并列。

例 3　一些人已经有环保意识了，他们用布袋代替塑料袋，不乱丢垃圾，还自愿种树以对抗沙尘暴。

① Some people have their awareness of environmental protection, so they use cloth bags to replace plastic bags; no littering and planting trees to combat sandstorms.

② Some people have already been aware of the importance of environmental protection, so they use cloth bags to replace plastic bags, refuse to litter, and plant trees to combat sandstorms.

这个例子更为复杂。"用布袋代替塑料袋""不乱丢垃圾""自愿种树以对抗沙尘暴"是三个并列成分，用来说明"他们"所做的事情。汉语的形式何其灵活！句①先用 they use cloth bags to replace plastic bags，随后却用 no littering 这个与前面完全不同的结构。句②则把三个并列成分都处理为由 they 发出的动作，从而在语法形式上将它们统一起来。

例 4 心理健康让我们拥有良好的个性，比如稳定的情感，温柔的性情，坚强的信念，容易与人相处，能适应复杂的情况，以及与他人保持良好的关系。

① Psychological health let us have good individual character including steady feeling, gentle disposition, and strong will, easy to get along with other person, can adapt oneself to complicated circumstances as well as have good relation with other people.

② Mental health gives us desirable personalities such as stable feeling, gentle disposition, and strong will, which makes it easy for us to get along with others, to adapt ourselves to the complicated circumstances, and to maintain favourable interpersonal relationships.

这个例子无疑更为极端。"稳定的情感，温柔的性情，坚强的信念，容易与人相处，能适应复杂的情况，以及与他人保持良好的关系"是并列成分，但"任性"的汉语综合使用了各种语法形式来展现这些并列成分：前三个成分是"形容词＋名词"，后三个成分是省略了主语的句子。句①跟着汉语的结构走，把英语句子写下来，其结果当然就是一塌糊涂！句②则根据英语习惯做了变通，先并列 stable feeling、gentle disposition、strong will，然后改用非限定性定语从句将后面三个成分重新处理，使句子显得平衡稳定，展示出高人一筹的英语句子把控能力。

5.4 句型多样性

5.4.1 主从复合句

句型的多样性并不简单等同于写复合句，虽然写一定数量的复合句是雅思高分段作文所要求的。当要表达几个意思时，我们可以用独立的单句来表达每一个意思，也可以把这几个意思放在同一个句子里，在后一种情况下就需要写复合句。

写复合句的时候，首先要确定哪一个意思是最主要的，把它作为主干句子来表达，然后把次要的意思放置在从句中。请看一例学生习作：

This policy would affect the cost of public transport. Some people need to travel on the roads every day. This policy would be very unpopular with them.

这里有三个意思需要表达：这项政策会影响到公共交通的成本；有些人需要每天乘坐公共交通；这项政策不受他们欢迎。如果以"这项政策不受他们欢迎"为主句，那么"这项政策会影响到公共交通的成本"就可以安排成原因状语从句，而"有些人需要每天乘坐公共交通"则可以安排为定语从句来修饰"他们"。于是，上面三个句子就可合并为：

As this policy would affect the cost of public transport, it would be very unpopular with those who need to travel on the roads every day.

以下介绍几个常见且容易模仿的主从复合句型。

1. It is believed/suggested/reported/well-known/argued/assumed that...

例 1　With the expansion of cities, people have to spend more and more time travelling to and from work. As one solution to this problem, **it is suggested that** apartment buildings should be planted near the city centre in place of parks and gardens.（190406，在城市中心建公寓楼可减少通勤时间吗？）

例 2　Meanwhile, **it is not uncommon at all that** the rivers and streams around paper factories (or other manufacturing factories) are so polluted that the water is no longer drinkable.（190907，经济发展与环境保护的关系）

例 3　**It is argued that**, when a teenager commits a crime, even a serious crime such as robbery or sexual harassment, he should not be given the same punishment as an adult criminal.（180506，未成年人犯法是否该受同样惩罚）

2. which 引导的非限定性定语从句

例 1　Undoubtedly, the increased price of cars and petrol will discourage people from owning and using their own cars, **which will surely contribute to the solution of traffic congestion and make big cities cleaner**.（210718，提高车价和油价是解决交通和污染问题的最好办法吗？）

例 2　Nowadays, there is a growing tendency that many museums and historical sites, **which seem less attractive for local dwellers**, are mainly visited by tourists from other parts of the world.（210809，本地人不参观当地博物馆的原因及解决办法）

例 3 As a matter of fact, parenting is about loving children without spoiling them, **which means that parents have to reinforce good discipline in their children**.（190727，溺爱孩子的后果）

3. what 引导的主语从句

例 1 With laptops, cell-phones, and tablets being widely used at school and at home, educators have been focusing on teaching their students keyboarding skills, for students can finish almost all their assignments with clicks of keyboard. **What they are supposed to do** is type their answers into the computer and submit them online to the teacher.（191123，当今时代，应该教孩子学习书法吗？）

例 2 My opinion, then, is that economic growth is forever needed in spite of its potential risks to the environment. **What we ought to do** is try to find ways of reducing its effect on the environment, rather than give up economic development altogether.（190907，经济发展与环境保护的关系）

例 3 If in the past they were able to engage in such activities as walking, gardening, weeding, and planting in their backyard, when they got back home from work, now **what people can do** is sitting in the sofa and watching TV.（200116，没有室外空间，好还是坏？）

4. while 引导的转折和让步从句

例 1 **While it is a clear indicator of a country's prosperity and thus can strengthen the confidence of people in their government**, a longer life span also results in the ageing problem.（210121，寿命延长对个人和社会的影响）

例 2 In the first place, culture determines what kind of music is more popular with people. Chinese people, for instance, are fond of music that is soft, familiar, and slow, **while Western people prefer something fast, strange, and strong**.（210313，音乐是人类的共同语言吗？）

例 3 **While it is hard to determine how the visual uniformity is related to quality at work**, having a dress code in place may help the way a corporation wants to be perceived.（180113，员工着装和工作品质有何关系？）

5.4.2 其他多样性手段

如前所述，句子的多样性不能仅由主从复合句来实现。事实上，如果学生作文段落里充满了复合句，这不仅会破坏作文的行文节奏，而且也是有风险的。复杂句用得越多，学生犯错的概率就越大，即使没有造成理解困难，也容易淹没学生想表达的主要意思，从而造成行文不连贯。笔者的经验表明，一篇 250 词左右的雅思范文，有 3—5 个复合句即可。

句子的多样性还可通过其他手段来实现。以下介绍几种实现句子多样性的常见方法。

1. 状语前置

英语中状语通常置于句末或动词之后，但我们可以将状语前置，让句子显得具有多样性。

例 1 **Instead of the Internet**, I would label language as "the most important invention", because it was the invention of language that ultimately distinguished humans from animals and made possible everything we have now in the human world.（201025，互联网是人类最重要的发明吗？）

例 2 **Far from being just a personal matter**, our health is something that largely guarantees the health of the community, as have been repeatedly evidenced in the Covid-19 pandemic that is still troubling the world today.（210515，照顾好自己的身体，是我们对社会应尽的义务吗？）

例 3 Then, **in face of climate change, rather than trying to prevent it**, we'd better try to find a way to live with it. For instance, when the hotter climate makes it impossible to grow a certain vegetable in summer, we can grow it earlier than now, store it and then eat it when the weather becomes too hot.（160716，避免还是接受气候变化）

2. 插入语

插入语在汉语中使用较少，但在英语中非常常见。

例 1 If other life forms do exist, **an idea I strongly support**, should we, **as human beings on the Earth**, try to reach out and communicate with them?（201005，应该与外星生命联系吗？）

例 2 Another possible downside of this rural-urban mobility is that, **without proper training**, the young rural people moving into cities may not be able to find a job, which, **then**, will bring about a series of social problems.（190425，乡村年轻人进城读书和工作的原因及利弊）

例 3 In the first place, it is difficult for many families to afford a retirement home's services which are typically very costly. It is, **therefore**, a great financial burden for families to have their old parents living in a retirement community.（191207，老年人住退休社区是好是坏？）

3. 句首或句末用分词短语作状语

这个用法在汉语中不会出现，但在英语里则是常用的。

例 1 When **put into prison**, the young people will have nothing to do but read and think about their past.（180516，未成年人犯法是否该受同样惩罚？）

例 2 The fierce competition that exists everywhere in big cities is destructive to our relationship with our colleagues, neighbours, and even friends, **resulting in our isolation and loneliness**.（180603，生活在大城市不利于身体健康吗？）

例 3 People can take a walk in the park together with their family members, **chatting and having a lot of fun**. This is of course much beneficial to their health than staying at home, **sitting in front of TV or a computer like a couch potato**.（190112，要体育设施还是购物中心？）

例 4 Many criminals find they simply cannot find a job to support themselves after being freed from prison. **Having been secluded from the real world for a long while**, they find themselves no longer needed by the world that changes on a daily basis. Then, without a choice, they have to steal, rob, or even kill people, just for survival's sake.（201107，被惩罚后罪犯继续犯罪的原因及解决办法）

4. 倒装句

恰当使用倒装句，可以增加句子的多样性。

例 1 However, others hold the opposite opinion that individual efforts, **small as they may be**, are also crucial to improve the environment, so each individual should take action.（201114，个人无助于解决环境问题吗？）

例 2 Finally, **not only is taking drugs itself a crime** but it may also lead to various other crimes that young people never intended to commit in the first place.（190523，青少年犯罪越来越多的原因及惩罚办法）

例 3　This is probably the reason why in the movie "Superman", Clark has to be working together with others as a newspaper man. **Only in this way can the superhero understand human problems and then figure out the way to solve them**.（160507，分班还是和班教学？）

5. 强调句

"It is... that/who..." 是英语里一种特有的强调句型，用来突出显示需要强调的句子成分。

例 1　Furthermore, if a woman plans to join the armed forces, she will have to tackle a number of other social issues. For instance, her parents may have strong objections to this choice of hers, because they cannot see their daughter for a long time. **It was for this reason that my cousin sister had to give up her dream of becoming a soldier.**（160519，女性应该参军吗？）

例 2　Science and technology improves our knowledge about the world by telling us what it is like, or can be like. **It was Newton, for instance, who told us why objects move and stop moving, and Einstein who told us that time is the fourth dimension of space.**（200912，艺术能告诉我们什么？）

例 3　When watching how criminals are tried and sentenced, TV viewers will learn a great deal about the law and the legal system. In fact, **it was from a televised trial that I finally understood it is a violation of law if you do not stop your car when you see a stop sign.**（200104，电视播放审判现场是好还是坏？）

6. 被动语态

被动语态在汉语中使用较少，但在英语中使用比较频繁。雅思写作属于正规文体的议论文写作，被动语态出现的概率更大。

例 1　What a student learns from books often does not include some useful everyday words and unique lifestyle **that could only be learned** by personally interacting with local people.（190309，需要去国外学习外语和文化吗？）

例 2　Just focusing on a certain limited number of practical skills, be it plumbing, carpentry, or mechanics, the students will soon find themselves out of joint with the world, because **these jobs may be performed by machines or**

may not be needed at all.（190912，普通教育还是职业教育）

例 3　To start with, the old buildings are no longer suitable for people to live in, therefore **they should be destroyed** and give way to new buildings so that people, especially young people in the cities have more living spaces.（190718，重修老建筑还是建新住房和道路？）

5.4.3 克服 if、though、because 冲动

英语写作中常常需要表达条件、让步和原因，而最常用的连接词就是 if、though、because，这本身并没错，但有些学生似乎只会使用这三个连接词，在同一篇文章中连续使用，从而造成句式单调的感觉。笔者建议，如果在写作中有 if、though、because 冲动时，考生可以考虑更换句型，使句子呈现多样性。

1. if 冲动

不是所有"如果"都用 if! 请看下面几例对 if 句子的改写。

例 1　If the government makes greater efforts, the pollution problem can be brought under control.

改写 1：**With greater efforts made by the government**, the pollution problem can be brought under control.

改写 2：**Greater efforts made by the government** can bring the pollution problem under control.

例 2　If people were allowed to carry guns, the world would become more dangerous.

改写 1：**Were people allowed to carry guns**, the world would become more dangerous.

改写 2：**The permission to carry guns** would make the world more dangerous.

例 3　If the female students and male students are encouraged to learn different subjects in school, the inequality between them will become intensified.

改写 1：**Encouraged to learn different subjects in school**, the female students and male students will become wider apart from each other.

改写 2：**Learning different subjects in school** will intensify the inequality between male students and female students.

2. though 冲动

不是所有"尽管"都用 though！请看下面几例对 though 句子的改写。

例 1 <u>Though children should be made to obey the rules</u>, they should also be given enough freedom to make their own choices.

改写 1：**While children should be made to obey the rules**, they should also be given enough freedom to make their own choices.

改写 2：**Despite that children should be made to obey the rules**, they should also be given enough freedom to make their own choices.

改写 3：**Children should be made to obey the rules, yet** they should also be given enough freedom to make their own choices.

例 2 <u>Though the cheaper air travel has brought about many benefits</u>, it has also posed a great threat to the resources and environment.

改写：**For all the benefits the cheaper air travel has brought about**, it has also posed a great threat to the resources and environment.

例 3 <u>Though the job is difficult</u>, we should set about doing it immediately.

改写：**Difficult as the job is**, we should set about doing it immediately.

3. because 冲动

不是所有"因为"都用 because！请看下面几例对 because 句子的改写。

例 1 <u>Because of the Internet</u>, we can gain access to large amount of information in the blink of an eye.

改写 1：**Thanks to the Internet**, we can gain access to large amount of information in the blink of an eye.

改写 2：**The Internet enables us** to gain access to large amount of information in the blink of an eye.

改写 3：**The Internet makes it possible for us** to gain access to large amount of information in the blink of an eye.

例 2 We must protect the wild animals, <u>because many of them are on the verge of extinction</u>.

改写 1：We must protect the wild animals, **for many of them are on the verge of extinction**.

改写 2：**As many of the wild animals are on the verge of extinction**, we must protect them.

改写 3：We must protect the wild animals, **many of whom are on the verge of extinction**.

5.5 长短句混合使用

雅思作文一般在 250—300 单词之间，句子数量大约 15—20 句。那么怎么来安排这些句子呢？很多同学已经注意到，一篇作文中若全是短句，自然是不好的，但若都是长句，读起来的感觉也不会很舒服，因此雅思作文中的句子应该是长短句混合使用。但问题是：什么时候该用短句，什么时候该用长句？

我们先来看一个段落：

例 1 ① Earlier scientists thought that during a man's lifetime the power of his brain decreased. ② But it is now thought that this is not so. ③ As long as the brain is given plenty of exercise it keeps its power. ④ It has been found that an old person who has always been mentally active has a quicker mind than a young person who has done only physical work. ⑤ It is now thought that the more work we give our brains, the more work they are able to do.

本段讨论的主题是：只要给大脑足够的锻炼，它就会保持活力。我们来仔细看看这段的句子安排情况。句①是短句，提出错误的观念，即以前的科学家认为随着人的年龄增加，大脑的功能会减退。句②是短句，对错误的观念进行否定。句③是短句，提出正确的观点。句④是长句，对正确的观点进行论证。句⑤是短句，换一种表达方式重申段落观点。5 个句子错落有致，读起来观点明确，论证有力。

大家知道，英语中有短句，也有长句。短句结构简单，意义清楚，易产生生动活泼、干脆利落的表达效果；长句则用严谨的语法结构来表达事物间更为复杂的内在联系。因此，**在表达段落重要观点的时候，我们通常用短句，而对观点进行说理论证或举例论证的时候，我们通常用长句**。用短句表达重要观点，很容易让读者抓住段落的重心所在，而用长句来论证，则使论证显得内容丰富，从而实现"观点明确，论证丰富"的表达效果。在上面引用的段落中，前三句旨在引出观点，都用短句，句④是在论证，使用长句，句⑤再次表达观点，因此也用短句。

下面，我们来看雅思考官给出的高分作文中的一个段落：

例2　① There are, however, some disadvantages. ② Primary school teachers are generalists, and may not have the necessary language skills themselves. ③ If specialists have to be brought in to deliver these sessions, the flexibility referred to above is diminished. ④ If primary language teaching is not standardised, secondary schools could be faced with a great variety of levels in different languages within their intake, resulting in a classroom experience which undoes the earlier gains. ⑤ There is no advantage if enthusiastic primary pupils become demotivated as soon as they change schools. ⑥ However, these issues can be addressed strategically within the policy adopted. (《剑桥雅思9》，Test 1，孩子应该从小学开始学外语吗？)

本段论证的是"从小学开始学外语的劣势"，一共6句，在段落中分别扮演四个功能。句①表达段落主题。句②指出小学外语教师的问题，即这些老师自身可能缺乏足够的语言技能。句③论证这个问题带来的后果之一，即需要从外面请老师来给小学生上外语课。句④和句⑤则论证另外一个后果，即小学外语教学若不均衡，中学生的语言技能就会有不同层次，从而让那些积极性很高的小学生进入中学后对语言学习不再有动力。句⑥说明这些问题可以得到解决。

现在我们来看看这个段落中句子的长短如何对应其功能。句①表达段落主题，明显用了短句，这是整个段落中最为简短的句子。句②提出具体问题，其功能是引发后面的讨论，也用了比较短的句子，使其意义非常清楚。句③至句⑤论证这个问题产生的后果，句子明显变长。句⑥再次表达观点，回归到短句。这样，整个段落的句子长短安排就呈现如下节奏：

短句—较短句—较长句—长句—较长句—短句

段落以短句开始，用较长句过渡到长句，然后又由较长句回归到短句。这个结构让笔者想到讲故事的结构。会讲故事的人，也总是从事件的开端讲起，然后营造氛围，最终达到高潮，之后再慢慢让故事走向结尾。本段为什么读起来让大家觉得舒服？笔者认为，重要原因就是其句子长短安排暗合了我们听故事的心理节奏。

通过这两个例子，可以总结出，雅思作文标准段落一般由 5 句构成，其句子长短的分布如下：短句 — 较长句 — 长句 — 较长句 — 短句。当然，在实际写作中，我们根据具体情况，大致遵从这个结构就可以了，不必完全拘泥于此。下面先来看一篇学生习作的段落：

① The situation would be better if people really tried their best to save the creature. ② Panda is a good example. ③ Panda is a typical endangered animal which only lives in China. ④ The number of Panda used to be less than 200. ⑤ Nevertheless, the lovely appearance of panda attract the world's attention. ⑥ It is favoured by people all over the world. ⑦ Finally, though it is still endangered, the number of panda grows to 1000. ⑧ According to these, it is obvious that the situation can be changed.

这里的论点是，如果我们尽力挽救动物，动物灭绝的情形就会改变。怎么论证？该同学举了熊猫的例子。她的思路是这样的：熊猫是一种濒危动物，只有中国才有。熊猫以前的数量不足 200。然而，熊猫的可爱模样吸引了世界的注意力。全世界的人都喜欢熊猫。虽然还是濒危动物，但其数量增长到了 1000。这就说明，情形显然是可以改变的。这个举例内容很合适，完全说明了观点，举例的语言大体也清楚，这样的作文可得 6 分，若要更上一层楼，则必须改进。该段共包含 8 个句子，但几乎所有句子都是短句，没有营造出合理安排长短句产生的节奏感。笔者这样改写：

① The situation would be better if people really tried their best to save the creature. ② Panda is a good example. ③ As an endangered species found only in China, pandas have grown in number from 200 a decade ago to 1,000 today, thanks to the protection from people all over the world attracted by their lovely appearance. ④ This example shows obviously that the situation can be changed.

改写的版本中，句①是短句，表达段落主题；句②是短句，引出后面的长句；句③是长句，具体举例论证；句④是短句，重申段落观点。这样改写后，句子长度的安排就基本符合标准的雅思段落了。

现在，我们再来分析以下几例中的句子长度安排。

例 3 ① However, the increased use of cars has caused serious consequences for our environment. ② Many experts, for instance, attribute the worsening air quality in big cities to the cars' exhaust gas emission and the dust that rises after them. ③ This accusation is perhaps well-grounded if you make a little comparison between the air quality 50 years ago and that now. ④ In addition to the waste gas and dust, cars also make unbearable noises, which is a headache to all city dwellers. ⑤ Just imagine a time you are shocked awake from your cozy dream by the sharp braking screech of a car passing by your house! (160915, 私家车的好处和坏处)

本段共 5 个句子。句①是短句，表达段落主题，即私家车增加对环境造成严重后果。句②和句③是较长句，论证第一个后果，即私家车污染空气。句④和句⑤是较长句，论证第二个后果，即私家车制造噪音。本段没有总结句，因此没有呼应的短句。

例 4　① Online shopping has many advantages, especially when it is compared with the store shopping. ② Sitting comfortably at home, no matter how terrible the weather outside might be, and with a few simple clicks on our computer or smartphone screen, we can order almost everything we need from clothes to books and from electric appliances to air tickets. ③ Then what we have to do is wait one or two days for the delivery of our order. ④ The whole process is really easy and simple and thus can save us a lot of time, not to mention the reduced prices we often enjoy when we shop online. (181111, 网上购物能否取代商店购物？)

本段共 4 个句子。句①是短句，表达段落主题，即网上购物有优势。句②是长句，具体描写网络购物的优势。句③是短句，继续描写网络购物的优势。句④是较短句，总结网络购物的优势，呼应第一句。

例 5　① Another important factor that affects the students' attitude towards learning is that a good education seems not as important as before. ② For quite a long time, receiving a good education was the only way for young people to get a decent job and earn a high salary. ③ But now, this is apparently not the case any more. ④ Influenced by business stars like Bill Gates and Steve Jobs, many young people now begin to believe that one's success is not in proportion to the education she/he receives. ⑤ The students, therefore, are not motivated enough to focus on their learning. (170304, 现在学生不爱上学的原因及解决办法)

本段共 5 个句子。句①是短句，表达段落主题，即影响孩子学习态度的是教育不再重要。句②是较短句，提出以前的情形。句③是短句，否定以前的情形。句④是长句，具体论证为什么孩子们不再认为教育与成功有联系。句⑤是短句，总结重申段落观点。这是一个标准的雅思作文段落。

5.6 提升句子语义密度

汉语的一个特点是不喜欢在一个句子里增加修饰语，如果要修饰，一般做法是重新写一句，而英语则不同。考生要想办法给过于单薄的句子增加语义密度，也就是在一个句子中容纳更多的内容。也许可以这样说：汉语是一种外展的语言，把复杂的意义外展出来，因此每个句子显得很单薄；而英语是一种内卷的语言，把复杂的意义内卷到句子中去，因此句子往往包含更丰富的内容。

为了把单薄的句子写得复杂一些，很多同学马上就想到复合句，即写一些定语从句或状语从句。的确，写定语从句或状语从句可以增加句子的语义密度，但笔者今天讨论的增加语义密度的方法远不止写从句。

那么，我们为什么要强调增加句子语义密度？这里有两个方面的原因。第一，雅思写作的评分标准中，有一条明确指向句子结构的多样性，句子结构越多样，就越可能得到高分。增加句子语义密度，势必要在句子主干周围增加其他成分，因此能让句子结构变得多样化。第二，汉语倾向单句表意，不在一个单句中融入很多意思，而是将不同意思用不同句子来表达。受其影响，中国学生在写英语作文的时候，往往罗列很多意义单薄的单句，而无法用恰当的办法将这些单句中的意思连接起来，因此形成的英文句子读起来不地道。

句子过于单薄是很多中国学生的通病所在。如果写作目标是 6 分或 5.5 分，然后去国外读预科，那这个句子单薄的毛病也不算什么，只要把单薄的句子写利索即可，待未来英语水平提升后再来写语义密度更高的句子。然而，对于那些目标为 7 分或以上的同学来说，就必须学会如何写出语义密度更高的句子了。

自然，一篇雅思作文区区 250 词左右，15—20 句之间，把每句的语义密度都无限放大，既无可能，也无必要。在这 15—20 句之中，有那么 3—5 句高语义密度的句子就可以了。其他句子，简单也好，复杂也好，对得分的影响不大，以不出错为原则。

现在，我们来看一段雅思高分范文：

Over the last half century the pace of change in the life of human beings has increased **beyond our wildest expectations**. This has been driven by technological and scientific breakthroughs **that are changing the whole way we view the world on an almost daily basis**. This means that change is **not always a personal option**, **but** an inescapable fact of life, and we need to **constantly** adapt to keep pace with it. (《剑桥雅思 6》，Test 4，变化是好事吗？)

这是一个开头段，第一句提供背景，第二句给出原因，第三句表明自己的观点。翻译成汉语大致是这样的：

在过去半个世纪中，人类生活的变化速度已经远远超乎预期。推动这一变化的是科技突破，这些突破几乎每天都在改变我们看待世界的方式。这意味着改变并不总是个人的选择，而是生活中不可避免的事实，我们需要不断地适应，以追上变化的步伐。

显然，无论从内容还是语言表达方式来看，这个开头段都颇具高分之相，但这里，笔者单谈这个开头段的句子语义密度。为了看清楚本段中句子如何实现语义密度，我们不妨把黑体部分抽掉，看看会是一种什么结果：

The pace of change in the life of human beings has increased. This has been driven by technological and scientific breakthroughs. This means that change is an inescapable fact of life, and we need to adapt to keep pace with it.

将这个段落翻译成汉语就是：

人类生活的变化速度加快了。这是由技术和科学突破推动的。这意味着改变是生活中不可避免的事实，我们需要适应，以追上变化的步伐。

拿掉黑体部分后，这个段落依然连贯，而且也表达出了基本意思！但是，请注意，拿掉黑体部分后的段落，句子的语义密度大大下降了，虽然读起来容易理解了很多，但也生硬了很多，单调了很多，就像失去了装饰的舞台。如果原来的段落是一碗营养丰富的米饭，现在剩下的就只是一碗稀粥了。而这，像极了很多中国学生的英语作文！

那么，我们来比较一下，之前和之后的句子到底发生了哪些变化？

原句：Over the last half century the pace of change in the life of human beings has increased beyond our wildest expectations.

改写句：The pace of change in the life of human beings has increased.

原句中有表示时间的短语 over the last half century，有表示程度的短语 beyond our wildest expectations。

原句：This has been driven by technological and scientific breakthroughs that are changing the whole way we view the world on an almost daily basis.

改写句：This has been driven by technological and scientific breakthroughs.

原句中有修饰 technological and scientific breakthroughs 的定语从句 that are changing the whole way we view the world，有表示程度的短语 on an almost daily basis。

原句：This means that change is not always a personal option, but an inescapable fact of life, and we need to constantly adapt to keep pace with it.

改写句：This means that change is an inescapable fact of life, and we need to adapt to keep pace with it.

原句中有对照的表达 "... not always a personal option, but..."，有表示程度的副词 constantly。

可以看出，改写句从原句中拿掉的成分都属于修饰语，这意味着什么呢？这意味着，**为了增加语义密度，我们需要对句子中"赤裸裸"的思想加以装饰。**如何装饰？很简单，就是为我们的基本思想提供细节。我们可以**解释**，让思想更具体，比如前面例子中用定语从句的方式来进一步解释 technological and scientific breakthroughs；可以描写某个思想的**程度**，比如上面例子中用 beyond our wildest expectations 来说明人类生活变化加快的程度；可以给思想装上**时间**的维度，比如前面例子中用 over the last half century 来明确人类生活变化加快发生的时间；可以通过**对照**来说明思想，比如前面例子中在说"变化是生活中不可避免的现实"之前，先说"变化不是某个人的选择"等。在主要思想上，附加解释、程度、时间、对照这些信息，句子的语义密度就增加了。一篇雅思作文，写出 3—5 个这样的句子，就足以显示 7 分水平了。

大家可以随便写一个简单的句子，然后按照以上提示的维度添加信息，就能体会到句子语义密度增加的乐趣。现在我们来做一些相关练习。

原句：When you plan to take your family for a trip, you may enjoy the flexibility of time.

拓展句：When you plan to take your family for a trip **out of town**, you may also enjoy the flexibility of **when to start off and when to return, rather than spending time waiting for the bus to come**.（160915，私家车的好处和坏处）

拓展句增加了 out of town，是对 trip 进行修饰，补充了关于 where 的具体信息；拓展句增加了 "when to start off and when to return, rather than spending time waiting for the bus to come"，是对 flexibility 进行具体解释，其中还融入了一个由 rather than 连接的对照，以突出这个 flexibility。

原句：In fact, all individuals have created the environmental problems, and this means that together they can fix these problems.

拓展句：In fact, all individuals have created the environmental problems **by neglecting the environment**, and this means that together they can fix these problems, **whether they are making large or small contributions**.（180421，政府还是个人该对环境负责？）

拓展句增加了 by neglecting the environment，是对 create 进一步说明，即如何 "制造了环境问题"；拓展句增加了 whether they are making large or small contributions 是对 fix these problems 补充说明，即 "解决问题" 的方式（无论贡献大还是小）。

原句：With good soft skills, one is able to connect with others as he/she will feel more comfortable in job situations.

拓展句：With good soft skills, one is able to connect **emotionally** with **his/her co-workers, clients and superiors** as he/she will feel more comfortable **and therefore more confident and efficient** in job situations.（181110，资历与社交能力同等重要吗？）

拓展句增加了 "his/her co-workers, clients and superiors"，这是细化原句中的 others，即到底是哪些人；拓展句增加了 and therefore more confident and efficient，这是扩展原句中的 comfortable，让句子的意思更加丰富。

原句：The new comers have to spend tremendous amount of time adjusting themselves to a new environment and culture. ... Furthermore, people living in a foreign country may very likely be subject to the racial discrimination.

拓展句：The new comers have to spend tremendous amount of time **making new friends** and adjusting themselves to a new environment and culture **completely different from that in their home country**. ... Furthermore, people living in a foreign country may very likely be subject to the racial discrimination, **which will make their work and living unbearable**. （220507，工作生活，国内还是国外好？）

拓展句增加了 making new friends，这是对 spend tremendous amount of time 进行补充；拓展句增加了 completely different from that in their home country 以对 environment and culture 进行描写（与本国完全不同的环境和文化）；拓展句增加了 which will make their work and living unbearable，相当于具体说明了 racial discrimination 产生的后果。

以上例子表明，我们可以通过多种方式（不仅仅是写从句）来拓展句子的语义，其核心是在一个句子中包含更多信息。这些信息也许不是我们要表达的关键信息，但是它们可以让句子显得更加丰厚，因此也更接近地道的英语。雅思写作高分需要考生具备写这种句子的能力。

5.7 句法练习

I. 下列句子存在问题，请尝试修改。

（1）Third, there are many people like to follow another. When someone around them feed pets, they will feed too.

（2）The level of life has improved, people can afford the expensive bill on pet.

（3）However, in my opinion that the pets are not very well.

（4）Nowadays, keeping pets increasingly becomes popularity in our society.

（5）In the urban, typically, to feed dogs, cats and birds even mice as pets are always regarded as a symbol of wealth or pleasure.

（6）… the sincere relationship between the host and the pet is contemporary people longing for, but can hardly get from the true-life people.

（7）Therefore we everyone should cultivate own hobbies.

（8）Having hobbies do some good for people.

（9）When people choose hobbies they must pay attention to which hobbies are fit them and which are not.

（10）Everybody has different hobbies.

（11）If the student only study hardly, we think that he is not a good student now.

（12）There are so many kinds of hobbies but one may has only some kinds of hobbies. Those hobbies may help one in different aspects as well as they may harm someone.

（13）Hobbies are interesting, generally speaking, benefit to people.

（14）We must pay attention to the latent problems of hobbies maybe carry when we enjoy the pleasure of hobbies.

（15）A lot international meetings on environment are hold, at which scientists from different countries are exchanging their ideas and are learning each other.

（16）But on my opinion, there is not enough yet. Environment protection can be a short term business, but a long and difficult undertaking.

（17）Environment problem has been so serious than ever that we could feel the threat every day.

（18）Secondly you should analyze the cause of being misunderstood. Because misunderstanding always happens by poor communication.

（19）But because there are different customs, habits, and opinions, misunderstood is hard to avoid.

（20）First, we should aware of that the misunderstanding is not avoidable in our daily life so that we could keep with a quiet mood.

（21）Besides, a same gesture may express different meanings for different areas people, it causes misunderstanding too if they communicate with nonverbal behaviour.

参考答案

（1）Third, **there are many people who like to follow others**. When some people around them keep pets, they will keep, too.

原句为 there be 引起的破碎句（见错误类型 12）。

（2）As the living standard has been improved, people can afford the expenses on pets.

原句为流水句（见错误类型 13）。

（3）In my opinion, however, pets are not all good.

原句为 that 从句引起的破碎句，句子缺主语（见错误类型 12）。

（4）Nowadays, keeping pets becomes increasingly **popular** in society.

原句为词性误用。

（5）In the urban, keeping dogs, cats, birds and even mice as pets **is** always regarded as a sign of wealthy and leisurely life.

原句主谓语形式不一致，当主语为动词不定式或其他非谓语形式及从句时，谓语用单数形式（见错误类型 2）。

（6）… the sincere relationship between the pets and their masters is **what modern people are longing for** but can hardly get from their real life.

原句从句部分缺少必需的宾语成分（见错误类型 6）。

（7）Therefore, **we all** should cultivate our own hobbies.

原句中，we 和 everyone 不能连用。

（8）Having hobbies **does** good to people.

原句主语为动名词，谓语使用了复数形式（见错误类型 2）。

（9）When people choose hobbies, they must know what hobbies **suit** them and what do not.

原句为搭配错误，fit 为动词，不与 be 搭配。

（10）Everybody has his own hobbies. (Or: Different people have different hobbies. Or: Hobbies vary/differ from one person to another.)

原句为物主代词漏用，hobbies 之前应该用物主代词（见错误类型 3）。

（11）He who studies hard only is no longer thought of as a good student now.

原句为搭配错误，"努力学习"应为 study hard，不是 study hardly。

（12）There are so many kinds of hobbies that one can choose only some of them. **Hobbies may help one in different ways, but may harm him too.**

原句为句型错误（见错误类型 8）。

（13）Hobbies are interesting and generally **beneficial** to people.

原句为不平衡结构，先使用形容词，后使用动词（见错误类型 10）。

（14）We must pay attention to the hidden problems **that hobbies may carry** when we enjoy the pleasure brought with them.

原句该用从句，却使用了 of 介词结构（见错误类型 6）。

（15）Many international meetings on environment **are held**, at which scientists from different countries **exchange their ideas** and **learn from each other**.

原句谈论一般情况，但使用了正在进行时（见错误类型 1）。

（16）But **in my opinion**, this is not enough. Environment protection **should not** be a short-term business, but a long and assiduous undertaking.

原句为介词词组搭配错误（见错误类型 7）。

（17）Environment problem **has become so much more serious** than ever before that we could feel **its threat** every day.

原句没有使用形容词比较形式，却用了 than（见错误类型 4）。

（18）Secondly you should **find out why you have been misunderstood, because** misunderstanding always results from the lack of communication.

原句将 because 用成独立分句，是破碎句（见错误类型 12）。

（19）But because there are different customs, habits and opinions, **being misunderstood** is hard to avoid.

原句用过去分词作主语，应该用动名词的被动语态。

（20）First, we should be aware that misunderstanding is unavoidable in our daily life, so we **would not make a fuss over it.**

原句为搭配错误，原文不符合英语习惯用法（见错误类型 7）。

（21）Besides, the same gesture may convey different meanings to **people from different areas**, **thus causing misunderstanding in the nonverbal communications.**

原句将两个独立分句用逗号相连，是流水句（见错误类型 13）。

II. 阅读以下雅思真题范文中的句子，在空白处填入适当的代词。

（1）In modern society, young people prefer to stay apart from _____ parents and live alone in big cities. Further, they have a tendency of postponing _____ parenthood until late 30's or even early 40's.（161109，人们喜欢独住的原因及影响）

（2）We all need news for information and knowledge, and in order for news to be reliable rather than misleading, a journalist must have a willing heart to pursue truth, a fair judgment and most important of all, a strong ability to express _____ mind with words. （160305，我们为什么不相信记者？）

（3）When a historic structure has become a threat to society, for example, having _____ removed can actually add more value to the area around _____. （190427，应该保存哪些老建筑？）

（4）The second reason is that by doing different jobs or careers, young people can increase _____ work experience and eventually become more versatile. This may give _____ a competitive edge, especially in today's job market where an all-round employee is always preferred. （191212，年轻人频繁更换工作的原因及利弊）

（5）A friend of _____ got married after having been single and living by _____ for many years, only to find that _____ was always quarrelling with _____ wife because, in _____ words, _____ was constantly picking faults with _____ habits and lifestyle. （161109，人们喜欢独住的原因及影响）

参考答案

（1）their; their

（2）his/her

（3）it; it

（4）their; them

（5）mine; himself; he; his; his; she; his

第六章　雅思写作重点题材观点及表达

6.1 雅思作文重点题材

笔者对 2010—2022 年共 13 年的雅思考试作文题目进行了全面统计，发现近 98% 的雅思写作都可归入 15 类题材，分布如下表。

2010—2022 年雅思写作题材分布

定位	题材	题目总数	占比
第一梯队 占比 50% 左右	教育	109	19.4%
	社会	95	16.9%
	生活	78	13.9%
第二梯队 占比 30% 左右	政府	43	7.6%
	媒体	39	6.9%
	工作	38	6.7%
	环境与生态	37	6.6%
第三梯队 占比 15% 左右	科技	26	4.6%
	犯罪	24	4.2%
	语言文化	19	3.3%
	旅游	13	2.3%
第四梯队 占比 5% 左右	交通	10	1.7%
	动物	9	1.6%
	体育	8	1.4%
	性别	5	0.8%
	合计		**97.9%**

从表中数据可以看出，在过去 13 年中，教育、社会、生活是当仁不让的

三大热门题材，总占比超过 50%。换句话说，每两次雅思考试，这三大话题就会出现一次，是雅思考试题材的第一梯队，所有考生都必须熟悉。接下来第二梯队是政府、媒体、工作、环境与生态四大题材，总占比接近 30%，即每三次雅思考试就会出现一次，因此也值得考生关注。第三梯队由科技、犯罪、语言文化、旅游四大题材构成，占比约 15%。第四梯队占比 5% 左右，由交通、动物、体育、性别这样的题材构成，它们偶尔会出现在考试题目中。需要说明的是，这个统计表里，性别和犯罪本来可归在社会题材中，动物也可归在环境与生态题材中，但由于性别、犯罪、动物这些题材出现频率较高，因此单独成类。

笔者拟对这些重点题材的基本观点和表达进行分类讲解。为讲解方便，仍将性别和犯罪归入社会题材，动物归入环境与生态题材。

6.2 教育类

"教育类"话题是雅思考试大作文常见话题，占所有考题的 20% 左右。主要涉及学什么、跟谁学、怎么学、如何评价学生、学习的目的等等。比如：

政府教育投资类，包括：支付大学学费是政府的责任还是个人的责任？政府奖学金应该颁给最好的学生还是进步最快的学生？

学习方向选择类，包括：成年人学习实际技能是自学较好还是从师更好？音乐和体育是否对学生的未来职业有用？儿童应该学习历史还是学习与生活更密切相关的课程？学校应该强调学生的竞争能力还是合作能力？

学生与老师或父母关系类，包括：学生应不应该评价老师？从老师那里学到的东西比从其他渠道要多吗？在大学读书是否在外面住比和父母一起住更好？孩子在家接受教育还是到学校接受教育更好？父母是否应该接受育儿类课程？由父母接送孩子还是学校接送？

其他，包括：网络学习是否对传统学习方式构成了挑战？大学是否应该无视经济背景给学生提供教育？成绩好的学生与成绩差的学生是否应该进行分班教学？

6.2.1 学习内容

母题：Some people think it is important for all children to learn history at school. Others believe that other subjects are more relevant to children's development today. Discuss both views and give your opinion. (190801)

子题 1: Some people say that in our modern age, it is unnecessary to teach children about the skills of handwriting. To what extent do you agree or disagree? (191123)

子题 2: Art classes like painting and drawing are important to students' development and should be made compulsory in high school. To what extent do you agree or disagree? (170701)

子题 3: Full-time university students need to spend a lot of time in studying, but it is essential to get involved in other activities. To what extent do you agree or disagree? (120225)

核心观点及表达

（1）教育不仅仅是教学生各种生活技能，还教他们成为对社会有用的人。

Education is not just about teaching students various life skills, but turning them into people useful to society.

（2）学校不应只教学生提升知识水平，还应该教各种软技能，如与人沟通、共事，以及明辨是非的能力。

Schools should not just tell students how to achieve high academic levels, but also teach them various soft skills such as how to communicate and work with others, and teach them how to tell right from wrong.

（3）学校不应强迫学生学习他们不感兴趣的东西，而应尊重学生未来的规划。

Schools cannot force students to learn things they are not interested in. Instead, schools should respect students' own ideas about their future.

（4）学校不应只教看起来对学生未来有利的课程，也应教有助于他们了解本国历史和文化的课程。

Schools should not just offer courses that seem to be useful to their students' future, but also courses that help students understand their own history and culture.

（5）学校应该给学生提供各种机会参加课外活动，以提高他们的实践能力，开阔眼界。

Schools should provide many kinds of opportunities for their students to engage in activities outside of the classroom so as to improve their practical skills and broaden their horizons.

（6）教育的目的不仅是让学生获得实用的基本生活技能，还是从身体上和精神上为他们的未来生活做好准备。

The objective of education is not just to let students acquire the basic practical survival skills, but to prepare them for the future life, both physically and mentally.

6.2.2 教、学方式

母题： Some people think that computers and the Internet are more important to a child's education than going to school. However, others believe that schools and teachers are essential for children to learn effectively. Discuss both views and give your own opinion.（100515）

子题1：Someone believes that parents should read or tell stories to their children. However, some others find it unnecessary because children can read books and watch TV by themselves. Discuss both views and present your own opinion.（101104）

子题2：In some countries, many people choose to educate their children at home by themselves instead of sending them to school. Do you think the advantages outweigh the disadvantages?（180426）

子题3：Some people think that schools should select their pupils according to their academic abilities. Others believe that young people with different abilities should be educated together. Discuss both views and give your own opinion.（181208）

核心观点及表达

（1）孩子应该去学校接受教育，因为在家接受教育的孩子，无论考试分数有多高，都不过像温室花朵，一旦遭遇外面的风雨，很容易就凋谢。更重要的是，正是在像学校这样不那么纯的地方，孩子们才能够学会分辨正误和好坏，待他们长大之后，最终成为身心健康的人。

Kids should go to school. A home-educated kid, however well he achieves in tests, is just like a flower in greenhouse which easily withers when exposed to the rain outside. More importantly, it is just in not so pure a place as school that kids can learn to tell right from wrong, good from bad and eventually become physically and mentally healthy when they grow up.

（2）因此，在学业上真正杰出的儿童应当接受单独授课，因为这将帮他们保持对正在学习的科目的兴趣。然而就其他能力而言，比如说领导能力以及合作能力，我确实相信只有所有孩子——不管聪明与否——都坐在同一个教室里，才能得到更好的发展。

So academically the really outstanding children should be taught separately because this could help maintain their interest in the subjects they are learning, yet when it comes to other abilities such as the ability to lead a team and to work with others, I do believe they can be better developed if all the kids—smart or not—sit in the same classroom.

（3）学校不应该仅提高学生的学习成绩，还应培养孩子的责任感，以及批判思维能力、合作能力、领导能力和明辨是非的能力。

Schools should not just try to improve their students' academic performance, but also cultivate their sense of responsibility and their ability to think critically, work with others, lead a team, and tell right from wrong.

（4）我们应该为观看电视设定时间限度，这样孩子们才能找到时间去从事其他可以提高他们个性、想象力和人际交往技能的活动。

We should set a limit on the screen time so that our children can find time for other activities that may help improve their personalities, imagination and interpersonal skills.

（5）与"冰冷"而"漠然"的网络相比，在课堂上听老师授课经常自带一丝温情，而这种个人化的情感有时候甚至比知识本身还重要，并变成我们学校生活的一部分记忆。

Compared with the "cold" and "indifferent" Internet, learning with teachers in classroom often carries a touch of human warmth and that personal feeling is sometimes even more important than the knowledge itself and becomes part of our memory of school life.

（6）来自网络的东西往往是有偏见的、不完整的、零碎的，甚至是错误的。

What we take from the Internet is often biased, incomplete, fragmentary, or simply erroneous.

6.2.3 教育类题材参考词汇

（1）**subject** 科目

（2）**optional/selective course** 选修课

（3）**required/mandatory course** 必修课

（4）**awareness** 意识

（5）**creative** 有创造性的

（6）**original** 新颖的，原创的

（7）**physical** 身体上的

（8）**emotional** 情感上的

（9）**psychological** 心理上的

（10）**peers** 同龄人

（11）**peer pressure** 同辈压力

（12）**motivation** 动力

（13）**highly motivated student** 有很强动力的学生

（14）**stimulating** 令人激动的（= very interesting）

（15）**acquire** 获取（acquire knowledge 获取知识，不能说 learn knowledge）

（16）**practical** 实际的

（17）**philosophical** 哲学的

（18）**develop** 培养（develop a sense of responsibility 培养责任心）

（19）**humanities** 人文学科

（20）**social science** 社会科学

（21）**economics** 经济学

（22）**sociology** 社会学

（23）**psychology** 心理学

（24）**natural science** 自然科学

（25）**basic science** 基础科学

（26）**applied science** 应用科学

（27）**distance education** 远程教育

（28）**versatile** 全面发展的；多才多艺的

（29）**theoretical knowledge** 理论知识

（30）**draw inspiration** 获取灵感

（31）**teaching method** 教学方法

（32）**job skills** 就业技能

（33）**soft skills** 软技能

（34）**expectation** 期望

（35）**aspiration** 志向

（36）**competitive** 竞争激烈的

（37）**self-esteem** 自尊（＝self-respect）

（38）**think independently** 独立思考

（39）**think critically** 批判性思考

（40）**evaluate** 评价

（41）**feedback** 反馈

（42）**sense of frustration** 挫败感

（43）**positive attitude toward life** 积极的人生态度

6.2.4 教育类题材句子写作练习

（1）与将孩子送到学校这一传统做法相反的是，越来越多的父母现在选择自己在家教育孩子。

（2）学校的老师不可能在一个孩子身上花那么多时间，因为他们得照顾其他几十个孩子。这种情况的自然结果是，在家接受教育的孩子可以得到全部关照，而他在学校读书的伙伴则完全可能被老师忽视。

（3）在我看来，教育更重要的是教会孩子成为一个更好的人，而实现这一目标的第一步就是学会如何与人相处。

（4）在家接受教育的孩子，无论考试分数有多高，都不过像温室花朵，一旦遭遇外面的风雨，很容易就凋谢。

（5）更重要的是，正是在像学校这样不那么纯的地方，孩子们才能够学会分辨正误和好坏，待他们长大之后，最终成为身心健康的人。

（6）在我看来，如果学生被赋予权利表达对老师的观点，尤其是表达关于老师教学有效性的观点，那么，学生和老师都会从中获益。

（7）如果学生对老师教的东西没有发言权，他们就不会知道自己是否在学正确的东西，也不知道自己学得是否有效率。

（8）比如，当我上 11 年级时，我发现数学老师要讲解的一道数学题对我们来说太难。绝大多数同学都不发言，但我站起来，勇敢地告诉老师我对他的看法。听到我的抱怨后，数学老师很快就纠正了他的教案。

（9）同时，如果老师虚心接受学生的批评，他们就能理解学生所想，从而能够提供最符合学生需求的教学。

（10）学生应该将大部分时间用在学习上，但现在很常见的是，学生根本无法专注于学习。

（11）20 年前，学生们几乎别无选择，只能将自己关在书房读书，而现在他们可以又快又容易地连入因特网，在因特网上他们什么都可以做。

（12）因特网是个绝好的发明，但是若沉迷于它，则无疑会减少本应用于更严肃工作的时间。

（13）不消说，想变得比别人优秀通常会使学生产生强烈的动力去努力学习，所以他们才能让自己变得越来越好。

（14）由于缺乏和其他学生足够的沟通，这些顶尖的学生不知道如何与周围的人相处，因此当他们进入需要更多合作的就业市场时，往往会一片茫然，不知所措。

（15）正如在篮球比赛中，个人表现都不是最好但懂得如何合作的球队，往往会战胜一个由最顶尖球员组成但各自为战的球队。

（16）因此，全国各地的学校应当鼓励学生相互竞争，同时要让他们知道，如何为了整体的利益而与他人合作。

（17）比如，如果有个 11 岁的孩子在数学上出类拔萃，能解决九年级的问题，那把他放在七年级的数学班是十分愚蠢的。因为所有七年级数学的问题对他而言都太简单了，他可能觉得完全没有挑战性，从而失去对数学的兴趣。

（18）不管一个人有多聪明，他都不太可能独自成功解决一个十分复杂的问题。

（19）因此，在学业上真正杰出的儿童应当接受单独授课，因为这将帮他们保持对正在学习的科目的兴趣。然而就其他能力而言，比如说领导能力，我确实相信只有所有孩子——不管聪明与否——都坐在同一个教室里，才能得到更好的发展。

（20）我所在的高中里，诸如音乐、绘画等艺术课程被列为必修课。

（21）艺术对学生的成长非常重要，因此应该成为必修课。

（22）通过学习艺术课，学生可以走出自我束缚，与具有相同兴趣的人交朋友。

（23）反对将艺术课程列为必修的声音主要来自那些认为艺术课程对学生没有用处从而是浪费时间的人。

（24）教育的目的不仅是让学生获得实用的基本生活技能，还是从身体上和精神上为他们的未来生活做好准备。

（25）我们可以有把握地做出结论：花在艺术上的时间从长远看会有回报的。

（26）今天的学生被众多诱惑包围着，他们慢慢发现学习太过单调无趣。

（27）学校和父母应该合作，给孩子的上网时间设限，鼓励他们投入更多时间去学习。

（28）通常，电视呈现知识的方式远比书本和老师更加生动，这让通过电视来学习的过程变得非常快乐和高效。

（29）观看太多电视意味着孩子们必须牺牲阅读和其他有创造性活动的时间。

（30）如果孩子们在电视前坐得太久，他们就没有多少时间和其他孩子相处，这会危及他们的人际交往技能。

（31）我们应该为观看电视设定时间限度，这样孩子们才能找到时间去从事其他可以提高他们个性、想象力和人际交往技能的活动。

（32）学生手头有更多的信息渠道，不必像以前那般依靠老师来获取他们想知道的东西了。

（33）网络上的信息可能不可靠，甚至不准确。

（34）主要依靠网络来获取知识的学生也许会成为一个什么都懂却什么都不专的人。

（35）与"冰冷"而"漠然"的网络相比，在课堂上听老师授课经常自带一丝温情，而这种个人化的情感有时候甚至比知识本身还重要，并变成我们学校生活的一部分记忆。

（36）由于每个学生都有自己的独特之处，那么选出一些并标之以"优秀学生"就没有意义而且具有误导性。

（37）没有父母和老师的监管，很多孩子最终沉迷于电脑游戏或者其他不健康的习惯。

（38）当孩子们有了时间和心灵的自由，他们就可以彻底地开发自己的潜能，而不是由别人来告诉他们做自己不感兴趣的事情。

（39）自己能自由做决定时，很多孩子实际上变得更独立、更负责任。

（40）读或讲故事除了给父母提供机会与孩子待在一起，还通常被认为是父母向孩子分享人生经验或智慧的绝佳机会。

（41）父母不应该停止给孩子读讲故事，直到他们大到可以独立阅读。

（42）因此，如果没有很多其他课程的知识，真正掌握某一门课程是不可能的。

（43）选择一门特定课程也许可以帮助你离开学校后找到一份工作，但是，如果你希望熟练掌握你选择的课程，希望实现更好的职业发展，希望过更加有趣的生活，那么，接纳尽量多的其他课程是更为可取的。

（44）当孩子应该与其他孩子一起在外玩耍时，却强迫他／她坐在家里学习完全不感兴趣的东西，这可能最终会浇灭孩子的学习热情。

（45）强迫孩子在很小的时候学习可能会给他们一种有害的印象，认为生活就像是一场必胜的战争，他们除了更加努力地工作别无选择。

（46）大学最令人惊喜的事情之一是，学生可以参加各种各样的俱乐部，如瑜伽俱乐部、国际象棋俱乐部、文学俱乐部等等。

（47）成为某个专业领域的专家，并为未来生活做好准备应该成为所有大学生的主要关注点，这些也是学生们支付学费的原因。

（48）那些更悠闲的活动，如弹吉他或唱歌，可以缓解他们沉重的学习负荷，让他们更具韧性，来对付生活中的身心压力。

（49）说到该在这些活动上花多少时间时，大学生必须记住，学业永远是首位，无论活动多么有趣，都绝不能为之牺牲学业。

（50）的确很难想象，没有教育我们的社会会是什么样子。

（51）因此，可以合理地得出结论，那就是，教育最主要的目的之一是让人们成为自己所向往的人。

参考答案

（1）Contrary to the conventional practice of sending their kids to school, more and more parents today choose to educate their children themselves at home.

（2）The teachers in school cannot spend that much time on the same kid because they have dozens of others to take care of. The natural result of this is that the home-educated kid may be given full attention to while his counterparts in school may well be ignored by his teachers.

（3）As far as I understand, education is more about telling a kid to become a better person and the first step towards this aim is learning to get along with people.

（4）A home-educated kid, however well he achieves in tests, is just like a flower in greenhouse which easily withers when exposed to the rain outside.

（5）Most important of all, it is just in not so pure a place as school that kids can learn to tell right from wrong, good from bad and eventually become physically and mentally healthy when they grow up.

（6）To my mind, if students are given the right to show their opinions about their teachers, especially about their teaching effectiveness, both the students and teachers will benefit.

（7）If they had no say about what their teachers tell them, they would not know whether they are learning the right thing or whether they are learning it in the most efficient way.

（8）For instance, when I was an eleventh-grader, I found my math teacher trying to explain a problem which was far too difficult for us. While most of my classmates remained silent about it, I stood up and told my teacher boldly what I thought he was doing. Upon my complaints, our math teacher made quick changes about his teaching plan.

（9）Meanwhile, if the teachers are open to their students' criticism, they will be able to understand what their students think, so they can give the kind of teaching that best suits the need of their students.

（10）Students ought to spend most of their time on the school work, but nowadays it is not uncommon that students are simply not able to put their heart to study.

（11）While students two decades ago had nearly no choice but get themselves shut in their study room and read books, students today have easy and fast access to the Internet, on which they can do almost all things.

（12）The Internet is a good great invention, yet obsession with it will certainly reduce the time that should have been put to more serious work.

（13）Needless to say, becoming better than others often gives students strong motivations to study hard so that they can become better and better themselves.

（14）Without enough communication with other students, these top students do not know how to get along with people around them and so when they go into job market where more cooperation is needed, they are often at a loss what to do.

（15）Just like in a basketball game, the team whose members are not the best individually but know how to work together often defeats the team which has the best players but they just play for themselves.

（16）Therefore, all schools across the country should encourage their students to compete with their peers and at the same time let them know how to work with others for the benefits of all members.

（17）For example, if an 11-year-old kid is exceptionally good at maths and he is able to solve k9 maths problems, it is truly stupid to put him in a k7 maths class. Since all these k7 maths problems are far too easy for him, he may not feel challenged at all and therefore lose all his interest in maths.

（18）No matter how smart a person might be, he could not possibly succeed in solving a highly complex problem all by himself.

（19）So academically the really outstanding children should be taught separately because this could help maintain their interest in the subjects they are learning, yet when it comes to other abilities such as leadership, I do believe they can be better developed if all the kids—smart or not—sit in the same classroom.

（20）Art classes such as music, painting and drawing are made mandatory in my high school.

（21）Art is so important to the students' development that it should be made compulsory.

（22）By taking art classes, students may come out of their shell socially and make friends with those with similar interests.

（23）Objections of art classes as required mainly come from those who think art classes are a waste of time because they are not useful to students.

（24）The objective of education is not just to let students acquire the basic practical survival skills, but to prepare them for the future life, both physically and mentally.

（25）We can safely conclude that the time spent on art will be rewarding in the long run.

（26）Today students are surrounded by so many distractions that they gradually find that learning is too boring and uninteresting.

（27）The school and parents should work together to set limits on the time children spend online and encourage them to devote more time to learning.

（28）TV often presents knowledge in far more vivid ways than books and teachers, which makes learning from TV a very enjoyable and efficient process.

（29）Watching too much TV means the children have to sacrifice their time for reading and other creative activities.

（30）If children sit in front of TV for too long, they will have little time to mix up with other children, which may put their interpersonal skills at stake.

（31）We should set a limit on the TV-watching time so that our children can find time for other activities that may help improve their personalities, imagination and interpersonal skills.

（32）With more sources of information at hand, students do not have to rely on their teachers as much as before for things they want to know.

（33）Information on Internet may be unreliable, or even incorrect.

（34）A student who mainly depends on the Internet for knowledge may end up a Jack of all trades but master of none.

（35）Compared with the "cold" and "indifferent" Internet, the communication with teachers in classroom often carries a touch of human warmth and that personal feeling is sometimes even more important than the knowledge it-self and becomes part of our memory of school life.

（36）As each student is unique in his/her own way, to sort out a few and label them as "top students" is senseless and misleading.

（37）Without the supervision of their parents and teachers, many children end up being addicted to computer games or other unhealthy habits.

（38）When given the freedom of time and mind, the children can fully explore their own potentials instead of being told to do things they are not really interested in.

（39）When left free to make their own decisions, many children actually become more independent and responsible.

（40）Reading or telling stories, besides providing an opportunity for the parents to stay together with their children, is also often considered as a wonder-ful occasion for parents to share their life's lesson or wisdom with their children.

（41）Parents should not stop reading and telling stories to their kids until they become old enough to read independently.

（42）It is thus very unlikely to really master a subject without much knowledge from other subjects.

（43）To choose one particular subject, then, may help you get a job after you leave the university, but to be open to as many other subjects as possible is more advisable if your wish is to have a masterful command of the subject you choose, to achieve a better career development, and to live a more interesting life.

（44）Forcing a kid to sit at home and learn things in which he/she does not have any interest at all when he/she is supposed to play with other kids out-side might eventually kill the kid's passion for learning.

（45）Pushing the kids to learn at their early age may give them the harm-ful impression that life is just like a must-win battle in which they have no alter-native but work still harder.

（46）One of the most amazing things about the university is that it always has a great variety of clubs that the students can join such as yoga club, interna-tional chess club, literature club, to name only a few.

（47）To become expert in one specialized field and get prepared for future life should become the major concerns for all university students, and these are also what the students pay their tuition for.

（48）Those more leisurely activities such as guitar playing or singing can relieve the students of their heavy load of academic work and make them more resilient to physical and emotional stresses in life.

（49）When it comes to the amount of time they should give to these activities, the university students must remember that their top priority should always be placed on the academic development, which can never be sacrificed for any other activities, no matter how interesting they might be to the students.

（50）It is indeed impossible to imagine what our society would be like without education.

（51）It is, therefore, reasonable to conclude that one of the primary purposes of education is to make people into what they aspire to.

6.3 社会类

"社会/犯罪/性别类"涉及的话题非常广泛，绝对是雅思作文高频话题，平均每年出现10—15次，与教育类话题不相上下。考点及分布如下：

青少年犯罪类，包括：未成年犯罪是否应承受和成年人一样的罪罚？应该请坐过牢的人去学校谈谈犯罪的危害性吗？能否有更多办法来遏制犯罪？

社会与生活类，包括：生活在大城市有害健康吗？鼓励消费对社会是好还是坏？发展中国家的人感觉比以前幸福而发达国家的人感觉不比以前幸福的原因以及教训；男女是否应该共同承担家务？晚育的原因及其劣势。

社会问题类，包括：人口老龄化是否利大于弊？警察带枪是否会导致更多的暴力？导致贫富差距的原因以及解决办法；女性可以参军吗？

6.3.1 犯罪

母题： In many parts of the world children and teenagers are committing more crimes. What are the causes? How should these young criminals be punished? （190523）

子题 1：Some think most crime is the result of circumstances e.g. poverty and other social problems. Other believe that most crime is caused by people who are bad by nature. Discuss both views and give your own opinion. (141118)

子题 2：In many countries, prison is the most common solution to the problem of crime. However, another effective way is to provide people with higher education so that they can not become criminals. To what extent do you agree or disagree? (180303)

子题 3：Many criminals continue to commit crimes even after being punished for them. Why do you think this happen? How can we solve this problem? (201107)

核心观点及表达

（1）一些人天性上比别人更容易犯罪，但教育可以在很大程度上阻止他们犯罪。

Though some people are more likely to commit crimes by nature, education can largely stop them from doing so.

（2）我们都知道，人类有跟随他人的天然倾向，尤其在伤害他人方面。

We all know about human's natural inclination to follow others, especially when it comes to doing harms to other people.

（3）犯罪的原因是多种多样的，包括家庭影响、社会影响和媒体影响。

The reasons vary why people commit crimes, including the influences from family, society, and the media.

（4）青少年犯罪率上升的原因在于破裂家庭和暴力影视节目变多，社会竞争压力增大。

The reasons for the growing juvenile crime rate include the greater number of broken families, violence movies and TV programmes, and the greater pressure from competition.

（5）过多接触电视中的暴力场景会极大影响影视观众，从而增加他们在实际生活中犯下同样暴力罪行的可能性。

The excessive exposure to the violent scenes on TV will greatly affect the theatre-goers and TV viewers, thus increasing the likelihood of their committing the same violent crimes in real life.

（6）随着破碎家庭数量的增加，越来越多被忽视的孩子触犯法律，因为缺乏家庭的关爱和感情使他们变得愤怒、暴力。

With the number of broken families going up, more and more neglected children have trouble with the law, as the lack of love and affection from their families makes them angry and violent.

（7）监狱是遏制犯罪率上升的有效办法之一，但从根本上说，解决犯罪的办法是让人们接受更多教育。

Prison may be one effective solution to the rising crime rate, but fundamentally, more education is the way out.

6.3.2 性别

母题： In many countries today, women as well as men work full-time, so it is logical for women and men to share household tasks equally. To what extent do you agree or disagree? （140501）

子题1：Some people believe that women should play an equal role as men in a country's police force or military force, while others think women are not suitable for these kinds of jobs. Discuss both views and give your opinion. （190126）

子题2：In many countries women are allowed to take maternity leave from their jobs during the first month after the birth of their baby. Do advantages outweigh disadvantages? （181013）

子题3：The workplace nowadays is trying to employ the equal number of females and males. Do you think it is a positive or negative trend? （110115）

核心观点及表达

（1）性别平等是社会进步的标志，但其实质是互相尊重，而不是忽略性别差异。因此，不宜要求男女做同样数量的工作。

Gender equality is a sign of social progress, but what gender equality really means is the mutual respect between men and women, not the disregard of their differences. It is, therefore, not reasonable to ask them to do the same amount of work.

（2）无论身体、情感还是社会层面，女性都不适合从警或参军，但女性可以以其他方式为国家做出贡献。

Physically, emotionally, and socially speaking, women are not suitable to serve in the police or armed forces. However, women can contribute to their country in other ways.

（3）现在越来越多的男性愿意在家照顾家庭，其中一个原因是，机器的广泛使用使他们能找到的工作越来越少了。

One of the important reasons why more and more men are willing to stay at home and look after the family is that, with the wide use of machines, the number of jobs available to men is shrinking quickly.

6.3.3 城市化与全球化

母题：With major cities continuing to grow, are there any problems to young people? How to solve these problems?（140906）

子题1：Young people are leaving their homes from rural areas to study or work in the cities. What are the reasons? Do advantages of this development outweigh its disadvantages?（131214）

子题2：A rise in the standard of living in a country often only seems to benefit cities rather than rural areas. What problems might this difference cause? How might these problems be reduced?（171219）

子题3：More and more people move from the countryside to big cities. Does this development bring more advantages or disadvantages to the environment?（220723）

核心观点及表达

（1）城市化有助于提高人们的生活水平，为城市发展提供劳动力，但也造成了很多社会问题和环境问题。

The urbanisation helps to improve the quality of our life and provide labour force for the urban development, yet it also creates many social and environmental problems.

（2）全球化让人们的生活更加便利，但也剥夺了本地人的工作机会，让本地的很多文化消失。

Globalisation, while making our life more convenient, robs the local people of their job opportunities and eliminates much of the local culture.

（3）随着城市化进程在全球疯狂地推进，动植物的生存空间越来越少。这种情况的确很糟糕，而且没有半点积极改变的迹象。

As the urbanisation process goes on ruthlessly throughout the world, plants and animals find less and less space to live in. This situation is bad enough, and shows no positive sign of change.

（4）随着经济的繁荣和城市化的快速发展，越来越多的人涌入大城市，这给城市的住房和交通带来了巨大的压力。

With the economic boom and rapid development of urbanisation, more and more people are now rushing into big cities, which has imposed great pressure on the urban housing and traffic.

（5）比如，大肆的城市化进程摧毁了众多自然空地和动物栖息地，并在其上建起了了无生趣的混凝土建筑。

The relentless urbanisation process, for example, has destroyed numerous natural open spaces and animal habitat, and had the dull concrete buildings in their place.

（6）随着城市化进程在全球快速开展，越来越多原来住在乡村的人涌入城市，尤其是大城市。我认为，这种情况已经给环境带来了很多问题，不管是城市的环境还是乡村的环境。

With urbanisation process going fast in the world, more and more people originally living in the countryside are moving to cities, especially big cities. This development, in my view, has created a lot of problems for the environment, both in the cities and in the countryside.

（7）贸易的增长要求增加使用化石燃料的交通方式，从而导致污染加重，引发气候变化，现今气候变化对人类和世界的未来造成了严重威胁。

Increased trade calls for more transport, which uses fossil fuels. As a result, pollution has increased, leading to climate change, which is now a serious threat to humanity and the future of the world.

（8）全球化带来本地文化的丢失。在世界很多地区，随着另一文化占据主导地位，本地文化消失了。

Globalisation may lead to loss of local culture. In many parts of the world, the local culture disappears with the domination by another culture.

6.3.4 人口、寿命与健康

母题：Today people live longer after retiring from work. What problems does this cause for individuals and society? What can be done?（220611）

子题1：Nowadays some older people choose to live in retirement communities with other older people, rather than living with their adult children. Is it a positive or negative development?（191207）

子题2：In some countries, the difference in age between parents and their children is generally greater than it was in the past. Do you think the advantages of this trend outweigh the disadvantages?（190928）

子题3：Figures show that in some countries, there is an ever-increasing proportion of population aged 15 or younger. What do you think are the effects of current and future on those countries?（180201）

子题4：In many countries, the proportion of elderly people is increasing. Do you think the positive effects of this trend outweigh its negative influence on society?（111008）

子题5：There are a higher proportion of older people than younger people. Do you think it is a positive or negative development?（120310）

核心观点及表达

（1）人类寿命延长的原因包括医疗进步、生活水平提高、机器承担了很多危险的工作。寿命延长的确是一件好事，但这也会导致老龄化，引起社会生产力下降、消费能力下降、社会福利成本增加等问题。

We live longer today because we have better medical services and better living standards, and also because machines have done many dangerous jobs for us. Living longer is of course a good thing, but it also brings about many problems such as aging, the reduced productivity, shrinking consumption, and the increased burden on social pension.

（2）退休后活得长久一些是件好事，因为这样人们就可以看到更多的世界，并能更多地参与孩子，甚至孙辈的生活，分享他们的悲喜，必要的时候给他们建议。

Living longer than before after retirement is a good thing, as it enables people to see more of the world and take greater part in the life of their children, or even grandchildren, sharing their happiness and sadness, and giving advice when necessary.

（3）活得更长有时候也不像所想的那样好。比如，很多人害怕在这无聊的 20 甚至 30 年的退休生活中，自己不再被别人需要。更糟的是，很多人退休后可能不得不长期住院。长期住院不仅自己痛苦，对孩子也是负担。

But a longer life sometimes is not as good as we may think. Many people, for instance, shudder at the thought that they will no longer be needed in the boring twenty or even thirty years of their retirement life. Worse still, many others may have to spend their long retirement years in hospital, which is not only painful to themselves, but also burdensome to their children.

（4）当 60 岁以上的人数达到一定程度时，会产生各种各样的社会问题，如医疗问题、福利问题、劳动力减少及消费降低等。

When the proportion of people over 60 years old reaches a certain limit, the entire society will have to face a great variety of problems related to medical care, social welfare, labour shortage, and the reduced overall consumption.

6.3.5 幸福社会

母题： What is the most important element you think to make a perfect society? How to achieve an ideal society?（130921）

子题 1：Many people nowadays do not feel safe either when they are at home or go out. What are the reasons? How to solve this problem?（150627）

子题 2：Some people believe that the best way to produce a happier society is to ensure that there are only small differences between the richest and the poorest members. To what extent do you agree or disagree?（140201）

子题 3：Economic progress is one way to measure a country's success. Other people think other factors are also important. To what extent do you agree or disagree?（131012）

子题 4：Individual greed and selfishness has been the basis of the modern society. Some people think that we must return to the older and more traditional values of respect for the family and the local community in order to create a better world to live in. To what extent do you agree or disagree?（150618）

子题 5：Many people in developing countries feel happier than before while many people in developed countries do not feel as happy as they used to be. Why? What lesson can you learn from this?（111126）

子题 6：Multicultural societies, where people of different ethnic groups live together, can bring more benefits than drawbacks to a country. To what extent do you agree or disagree?（160402）

子题 7：If a country is already rich, any additional economic wealth does not make its citizens happier. To what extent do you agree or disagree?（210918）

核心观点及表达

（1）每个人对"完美社会"的定义可能都不同，但每个完美社会都应该保障其成员安全和物质充足，让成员有归属感，给成员提供实现梦想的机会。

The definition of a "perfect society" may vary from one individual to another, yet there are things that every perfect society must provide to its members: the personal security, material satisfaction, sense of belonging, and the opportunity to fulfill their dreams.

（2）物质充足是社会幸福的必要条件，但不是充分条件。

Material abundance is a necessary, but not sufficient condition for a happy society.

（3）缩小贫富差距有助于构建和谐社会，但也可能让社会失去发展动力。

A small difference between the rich and the poor is helpful to create a happy society, yet it may also shut down the engine for the development of society.

（4）传统社会价值观能解决当今社会的某些问题，但不能解决所有问题。

The traditional social values can solve some of the problems we face now, but surely not all of them.

（5）一个完美的社会不仅仅取决于物质财富。

A perfect society does not just rest on its material wealth.

6.3.6 社会类题材参考词汇

（1）**commit a crime** 犯罪

（2）**criminal** 罪犯

（3）**victim** 受害者

（4）**violate the law** 违法

（5）**consequence** 后果

（6）**juvenile crime** 青少年犯罪

（7）**youngster** 年轻人

（8）**teenager** 青少年

（9）**punishment** 惩罚

（10）**capital punishment** 死刑

（11）**life imprisonment** 无期徒刑；终身监禁

（12）**law-abiding citizens** 守法的公民

（13）**crime** 罪行

（14）**crime rate** 犯罪率

（15）**gender equality** 性别平等

（16）**gender role** 性别角色

（17）**gender difference** 性别差异

（18）**stereotype** 刻板印象，思维定式 （stereotyped image of a woman 对女性的刻板印象）

（19）**feminism** 女性主义

（20）**household chores** 家务活

（21）**physical strength** 体力

（22）**intellectual** 智力的

（23）**liberation** 解放

（24）**job market** 就业市场

（25）**gender discrimination** 性别歧视

（26）**urbanisation** 城市化

（27）**infrastructure** 基础设施

（28）**tertiary industry** 第三产业

（29）**unemployment** 失业

（30）**population explosion** 人口爆炸

（31）**job opportunities** 就业机会

（32）**social welfare** 社会福利

（33）**medical services** 医疗服务

（34）**cultural diversity** 文化多样性

（35）**labour shortage** 劳动力不足

（36）**birth rate** 出生率

（37）**aging of population** 人口老龄化

（38）**longevity** 长寿

（39）**life expectancy** 预期寿命

（40）**life span** 寿命

（41）**retirement life** 退休生活

（42）**sense of belonging** 归属感

（43）**material wealth** 物质财富

（44）**gap between the rich and the poor** 贫富差距

6.3.7 社会类题材句子写作练习

（1）我认为所有的罪犯，无论年龄多小，都应该被关进监狱，而在监狱关多久取决于罪行的严重程度。

（2）对于年轻人来说，监狱是个很好的地方来让他们反思其所做的错事。

（3）我的看法是，青少年如果犯下严重罪行，就应该像成年罪犯一样被关进监狱，因为监狱的经历会让他们成为更好的人。

（4）过多接触电视中的暴力场景会极大影响影视观众，从而增加他们在实际生活中犯下同样暴力罪行的可能性。

（5）我们都知道，人类有跟随他人的天然倾向，尤其在伤害他人方面。

（6）今天的娱乐节目制片人往往将暴力行为表达为一种英雄行为，而且为其辩护，这是很有误导性的，给观众，尤其是年轻观众，一种错误的印象，即暴力是一件很酷也总是正确的事情。

（7）显然，前囚犯比任何人都更能让青少年了解违法的后果。他们亲身参与了犯罪，非常清楚他们的行为给受害者及其家人带来的痛苦。

（8）除了补救功能外，监狱还可以对那些有犯罪倾向的人起到威慑作用。在监狱里失去自由的可能性能最有效地阻止他们对社会和其他人造成伤害。

（9）首先，教育提高了人们的道德水平，使他们能够分辨是非，从而在心里建立起坚固的高墙，抵御做任何反社会行为。更重要的是，受过良好教育的人总是能找到满意的工作，这份工作会让他们过上体面的生活，让他们永远都不会想到犯罪。

（10）有证据表明，在监狱里教育罪犯在某种程度上是有效的，因为这可以帮助他们在获释后尽快找到一份好工作，恢复正常生活。

（11）政府最近制定的一项政策值得推荐，即禁止15岁以下的年轻人进入酒吧和网吧。这项政策使孩子们有可能花更多的时间与父母和老师在一起，从而减少他们行为不端的可能性。

（12）我刚看过的一则报纸报道比较了有产假的国家和没有产假的国家的婴儿死亡率，得出的结论是前者婴儿的死亡率比后者低25%。

（13）经常的情况是，新婚夫妇才刚刚开始工作，仍努力维持生计，家添新丁将是一个很重的负担。然而，即使没有经济问题，很多年轻夫妇仍然拒绝要孩子，因为他们希望在生孩子前开发自己的各种潜能，或者体验这个世界。

（14）男人和女人都在朝九晚五地供养家庭，因此应该平等分担家务，在这个意义上，零性别差异表面上正在成为现实。

（15）新技术使许多以前由男性担任的职位不复存在。例如，建筑工地上的许多工作现在都是由机器完成，从而使许多建筑工人失业。

（16）现在，家庭煮男们不必再为自己感到羞耻，而在外工作的妻子则有更多的机会去实现个人理想。

（17）可以得出这样的结论：幸福的两性关系与分担同样数量的家务活没有什么联系，即使女人和男人一样有全职工作。在这方面，两性平等和幸福婚姻的逻辑可能不同于平等分担家务。

（18）全球化导致了全球层面上的竞争，这使我们能够享受到质量更高、价格更低的产品。如果我们以前不得不花很多钱购买一辆当地品牌的汽车，那么随着从生产成本低得多的其他国家进口汽车，其价格可能会减半。

（19）全球化也会对我们所生活的自然环境产生负面影响。增加产量意味着增加对自然资源的利用。此外，贸易的增长要求增加使用化石燃料的交通方式，从而导致污染加重，引发气候变化，现今气候变化对人类和世界的未来造成了严重威胁。

（20）预期寿命的延长可能对社会产生更大的影响。虽然它是一个国家繁荣的明显指标，因此可以加强人们对政府的信心，但寿命的延长也会导致老龄化问题。

参考答案

（1）I think all criminals, no matter how young they are, should be put into jail and how long they should stay there depends on the severity of their crime.

（2）Prison is a good place for young people to think again what wrong they have done to other people.

（3）My opinion is that, like an adult law violator, the teenager should also go to prison when he commits serious crimes because this experience in prison may enable them to become a better person.

（4）The excessive exposure to the violent scenes on TV will greatly affect the theatre-goers and TV viewers, thus increasing the likelihood of their committing the same violent crimes in real life.

（5）We all know about human's natural inclination to follow others, especially when it comes to doing harms to other people.

（6）Entertainment producers these days tend to present, quite misleadingly, violent acts as an expression of heroism and have them well justified, giving the viewers, especially those young viewers, a false impression that violence is a cool and always right thing to do.

（7）Obviously, ex-prisoners are in a better position than anybody else to let teenagers understand the consequences of violating the law. They were personally involved in crimes and know very well how much pain their behaviour has inflicted upon the victims and their families.

（8）On top of the remedial function, prison can serve as a deterrent for those with an inclination to crime. The likelihood of losing freedom in prison can most effectively stop them from doing harms to society and other individuals.

（9）To start with, education improves people's moral standards which enable them to tell right from wrong so that they will build a robust inner wall against any antisocial behaviours. More importantly, people with better education are always able to find a satisfying career that will reward them with a decent life, and they will never think of committing any crime.

（10）There is evidence that educating criminals in prison does work to some extent, for it can help them secure a good job as soon as possible after being set free and returning to normal life.

(11) One recommendable policy the government has made recently is to ban the entry of young people under 15 to the bars and the Internet cafes. This policy makes it possible for children to spend more time with their parents and teachers, thus reducing the likelihood of their misconducts.

(12) I have just read a newspaper report which compares the infant mortality rate between the countries which practise maternity leave and those which do not and concludes that infant death rate in the former is 25% lower than that in the latter.

(13) More often than not, the newly married couples have just started their career and are still struggling to make their ends meet, and an additional member would be a great burden. But even if free from financial problems, many young couples still refuse to start a family with kids because they wish to develop their various potentials or experience the world before they have kids.

(14) In appearance, the zero gender gap is becoming a reality, in the sense that, since both men and women are equally the family's bread-earners working from nine to five, both should share the housework equally.

(15) New technologies have made many positions previously held by men unavailable any more. For instance, much work in a construction site is now done by machines, rendering many construction workers jobless.

(16) Now the househusbands no longer have to feel ashamed of themselves and the working wives have more opportunities to realize their personal ambitions.

(17) It is proper to conclude that happy relationships have little to do with sharing the same amount of housework, even when women like men have full-time jobs. In this regard, gender equality and a happy marriage may have a logic different from equally sharing the housework.

(18) Globalisation leads to competition at a global level, which enables us to enjoy products of higher quality at lower prices. If we had to spend a lot of money purchasing a car of local brand, then the price may be halved with the importation of cars from other countries where the production cost is much lower.

（19）Globalisation also has negative effects on the natural environment we live in. Increased production means increased utilization of natural resources. Besides, increased trade calls for increased transport, which uses fossil fuels. As a result, pollution has increased, leading to climate change, which is now a serious threat to humanity and the future of the world.

（20）The increased life expectancy can have an even stronger impact on society. While it is a clear indicator of a country's prosperity and thus can strengthen the confidence of people in their government, a longer life span also results in the aging problem.

6.4 生活类

"生活类"话题属雅思写作高频话题，该话题分布广泛，考点及分布如下：

日常生活类，如：购买名牌是好是坏？生活质量降低的原因；要不要成为素食者？食用异地生产的食品是好还是坏？

社交类，如：现代社会通过网络购物、工作和交流是好是坏？手机和网络对人们的联系起重要作用是好是坏？写信会否消失？写信是否重要？

生活方式类，如：为什么人们继续以不健康的生活方式生活？现在人们扔掉旧的东西再买新的东西的原因和影响。

其他，如：极限运动应该被制止还是让人们自由选择？

6.4.1 日常生活

母题： In many countries, people are wearing more western-style clothes (suits and jeans) rather than their traditional clothes. Why? Is this a positive or negative development?（201226）

子题 1： Health experts claim that walking is the best exercise. However, people are walking less on a daily basis. What has made it happen and how to deal with this?（210327）

子题 2： During holidays and weekends, young people spend less time on outdoor activities in natural environment, such as hiking and mountain climbing. Why? What can be done to encourage them to go out?（210417）

子题 3：Research shows that some people continue to eat unhealthy food even though they know it is bad for them. Why? What are the most efficient ways to improve their eating habits?（211218）

子题 4：Some people think everyone should be a vegetarian, because they do not eat meat to stay healthy. To what extent do you agree or disagree?（150919）

子题 5：On the vehicle-free day, private cars, trucks and motorcycles are banned in the city centre while the public transport is permitted such as bicycles, buses and taxis. Do the benefits of the vehicle-free day outweigh the disadvantages?（170112）

核心观点及表达

日常生活类话题看似简单，但其实每一个选择后面都有很多原因，并会产生重要后果。比如：

孩子不愿去自然环境中从事户外活动。原因：孩子太忙，自然环境中的户外活动很枯燥。后果：孩子身体变差。

私家车越来越多。原因：方便，住的地方越来越远离工作地点。后果：城市变得拥挤，产生污染，个人身体越来越差。

人们愿意买名牌。原因：质量更好，身份象征。后果：价格更高，以貌取人（people are valued according to what they have, not what they are）。

人们愿意吃外国快餐。原因：快捷，便宜。后果：不健康，丢失本地食品传统，减少就业机会。

看以下观点及表达：

（1）如果崇拜名牌成风，这个世界可能变得不公平，因为人们会歧视买不起名牌的人。

If everybody in society worships the famous brands, then the world may become an unjust place to live in because people will develop a biased attitude to those who cannot afford these brands.

（2）30 年前，诸如麦当劳、肯德基和赛百味这样的美国快餐食品在中国几乎闻所未闻，然而现在它们对多数中国人而言已经是耳熟能详，中国也许已经成为世界上食用美国快餐食品最多的国家。

30 years ago, American fast food such as McDonald's, KFC, and Subway was basically unheard of in China, but now they have become everyday words

to most Chinese people and China has probably consumed the greatest amount of American fast food in the world.

（3）当更多种类的食品从外而来时，我们就拥有了更好的营养结构，以及更多自由来选择自己喜爱的食品。

With greater variety of food coming from outside, we can enjoy a better nutritional structure and greater freedom to choose our favourite food.

（4）我相信，随着外国食品到来而引起的激烈竞争对本地食品业的长远发展是有好处的，因为这会迫使本地食品公司改进产品质量，反过来会让它们在国际市场上更具竞争力。

I believe the intensified competition resulting from the arrival of the foreign food is beneficial to the long-term development of the local food industry, because it will compel the local food companies to improve the quality of their products, which in turn will make them more competitive in the global market.

（5）汽车和摩托车的一个重要优势是让生活变得更高效，因为它们能快速把我们送到某地，这在以前是无法想象的。

One important advantage of cars and motorcycles is that they make our life more efficient. They can transport us to a place in a quick manner unimaginable prior to their invention.

6.4.2 网络社交

母题：Mobile/cell phones and the Internet play an important role in the way in which people relate to one another socially. Is this a positive or negative development? What is your opinion?（120809）

子题 1：Online shopping is now replacing shopping in stores. Do you think it is a positive or negative development?（141122）

子题 2：With the increasing use of mobile phone and computer, the number of people who write letter has decreased. As a result, letter writing will disappear soon. Do you agree or disagree?（121124）

子题 3：Many people today prefer socializing online to spending time with friends in local community. Do advantages outweigh the disadvantages?（180602）

核心观点及表达

网络交流快捷方便，但可能影响我们面对面的交流能力，减少我们与家人朋友共处的时间，同时存在虚假欺诈的可能性。传统的社交方式，比如写信已经逐渐被网络社交取代。看以下观点及表达：

（1）在有手机之前，我们不得不花几个小时写一封信，接着去几英里外的邮局寄给朋友，然后等很多天才收到回复。但现在只是点击几下而已。

Before we had mobile phones, we had to spend hours writing a letter and then travelling a few miles to the post office to send it to our friends, and then waited many days for the reply. But now it is a matter of just a few clicks.

（2）与实体商店购物不同的是，网上购物剥夺了我们与家人共度一段美好时光的机会。

Unlike the store shopping, online shopping deprives us of the opportunities to spend quality time together with our family members.

（3）手机使用的增加大大减少了人们面对面交流的机会。没有肢体语言和面部表情的帮助，手机上的交流很容易以误解告终。当然，过度依赖手机获取信息也可能导致手机用户之间的疏远。

The increased use of mobile phones has greatly reduced the opportunities for people to engage in face-to-face communication. Without the help of body language and facial expression, the communication over mobile phones may easily end up in misunderstanding. Of course, the excessive dependence upon mobile phones for information may also contribute to the estrangement among their users.

（4）与真实生活中的朋友交谈，比有上千个素不相识的网上朋友更有好处。

Talking with our friends in real life is much more rewarding than having thousands of virtual friends who do not really know us.

6.4.3 生活方式

母题：Nowadays, many people spend less and less time at home. What are the reasons and what are the effects of this trend on individuals and on society? （191221）

子题 1：Some people think that young people should spend more of their free time at home with their family instead of entertaining outside. Others disagree. Discuss both views and give your own opinion. (181027)

子题 2: In some countries, more people choose to live by themselves in recent years. Why is the case? Is it a positive or negative development for society? (161119)

子题 3: These days an increasing number of people in many cities know little about their neighbours and do not have a sense of community. What do you think are the causes and what solutions can you suggest? (180719)

子题 4: Nowadays, people spend more and more time away from their families. Why is this? What effect will it have on themselves and their families? (220430)

子题 5: Scientists keep telling people to lead a healthy lifestyle, but most people continue with unhealthy activities. Please analyse the reasons. (131221)

核心观点及表达

现代生活方式有四个特点：一是独居的人越来越多，二是在家的时间越来越少，三是网上时间越来越多，四是流动性更大。其原因是多方面的：工作压力（work pressure）变大，不结婚的人越来越多（high celibacy rate），网络越来越发达，全球化导致工作流动性（mobility）更大。看以下观点及表达：

（1）没有他人在场，没有他人的眼睛盯着，独居者自由地沉溺于自己奇怪的习惯：吃完饭不洗碗，凌晨 2 点赤身裸体站在厨房，从罐里抓花生酱吃，等等。

In the absence of anybody else and his/her watchful eyes, the solo dweller is free to indulge his or her odd habits: no dish washing after dinner, standing naked in the kitchen at 2 a.m., eating peanut butter from the jar, and so on.

（2）即使愿意，许多人也根本不能像以前那样有那么多时间在家，因为他们面临着越来越大的工作压力。有些人可能被迫加班，另一些人可能不得不长途跋涉去谈商务合同。

Many people simply cannot spend as much time at home as before, even if they want to, because they face increasing pressure from work. Some may be forced to work extra hours, and others may have to travel long distances for a business contract.

（3）众所周知，父母在家陪伴是孩子健康发展的关键。许多经常看不到父母的孩子表现出一种被称为情绪缺失的症状。

As is known to all, the presence of parents at home is key to the healthy development of their kids. Many children who cannot often see their parents show a symptom known as emotional deficiency.

6.4.4 生活类题材参考词汇

（1）**family member** 家庭成员

（2）**spoil** 溺爱

（3）**community** 社区

（4）**generation gap** 代沟

（5）**harmony** 和谐

（6）**protective** 保护性的

（7）**excessive** 过多的

（8）**emotional refuge** 情感避难所

（9）**life expectancy** 预期寿命

（10）**single-parent family** 单亲家庭

（11）**broken family** 破裂的家庭

（12）**domestic violence** 家庭暴力

（13）**nuclear family** 小家庭（只包括父母和子女）

（14）**extended family** 大家庭（几代同堂的家庭）

（15）**maternity leave** 产假

（16）**work extra hours** 加班

（17）**outdoor activities** 户外活动

（18）**sports facilities** 运动设施

（19）**prime family time** 黄金家庭时间

（20）**obesity** 肥胖症

（21）**productive** 有生产力的

（22）**maintain good health** 保持身体健康

（23）**medical resources** 医疗资源

（24）**balanced diet** 均衡的饮食

（25）**identity** 身份

（26）**city dweller** 城市居民

6.4.5 生活类题材句子写作练习

（1）晚育有独特的好处：晚育有利于孩子，因为此时父母在经济上和情感上的境况都更好了；晚育有利于父母，因为现在他们事业有成，有更多时间来照顾孩子。

（2）解决这个问题的一种方法是，人们把车停在远离住处或办公室的地方，这样他们上下班都必须走一定的距离。

（3）快餐带来的一个重要好处是提高了效率。吃传统食物可能需要两三个小时，但我们吃快餐只需要几分钟。快餐为我们节省的时间可以用于更有成效的工作，从而提高社会的整体效率。

（4）我们的健康远不仅仅是个人问题，它在很大程度上保证了社区的健康，这被今天仍困扰世界的新冠大流行一再证明。

（5）不健康的食物总是美味、便宜、容易获得的。只要有机会，没有多少人能真正抵挡住煎培根、汉堡和热狗等食物的诱惑。这些食物从超市到剧院都可以买到，通常只需要几美元。

（6）缺乏锻炼也是导致肥胖水平飞升的一个关键因素，因为普通青少年每天花很长时间玩电子游戏，很少做户外运动。

（7）大城市里无处不在的激烈竞争破坏我们与同事、邻居乃至朋友的关系，导致我们孤独寂寞。

（8）现代城市规划者倾向于根据功能将城市划分为不同的区域，如大学区、商业区、医院区、居住区等。基于明确功能划分的城市能使我们的生活更轻松、更有效。

（9）在"无车日"这天，人们会产生一种意识，那就是他们不应该再把有车的生活视为理所当然。他们将会明白，开车的好处是用代价换来的。

（10）很多人认为，推迟做父母可能会给夫妇，尤其是大龄妈妈，带来身体上的挑战，同时父母年龄大对孩子也不公平，因为他们有可能活不了那么久，看不到孩子的成长。

（11）此外，对名牌的强烈渴望可能会使我们变成非理性的消费者，促使我们去尝试所有的，甚至是非法的手段来买下它们。

（12）创造工作与生活的平衡对于改善人们的整体幸福感是至关重要的，

然而对于现代的许多人来说，实现这种平衡只是一项"不可能完成的任务"。

（13）如果整容手术培养了一种只重视外表的社会氛围，那么就没有人会关心培养内在性格和个性了。更重要的是，由于整容手术往往非常昂贵，只有富人才能负担得起，这意味着只有富人才能从手术中受益。因此，整容手术造成了贫富差距不断扩大。

（14）正如老话"自助者天助"所说的那样，我认为努力工作应该成为我们生活的引擎，运气充其量只能是加速器。

（15）今天，我们都相信知识就在指尖，因为所有知识似乎都已经电子化存储，很容易在网上获取。

（16）网络的空间几乎是无限的，因此可以储存世界上所有的知识，我们没有太大必要花那么多钱修建实体图书馆了。

（17）很多人就是喜欢阅读实体书籍来学知识，而不是使用网络资源，因为他们相信书籍更可靠，而且他们发现自己在情感上和智力上都与书本知识更紧密。

（18）今天，电子邮件、推特、微信、脸书之类的现代通信技术已经主导了我们的生活，以至于我们不再需要写信或打电话了。

（19）为现代通信科技的到来而欢呼的人发现，与传统相比，这些新型的通信方式可以有效降低人们交流的时间和成本。

（20）缺乏面对面沟通可能损害我们恰当表达个人情感和意见的能力。

（21）由于没有多少人的温暖，这种基于技术的通信方式会给人们制造距离，让他们不太关心彼此，从而让这个世界冷漠得多。

（22）在家工作的人经常发现他们变得不那么有效率，因为分心的事更多，并且同事压力变小了，而住在离办公室很远的地方意味着他们与同事和上级面对面交流的机会减少，这会导致业务受损，甚至丧失晋升的机会。

（23）因此，我的结论是知识会越来越多地走向网络，这会让知识存储变得更加经济和便捷，但是书籍永远不会消失，因为总会有人喜欢拥抱以印刷形式出现的知识。

参考答案

（1）Having kids later in life can be beneficial in unique ways: it is good to the babies because their parents are now financially and emotionally better conditioned; it is good to the parents because now they have been well established so that they have more time for their kids.

（2）One way to solve the problem is that people park their cars away from their houses or offices so that they will have to walk a certain distance to their cars both when they go to work and return home from their work.

（3）One important benefit fast food brings is the improved efficiency. Eating traditional food may take us two or three hours, but it is a matter of just a few minutes when we eat fast food. The time saved for us by fast food can be used in more productive work so that the general efficiency of society will be enhanced.

（4）Far from being just a personal matter, our health is something that largely guarantees the health of the community, as has been repeatedly evidenced in the Covid-19 pandemic that is still troubling the world today.

（5）Unhealthy food is always tasty, cheap, and readily available. Not many people can really resist the temptation to enjoy the fried bacon, hamburger, and hot dog, to name just a few, whenever they have a chance. These food, available everywhere from the supermarkets to the theatres, usually costs only a few dollars.

（6）Lack of exercise is also a key factor behind soaring levels of obesity, with the average youngster spending long hours daily playing video games, and little time doing outdoor activities.

（7）The fierce competition that exists everywhere in big cities is destructive to our relationship with our colleagues, neighbours, and even friends, resulting in our isolation and loneliness.

（8）Modern city planners tend to separate a city into different areas according to their functions, such as the university area, business area, hospital area, residential area and so on. A city arranged on the basis of clearly-defined functional areas can make our life a lot easier and more efficient.

（9）On this "vehicle-free" day, the awareness will dawn on people that they should no longer take for granted their life with cars. They will be made to understand that the benefits of driving cars do not come without prices.

（10）Many people argue that the delayed parenthood may pose physical challenges to couples, especially the older mom, and it is quite unfair on the child to have old parents because they probably won't live long enough to see the child grow up.

（11）Besides, the strong desire for famous brands may turn us into irrational consumers and prompt us to try all, even illegal, means to buy them.

（12）Creating a work-life balance is critical to improving people's overall well-being, yet for many people in the modern age, to achieve such a balance is just a "mission impossible".

（13）If cosmetic surgery fosters a social atmosphere in which only appearance is valued, then no one will care about developing their inner character and personalities. More importantly, as cosmetic surgery is often very costly, only the rich people can afford the operation, which means only the rich people can benefit from the surgery. Consequently, cosmetic surgery has contributed to the ever-widening gap between the rich and the poor.

（14）As is suggested in the old saying "God helps those who help themselves", I believe hard work should become the engine of our life, and luck can at best be the accelerator.

（15）Today we all believe that knowledge is just at the tip of our fingers because all knowledge seems to have been stored electronically and is easily accessible on the Internet.

（16）Owing to its virtually unlimited capacity, the Internet can store all knowledge in the world. This makes it quite unnecessary for us to spend that much money constructing the brick-and-mortar libraries.

（17）Many people simply prefer reading real books for knowledge to online sources, because they believe books are more reliable and they find themselves emotionally and intellectually more attached to knowledge in books.

（18）Nowadays, modern communication technologies such as email, twitter, We-Chat and Facebook have dominated our life in such a way that we no longer need to write letters or make phone calls.

（19）People rooting for the advent of modern communication technologies find these new ways of communication, compared with the traditional ones, can effectively reduce the time and costs of communication among people.

（20）The lack of face-to-face exchange may actually impair our ability to properly express our personal feelings or opinions.

（21）Without much personal warmth, this technology-based communication creates distances among people and makes them care less about each other, turning this world into a much colder place.

（22）People who work from home often find they become less efficient because they have more distractions and less peer pressure and living far away from office means less opportunity to have face-to-face interactions with their colleagues and superiors, which may result in the loss of business and even chances of promotion.

（23）My conclusion, then, is that knowledge will increasingly find its way to the Internet and it will make knowledge storage more economical and convenient, yet books will never vanish because there are always people who would like to embrace knowledge in printed form.

6.5 政府类

政府类内容涉及广泛，常见考点如下：

政府投资，例如：政府资金拨款应该首先考虑医疗还是其他方面？为了解决交通堵塞问题，政府应不应该免费提供公交？政府资金是否应该用于更重要的事情而不是艺术上面？政府的资金支持是否应该仅仅提供给科学研究？政府支付大学学费是否利大于弊？政府应该在每个乡镇建设公共图书馆，这是否浪费钱？政府资金是否应该用于教育而不是其他东西？政府应提供资金赡养老人还是老年人自己承担？政府应该投资提高文盲的知识水平吗？

政府与个人生活，例如：政府或个人，谁应该对健康饮食负责？年轻人是否适合在政府中担任重要职位？政府和个人，谁对环境保护负责？政府和个人，谁对接送孩子上学负责？

6.5.1 政府投资

母题：Some people think people working in creative arts should be financially supported by government. Others think they should find financial support from other resources. Discuss both sides and give your opinion. （151031）

子题 1：Children's education is expensive. In some countries, the government pays some of or all of the costs. Do the advantages outweigh its disadvantages? （140222）

子题 2：Some countries achieve international sporting success by building specialized facilities to train top athletes instead of providing sports facilities that everyone can use. Do you think it is a positive or negative development? （161203）

子题 3：Education of young people is highly prioritized in many countries today. However some believe that educating the adults who cannot read and write is also important so more public money should be spent on this. To what extent do you agree or disagree? （210710）

子题 4：Government should offer financial support to the care of the old people, while others think old people should save money for their own future life. Give your opinion on this topic. （160319）

子题 5：The best way for the government to solve traffic congestion is to provide free public transport 24 hours a day, 7 days a week. To what extent do you agree or disagree? （140109）

核心观点及表达

任何一项政府投资都是有实际或潜在好处的（actual or potential benefits），但政府投资的预算（budget）是有限的，在一个领域的投资就会影响在另一个领域（sector）的投入，即一部分人获益时，就必然有另一部人受损。因此，政府投资问题往往不是讨论某个领域是否重要，而是要结合投资成本（investment costs）和投资效益/回报（investment return）来讨论。比如，政府是否应该给所有人提供免费医疗？首先，免费医疗当然是好事，能让所有人病有所医，但是若政府投资医疗，那么政府在其他领域（如教育和技术）的投资就会相应减少。因此，建议设置一个收入基准线，低于该线的家庭可以获得免费医疗，高于该线的家庭则自己支付。看以下观点及表达：

（1）由于公共资金总是有限的，因此增加对免费医疗保健的投资，肯定会导致对教育和技术等其他部门的投资减少。

As the public money is always limited, the increased investment on free medical care will surely result in the reduced investment in other sectors such as education and technology.

（2）他们认为，免费医疗保健将给政府预算带来巨大的财政负担，政府预算应该流向教育和环境保护等更重要的部门。

Free health care, in their opinion, will put a huge amount of financial burden onto the government budget, which should go to more important sectors such as education and environmental protection.

（3）对于 50 岁以上的人，政府应该鼓励他们学习，但不应该在他们身上花费公共预算，因为这种投资的回报即使有，也将是非常小的。

For those over the age of fifty, the government should encourage them to learn, but no public money should be spent on them, because the return of such investment will be, if any, extremely marginal/small.

（4）即使与教育、医疗保健系统和技术相比，艺术对我们的物质生活方面没有太大帮助，但它们与我们的情感和精神生活的确有很大关系。

Even if arts, when compared with education, health care system, and technologies, do not help much with the material aspects of our life, they do have much to do with our emotional and spiritual life.

6.5.2 政府和个人

母题：Some believe governments should do more to make citizens have a healthy diet, others believe individuals must take responsibility for their diets and health. Discuss both views and give your own opinion.（140719）

子题 1：The use of mobile phone in certain places is just as antisocial as smoking. Do you think mobile phones should be banned like smoking?（150214）

子题 2：Some people think younger people are not suitable for important positions in governments of countries. Some think it will be a good idea for younger people to take on these positions. Discuss both views and give your own opinion.（140712）

子题 3：Many people believe that scientific research should be carried out and controlled by the governments rather than private companies. To what extent do you agree or disagree with this opinion? （210821）

子题 4：Some people think that it is government's responsibility to transport children to school, while others think parents should get their children to school. Discuss both views and give your own opinion. （211127）

核心观点及表达

某件事情到底由个人负责，还是政府负责？这样的题目，应该考虑政府的公益性质，以及政府是立法（make laws）和监督（supervise）机构，并能大规模（on a large scale）、大范围采取行动，个人一般仅能从自己做起。看以下观点及表达：

（1）政府和私营企业都应该负责科学研究，不过前者应该关注基础研究，而后者应该关注应用研究。

Both government and private companies should be responsible for the scientific research, although the former should focus on basic research while the latter on applied research.

（2）在很大程度上，保护当地环境的责任必须由政府和个人共同承担。政府应该让公众知道，环境保护是每个人的事。否则，看似众人负责就会变成无人负责。

To a great extent, the responsibility for looking after the local environment must be shared by the government and individuals. The government should let the public know that environmental protection is everybody's business. Otherwise, what seems to be everybody's business would become nobody's business.

（3）因此，很难就年轻人是否应该担任政府要职得出一个普遍的结论。对于一些更基于经验的职位，老年人是更适合的人选，而对于其他需要更多激情而非经验的职位，年轻人可能比老年同行做得更好。

It is, therefore, difficult to draw a general conclusion about whether young people should hold important government positions. For some positions which are more experience-based, the elderly people are more suitable candidates, yet for other positions which require more passionate spirit than experience, young people can perhaps do a better job than their elderly counterparts.

（4）食物不是一个简单的个人问题，在食物的生产、分配和消费方面，也一直是一个社会问题。

Rather than a simply personal issue, food is always also a social issue in terms of its production, distribution and consumption.

（5）虽然个人很难解决这些大的环境问题，但个人仍然负有环境保护责任。事实上，如果每个人在日常生活中做正确的事情，那么像全球变暖或海平面上升之类的重大环境问题可能根本就不会发生。

Although it is very difficult for individuals to solve those big environmental problems, individuals still have their share of responsibility for environmental protection. Indeed, if everyone does the right thing in everyday life, such big environmental problems as global warming or sea level rise may not have happened at all.

6.5.3 政府类题材参考词汇

（1）**establish** 建立

（2）**alleviate** 减轻

（3）**authorities** 当局；主管部门

（4）**impose** 强加于

（5）**efficient** 有效率的

（6）**effective** 有效的

（7）**enact** 通过（法律）

（8）**sensible policy** 明智的政策

（9）**long-term solution** 长远的解决方案

（10）**eventually** 最后，终于，从长远看（= in the long run）

（11）**give priority to...** 优先处理……

（12）**unemployment rate** 失业率

（13）**be indifferent to...** 对……漠不关心

（14）**means of transportation** 交通工具

（15）**urbanisation** 城市化

（16）**rewarding** 有回报的

（17）**flexible** 灵活的

（18）**investment return** 投资回报

（19）**investment costs** 投资成本

（20）**make laws and regulations** 制定法律法规

（21）**introduce** 引进；介绍

（22）**international aid** 国际援助

（23）**create job opportunities** 创造就业机会

（24）**investment sector** 投资领域

6.5.4 政府类题材句子写作练习

（1）有了免费医疗，他们一旦发现自己的健康有问题，就能随时去医院，而无须担心金钱问题。这当然能提高他们的幸福感，整个社会将会变得更加和谐。

（2）艺术可以改善人的心理状态，使人团结起来，尤其是当一个国家处于危机时。比如，9·11 恐怖袭击后，整个美国处于瘫痪状态，但它很快就从这种瘫痪状态中复苏了，很大程度上就是因为美国人受到艺术作品的鼓舞，这些作品鼓励他们面对现实，继续前进。

（3）政府应制定严格的法律法规，确保生产和销售的食品的质量。

（4）我们需要照顾好这些建筑物，并尽可能长时间地保存它们，不管这需要多少金钱，这样它们就可以向我们的后代讲述城市或国家的故事。

（5）免费公共交通将给政府预算带来沉重负担，因此政府将不得不削减在教育、医疗、技术开发等部门的投资。

（6）当公共交通免费的时候，许多本来会留在家里的人可能选择乘坐免费的交通工具出行。这就会在很大程度上抵消路上私家车数量减少带来的益处，甚至可能使公共交通系统瘫痪，尤其是在交通高峰期。

（7）很多人认为，政府对艺术家（如画家、音乐家和诗人）的任何投资都是浪费，因为政府应该把纳税人的钱投放到更重要的事情上。

（8）由于任何国家的政府都主要负责保护本国公民免受任何形式的伤害，因此当本国公民遭受贫困的时候却把钱给外国人似乎是相当荒谬的。例如，如果仍然有许多人失业，买不起自己的房子，政府就应该尽最大努力创造更多的就业机会来帮助他们，而不是把钱用于国际援助。

（9）总之，提供国际援助绝不仅仅是金钱问题。它远非浪费金钱，而是提供了一个融入国际大家庭的机会。因此，我的论点是，给予其他国家适当的财政帮助总是必要的，即使在国内仍然有一些人生活不富裕。

（10）因此，我的建议是富国向穷国提供智力和技术援助，只有在绝对必要时才提供经济援助。

参考答案

（1）With free health care, they can go to hospital whenever they find there is anything wrong with their health without worrying about money. This will, of course, enhance their sense of well-being and the entire society will become much more harmonious.

（2）Art can improve people's mental state and bring them together, especially when a country is in crisis. The entire United States, for example, was paralyzed right after the 911 terrorist attack, but it quickly recovered from that paralysis, largely because American people were inspired by the artistic works which encouraged them to face the reality and move on.

（3）The government should make strict laws and regulations to ensure the quality of food produced and sold in market.

（4）We need to take good care of these buildings and keep them as long as possible, however much money it may involve, so that they can tell the stories of the city or the nation to our future generations.

（5）Free public transport will put a heavy burden on the government's budget so that the government will have to cut down on its investment in such sectors as education, medical care, and technological development, to mention just the three.

（6）When public transport goes free, many people who otherwise would stay at home may choose to go out by taking the free transport. This will greatly undo the benefits brought by the reduced number of private cars on road and may even paralyze the public transport system, especially during the rush hours.

（7）Many people consider any government investment on artists such as painters, musicians, and poets as wasteful because the government should put the tax-payers' money to more important things.

（8）As the government of any country is mainly responsible for protecting its own citizens from harm of any kind, it seems quite absurd to give money to people in other countries when the citizens at home are suffering from poverty. For example, if there are still many people who are jobless and cannot afford their own houses, the government should try its best to help them by creating more jobs rather than paying money for international aid.

（9）To conclude, offering international aid is never just a matter of money. Far from being a waste of money, it actually gives the country an opportunity to become a member of the international big family. My argument, then, is that giving appropriate financial help to other countries is always necessary, even when there are still some disadvantaged people at home.

（10）My suggestion, then, is that rich countries provide intellectual and technological aid to poor countries and offer financial aid only when it is absolutely necessary.

6.6 媒体类

媒体类属于中频题材，考点及分布如下：

广告的利弊，例如：广告使人变得同质化；广告影响人的想法并造成负面影响；广告对我们生活有着极大的影响，是否利大于弊？食品广告是否应该像烟草广告那样被禁止？广告是否只是说服人们去买产品而没有使得产品质量有所提高？消费者是否被广告影响？有什么方法保护他们？

媒体对儿童的影响，例如：针对孩子而设计的广告日渐增多是不是件坏事？儿童对电视的兴趣比创造性活动的要大的原因以及解决办法。

新媒体的影响，例如：人们在网上学习、工作的优缺点；新媒体为什么对现代社会很重要，它们的影响是好是坏？信息能被随便地传到网上是否使人们无法获得准确的信息？

其他，例如：我们是否能够相信记者？一个成功的记者应该有怎样的品质？媒体倾向于报道社会问题及紧急情况是否对个人和社会有害？观看外国电影的人比观看本地电影的人多的原因，以及政府应该怎样做以支持本地电影业？读报纸和看电视新闻是否是浪费时间？

6.6.1 广告的利弊

母题：People are surrounded by many kinds of advertising, which can in-

fluence their life. Does the positive effect of this trend outweigh negative effect?
（151205）

子题1：Some people think advertising may have positive economic effects. Others think it has negative social effects because advertising makes individuals not satisfied with what they are and what they have. Discuss both views and give your own opinion.（170422）

子题2：Nowadays consumers are faced with the advertisements from competitive companies. To what extent do you agree that consumers are influenced by advertisements? What measures should be taken to protect them?（120510）

子题3：To what extent do you agree or disagree with the following statement? Advertising usually encourages consumers to buy a product or service in quantity rather than promoting its quality.（120707）

子题4：The main aim of advertisements is increasing sales of products that people do not really need. To what extent do you agree or disagree?（210717）

核心观点及表达

广告可传递信息（informative），而且设计美观（colourfully designed），可以给我们的生活增添亮色，甚至也是一个国家经济繁荣的标志。但广告往往夸大其词（exaggerate），误导性强（misleading），从而让消费者上当受骗。广告往往通过各种方式制造消费欲望，让消费者花钱购买很多不必要的商品（buy things they do not really need），从而引发一系列社会问题（result in many social problems）。看以下观点及表达：

（1）广告对我们生活的渗透已经如此之深，有时候我们甚至惊叹其无所不在。

The penetration of advertising into our life has gone so far that sometimes we even feel amazed by its ubiquity.

（2）除了提供信息，广告还用吸引人的设计和图像试图劝说人们花钱购买其推销的商品或服务。

With attractive designs and images, advertising, on top of being informative, tries to persuade people to spend money on the commodities or services it promotes.

（3）事实上，我们甚至能发现一个国家的经济实力与广告的可见度之间有紧密联系。

As a matter of fact, we can even find a close association between the strength of a country's economy and the visibility of its advertising.

（4）广告可能让我们对已经拥有的东西和现在的地位不满，让我们十分渴望那些得不到的东西。

Advertising may make us less content with what we have and what we are now and leave us craving hopelessly for those unattainable commodities.

（5）因此，广告在给我们提供有用的商品信息时，也在我们内心制造了不合适的欲望，让我们不幸福。

Advertising, then, while providing us with useful commodities information, also creates the unwanted desire in our hearts and makes us unhappy.

6.6.2. 媒体对儿童的影响

母题：Nowadays, there is a large amount of advertising aimed at children. Some people think they have negative effects on children and should be banned. To what extent do you agree or disagree?（160220）

子题 1：Nowadays a large amount of advertising is aimed at children. Some people think this can have negative effects on children and should be banned. To what extent do you agree or disagree?（180811）

子题 2：In some countries advertising aimed at children persuades them to buy snack, toys and other products. Some parents object to this pressure on children, but some advertisers suggest they provide useful information. Discuss both views and give your own opinion.（160709）

核心观点及表达

孩子可以通过电视这样的媒体学习很多有用的知识，但电视媒体是单向的（one-way communication），观众处于被动接受的位置，因此有可能影响孩子的创造力（creativity），看太多电视甚至会引发孩子的性格问题（personality disorder）。就广告而言，针对儿童的广告虽然也能提供信息，但总体来说弊大于利。看下面的句子及表达：

（1）虽然这些广告确实有一些好处——它们至少提供了信息，但我非常确信它们对儿童是弊大于利。

While these advertisements do have some benefits—they are informative at least, I am quite convinced that they are more harmful than beneficial to children.

（2）即使广告商在为学习辅助产品做广告时，经常声称他们的产品会让孩子们的学习过程充满乐趣，这也是很不好的，因为这会给孩子们一种错误的印象，即不必认真地投入学习。

Even when they are advertising learning-aid products, the advertisers often claim their products will make children's learning process full of fun. This is really bad because it gives children a false impression that they do not have to put serious efforts into their study.

（3）为了迎合儿童的心理需求，许多广告以极具想象力和不切实际的方式来描述这个世界。例如，当要推广玩具武器时，广告会把这个世界描述为坏人横行之处。接触这种广告的孩子可能会对世界产生深深的敌意。

Catering to the psychological needs of children, many advertisements describe the world in highly imaginative and unrealistic manners. For instance, when they want to promote their doll weapons, they will describe the world as a place full of bad guys. A child exposed to such advertising may develop a deep sense of hostility to the world.

（4）另一方面，当他们想向孩子兜售游乐园的门票时，他们会把这个世界描述为一个充满爱、完全没有任何危险的地方。相信这种广告的孩子很难对付现实生活中的麻烦。

On the other hand, when they want to sell entertainment park tickets to children, they will describe the world as a place full of love and without any danger at all. A child who has been made to believe this kind of advertising will have a hard time dealing with troubles in real life.

6.6.3 新媒体

母题： News media are important in modern society. Why are they important? And are their influences generally positive or negative?（120317）

子题 1： More and more people no longer read newspaper or watch TV programmes to get news. They get news about the world through the Internet. Is this a positive or negative development?（210403）

子题 2：Nowadays many people use social media every day to keep in touch with others and news events. Do you think the advantages outweigh the disadvantages?（211106）

子题 3：Some people think visual images (like photograph or video) can tell information more accurately in a news story, while others think they are not reliable sources. Discuss both views and give your opinion.（220806）

核心观点及表达

网络加快了我们的信息交流速度，多媒体交流方式更是提高了交流效率和效力（efficiency and effectiveness），但是不见面的交流有可能让人与人之间的关系变得疏远（alienated）和冷漠（cold）。因特网能提高我们获取信息的速度，节约时间，但这些信息往往是碎片化的（fragmented）、不完整的（incomplete），甚至是错误的（erroneous），此外，从网上获取知识缺乏人与人之间的温度（warmth），因此我们很难与知识建立起个人感情（personal feeling），其后果是我们学到了很多硬事实（hard facts），却无法对知识产生敬畏感（respect and awe）。不管什么媒体，所报道的内容都是选择性的（selective），因此读者应该有批判的眼光（read them in a critical way）。网络社交中，个人隐私无法得到有效保护，有些人甚至利用社交媒体来诬陷别人或从事诈骗，从而造成极坏的影响。看以下观点及表达：

（1）重要的是，我们要记住任何一种再现，无论是口头上的还是视觉上的，一定都是选择性的。

It is important that we remember any representation, be it verbal or visual, must be selective.

（2）互联网上的新闻可以以无与伦比的速度和规模传播。有了互联网，来自世界任何一个角落的人都可以快速了解所有地方正在发生的事情，从纽约和上海等大城市到非洲的一些偏远村庄。

News on the Internet can spread at unmatched speed and scale. With the Internet, people from any corner of the world can have quick access to what is going on in all places, ranging from big cities such as New York and Shanghai, to some remote villages in Africa.

（3）另一方面，正如我们很多人可能已经经历的那样，来自互联网的新闻往往是不准确的，有时甚至具有误导性。我们已经多次发现，在互联网上，同一事件的不同版本是相互矛盾的，所以我们不知道该相信什么。

On the other hand, as many of us may have experienced, news from the Internet is often inaccurate, sometimes even misleading. Many times we have found that the different versions of the same event on the Internet are contradicting each other and so we do not know what to believe.

6.6.4 记者

母题：We can get knowledge from news. But some people even think we should not trust the journalists. What do you think? And what do you think are the important qualities that a journalist should have?（160305）

子题：A tendency of news reported in the media about problems and emergencies rather than positive developments is more harmful to the individual and to society. Do you agree or disagree?（120414）

核心观点及表达

（1）在我看来，良好的判断力是一个记者需要拥有的首要品质。当面临一系列复杂的事件时，一个记者需要做很多决定：要报道什么？从什么角度报道？为了什么目的？一个记者只有拥有良好的判断力和维护公正的意愿，才能使新闻报道最接近事实真相。

To my mind, the ability to make fair judgment is the first important quality that a journalist should have. When faced with a series of complicated events, a journalist will have many decisions to make: what to report, from whose perspectives, for what purposes? Only with a fair sense of judgment and the willingness to make things right can a journalist bring out a news report closest to the real state of affairs.

（2）我们都需要从新闻中获取信息和知识。为使新闻是可靠的而非误导性的，一个记者必须有决心追求真理，有良好的判断力，而最重要的是，有很强的能力用文字表达自己的观点。

We all need news for information and knowledge, and in order for news to be reliable rather than misleading, a journalist must have a willing heart to pursue truth, a fair judgment and most important of all, a strong ability to express his/her mind with words.

（3）重要的是媒体同时报道社会的消极和积极发展。只有这样，我们才能了解到周围世界的全貌。

It is important that the media report both the negative and positive developments of society. Only in this way can we gain access to the whole picture of the world around us.

6.6.5 媒体类题材参考词汇

（1）**popular** 流行的；受欢迎的

（2）**objective** 客观的

（3）**be biased against...** 对……有偏见的

（4）**celebrity** 名人

（5）**journalist** 记者

（6）**cover** 报道（＝report）

（7）**misleading** 误导性的

（8）**trustworthy** 值得信任的

（9）**informative** 信息量大的

（10）**entertaining** 娱乐性质的

（11）**responsible** 负责任的；有责任心的

（12）**rising star** 新星

（13）**advertising** 广告

（14）**commercial** 电视广告

（15）**current affairs** 时事

（16）**have access to...** 获取或者使用……

（17）**exaggerate** 夸大（＝overstate）

（18）**insight** 洞察力

（19）**exaggerating** 夸大其词的

6.6.6 媒体类题材句子写作练习

（1）广告当然是非常有用的，它告诉我们该买什么，在哪里买，怎样买，但它也有负面影响，尤其是通过改变我们认为在生活中重要的东西。

（2）我们被广告包围，很容易就相信我们的生活就是买东西。这种广泛的消费主义一方面可以说服我们购买许多我们并不真正需要的东西，另一方面也让我们对自己拥有的东西不那么满意，而对那些无法负担的商品孜孜以求。

（3）印刷新闻的黄金时代已经一去不返，但没有什么比得上手拿报纸的感觉了。毕竟，获知新闻的不同方式之间并不相互排斥，每一种新闻媒体都以自己的方式产生作用。

（4）大多数儿童广告有误导性，对那些年龄尚小、还不能区分想象和现实的孩子来说危害真的很大。

（5）根据新闻业的研究报告，本地电视台是大多数人的第一新闻渠道，数字化新闻排在第二位，其次是电台，最后是报纸。

（6）尽管报纸逐渐被电视、广播和最近的互联网取代，但对大多数人来说，报纸仍然是主要的信息来源，尤其是在政治和商业领域，可能会在未来的一段时间内保持这种状态。这主要是因为，传统上大家认为报纸是最严肃的新闻渠道，而相比之下，电视、广播和网络通常被视为娱乐媒体。

（7）在我看来，虽然通过互联网获取新闻可能存在某些问题，特别是在其准确性和客观性方面，但它的速度和规模是我们永远不能忽视的优势。在当今这个强调速度的社会中，转向互联网获取新闻也许是一个不可逆转的趋势，也是一个积极的发展。既然如此，政府应该制定规则来提高在线新闻的质量，我们也应该擦亮眼睛，学会辨别真实新闻和假新闻。

（8）诚然，许多广告都在推广消费者并不真正需要的产品。通过创造对消费的欲望，这些广告促使消费者不去思索购买原因便去购买尽可能多的产品。

（9）总之，人们发现，许多广告都试图通过鼓励我们购买他们的产品来刺激我们隐藏的消费欲望，但我确实相信广告的主要目的是提供信息。毕竟，是否购买要由消费者自己来决定。

（10）只需简单点击几下，他们就可以立即把自己的消息发送给世界各地的朋友，而不必像以往写信那样等上几天。

参考答案

（1）Advertising is, of course, very useful, informing us about what to buy, where to buy and how to buy, but it also has negative effects, especially by transforming what we regard as important in our life.

（2）Surrounded by advertisements, we can easily be led to a belief that our life is all about buying things. This widespread consumerism can persuade us into buying many things we do not really need on the one hand, and make us less content with what we have and crave hopelessly for things we cannot afford on the other.

（3）The golden days of print news are gone forever, but nothing is like the feeling of physically holding a newspaper in hands. After all, the different ways of learning about news are not mutually exclusive. Each news media outlet is effective in its own way.

（4）Since most children advertisements are misleading, they are really harmful to children who are not old enough to tell the difference between imagination and reality.

（5）According to research reports on the news industry, local television is the number one source of news for the majority of people, with digital news coming in second, followed by the radio, and then by the newspaper.

（6）Even though gradually being eclipsed by TV, radio, and more recently the Internet, newspapers are still the dominant source of information for most people, especially in the political and business landscape, and likely to remain in that position for some time to come. This is mainly because newspapers are traditionally thought of as the most serious news channel compared with TV, radio, and the Internet, which are often treated as media of entertainment.

（7）In my view, though getting news through the Internet may involve certain problems, especially in terms of its accuracy and objectivity, its speed and scale are the advantages that we can never ignore. Turning to the Internet for news is perhaps an irreversible trend and a positive development as well today in a society that emphasizes speed. That said, the government should make rules to improve the quality of online news, and we should also sharpen our eyes and learn to discern real news from fake ones.

（8）Admittedly, a lot of advertisements are promoting products that consumers do not really need. By creating the desire to consume, these advertisements push consumers to purchase as many products as possible without thinking why they should.

（9）To conclude, it has been found that many advertisements are trying to stimulate our hidden consumption desire by encouraging us to buy their products, but I do believe the main aim of advertisements is to inform. After all, it is up to the consumers themselves to decide whether to buy or not.

（10）With a few simple clicks, they can send news about themselves to all their friends around the globe instantly instead of having had to wait a few days when they used to write letters.

6.7 工作类

工作类话题考点主要包括：工作时间、工作地点的选择；工作的价值及满意度；领导应该由年轻人还是老年人担任？从事同一件工作，还是换多种工作？大学毕业生增加会导致失业率增加吗？招聘时应该看重哪些因素？

母题： Some people say job satisfaction is more important than job security, while others believe that having a permanent job is better than enjoying the job. Discuss both views and give your own opinion.（141025）

子题1：An increasing number of people are changing careers during the working life. What do you think are the reasons? Do you think it is a positive or a negative trend?（140621）

子题2：After high school, some people go to college to prepare themselves for future career, while others go to the job market to increase their work experience. Discuss both views and give your own opinion.（130309）

子题3：It is a good thing for those in the senior management position to have much higher salaries than other workers in the same company or organisation. To what extent do you agree or disagree?（161029）

子题4：Nowadays, many employers think that social skills are as important as good qualifications for employing people. To what extent do you agree or disagree?（181110）

核心观点及表达

（1）人们需要工作养家糊口，但人们也期待从中获得满足感。

We need to work to make a living, but we also expect to derive satisfaction from our work.

（2）随着互联网的广泛使用，我们的工作和生活往往息息相关，因为很多人在家办公。

With the wide use of the Internet, our life and work are often inseparable, since many of us work from home.

（3）很多人为了挣更多钱而加班工作，其结果是陪伴家人的时间越来越少，反而降低了生活质量。

Many people work extra hours in order to make more money, only to find that they have less and less time for their families. As a result, the quality of their life is reduced rather than improved.

（4）经常更换工作可能有助于自我提升，但不稳定也可能导致生活不幸福。

Changing jobs frequently may help to perfect ourselves, but the instability may also lead to an unhappy life.

（5）招聘时看重什么取决于工作岗位的性质。

What should be valued in a job interview depends upon the nature of the position.

6.7.1 工作类题材参考词汇

（1）**demanding** 苛刻的；要求高的

（2）**productive** 有生产力的；高效率的

（3）**boost productivity** 提高生产力

（4）**mandatory** 强制的；要求的

（5）**job seekers** 求职的人

（6）**stay on the same job** 坚持做同一份工作

（7）**hop from one job to another** 从一份工作跳到另一份工作

（8）**versatile** 全能的

（9）**give sb a competitive edge** 给某人竞争优势

（10）**Jack of all trades and master of none** 什么都会但什么都不专的人

（11）**win-win situation** 双赢局面

（12）**competent** 胜任的

（13）**dress code** 着装标准 / 规范

（14）**individuality** 个性

（15）**soft skills** 软技能

（16）**qualifications** 资历

（17）**expertise** 专业知识

（18）**specialty** 专业

（19）**vacation** 假期

（20）**professional** 职业的

（21）**creative** 创新的

（22）**paid leave** 带薪休假

6.7.2 工作类题材句子写作练习

（1）虽然很多人认为老年人更富有经验和能力，但我想说，政府的一些重要职位也应开放给年轻人。

（2）年轻人比老年人更开放，更能接受新想法，更有可能以创新的方式解决问题，并把自己新颖的想法付诸行动，这可能会带来意想不到的好处。

（3）对于一些更基于经验的职位，老年人是更合适的人选，而对于其他需要更多激情而非经验的职位，年轻人可能比老年同行做得更好。

（4）到了退休年龄继续工作使得他们的大脑保持积极运转状态，这样，他们患上大脑疾病（比如老年痴呆症）的概率就会下降，老年人便有可能过上更有意义、更加健康的生活。

（5）有些人坚持认为忠于一个工作和地方是更好的选择，但我相信，改变工作和住址带来的消极影响与其好处相比是微不足道的。

（6）如果我们所说的"令人满意的职业生活"是指赚更多的钱，过上更充实的生活，那么，频繁地换工作是一个更好的选择……另一方面，如果将"令人满意的职业生活"理解为提供高度专业的服务，爬上公司的顶端，那么，最好确定职业道路并坚持下去……总之，频繁换工作和坚持一份工作都可能带来令人满意的职业生活，但什么是令人满意的职业生活因人而异。

（7）总之，雇主应该关注工作质量，但着装要求对职场而言是否有意义，这是一个只有雇主才能回答的问题。

（8）资历和软技能并不是相互排斥的，因为这两种东西在就业市场上同样重要。就工作而言，没有"非此即彼"的问题，因为答案必须是两者兼而有之。

（9）有良好的软技能，一个人能够和他/她的同事、客户和上级建立感情上的联系，因为在工作环境中，这样的人看起来更加轻松自如，因而也更有信心和效率。

（10）我们应该始终努力在工作和生活之间取得平衡，这样我们才能有足够的时间陪伴家庭。

（11）休假可以让员工换换节奏，使他们从"工作模式"中解脱出来，这样，当他们回到工作岗位时，就能做更多的事情。

（12）但是，如果一个人发现他所从事的工作没有意义或没有成就感，那么换工作对公司和员工来说都是双赢的策略。

（13）因此，说一个人拥有享受带薪年假的合法权利是一回事，说假期总是能提高生产力却是另一回事。

（14）综上所述，传统思想认为，老年求职者与年轻求职者相比，没有那么"精通技术"。然而，在我看来，"技术"和"老"并不是对立的，而且雇主做决定时，考虑的因素远不止技术技能这一项。

（15）鉴于自动化有可能让人们失去工作，人们应该为未来能继续就业做准备，学习沟通技巧，同时与新技术保持同步。

（16）因此，除了掌握不断进步的技术，优秀的人际交往技巧可能在未来的就业市场中起着至关重要的作用，认识到这一点也很重要。

（17）因此，仅凭学历并不足以取得成功。事实上，我们已经看到许多高学历的人因为这样或那样的原因彻底失败。因此，我的结论是，即使它们之间存在着某种正相关，学历也不一定会带来成功的生活，因为除学历之外，成功还涉及其他许多因素。

参考答案

（1）While it is assumed by many that the elderly people are more experienced and capable, I would say that some important government positions should also be open to young people.

（2）Young people who are more open-minded and receptive to new ideas than the elderly, are more likely to solve problems in an innovative way, and to put their original ideas into action, which may lead to unexpected benefits.

（3）For some positions which are more experience-based, the elderly people are more suitable candidates, yet for other positions which require more passionate spirit than experience, young people can perhaps do a better job than their elderly counterparts.

（4）Continuing to work even after their retirement age enables their brains to keep functioning actively so that they may suffer fewer chances of brain disorders such as Alzheimer's disease, which makes it possible for elder people to lead a more meaningful and healthier life.

（5）Some may insist that being loyal to one job and place be a better choice, but I believe that when compared with the benefits, the negative effects that change of jobs and accommodating locations may cause are insignificant.

（6）If by "a satisfying career life," we mean earning more money and leading a fuller life, then, frequently changing jobs is a better choice. ... On the other hand, if "a satisfying career life" is understood as providing the highly professional service and climbing to the top of the corporate ladder, then, it is advisable to decide on a career path and keep to it. ... To conclude, both changing jobs frequently and keeping to one job permanently may lead to a satisfying career life, but what constitutes a satisfying career life varies from one individual to another.

（7）To conclude, employers should be concerned about the quality at work, but whether a dress code makes sense for a workplace is a question only employers can answer.

（8）Qualifications and soft skills are not mutually exclusive as both of them are important in the job market. As far as employability is concerned, there is no "either/or" question since the answer must necessarily be both.

（9）With good soft skills, one is able to connect emotionally with his/her co-workers, clients and superiors as one will look and feel more comfortable and therefore more confident and efficient in job situations.

（10）We should always try to strike a balance between our work and life so that we will be able to have enough time for our families.

（11）Vacations could give workers a change of pace and a break from the "work mode", so that they can be expected to do more when they get back to work.

（12）However, if a person does not find the job he is doing interesting or fulfilling, then quitting the job and getting a new one could be a win-win strategy both for the companies and employees.

（13）So it is one thing to say that one has the legal right to enjoy a paid annual leave, but it is quite another to conclude that vacations can always boost productivity.

（14）To sum up, conventional thinking assumes that older job-seekers are relatively not as "tech-savvy" as younger ones. To my mind, however, "tech" and "old" are not opposites, and there are far more factors than technology skills to consider in the decision of the employers.

（15）Given the potential of automation to put jobs at risk, people should prepare to remain employable in the future by learning communication skills while keeping steps with new technologies.

（16）In addition to working with the ever advancing technologies, therefore, it is important to realize that excellent interpersonal skills may play a vital role in future job market.

（17）Therefore, educational qualifications alone are not sufficient for success. In fact, we have seen many people with high educational qualifications whose life turns out to be a complete failure for one reason or another. My conclusion, then, is that, even though there is a certain positive co-relation between them, educational qualifications do not necessarily lead to a successful life, for success involves many factors other than educational qualifications.

6.8 环境与生态类

该题材考点及分布如下：

环境问题的解决办法，例如：自然资源消耗过快的后果和解决办法；缺乏可循环利用材料的原因和解决办法；为什么个人保护环境很重要，我们应该怎样做？保护环境是否只能靠将其上升到国际的高度？国际社会应不应该马上减少化石燃油的使用？个人力量能否改善环境？

环境与资源，例如：保护动物上是否使用过多资源？核能是不是满足日益增长的能源需求的更好选择？随意使用水资源还是应该严格限制水资源的使用？人们在偏僻地区寻找资源的利弊。

人类活动对环境的影响，例如：科学家和游客去南极的优缺点；消除人类活动对动植物的消极影响是否已经太迟，还是说能找到有效的方法改善现状？由发展引起的污染和环境问题是否无法避免？

其他，例如：应不应该严格控制人为的噪声？廉价航空让人们更自由地向远方旅行因而应该受到鼓励，还是说它会导致环境问题因而应该不再发展？多种点树还是多建点房子？

6.8.1 能源和能源危机

母题：The natural resources such as oil, forests and fresh water are being consumed at an alarming rate. What problems does it cause? How can we solve these problems?（150801）

子题 1：The international community should act immediately to reduce the use of fossil fuels. To what extent do you agree or disagree?（140125）

子题 2：With the increasing demand for energy sources of oil and gas, people should look for sources of oil and gas in remote and untouched places. Do the advantages outweigh the disadvantages of damaging such areas?（220625）

核心观点及表达

自然资源消耗过快已经给我们这一代人及未来子孙（the future generations）造成了严峻威胁（a huge threat），但是减少使用化石燃料（fossil fuels）会极大影响我们现有的生活水准。因此，解决能源危机的最好办法是开发新型的替代能源（alternative energy），如太阳能（solar energy）、水能（water energy）、风能（wind power）等。看以下观点及表达：

（1）半个多世纪以来，对自然资源的过度消耗一直是和公众利益相关、受公众关注的问题，但这个问题从未真正得到解决。

The excessive consumption of natural resources has been a subject of public interest and concern for over half a century, but the problem has never really been addressed.

（2）为了降低自然资源的消耗率，首先要做的就是鼓励人们过低碳生活……此外，政府有必要投资开发使用环保替代能源的技术，如太阳能和水能。

To reduce the consumption rate of natural resources, the first and foremost thing to do is to encourage people to live a low-carbon life. ... Besides, it is necessary that governments invest in developing technologies to use environmentally friendly alternative energy such as solar and water energy.

（3）然而，目前的能源需求使任何国家都难以大幅减少对化石燃料的使用。因此，问题也许不在于如何减少化石燃料的使用，而在于如何减少对化石燃料的过度依赖。一个解决办法是开发更多的可再生能源，如太阳能和风能。

Nevertheless, the current energy demand makes it hard for any country to significantly decrease its use of fossil fuels. So the issue is perhaps not how to reduce the use of fossil fuels, but how to reduce the heavy reliance on them. One solution is to develop more renewable sources of energy such as solar and wind power.

6.8.2 环境和生态保护

母题：Pollution and environmental problems are caused by the development of a country. Therefore, someone believes that it cannot be avoided. To what extent do you agree or disagree?（101023）

子题1：The key to solving environmental problems is simple: the present generation must have a less comfortable life for the sake of future generations. To what extent do you agree or disagree?（220822）

子题2：Some people think that instead of preventing climate change, we need to find a way to live with it. Do you agree or disagree?（160716）

子题3：Human activities have negative effects on plants and animal species. Some people think that it is too late to do anything about this problem. Other people believe that effective measures can be taken to improve this situation. Discuss both views and give your opinion.（200808）

子题4：Some people think that environmental problems are too big for individuals to solve. Others, however, believe that these problems cannot be solved if individuals do not take actions. Discuss both views and give your own opinion.（201114）

子题5：Some people think that climate change could have a negative effect on business. Other people think that climate change could create more business opportunities. Discuss both views and give your own opinion.（200111）

核心观点及表达

人类文明已经在很大程度上破坏了生态环境，但亡羊补牢，犹未为晚，我们需要从自身出发，保护环境。保护生态并不仅仅是利他行为，更是为了保护人类自身，因为一旦生态遭到破坏，人类就不复生存，因此无论花费多少去保护生态都是值得的。看下面观点及表达：

（1）人类文明已经在很大程度上摧毁了许多动植物的栖息地，让一些物种完全从地球上消失了。这种情形让很多人产生了强烈的悲观情绪，认为现在已经太晚而无法挽回了。虽然人们有足够的理由来坚持这个悲观的观点，但我还是乐观地相信，通过采取有效措施，我们可以挽救这种情形。

Human civilisation has largely destroyed the habitats of many plants and animals so that some species have disappeared entirely from the earth. This situation has caused a strong sense of pessimism among many people that it is already too late for us to do anything about it. Though people have enough reasons to hold this pessimistic view, I am still positive that we can save the situation by taking effective measures.

（2）当然，更重要的是应该教育人们，使其明白，如果整个生态系统被破坏，人类自身也会受害。我们的存在非常依赖于周围的动植物，一旦它们死亡，我们也会死亡。如果这种理念深入人心，那么人类就会尽力保持他们与自然世界的和谐关系。

More important is, of course, that people should be educated to understand that human beings themselves would suffer if the entire ecological system were destroyed. Our own existence is so dependent on the plants and animals around us that if they die, we will die, too. With this understanding deep in mind, human beings will try their best to maintain a harmonious relationship with the natural world.

（3）当然，如果我们选择过不那么舒适的生活，环境会有很大的改善。然而，问题是，很少有人愿意放弃已经拥有的东西。一旦习惯了现代生活方式的便利，他们会发现很难没有它们，即使是为了环境。此外，在世界上大多数国家，如果强迫人们采纳父母和祖父母的更简单的生活方式，那就太过分了。

To be sure, the environment would be considerably improved if we chose to live a less comfortable life. The issue is, however, that few people would like to give up what they have already had. Once having been used to the conveniences of modern lifestyle, they may find it hard to go without them, even if for the sake of the environment. Furthermore, in most countries in the world, it would be too much to force people to adopt the simpler lifestyles of their parents and grand-parents.

（4）事实上，如果每个人在日常生活中做正确的事情，那么像全球变暖或海平面上升之类的重大环境问题可能根本就不会发生。

Indeed, if everyone does the right thing in everyday life, such big environ-mental problems as global warming or sea level rise may not have happened at all.

6.8.3 动物

母题： Humans should not use animals as sources of food and clothing. To what extent do you agree or disagree with this view? （120428）

子题1：It is a natural process of animal species to become extinct (e.g. di-nosaurs, dodos, etc.). There is no reason why people should stop this from hap-pening. Do you agree or disagree? （190914）

子题2：Some people think that it is acceptable to use animals in medical research for the benefit of human beings, while other people argue that it is wrong. Discuss both views and give your opinion. （130418）

核心观点及表达

我们要保护野生动物（wild animals），尤其是那些濒临灭绝的（endangered / on the verge of extinction）动物，因为动物多样性（diversity）不仅有关生活乐趣，更是关涉自然平衡（balance）。我们总体上反对随意将动物用于医学实验，因为这既残忍（cruel），也侵害了动物权利（violate the animal rights），但是在某些情况下，动物实验也是必要的，因为动物实验推动的医学技术，既有利于人类，也有利于动物自身长期繁衍。我们强烈反对将兽皮用作装饰性的衣物，这种为了人类自身虚荣而剥夺野生动物生命的行为，纯粹是谋杀（murder）；我们也强烈反对食用野生动物，这既残忍也会破坏生态平衡。

但人类为了自身营养需要，可以食用某些家畜，因为从某种意义上说，人类能健康繁衍下去，这些家畜的种族才能够繁衍下去。看以下观点及表达：

（1）现在，一些人认为我们不再有必要使用动物制成的食物、衣服和药品，因为现代科技已经找到了它们的代替品。

Nowadays, some people think it unnecessary for us to use animals for food, clothing, or medicines any longer because modern technology has found the substitutes for them.

（2）猎杀珍稀动物将会导致其灭绝，影响生物多样性，这对动物和自然界之间的平衡十分有害。

Hunting rare animals will lead to their extinction and affect the bio-diversity, which is detrimental to the balance between nature and animal.

（3）为了人类的健康，我们需要平衡饮食结构，既要有肉类也要有蔬菜。

For the sake of human beings' health, we need to balance our diet so that it contains both meat and vegetables.

（4）总的来说，尽管现代科技使我们没有必要通过杀害野生动物来远离饥饿和寒冷，但为了自身的利益，我们仍十分需要动物产品。

To sum up, while modern technology has made it quite unnecessary for us to kill wild animals to keep us from hunger and cold, we are still in great need of animal products for our own benefits.

6.8.4 环境与生态类题材参考词汇

（1）**energy crisis** 能源危机

（2）**animal species** 动物物种

（3）**resource scarcity** 资源匮乏

（4）**become extinct** 灭绝

（5）**panic** 恐慌

（6）**catalyst for conflict** 冲突的催化剂

（7）**destructive blow** 毁灭性的打击

（8）**future generations** 后代

（9）**environmentally friendly** 对环境友好的

（10）**minimalist style** 极简风格

（11）**excessive use of...** 过度使用……

（12）**low carbon life** 低碳生活

（13）**traffic congestion** 交通堵塞

（14）**economical** 省钱的；经济的

（15）**exhaust gas emission** 尾气排放

（16）**sustainable development** 可持续发展

（17）**exploit** 开发；利用

（18）**ecosystem** 生态系统

（19）**disposable** 一次性的（使用完即丢弃的）

（20）**pollute** 污染

（21）**consume** 消费

（22）**consumerism** 消费主义

（23）**shortage** 短缺

（24）**recycle** 循环利用

（25）**ecological balance** 生态平衡

（26）**environmentalist** 环保主义者

（27）**deforestation** 砍伐森林

（28）**renewable energy** 可再生能源

（29）**alternative energy** 替代能源

（30）**chain reaction** 连锁反应

（31）**greenhouse effect** 温室效应

（32）**global warming** 全球变暖

（33）**environmentally friendly energy** 对环境友好的能源

（34）**climate change** 气候变化

（35）**solar energy** 太阳能

（36）**wind power** 风能

（37）**water power** 水能

（38）**endangered species** 濒危物种

（39）**on the verge of extinction** 处于灭绝边缘

（40）**companion** 伴侣

（41）**harmonious** 和谐的

（42）**co-exist** 共存

（43）**animal rights** 动物权益

（44）**artificial** 人造的

（45）**food chain** 食物链

（46）**habitat** （动物）栖息地

（47）**migrate** 迁徙

（48）**migratory birds** 候鸟

（49）**sea-level rise** 海平面上升

6.8.5 环境与生态类题材句子写作练习

（1）我们的社会是一个消费主义和一次性物品充斥的社会，其中一个严重的问题是塑料垃圾的污染，从农村到城市到海洋，随处可见，给人类和非人类都带来了大量的问题。

（2）为了保护环境免受塑料垃圾影响，我相信首先要做的是鼓励人们采取简单的生活方式，尽量减少使用塑料产品。如果人们不过多使用塑料产品，塑料垃圾将大大减少。

（3）尽管要彻底消耗完自然资源还有很长时间，但现在惊人的消耗速度已经在世界各国中引起了相当大的恐慌。其结果是，所有国家都会参与争夺资源的战争，迟早会把地球拖入地狱般的战场。

（4）为了降低自然资源的消耗率，首先要做的事情是鼓励人们过低碳生活。例如，人们可以乘坐地铁和公共汽车等公共交通工具来通勤，而不是自己开车。他们应该明白这一点，即使低碳生活现在不能使自己受益，也将使他们的子孙受益。

（5）当然，如果我们选择过不那么舒适的生活，环境会有很大的改善。事实上，我们目前的生活方式在很大程度上是造成许多环境问题的原因。随着越来越多的汽车进入家庭，汽车排放的废气已经成为空气污染甚至全球变暖的罪魁祸首。

（6）众所周知，有些环境问题确实太重大，个人无法解决。例如，面对全球变暖等气候变化问题，个人几乎无能为力，只有政府有能力应对。

（7）事实上，如果每个人在日常生活中做正确的事情，那么像全球变暖或海平面上升之类的重大环境问题可能根本就不会发生。

（8）气候变化不是好事，但目前我认为人们不应该采取代价昂贵的措施去阻止它，相反，我认为我们应该设法去适应它。

（9）我们的存在非常依赖于周围的动植物，一旦它们死亡，我们也会死亡。如果这种理念深入人心，那么人类就会尽力保持他们与自然世界的和谐关系。

（10）虽然在自然保护和人类发展中取得平衡殊为不易，但我们总能找到出路。采取行动改变现状永远都不晚，因为只要我们行动早1分钟，我们活下来的机会就可增加1%。

（11）然而，如果一个城市连住房都不够，却要求人们去植树，这是很愚蠢的。毫无疑问，植树对环境更有利，但是找个遮风避雨的地方对所有人来说一直都是需要首先考虑的。

（12）我认为，政府禁止拥有或使用汽车是不现实的，因为汽车在我们的日常生活中已经非常重要，但是我们也不能忽视汽车给环境带来的负面影响。我觉得，为了走出这个困境，我们有两个选择：其一，发展汽车科技，制造出较少耗费燃料的汽车；其二，鼓励汽车拥有者尽可能使用公共交通。

（13）在很大程度上，保护当地环境的责任必须由政府和个人共同承担。政府应该让公众知道，环境保护是每个人的事。否则，看似众人负责就会变成无人负责。

（14）每年要花费数十亿美元来保护濒临灭绝的野生动物。对许多人来说，这是不可想象的，因为数以百万计的人仍在遭受粮食短缺的痛苦，而且由于贫困，更多的人被剥夺了接受教育的机会。

（15）总之，各国有理由减少石油、煤炭和天然气等化石燃料的消耗，但更现实的是，它们应该找到方法来产生和储存替代能源，如太阳能和风能。

（16）如今，新技术的发展速度比以往任何时候都快，其后果是，产品很快就被更新更好的版本取代，而用户必须购买这些版本才能享受其新功能。

参考答案

（1）Ours is a consumerist and throw-away society, in which one serious problem is the pollution of plastic waste that can be seen everywhere from the countryside to the cities and to the oceans, causing tons of problems for humans and non-humans alike.

（2）In order to save the environment from plastic waste, I believe the first and foremost thing to do is encourage people to live a simple lifestyle and minimize the use of plastic products. Plastic waste will be greatly reduced if people do not use plastic products that much.

（3）Even though it will take a long time for natural resources to be completely consumed, the alarming rate at which they are consumed nowadays has caused considerable panic among countries in the world. The result is that all countries are involved in the war for resources which will sooner or later drag the earth into a hellish battlefield.

（4）To reduce the consumption rate of natural resources, the first and foremost thing to do is encourage people to live a low-carbon life. For instance, instead of driving their own cars, people can commute by taking public transportation such as metro and buses. They should be made to understand that even if the low-carbon life does not benefit themselves now, it will benefit their children or grandchildren.

（5）To be sure, the environment would be considerably improved if we chose to live a less comfortable life. As a matter of fact, our present lifestyle is largely responsible for many environmental problems. As more and more cars find their way into households, the exhaust gas emissions from cars have become the major culprit in the air pollution and even global warming.

（6）As we all know, there are some environmental problems which are indeed too big for individuals to solve. For example, in face of climate change such as global warming, individuals can do very little and only the governments have the ability to deal with it.

（7）Indeed, if everyone does the right thing in everyday life, such big environmental problems as global warming or sea level rise may not have happened at all.

（8）Climate change is not a good thing, but for the time being, I do not think we should take expensive and costly measures to prevent it. Rather, I believe we should find a way to live with it.

（9）Our own existence is so dependent on the plants and animals around us that if they die, we will die, too. With this understanding deep in mind, human beings will try their best to maintain a harmonious relationship with the natural world.

（10）Though keeping balance between the natural protection and human development is never easy, we can always find a way out. It is never too late to take measures to change the situation, for if we take actions one minute earlier, our chance of survival will increase by one percent.

（11）Yet, it would be stupid to ask people to plant trees in a city or town where they cannot find enough houses to live in. Planting trees is undoubtedly more environmentally friendly, but getting a shelter to keep off rain and snow is always the top concern for all people.

（12）In my view, it is unrealistic for the government to put a ban on the car ownership or use since the cars have been so important in our daily life, yet we cannot overlook the negative effects they have on the environment. To get out of this dilemma, to my mind, there are two options, the first being to develop car technology and produce cars that burn less fuel and the second, encouraging car owners to use public transportation whenever possible.

（13）To a great extent, the responsibility for looking after the local environment must be shared by the government and individuals. The government should let the public know that environmental protection is everybody's business. Otherwise, what seems to be everybody's business would become nobody's business.

（14）It would cost billions of dollars a year to preserve endangered wild animals. This is unthinkable for many, since millions of people are still suffering from food shortage and even more deprived of the opportunity to receive education because of poverty.

（15）In conclusion, there are reasons why countries should reduce their consumption of fossil fuels such as oil, coal and natural gas, but more realistically, they should find ways of generating and storing alternative sources such as solar and wind energy.

（16）Now new technologies are developing at a much faster speed than ever before, the consequence of which is that a product is quick to be replaced by its newer and better versions, and then the users have to buy them in order to enjoy their new features.

6.9 科技类

科技类题材主要涉及如下内容：科技发展的利弊；太空旅行的利弊；现代通信发展的利弊；外星人探索的利弊；科技和艺术的关系。

母题：Scientific progress always influences our daily life. Do you think these influences are positive or negative? Give your reasons.（130323）

子题 1：Some people think that robots are very important for humans' future development. Others, however, think that robots are a dangerous invention that could have negative effects on society. Discuss both views and give your opinion.（110108）

子题 2：Research has shown that nowadays business meetings and training are increasingly taking place online. Do you think the advantages outweigh the disadvantages on this matter?（190706）

子题 3：Air travel is only beneficial to the richest people. To what extent do you agree or disagree?（100206）

子题 4：In today's world of advanced science and technology, we still greatly value our artists and writers. What can arts tell us about life that science and technology can not?（200912）

核心观点及表达

科技带来的好处：让我们的生活更方便；提高我们的工作效率，替我们做危险的工作；让我们得以超越日常生活，体验以前不可想象的世界。

科技带来的坏处：发展科技需要大量人力物力，而这些资源可以用来改善人们更为迫切的日常生活；科技发展有可能让我们失业；科技可能让人与人之间的关系变得疏远；人类可能被科技所控制。

看以下观点及表达：

（1）科技不总是天使，相反，有些情况下，科技也许会变成魔鬼，让我们的生活相当痛苦和复杂。

Technology is not always an angel, rather, in some cases, it may turn out to be a devil making our life rather miserable and complicated.

（2）科技到底是扰你还是帮你，取决于你的生活态度。

Whether technology is a nuisance or a help depends upon your attitude towards life.

（3）这些人普遍更怀疑外太空是否存在其他生命，因此他们认为试图寻找这些生命纯粹是在浪费金钱，尤其是当这个星球尚有很多现实问题急需解决的时候。

They are generally more doubtful about the existence of other beings in the outer space, so they believe it is just a huge waste of money to try to look for them, especially when there still are so many practical problems on this planet crying for solution.

（4）今天，我们都相信知识就在指尖，因为所有知识似乎都已经电子化存储，很容易在网上获取。

Today we all believe that knowledge is just at the tip of our fingers because all knowledge seems to have been stored electronically and is easily accessible on the Internet.

（5）网络的空间几乎是无限的，因此可以存储世界上所有的知识，我们没有太大必要花那么多钱修建实体图书馆了。

Owing to its virtually unlimited capacity, the Internet can store all knowledge in the world. This makes it quite unnecessary for us to spend that much money constructing the brick-and-mortar libraries.

（6）在家工作的人经常发现他们变得不那么有效率，因为分心的事更多，并且同事压力变小了，而住在离办公室很远的地方意味着他们与同事和上级面对面交流的机会减少，这会导致业务受损，甚至丧失晋升的机会。

People who work from home often find they become less efficient because they have more distractions and less peer pressure and living far away from office means less opportunity to have face-to-face interactions with their colleagues and superiors, which may result in the loss of business and even chances of promotion.

6.9.1 科技类题材参考词汇

（1）**breakthrough** 突破

（2）**advance** 进展，发展

（3）**advanced** 高级的

（4）**potential** 潜在的

（5）**available** 可以得到的；可以使用的

（6）**enhance/promote** 提升

（7）**productivity** 生产力

（8）**beneficial** 有益的

（9）**positive** 积极的

（10）**negative** 消极的

（11）**double-edged sword** 双刃剑

（12）**labour-consuming** 费力的

（13）**time-consuming** 耗时的

（14）**labour-intensive industry** 劳动密集型产业

（15）**information explosion** 信息爆炸

（16）**virtual classroom** 虚拟教室

（17）**online fraud** 网络诈骗

（18）**artificial intelligence (AI)** 人工智能

（19）**modern communication technologies** 现代通信技术

6.9.2 科技类题材句子写作练习

（1）在他们看来，浪费在探索外星人的钱应该用来帮助那些无力支付大学费用的孩子，以及那些生病却无法享有良好医疗服务的人。

（2）人们应该有权选择在哪里工作和居住，尤其是新技术和交通已经使这成为可能。

（3）随着科学技术的进步，越来越多的发明出现在我们的生活和工作中，其中机器人可能是最有争议的发明。有些人担心机器人可能会破坏社会，而另一些人则认为机器人对我们的生活和工作有好处。

（4）正如许多科幻小说中所展示的，许多人担心，迟早有一天，机器人会做独立决定并自行行动，从而伤害甚至征服人类世界。

（5）我们必须承认，机器人确实可以减轻各种日常家务劳动，并为我们完成最困难和最危险的任务，从而给我们带来很多好处。我相信机器人绝对

可以使人类世界成为一个更好的生活场所。

（6）作为唯一的智能人，我们生活在这个宇宙已经太久，很多人觉得找到外星球的兄弟姐妹这个想法很有吸引力。

（7）正如很多科学家猜想的那样，地球终将死去并消失在黑洞，因此我们需要外星兄弟姐妹了解我们，这样，当那一天终于来临时，我们未来的子孙也不会消亡。

（8）总之，互联网是像电力、太阳能和原子弹一样伟大的发明，但如果我们必须选择人类历史上"最重要的发明"，我愿意投票给语言。

（9）因此，科技到底是扰你还是帮你，取决于你的生活态度。如果你喜欢过一种像隐士梭罗那般简单的生活，你最好远离任何科技，因为科技会让你的生活方式复杂化，甚至毁了你的生活方式；但是如果你的志向是成为一名成功的商人或从政的人，那么你就必须紧跟科技的最新发展，因为科技一定能帮助你实现梦想。

（10）我认为，现代数字化通信方式无疑是积极的进步，因为它们可以帮助我们解决很多问题。剩下要做的是充分利用它们，同时降低它们可能带来的风险。

参考答案

（1）The money squandered on the exploration of aliens, they argue, should go to helping children who are unable to pay for their college education and those who are ill but cannot enjoy decent medical services.

（2）People should be given the right to choose where to work and live, especially when the new technology and transport have already made this possible.

（3）With the advances of science and technology, more and more inventions have come into our life and work, among which robots might be the most debatable one. Some people worry that robots may destroy society, while others think they are good for our life and work.

（4）As is shown in many science fiction, many people are worried that the time will arrive sooner or later when robots make independent decisions and act on their own, and as a result, harm or even conquer the human world.

（5）What we have to admit is that robots do bring a lot of benefits by relieving us of various daily house chores and performing the most difficult and dangerous tasks for us. I believe robots can absolutely make human world a better place to live in.

（6）Having been living in the universe as the only intelligent being for too long, many people find it a very attractive idea to reach their brothers and sisters from other planets.

（7）As the Earth will surely die and disappear into the Black Hole as many scientists have speculated, we need to be known by our siblings on other planets so that when that day eventually does come, our future grand, grand children will not perish.

（8）To conclude, the Internet is an invention as great as electricity, solar energy, and the atomic bomb, but if we have to choose "the most important invention" in human history, I would give my vote to language.

（9）So whether technology is a nuisance or a help depends upon your attitude towards life. If you enjoy the simple life of a hermit like Thoreau, you'd better stay away from any technology, for it will complicate or even ruin your lifestyle. But if your ambition is to become a successful businessman or politician, you must keep abreast of the latest development of technology, for it will surely help you realize your dream.

（10）In my opinion, modern digital means of communication are certainly a positive development because they can help to solve many of our problems. What remains to be done is that we make the best use of them and reduce the risks they may involve.

6.10 语言文化类

语言文化题材在雅思考试中属于低频话题，平均每年出现 2—3 次。考点及分布如下：

网络对传统文化的冲击，例如：人们能从网上获取信息，因此博物馆是否不那么重要了？是否可以通过书籍、电影和网络而不需亲临其境去了解其他文化？

旅游和传统文化，例如：很多当地人不喜欢当地的旅游景点和博物馆的原因，以及可以采取哪些措施吸引他们？旅行者如何学习其他文化和传统？为什么有些旅行者对这些文化和传统没有兴趣？

对文化的不同看法，例如：对某些文化重视老年人而某些文化重视年轻人的看法；越来越多不同文化和民族的人共同生活的原因以及利弊；传统文化是否有必要保存？

语言保护，例如：出钱保护即将消失的语言是政府应该做的还是只是在浪费钱？某些语言更多地被使用而其他语言更加少用，这一趋势是好是坏？

母题： Some people think governments should spend money on measures to save languages with few speakers from dying out completely. Others think this is a waste of financial resources. Discuss both views and give your own opinion.（201220）

子题1：The customs and traditional ways of behaviour are no longer relevant to the modern world. So they are not worth keeping any more. To what extent do you agree or disagree?（160910）

子题2：Some people think that cultural traditions will be destroyed when they are used as money-making machines aiming at tourists, other people believe that it is the only way to save such conditions in the world today. Discuss both sides and give your own opinions.（151219）

子题3：Differences between countries are becoming less evident recently. People can see the same films, brands, fashion, advertisements and TV channels. To what extent do disadvantages outweigh advantages?（160109）

子题4：Some people think it's necessary to travel abroad to learn about other countries. However, other people think that it is not necessary to travel abroad because all the information can be seen on TV and the Internet. Discuss both opinions and give your own opinion.（160804）

核心观点及表达

传统文化需要保存（preserve），因为传统文化中包含了一个民族的历史和记忆。文化往往需要身临其境才能为人所真正理解。多元文化共存可以相互学习，消除偏见（remove prejudices），使世界更加和谐（more harmonious）。文化更多作用于一个人的精神世界，不能全部以实用性来衡量。应该保护语言多样性，因为一种语言消失，意味着一种文化消失。看以下观点及表达：

（1）总之，政府确实应该花钱来拯救那些少数语言，使其免于消亡，因为通过保护这些语言，政府不仅在保护文化，而且在促进民族团结与和谐。语言就是一块宝石，当然需要不惜任何代价来保存。

To sum up, governments should indeed spend money saving those languages of few speakers from dying out because by protecting these languages, the governments are not just protecting the culture, but also promoting the national unity and harmony. A language is such a gem that certainly needs preservation at any cost.

（2）总之，虽然许多传统习俗和做法看似与现代世界无关，但它们并不像有些人说的那样毫无用处。相反，它们很重要，帮助我们理解历史，塑造身份。在这个意义上，它们当然值得保存。

To conclude, though many traditional customs and ways of behaviour may appear irrelevant to our modern world, they are not useless as some people claim. On the contrary, they are important to help us understand our history and shape our identity. In this sense, they are certainly worth keeping.

（3）当来自不同文化背景的人一起互动，他们能相互分享和学习，能更好地理解彼此。比起让人们相互隔离，这样绝对更有利于世界的和平稳定。

When people from different cultural backgrounds interact together, they can share, learn from each other, and they can understand each other better. This is definitely more favourable for the world's stability and peace than making people live separately.

（4）总之，虽然一些大众媒体，如书籍、电影和互联网，在文化交流中起着不可或缺的作用，但为了亲身体验独特的文化和习俗（可能与我们从大众传媒中获得的不一样），旅行更具重要性。

To conclude, although some mass media, such as books, films and the Internet, play a necessary role in cultural exchange, travelling is of greater importance in order for us to personally experience the distinctive cultures and customs which may diverge from what we have acquired from mass media.

6.10.1 语言文化类题材参考词汇

（1）**preserve** 保存；保护

（2）**ancestor** 祖先

（3）**cultural heritage** 文化遗产

（4）**cultural diversity** 文化多样性

（5）**cultural conflict** 文化冲突

（6）**tradition** 传统

（7）**cultural relics/sites** 文化遗迹

（8）**custom** 习俗

（9）**pass down from generation to generation** 代代相传

（10）**conservative** 保守的

（11）**cling to old ideas** 守旧

（12）**cultural artifact** 文物

6.10.2 语言文化类题材句子写作练习

（1）首先，从书籍、电影和互联网获得的文化信息只显示某群人的意见或态度，这些人在某些情况下可能传达错误的信息，导致文化误解和歧视。例如，在一些书籍或电影中，英国人往往显得有些保守、世故、冷漠，但我们到英国旅行时，会发现那里的很多人很友好、外向，有时甚至有点疯狂。因此，旅行让我们有机会打破大众传媒创造的固定形象。

（2）尽管多元文化社会可能会引起一些问题，但我还是认为这样的社会更具有吸引力。当来自不同文化背景的人一起互动，他们能相互分享和学习，能更好地理解彼此。比起让人们相互隔离，这样绝对更有利于世界的和平稳定。

（3）我认为传统文化应该得到保留，即使它与我们的日常生活无关，它在我们理解历史、形成身份过程中却至关重要。

（4）那就是为什么作为中国大学生，我反对庆祝圣诞节而不反对庆祝春节，反对庆祝情人节而不反对庆祝七夕节。的确，我们一直都是从传统文化中发现自己的。

（5）考虑到博物馆为子孙后代保存一个国家的集体记忆，博物馆公共资金的重要性再怎么强调也不为过。

（6）只有当博物馆不能获得足够的政府支持时，私人领域的捐赠才是必要的，而且只有在不妨碍博物馆的公众功能的条件下才能接受。

（7）事实上，一个国家越尊重它的文化多样性，它的人民就越幸福、越团结。从这个意义上说，保护少数语言也有利于国家的经济发展。

参考答案

（1）Firstly, cultural items acquired from books, movies or the Internet only show the opinions or attitudes of a certain group of people, who in some circumstances may convey wrong messages and cause cultural misunderstanding and discrimination. For example, in some books or movies British people often appear a bit conservative, sophisticated and indifferent, but when we travel to the United Kingdom, we'll find many people there friendly, outgoing and sometimes even a little crazy. So travel grants us the opportunity to break the stereotypes created by mass media.

（2）Despite the problems that may arise from the multi-cultural societies, I still think such societies are more attractive. When people from different cultural backgrounds interact together, they can share, they can learn from each other, and they can understand each other better. This is definitely more favourable for the world's stability and peace than making people live separately.

（3）I believe the traditional culture should be preserved, for it plays a pivotal role in our understanding of history and formation of identity even if it is irrelevant to our daily life.

（4）That's why I, a Chinese university student, do not like the idea of celebrating Christmas instead of the Spring Festival, or Valentine's Day instead of the Double Seventh day. Indeed, it is in the traditional culture that we can always find ourselves.

（5）Considering that museums preserve a country's collective memory for future generations, the importance of public funding in museums could never be overestimated.

（6）Donations from the private sector are necessary only when the museum cannot obtain sufficient support from the government and are acceptable only on the condition that they do not interfere with the public roles of the museum.

（7）As a matter of fact, the more a country respects its cultural diversity, the happier and more united its people are. In this sense, protecting the minority languages is also conducive to the economic development of the country.

6.11 旅游类

"旅游类"话题在雅思考试中时有出现。主要涉及如下内容：

出国旅游的利弊，例如：出国旅游使人变得更加偏见的原因和解决办法；有些人觉得出国旅游不好，怎么改变他们的思想？出国旅游越来越容易是好是坏？人们会不会从国际旅游中受益？人们如何提高对其他国家的理解？

旅游收费问题，例如：外国人参观旅游景点时是否应该比本国人支付更多的费用？文化景点旅游收费是否有利于保护这些文化景点？

旅游者素质问题，例如：不能成为一个负责任的旅游者的原因和解决方法。

母题：Today, more and more developing countries are expanding tourist industry. Why is it the case? Do you regard it as positive or negative?（100617）

子题1：International travel makes people more prejudiced rather than broad-minded. Why? How to improve their understanding of countries they visit?（150813）

子题2：Foreign tourists abroad should be charged more than local people when visiting the local historical and cultural tourist attractions. To what extent do you agree or disagree?（110430）

子题3：It is not necessary to travel to other places to learn about culture and people, because people can learn from books, films or the Internet. To what extent do you agree or disagree?（171005）

核心观点及表达

支持旅游的理由：旅游可以让人放松身心（make us relax both physically and mentally）；可以让我们接触不同的文化，开阔视野（open up / broaden our vision）；可以让我们接触自然，激发我们热爱自然（inspire our love for nature）；旅游业能带来收入（generate income）。

反对旅游的理由：旅游浪费时间和金钱（a huge waste of time and money），尤其是节假日旅游；旅游往往污染环境（pollute the environment），破坏生态（ruin the ecosystem）；在网络时代，可以通过网络坐在家里看世界，不需要旅游了（travel is no longer necessary when we can sit at home in front of the computer and tour around the world）。

请看下面的观点及表达：

（1）在过去的几十年里，旅游业在世界各地蓬勃发展，这给当地环境和文化的保护带来了巨大的压力。

Tourism has boomed throughout the world in the past few decades, and this puts tremendous amount of pressure on the protection of local environment and culture.

（2）当越来越多的游客涌入这些地方，这些地方被污染，乃至最终毁灭只是一个时间问题。

When more and more tourists come rushing into these places, it will only be a matter of time when these places are contaminated and eventually ruined.

（3）人们应该得到足够的教育，认识到负责任的游客对环境的重要性。

People should be given enough education and made to realize how important the responsible tourists are to the environment.

（4）旅游通常被认为是了解其他国家或地区传统习俗和异域文化的良好途径。

Travel is commonly perceived as a good approach to learn about the traditional customs and exotic cultures of other countries or regions.

（5）从书籍、电影和互联网获得的文化信息只显示某群人的意见或态度，这些人在某些情况下可能传达错误的信息，导致文化误解和歧视。

Cultural items acquired from books, movies or the Internet only show the opinions or attitudes of a certain group of people, who in some circumstances may convey wrong messages and cause cultural misunderstanding and discrimination.

（6）虽然一些大众媒体，如书籍、电影和互联网，在文化交流中起着不可或缺的作用，但为了亲身体验独特的文化和习俗（可能与我们从大众传媒中获得的不一样），旅行更具重要性。

Although some mass media, such as books, films amd the Internet, play an indispensable role in cultural exchange, travelling is of greater importance in order for us to personally experience the distinctive cultures and customs which may diverge from what we have acquired from mass media.

6.11.1 旅游类题材参考词汇

（1）**expand** 拓展

（2）**culture shock** 文化冲击

（3）**explore** 探索；研究

（4）**conflict** 冲突

（5）**mutual understanding** 相互理解

（6）**tourist attraction** 旅游景点

（7）**prejudice** 偏见

（8）**overcome the prejudices** 克服偏见

（9）**exotic** 异族的；异域风情的

（10）**first-hand experience** 一手经验

（11）**refreshing** 提神的

6.11.2 旅游类题材句子写作练习

（1）人类的天性就是对自己熟悉的事物没有好奇心。因为大多数当地人对自己城市的历史和文化很熟悉，所以他们更喜欢去参观其他城市的博物馆和历史遗迹，这样他们可以体验不同的习俗和文化。

（2）游客和本地居民之间互动日益增加的自然结果是，他们能够更好地相互理解，并对文化差异更加宽容。

（3）因此，我的观点是，随着越来越多的人发现访问其他国家更容易、更实惠，游客和东道国都将受益。虽然这可能会引起一些问题，但总体上这是一个积极的趋势。

（4）有些人怀疑旅游的必要性，因为我们可以通过阅读书籍、看电影和上网来了解其他文化，这似乎更便宜、更省时、更容易获得。

（5）在旅行中，我们可以与当地人互动，深入体验他们的生活，如他们的饮食习惯、风土人情和独特的行为方式，同时在相互交流过程中将自己的文化传递给当地人。

（6）通过创造就业机会和带来收入，旅游业可以迅速提高当地人民的生活水平。我相信这就是发展中国家扩大其旅游业的动机所在。

（7）在我看来，旅游业对发展中国家是有利的，但它们不应该仅依赖旅游业。为了实现更可持续的增长，发展中国家必须找到提高其科学和教育水平的方法。

（8）为了金钱而对文化传统过度开发可能会破坏它们。游客们来自世界各地，他们有不同的品味，因此他们可能会要求文化传统适应他们的口味。比如，一个中国游客在参观埃文河畔斯特拉特福时可能期望莎士比亚的戏剧以一种和中国戏曲相似的风格呈现，以便他能更好地理解它们。

（9）尽管作为营利机器，有些传统可能会被破坏，但我坚信对游客开放它们是更好的选择。首先，不管多么古老、多么经典的文化传统都必须与时俱进。来自世界各地的游客可能会为之带来新的视角和灵感，从而增添新的生命力。同时，旅游开放带来的收益可以有效地减轻政府的财政负担。

参考答案

（1）Such is human nature that people do not have curiosity about what they are familiar with. As most local people are familiar with the history and culture of their own city, they prefer to pay a visit to the museums and historical sites in other cities, so that they can experience different customs and cultures.

（2）The natural result of the increasing interactions between the visitors and the native people is that they can understand each other better and grow more tolerant to their cultural differences.

（3）My view, therefore, is that as more people find it easier and more affordable to visit other countries, both the visitors and the host countries will benefit. Though it may cause some problems, it is generally a positive trend.

（4）Some people are suspicious of the necessity of travel as we can learn about other cultures by reading books, watching films and browsing the Internet, which seem cheaper, less time-consuming and more accessible.

（5）During travel, we can interact with local people and deeply experience their life, such as their dietary habit, peculiar customs and unique manners, while at the same time spreading our own culture to those local people in the process of mutual exchanges.

（6）Tourism can quickly improve the living standard of the local people by creating job opportunities and bringing income for them. I believe this explains the motivation of developing countries to expand their tourism industry.

（7）In my view, tourism is beneficial to developing countries, but they should not just rely on tourism. For a more sustainable growth, developing countries must find ways to uplift their scientific and education level.

（8）Over-exploitation of cultural traditions for money may really destroy them. As tourists come from different parts of the world, they have various kinds of taste, so they may want the cultural traditions to be adapted to their tastes. For instance, a Chinese visitor to Stratford-on-Avon may expect Shakespeare's plays to be performed in a style similar to Chinese plays so that he can understand them.

（9）While as money-making machines, some traditional cultures may suffer, I firmly believe opening them to tourists is a better choice. Firstly, cultural traditions, however ancient and classical, must change with time. Tourists from the world may bring new perspectives and inspirations, and thus new life to these traditions. At the same time, opening-to-tourism can also bring about profits which can effectively relieve government of the financial burden.

6.12 交通类

雅思考试中的交通类题材，均涉及解决交通拥堵或交通安全问题的措施，比如：高峰时期征收拥堵税能有效减轻城市交通拥挤吗？城市无车日可以解决城市交通问题吗？免费提供全天候公共交通服务是解决城市交通堵塞的最好办法吗？提高最小驾驶年龄有助于提高交通安全吗？

母题：The best way to solve traffic congestion is to provide free public transport 24 hours a day, 7 days a week. Do you agree or disagree?（171121）

子题 1：The best way to deal with the problem related to the traffic and transportation is to encourage people to live in cities rather than in suburbs and countryside. To what extent do you agree or disagree?（211120）

子题 2：Some countries spend a lot of money making it easier to use bicycles in cities. Why? Is it the best way to solve the transport problems?（220217）

核心观点及表达

试题中提出的解决交通堵塞和安全问题的方法都有一定道理，但也会带来问题，因此可以提出更好的解决方法。请看以下观点及表达：

（1）毫无疑问，汽车和汽油价格的上涨会阻止人们拥有和使用自己的汽车，这肯定有助于解决交通拥堵问题，并使大城市更加清洁。

Undoubtedly, the increased price of cars and petrol will discourage people from owning and using their own cars, which will surely contribute to solving the traffic congestion and making big cities cleaner.

（2）然而，提高汽车和汽油的价格可能会造成意想不到的问题。

However, increasing the price of cars and petrol may cause unexpected problems.

（3）因此，要处理交通和污染问题，只提高汽车和汽油的价格是不够的。对政府来说最好的做法也许是投资更多来修建新路，并引入更严格的交通法规和规章。

Therefore, to deal with the traffic and pollution problems, increasing the price of cars and petrol is not enough. The best thing for the government to do is perhaps make more investments on the construction of new roads, and introduce stricter traffic laws, rules and regulations.

（4）虽然现在大多数城市都有相当发达的交通系统，比如公共汽车和地铁，但它们容易变得非常拥挤，尤其是在上下班高峰期。

Though most cities today have fairly advanced transportation systems like the bus and metro, they tend to be extremely crowded, especially in rush hours.

6.12.1 交通类题材参考词汇

（1）**means of transport** 交通工具

（2）**public transportation** 公共交通

（3）**traffic congestion** 交通堵塞

（4）**traffic rules** 交通规则

（5）**pedestrian** 行人

（6）**commuter** 通勤人员

（7）**city dweller** 城市居民

（8）**rush hour** （上下班）交通高峰期

（9）**abide by** 遵守

（10）**alleviate** 减轻

（11）**road safety** 道路安全

6.12.2 交通类题材句子写作练习

（1）当街道上林立着各种商店时，将有无数的车辆来来往往；当购物者涌入商店时，他们将会发出城市居民难以忍受的噪音。

（2）毫无疑问，实行免费公共交通后，有些人会选择少开自己的车，这样有助于缓解交通，但是我不确定这种做法对交通有多大帮助。

（3）如果驾驶员和行人更加小心地遵守交通规则，也能有效缓解交通堵塞问题。

（4）最近，有人建议提高汽车和汽油的价格，以对付日益严重的交通和污染问题。虽然我认为这个建议在一定程度上是有帮助的，但它远非最好的解决方案。

（5）汽车和汽油的价格上涨，使普通收入的人不开车，但对那些真正富有的人则没有丝毫影响。这样，我们将面临一个尴尬的局面：富人享受汽车的奢华，而其他大多数人则不得不在拥挤的公共交通受苦。

（6）免费公共交通是个好主意，但在实践中并不总是好的。为了交通和环境，政府不应该为免费公共交通提供资金，而应该建设更多的道路，并引入更严格的汽车拥有和使用的规则。

（7）当公共交通免费的时候，许多本来会留在家里的人可能选择乘坐免费的交通工具出行。这将大大削弱路上私家车数量减少带来的好处，甚至可能使公共交通系统瘫痪，尤其是在交通高峰期。

（8）许多交通事故的发生是因为司机不擅长驾驶，而且他们不熟悉交通规则，所以每年参加考试将会提高他们的驾驶技能，并提醒他们遵守道路规则。因此，道路交通将变得更安全。

参考答案

（1）When the street is lined with all kinds of stores, there will be numerous vehicles coming and going, and when shoppers rush into these stores, they will make noise intolerable to the city dwellers.

（2）Undoubtedly, with the introduction of free public transport, some people may choose to drive less of their own cars, and this will be helpful to ease the traffic, though I doubt the extent to which this can help with the traffic.

（3）If the drivers and pedestrians were more careful in abiding by the traffic rules, the traffic problem could also be effectively alleviated.

（4）Recently, it is proposed that the price of cars and petrol be increased to combat the growing traffic and pollution problems. While I think this proposal may be helpful to a certain extent, it is far from the best solution.

（5）As the higher price of cars and petrol prevents people with average income from driving their cars, it can do nothing to those really wealthy. Then we will face an awkward situation where the rich people enjoy the luxury of cars while most others have to suffer in the crowded public transport.

（6）Free public transport is a good idea, but it is not always good in practice. For the sake of traffic and environment, the government, rather than providing funds for free public transport, should construct more roads and introduce stricter rules of car ownership and use.

（7）When public transport goes free, many people who otherwise would stay at home may choose to go out by taking the free transport. This will greatly undo the benefits afforded by the reduced number of private cars on road and may even paralyze the public transport system, especially during the rush hours.

（8）As many traffic accidents take place because drivers are not good at driving, and that they are not familiar with the traffic rules, taking the test each year will improve their driving skills and remind them of abiding by road rules. As a result, the road transport will become safer.

6.13 体育类

雅思考试中，体育类题材通常涉及如下问题：专业体育还是大众体育？是否应该禁止危险体育活动？团队活动还是个体活动？身体条件还是心态更重要？

母题： Some countries achieve international sporting success by building specialized facilities to train top athletes instead of providing sports facilities that everyone can use. Do you think it is a positive or negative development？（140710）

子题 1： Extreme sports such as sky diving and skiing are very dangerous and should be banned. To what extent do you agree or disagree with this view?

（201128）

子题 2：Some people think that the Olympic Games is an exciting event and can bring nations together. Others, however, think that it is a waste of money. Discuss both views and give your own opinion.（220716）

子题 3：Some people argue that the fittest and strongest individuals and teams can achieve the greatest success in sports. But other people think the success is much related to the mental attitude. Discuss both views and give your opinion.（190105）

子题 4：The best way to teach children to cooperate is through team sports at school. To what extent do you agree or disagree?（151114）

核心观点及表达

（1）总之，在个人或团队的比赛中，身体实现心中所想。这两样因素并不相互排斥，因为两者都是实现最大成功所必需的。

To sum up, in individual or team competitions, the body achieves what the mind believes. The two are not mutually exclusive as both are needed to make the greatest success happen.

（2）在我看来，运动是一种休闲活动，但只有在个人层面才是如此，因为在社会上，它远远不止于此。这就是为什么世界各国政府建造体育设施或训练顶级运动员参加国际体育比赛来鼓励其人民从事体育运动。

In my view, sport is a leisure activity, but it is true only at the individual level, because socially it is far more than that. That is exactly why all governments across the world would encourage their people to engage in sport by building sport facilities for them or training the top athletes to compete in international sport games.

（3）总之，极限运动必然会涉及一些风险，就此而言，所有运动都一样，但政府应该做的是防范这些风险，而不是阻止人们参加这些运动。

In conclusion, extreme sports, and all sports for that matter, may necessarily involve some risks, but what the government should do is take precautions against these risks, rather than prevent people from taking part in these sports.

（4）奥运会通常持续 20 天，各国的运动员，不论种族和国籍，不仅在同一舞台上比赛，而且相互交流和结识朋友。

In the Olympic Games, which usually lasts about 20 days, sportsmen from all countries, regardless of race and nationality, not only compete on the same stage, but also communicate and make friends with each other.

6.13.1 体育类题材参考词汇

（1）**team sport** 团队运动

（2）**solo sport** 个人运动

（3）**sportsmanship** 体育精神

（4）**leisure** 休闲

（5）**participant** 参与者

（6）**extreme sport** 极限运动

（7）**bungee jumping** 蹦极

（8）**sport facilities** 体育设施

6.13.2 体育类题材句子写作练习

（1）像足球和篮球这样的团体活动是否比像游泳和网球这样的单人活动更有益于我们？我认为，答案取决于我们讨论的是什么样的益处。

（2）单人活动可以培养我们自力更生和我们的责任感。这是因为在这些活动中，成功完全是个人努力的问题，我们将不得不学会依靠自己，学会面对我们的决定和行动产生的后果。

（3）当人们从事任何类型的运动，即使是简单的慢跑，他们也能够找到一种方法，摆脱正常的生活节奏，并感觉到一种变化在身上发生，而这正是"休闲"的意思。

（4）就像一个经常进行体育锻炼的人可能更善于处理生活中的问题，如果一个社区（或一个国家）的人民热爱运动，这个社区（或国家）也可能更和谐。

（5）最近一次事故发生在一名 20 岁的女孩身上，她在高空跳伞时死亡，在公众中引起了大量讨论，讨论这项运动是否应该被允许。

（6）禁止这些运动肯定会让那些愿意从这些运动中获得刺激甚至灵感的极限运动爱好者失望。事实上，人们参加极限运动，最重要的原因之一是这些运动可以刷新他们的生活感受，鼓励他们迎接生活中的挑战。

（7）总之，极限运动必然涉及一些风险，就此而言，所有运动都一样，但政府应该做的是防范这些风险，而不是阻止人们参加这些运动。

（8）由于技术的发展，当代城市居民已经从手工劳作中解脱出来，他们突然发现自己有大量空闲时间，但是数世纪前修建的城镇没有足够的娱乐和体育设施供他们使用。

（9）总之，花钱鼓励孩子们参加基层体育活动，同时在精英阶层培养有竞争力的选手，这么做不会让一个国家失去任何东西。两项投资都是有价值的，政府唯一要做的就是平衡它们。

（10）虽然团体活动可以教会人们许多重要的生活技能，但是人们也可以从个体活动中获得许多其他的基本技能。因为很难说哪组技能更重要，我们无法就哪种活动更有助于发展生活技能达成共识。

（11）尽管人们越来越关注科学、数学、语言和社会研究等核心学科，但学校有必要不去削减体育、艺术和音乐课程，因为它们能极大提高孩子们在核心学科中的表现，并能极大提高孩子们的整体健康和情感幸福。

（12）要想在体育运动中取得最大的成功，首先需要身体的能力。然而，在力量和健康相当的时候，胜败最终由正确的心态来决定。

（13）有正确心态的人知道，即使输了一场比赛，他们也绝不放弃，只要他们不放弃，就能东山再起。

参考答案

（1）Are activities played as a team like football and basketball more beneficial to us than those played individually like swimming and tennis? The answer, I think, depends on what kind of benefits we are talking about.

（2）Activities that are played alone can develop our sense of self-reliance and responsibility. This is because in such activities, success is entirely a matter of personal efforts, and we will have to learn to rely on ourselves and face the consequences of our own decisions and action.

（3）While they engage in sport of any sort, even simple as jogging, people will be able to find a way to get out of the normal rhythm of their life, and feel a change taking place in them. And this is exactly what "leisure" is supposed to mean.

（4）Just as an individual who does regular physical exercise may be better at dealing with the problems in his life, a community (or a country) may also be more harmonious if its people love sport.

（5）The recent accident that occurred to a 20-year-old girl who died in sky diving has aroused a lot of discussion in public about whether this sport should be allowed or not.

（6）To ban these sports would definitely disappoint the extreme sports lovers who are willing to draw excitement and even inspirations from these sports. In fact, one of the most important reasons why people participate in extreme sports is that these sports can refresh their feeling of life and encourage them to meet the challenges in life.

（7）In conclusion, extreme sports, and all sports for that matter, may necessarily involve some risks, but what the government should do is take precautions against these risks, rather than prevent people from taking part in these sports.

（8）Cities and towns built centuries ago do not have enough entertainment and sports facilities available to contemporary city dwellers who, relieved of the manual labor by the technological advances, suddenly find they have a great amount of free time.

（9）To conclude, a country has nothing to lose when spending money encouraging young children to be engaged in physical activities at grass-roots levels as well as preparing competitors at elite levels. Both investments are valuable, and the only thing for the government to do is balance them out.

（10）Though group activities can teach people many important life skills, people can gain a lot of other essential skills from solo activities as well. As it is hard to tell which set of skills is more important, we cannot reach the consensus of opinion as to which kind of activities is more useful in the development of our life skills.

（11）Despite the increasing focus on the core academic subjects like science, mathematics, language, and social studies, it is necessary for schools not to cut programs in PE, art and music, for they contribute a great deal to the enhanced achievement in the core academic subjects as well as the overall health and emotional well-being of young children.

（12）To achieve the greatest success in sports, first it requires physical ability. However, strength and fitness being equal, it is ultimately the right mental attitude that makes a big difference.

（13）People with the right mental attitude understand that they will never give up even when they have lost a game, and that they will make a comeback as long as they do not quit.

第七章　2010—2022 年雅思复现率最高的 20 篇作文解析及范文

　　众所周知，雅思作文是题库命题方式，考试题目重复出现并不令人惊讶。读者可能很关心，在过去 10 多年中，复现频率最高的题目到底是哪些呢？笔者统计了 2010—2022 年复现频率最高的 20 个题目，分别是：

　　（1）Children today find it difficult to concentrate on or pay attention to school. What are the reasons? How can we solve this problem? 孩子们现在很难专心学习的原因及解决办法

　　（2）Employers should give their staff at least a 4-week holiday a year to make employees better at their jobs. To what extent do you agree or disagree? 一年四周假期能让员工工作得更好吗？

　　（3）With the increasing demand for energy sources of oil and gas, people should look for sources of oil and gas in remote and untouched places. Do the advantages outweigh the disadvantages of damaging such areas? 应该去偏远地区开发能源吗？

　　（4）In many countries women are allowed to take maternity leave from their jobs during the first month after the birth of their baby. Do advantages outweigh disadvantages? 女性休产假的利弊

　　（5）City dwellers seldom socialize with their neighbours today and the sense of community has been lost. Why has this happened and how to solve this problem? 城市居民很少和邻居交流的原因及解决办法

　　（6）In many parts of the world children and teenagers are committing more crimes. What are the causes? How should these young criminals be punished? 青少年犯罪增加的原因？该如何惩罚他们？

（7）In some cultures the old age is highly valued, while in some cultures youth is highly valued. Discuss both views and give your own opinion. 不同文化对老年人和青年人的重视程度不同

（8）It is believed by many that those people who read for pleasure are better in imagination and language skills than those who prefer to watch TV. To what extent do you agree or disagree? 闲读比看电视更有利于培养想象力和语言能力吗？

（9）Many young people in the workforce today change their jobs or careers every few years. What do you think are the reasons for this? Do the advantages of this outweigh its disadvantages? 年轻人经常换工作的原因及利弊

（10）More and more people buy and use their own cars. Do you think the advantages of this trend for individuals outweigh its disadvantages for environment? 私家车对个人和环境的利弊

（11）More and more people want to buy famous brands with clothes, cars and other items. What are the reasons behind this? Do you think it is a positive or negative development? 越来越多的人喜欢名牌的原因及利弊

（12）Online shopping is now replacing shopping in store. Do you think it is a positive or negative development? 网上商店取代实体商店的利弊

（13）Art classes like painting and drawing are important to students' development and should be made compulsory in high school. To what extent do you agree or disagree? 艺术课应该成为高中必修课吗？

（14）Nowadays many people use social media every day to keep in touch with others and news events. Do you think the advantages outweigh the disadvantages? 用社交媒体联络和看新闻的利弊

（15）Some people think living in big cities is bad for people's health. To what extent do you agree or disagree? 生活在大城市不利于身体健康吗？

（16）The restoration of old buildings in major cities in the world costs numerous governments' expenditure. This money should be used in new housing and road development. To what extent do you agree or disagree? 在大城市重修老建筑不如建新房子和新道路吗？

（17）Young people are leaving their homes from rural areas to study or work in the cities. What are the reasons? Do advantages of this development outweigh its disadvantages? 年轻人离开乡村到城市去工作和学习的原因及利弊

（18）In some countries, the criminal trials are shown on TV and the general public can watch them. Do the advantages outweigh the disadvantages? 电视播放审判现场的利弊

（19）The best way for the government to solve the traffic congestion is to provide free public transport 24 hours a day, 7 days a week. To what extent do you agree or disagree? 解决交通堵塞问题的最好办法是政府免费提供全天候公交服务吗？

（20）Some people think that cultural traditions will be destroyed when they are used as money-making machines aiming at tourists, other people believe that it is the only way to save such conditions in the world today. Discuss both sides and give your own opinion. 将文化传统用于赚钱会毁掉这些传统还是挽救它们？

7.1 孩子们现在很难专心学习的原因及解决办法

题目

Children today find it difficult to concentrate on or pay attention to school. What are the reasons? How can we solve this problem?

解析

本题为报告类题目，关键词是 children，需要贴近孩子们的情况来讨论他们为什么不能专心学习。孩子们不能专心学习的原因无非就是内因和外因。外因很容易找到，比如网络游戏的干扰，电视节目的干扰，或者课本太枯燥无聊等；内因也容易发现，比如现在有很多人宣传不需要读书也能成功，这样孩子们就没有学习的动力了。解决办法也很简单、直接，比如控制孩子们使用网络的时间，同时告诉孩子们读书的重要性（即使不能挣钱，也能让生活更充实和幸福）。

范文讲解

Students ought to spend most of their time on the school work, but nowadays

it is not uncommon that students are simply not able to **put their heart to** study. There could be two reasons why this happens.

本段是开头段，使用开门见山法，直接提出现象，但在用词上并不照抄题目，而是体现出变化。最后一句提出有两个原因。

（1）**it is not uncommon that...** ……并不罕见

（2）**put one's heart to...** 集中精力做……

First, today students are surrounded by so many **distractions** that they gradually find that learning is too boring and uninteresting. While students two decades ago had nearly no choice but sit in the classroom and read books, students today have easy and fast **access** to the Internet, on which they can do almost all things. For instance, they can play computer games, watch videos, search for any information they need, and chat with their friends, **to mention just a few**. So, having been used to this kind of "easy" online life, many young people simply cannot put their heart into the more serious and **consuming** school work.

本段分析学生不喜欢学习的第一个理由，也是**浅层次的外部理由**，即学生因为外部干扰（尤其是互联网的干扰）而讨厌学习。本段的论证思路是：学生发现学习无趣 — 比较今天的学生和 20 年前的学生 — 举例今天的学生可以在网上做什么 — 上网的结果就是不愿意再认真学习。

（1）**distraction** 干扰

（2）**access** 进入；使用

（3）**to mention/name just a few** 如此等等；诸如此类

（4）**consuming** 耗费的（比如 time-consuming 耗时的；energy-consuming 耗能量的）

Another important **factor** that affects the students' attitude towards their school work is that a good education seems not as important as before. For quite a long time, receiving a good education was the only way for young people to get a **decent** job and earn a high salary. But now, this is **apparently** not the case any more. Influenced by business stars like Bill Gates and Steve Jobs, many young people now begin to believe that one's success does not have much to do with the education he/she receives. The students, therefore, are not **motivated** enough to focus on their learning.

本段讨论学生不喜欢学习的另一个原因，也是**更深层次的内在原因**，即学生不再相信只有受教育才能成功。本段的论证思路是：主题句 — 以前的情况 — 现在的情况 — 结论。在论证的过程中，顺便举出一些例子，可以展示考生的知识面，同时增强作文的语义密度。

（1）**factor** 因素

（2）**decent** 体面的

（3）**apparently** 表面看地；明显地

（4）**motivated** 有动力的

As education of the young is so important to the future of the world, we ought to find ways out of this **embarrassing** situation. For example, schools and parents should work together to **set limits on** the time children spend on-line. The Internet is a good great invention, yet **obsession with** it will certainly reduce the time that should have been put to more serious work. Besides, young people should be made to understand that life is not just about making money, but about having rich and colourful experience. Education is the best **gateway** to that **rewarding** life.

本段针对前面两个原因提出**解决方案**，论证思路是：需要找到解决办法 — 第一个办法是限制学生上网时间 — 过多上网的坏处 — 第二个办法是让学生明白读书的意义是拥有更丰富精彩的生活。

（1）**embarrassing** 令人尴尬的

（2）**set limits on...** 给……设限

（3）**obsession (with)** 沉迷（于……）

（4）**gateway** 途径

（5）**rewarding** 有回报的；有价值的

参考译文

学生应该将大部分时间花在学习上，但今天很常见的是学生根本无法专心学习。发生这种现象可能有两个理由。

首先，今天的学生被很多诱惑包围着，他们慢慢发现学习太过单调无趣。20年前的学生几无选择，只能坐在教室读书，而今天的学生可以又快又方便地进入因特网，在这里他们几乎什么事情都可以完成。比如，可以玩电脑游戏、看电影、查询需要的信息、和朋友聊天，诸如此类。因此，习惯这种"容易的"

网上生活后，很多年轻人根本无法把心思放到更严肃、更费精力的学业上。

另外一个影响学生学习态度的重要因素是，良好的教育似乎不像以往那么重要了。在很长一段时间内，接受好的教育是年轻人获得好工作、挣高工资的唯一路径，但是现在显然不再是那样了。受比尔·盖茨、史蒂夫·乔布斯这些商界明星的影响，很多年轻人现在开始相信，一个人的成功与他／她所受的教育并无多大关系，因此，这些学生就没有足够的动力来专心学习了。

年轻人的教育对世界的未来至关重要，因此我们应该找到办法走出这个尴尬的困境。比如，学校和父母应该合作，给孩子上网的时间设限。因特网是伟大的发明，然而沉迷于此必将减少用于更严肃的学业上的时间。此外，还应该让年轻人明白，生活不仅仅是挣钱，还在于拥有丰富精彩的体验，而教育是抵达那种有价值的生活的最佳通路。

7.2 一年四周假期能让员工工作得更好吗？

题目

Employers should give their staff at least a 4-week holiday a year to make employees better at their jobs. To what extent do you agree or disagree?

解析

本题实际是一个"手段—目的"类题目。手段是老板给员工一年至少四周假期，目的是让他们工作得更好。"手段—目的"类作文的标准答题方式是，先承认手段有一定效果，再提出该手段存在的问题，继而提出需要找到更好的办法。就本题而言，先讨论给员工放假的好处：长假能够让员工调整身体、享受家庭团聚；员工可以利用长假学习新技能；假期体现了公司对员工的关心，让员工感受到关爱。这样，员工回来后就能更加精力充沛，精神愉悦地工作。然后指出长假可能存在的问题：很多员工变得更懒，工作效率反而下降。最后提出其他办法：提高员工工作效率的最佳办法不是放假，而是鼓励他们多运动，健康生活，同时提供再培训的机会。

范文讲解

Countries around the world **vary** when it comes to the issue of how many vacation days employees should enjoy, though **typically** the annual leave lasts four weeks. **In theory** the 4-week holidays will make staff better at their work, but opinions differ **in practice**.

　　本段开门见山提出年假的话题，然后提出观点：理论上年假有助于工作人员提升效率，但实际上意见不一。

　　（1）**vary** 与……不同

　　（2）**typically** 一般地；典型地

　　（3）**in theory** 理论上

　　（4）**in practice** 实际上

Evidence has shown that taking an annual leave is good not only for workers but also for their bosses. To begin with, **it should come as no surprise to any one** (even the most **demanding** CEO) **that** a well-rested worker is healthier and more **productive**. Vacations could give workers a change of pace and a break from the "work mode", so that they can be expected to do more when they get back to work. Meanwhile, the **mandatory** four weeks off given to employees would be good for employers because the increased productivity of their employees will surely bring more profits, at least in theory.

　　本段讨论休年假的**好处**，涉及两个方面：对员工来说，休假可以提高效率；对老板来说，效率的提高就意味着更多利润。本段采取的是说理的论证方法，用 to begin with 和 meanwhile 列举了两个原因。

　　（1）**it should come as no surprise to any one that...** 任何人都不应感到奇怪……

　　（2）**demanding** 苛刻的；要求高的

　　（3）**productive** 有生产力的；高效率的

　　（4）**mandatory** 强制的；要求的

In practice, however, the expected increase in workers' **productivity** after holidays does not always **translate into** reality. **More often than not**, being away from work for as long as 4 weeks could put one at a disadvantage and decrease one's productivity. There will be a period of time for adjustment when one is less motivated right after being back from vacations. So **it is one thing to** say that one has the legal right to enjoy a **paid annual leave**, **but it is quite another** to conclude that vacations can always **boost productivity**. **As the saying goes**, "Too much work, too much vacation, too much of any one thing is unsound."

本段讨论休年假带来的**坏处**：不一定能提高员工生产力（同样采用说理的方式），并用俗语当作证据。值得一提的是，雅思作文中虽然并不明确反对使用俗语，但一定要使用恰当。最好使用英文中的俗语，汉语俗语翻译过去，通常难令人满意。

（1）**productivity** 生产力

（2）**translate into...** 变成……；转化成……

（3）**more often than not** 通常；经常

（4）**it is one thing to do..., but it is (quite) another to do...** 做……是一回事，但做……（完全）是另一回事

（5）**paid (annual) leave** 带薪（年）假期

（6）**boost productivity** 提升生产力

（7）**as the saying goes...** 常言道……

To sum up, while **legally** employers should give their staff a paid annual leave **in the hope of** making them better at their jobs, **it does not necessarily mean** that by so doing there will be as many benefits as expected. To increase efficiency, the employers may have to find other ways.

本段为**结论**：强调休假不一定能带来预期的好处。

（1）**legally** 依法地；法律上地

（2）**in the hope of...** 旨在；意在

（3）**it does not necessarily mean...** 这不一定意味着……

参考译文

在员工应该享受多少假期的问题上，世界各国均不相同，尽管年假通常为四周。从理论上讲，四周的假期会使员工工作得更好，但在实践中意见不一致。

有证据表明，休年假不仅对员工有益，而且对他们的老板也有好处。首先，任何人（甚至是最苛刻的首席执行官）都不会感到惊讶，即一个充分休息的员工更健康，更有生产力。休假可以让员工换换节奏，使他们从"工作模式"中解脱出来，这样，当他们回到工作岗位时，就能做更多的事情。同时，强制性地让员工休四周假期，对雇主也有利，因为员工生产力的提高，肯定会带来更多利润，至少在理论上是这样。

然而，在实践中，假期后员工生产力的预期增长并不总是成为现实。通常情况下，离开工作长达四周，会让人处于不利地位，并降低生产力。一个人刚从假期归来，不如以前那么有动力，会需要一段时间来调整。因此，说一个人拥有享受带薪年假的合法权利是一回事，说假期总是能提高生产力却是另一回事。俗话说："工作太多，休假太多，凡事皆过犹不及。"

总而言之，虽然雇主应依法给予员工带薪年假，指望他们能更好地工作，但这并不一定意味着这样做会带来预期中的那么多好处。为了提升效率，雇主们得找到其他办法。

7.3 应该去偏远地区开发能源吗？

题目

With the increasing demand for energy sources of oil and gas, people should look for sources of oil and gas in remote and untouched places. Do the advantages outweigh the disadvantages of damaging such areas?

解析

本题关键词包括 look for sources of oil and gas、in remote and untouched places，话题是，去偏远地区开发能源会导致这些地区遭到破坏，这样做是否有利？

仔细分析会发现，本题实际暗含了一个"手段—目的"关系：为了解决能源短缺问题，需要去偏远地区寻找能源。此类题型的一般解题思路为：先承认手段的合理性，再讨论手段带来的问题，最后提出比该手段更好的选择。遵循这个思路，本题可以首先讨论在偏远地区开发能源的好处，比如可以解决能源稀缺的问题，而且在偏远地区开发，对人类生活的短期影响较小；然后讨论在偏远地区开发能源的坏处，比如浪费大量人力物力，而且破坏生态环境，对人类生活的长期影响非常可怕；最后提出自己的观点：为解决能源问题，到偏远地区开发能源弊大于利，人们应该做的是节约能源，同时开发替代能源，比如太阳能和水能等。

范文讲解

The shortage of energy such as oil and gas has become one of the most **urgent** problems in the modern world. To solve the problem, many suggest that we go to the remote and untouched places for more sources of energy. **To my mind**, however, this is a suggestion that may produce **mixed results**.

本段共三句，每句承担不同的功能。第一句提供背景，第二句是对题目观点的改写，第三句表达自己的观点。这是一个标准的雅思作文开头段。

（1）**urgent** 紧迫的；急迫的

（2）**to my mind** 在我看来；我认为

（3）**mixed results** 好坏参半的结果

Looking for new energy in **uninhabited** areas is a very attractive idea. Such places always **abound with** energy **desperately** needed by human race, thus attracting generations of people to take their chances. Besides, the exploration of energy in these areas has little immediate impact on the everyday life of people since it happens far away from where they live.

本段讨论在偏远地区开发能源的**好处**：这些地区富含能源，且远离人类居住地，不影响人类的正常生活。使用 besides 来连接这两个好处。

（1）**uninhabited** 无人居住的

（2）**abound with** 富含……

（3）**desperately** 极端地；极其地

But doing so may have a lot of problems as well. To start with, it would **involve tremendous** costs to find energy in these places. People will have to build houses, and roads to transport food and other daily necessities, all of which will be so expensive that the costs may far **exceed** the benefits. More importantly, looking for energy in the remote areas will almost certainly damage their natural environment. As plants and animals die out, the whole **ecosystem** will be **upset**, the **long-term effect** of which would be **devastating**.

本段讨论在偏远地区开发能源带来的**问题**，主要涉及成本巨大和环境破坏两个方面。本段共五个句子，除了第一句主题句之外，其余每两句讨论一个问题。

（1）**involve** 涉及；包含

（2）**tremendous** 巨大的

（3）**exceed** 超过

（4）**ecosystem** 生态系统

（5）**upset** 扰乱

（6）**long-term effect** 长远的效果

（7）**devastating** 摧毁性的

In my personal opinion, therefore, people should not be encouraged to invade the **unpopulated** areas in order to protect themselves from the energy crisis, for the **aftermath** would be unbearable. To solve the energy problem, people should first of all learn to save energy whenever possible, and then develop **alternative** energy sources such as solar energy and water energy.

本段在前面优劣讨论的基础上，提出自己的观点：不宜到偏远地区开发能源，因为其后果的确太严重；为了解决能源问题，应该提倡节约，同时开发新型能源技术。

（1）**unpopulated** 无人居住的

（2）**aftermath** （不好的）后果

（3）**alternative** 替换的

参考译文

石油和天然气等能源短缺已成为现代世界最紧迫的问题之一。为了解决这个问题，许多人建议我们去偏远和人迹未至的地方寻找更多的能源。然而，在我看来，这个做法可能产生好坏参半的结果。

在无人居住的地区寻找新能源是一个非常有吸引力的想法。这样的地方总是充满了人类急需的能源，从而吸引了一代代的人去冒险。此外，在这些地域的能源探索对人们的日常生活几乎没有直接影响，因为它发生在远离人类居住的地方。

但这样做可能会有很多问题。首先，在这些地方寻找能源将需要巨大的成本。人们将不得不建造房屋并修建道路来运输食物和其他生活必需品，所有这些东西都将非常昂贵，以至于成本可能远远超过收益。更重要的是，在偏远地区寻找能源，几乎肯定会破坏这些地区的自然环境。随着动植物的消亡，整个生态系统将会被破坏，其长期影响将是毁灭性的。

因此，在我个人看来，不应该鼓励人们为自己免受能源危机的影响而入侵这些无人居住的地区，因为后果将是无法承受的。为了解决能源问题，人们首先应该学会尽可能节约能源，然后开发太阳能和水能等替代能源。

7.4 女性休产假的利弊

题目

In many countries women are allowed to take maternity leave from their jobs during the first months after the birth of their baby. Does the advantages outweigh the disadvantages?

解析

本题的核心是，女性生完小孩后是否该休产假？那么，休产假和不休产假各有什么利弊呢？休产假的好处容易想到，包括有时间陪孩子，有时间缓解怀孕和生育期间的紧张和不安，另外就是恢复身体。但是，休产假也有问题。比如有些通常由女性承担的工作可能就缺人手了；再比如，休产假几个月期间，女性完全脱离工作岗位，返岗后有可能对工作变得生疏；同时，由于不工作，营养过好，如果不锻炼，女性很容易变得过胖。但是，权衡休产假的好处和坏处后，还是觉得女性应该享有这个权利，虽然她们在享受这个权力的时候，要注意降低这个权利可能对工作和身体带来的负面影响。本范文采用双边讨论结构，因为女性休产假明显有好处和坏处，如果用一边倒结构，无论讨论好处或者坏处，都不具有说服力。

范文讲解

It is a **customary practice** for most countries in the world to give women a few months of **maternity leave** after they **give birth to** the baby. To spend a few months away from work after giving birth, however, has disadvantages as well as advantages.

本段先改写题目中提出的现象，然后提出自己的观点：女性休产假有利有弊。

（1）**customary practice** 常规做法

（2）**maternity leave** 产假

（3）**give birth to** 生育；使诞生

To be sure, the newly-born baby is the one who benefits the most from the maternity leave. As we know, the first few months of the new life are always the most dangerous time, during which the baby faces many dangers, some quite unexpected, that may be **deadly**. Therefore, the **intensive care** from the mother is critical for the survival of the baby. I have just read a newspaper report which compares the infant **mortality rate** between the countries which practise maternity leave and those which do not and concludes that infant death rate in the former is 25% lower than that in the latter. Besides, taking a few months off her work after the baby is born is also a good way to **release the anxiety and stress** the mother must have experienced during her pregnancy, so she will more likely behave normally after going back to work.

本段论述产假的**好处**，分成以下两个方面：其一是新生儿面临危险，母亲的照顾保证新生儿的存活；其二是母亲能释放产期焦虑以便正常回归工作。两个方面之间用 besides 连接。

（1）**to be sure** 毫无疑问（= it is sure that; certainly）

（2）**deadly** 致死的

（3）**intensive care** 精细的护理

（4）**mortality rate** 死亡率

（5）**release the anxiety and stress** 释放焦虑和压力

Like anything else, maternity leave may also bring about some negative effects. In some **female-dominated** professions like nursing, the few months leave may cause a serious **shortage of labour**. And we have seen many women who cannot **perform** their job well as usual because they are not familiar with their job after the long leave. Meanwhile, many women who used to be **slender** have become over-weight after the few months of no work and **overeating**.

本段主要论述产假的三方面的**坏处**：以女性为主的工作有时会出现严重的劳动力短缺；女性假后工作变生疏；女性产假期间变得过胖。第一、二层次用 and 连接，最后一个层次用 meanwhile 连接。

（1）**female-dominated** 女性为主的

（2）**shortage of labour** 劳动力短缺

（3）**perform** 完成；执行

（4）**slender** 苗条的

（5）**overeating** 暴食

Taking into account both the advantages and disadvantages, I believe maternity leave is a good thing. **After all**, the baby's survival and the mother's health are much more important than the possible **side effects** of labour short-age, temporary unfamiliarity with the work and out of shape. If the maternity leave time is wisely used, the new mothers **may just as well** return to their work as energetic as before.

本段结合前面的利弊分析提出自己的观点：产假是好事，有利于婴儿的存活和母亲的健康，其不利影响比起这两点就微不足道了。

（1）**take into account** 考虑在内

（2）**after all** 毕竟

（3）**side effect** 副作用

（4）**may just as well** 完全可能

参考译文

世界上大多数国家的习惯做法是在女性生完孩子之后给她们放几个月的产假。然而生完孩子之后离开工作几个月既有好处又有坏处。

新生儿无疑是产假最大的受益者。正如我们知道的，新生儿的前几个月总是最危险的时期，在这期间婴儿会遇到很多危险，有的根本意想不到，还有可能是致命的，因此，母亲专心细致的照顾对婴儿的存活十分关键。我刚看过的一则报纸报道比较了有产假的国家和没有产假的国家的婴儿死亡率，得出的结论是前者婴儿的死亡率比后者低 25%。此外，生完孩子之后休几个月也是母亲释放产期焦虑和压力的好方法，因此她在回到工作岗位后将更有可能表现如常。

就像其他事情一样，产假也会带来一些消极的影响。在某些以女性为主的行业，诸如护理，几个月的产假会造成严重的劳动力短缺。我们见过很多女性因为休很长的产假后对工作变得生疏，从而不能如往常一样胜任工作。同时，许多原本苗条的女性经过几个月的暴食和不工作之后会变得过胖。

同时考虑优缺点后，我相信产假是好事。毕竟，婴儿的存活和母亲的健康比起产假可能带来的诸如劳动力短缺、暂时的工作生疏和身体走样的副作用来说要重要得多。如果产假能被合理地利用，新妈妈可能会以之前那般充满活力的状态回归工作。

7.5 城市居民很少和邻居交流的原因及解决办法

题目

City dwellers seldom socialize with their neighbours today and the sense of community has been lost. Why has this happened and how to solve this problem?

解析

从什么时候开始，我们不再与邻里交往？从什么时候开始，我们不再愿意加入一个群体？本题给了一个机会来让我们思考。原因当然是多方面、多层次的，在短短的 250 词内不可能谈完谈深。我在想，也许是我受到了媒体的影响，认为邻居可能不是好人，可能会抢我，甚至害我；也许是家里的网络给了我太多归属感，让我沉醉在虚拟世界里。我知道，远离邻里，远离社区，害怕甚至拒绝与真人打交道，这是一种常见的现代人疾病。我决定，从今天写完这篇作文开始，每天抽出 1—2 小时，不带手机，不带平板电脑，也不带笔记本电脑，去与邻居交流，去加入社区活动；我决定，不再读，不再信，也不再传那些鸡鸣狗盗的媒体新闻，敞开心扉，将心比心，去交几个真正的朋友！请看本范文如何表达以上略带诗意的内容。

范文讲解

Recently I read a news report about a ninety-year-old poor woman dead at home for days without anybody knowing it. This report **points to** one key problem that faces dwellers in cities, especially big cities: they seldom **interact** with their neighbours, **much less to say** they care about their neighbours and as a result they feel lonely because they do not feel they belong to any community.

本段重述题目中提出的现象：城市居民互不来往，没有归属感。本段用举例方式来引出话题。这种方式其实是英语作文很常见的一种方式，但由于它难以融入国内雅思写作培训的所谓万能模板，因此很多培训老师都避而不讲。

（1）**point to** 指向；指明

（2）**interact** 互动

（3）**much less to say** 更不必说

When asked why they do not socialize with their neighbours, many people would **respond by saying** "Why should I? This is a dangerous city!" Indeed, modern media such as TV, newspaper and the Internet have had **way too much** coverage about the city's crimes like theft, robbery and murder. People **constantly exposed to** such reports of the dark side of the city life may **harbour the idea that** nobody is **trustworthy**, including their neighbours.

本段写城市居民不和邻居往来的**第一个理由**，即媒体的影响。本段开头句也可以这样写：Firstly, many people do not socialize with their neighbours because they think the city is a dangerous place. 当然，这样写显然平淡一些。

（1）**respond by saying** 这样回复（= answer）

（2）**way too much** （表示否定）太多，过多

（3）**constantly exposed to...** 长期长期暴露在……（此处指长期阅读）

（4）**harbour the idea that...** 抱有……的想法

（5）**trustworthy** 值得信任的

On the other hand, people now do not feel any more the **necessity** to communicate with their neighbours or become part of a community. Anyway, they do not need their neighbours like they did before. They work, earn money and go back home. When they want to talk, they can just pick up their cellphones and talk to anybody in the world; when they have some brilliant ideas they want to share, they can go online with **a few simple clicks** and then publish their ideas there.

本段写**第二个理由**，即现代人没有与邻居交往的实际需要。主要论述方式是举例：想与人交谈的时候……；想与人交流思想的时候……

（1）**necessity** 必要性

（2）**a few simple clicks** 简单点击几下

But we all know that this kind of **confinement** is no good, no matter how many friends or fans we may have online. As part of the solution to the problem, I would suggest everybody have an "Internet-free moment". **Simply put**, we can **set aside** an hour every day, in which we try to personally **reach out to** our neighbours. Once we begin to care about real people around us, we will suddenly find ourselves living in a community that also cares about us. This experience is much more **rewarding** than having thousands of **virtual** friends who do not really know us. At the same time, all media should **be fully aware of** their share of responsibility in this problem, and try to bring more positive stories about the city life.

本段写**解决办法**。提出了具体办法：每天抽出一个小时无网络时间去与邻居交流，然后对媒体提出建议。

（1）**confinement** 封闭

（2）**simply put** 简言之

（3）**set aside** 抽出；留出

（4）**reach out to...** 接触……；向……伸出手

（5）**rewarding** 有回报的

（6）**virtual** 虚拟的

（7）**be fully aware of...** 充分意识到……

参考译文

我最近读到一则新闻报道，说一个可怜的 90 岁老太太在家里死去数日却无人知晓。这则报道指向城市（尤其是大城市）居民面临的一个关键问题：他们很少与邻居互动，更不要说关心邻居；他们因没有群体归属感而感觉孤独。

当问及为什么不和邻居交往时，许多人的反应就是："为什么要交往？这个城市很危险！"的确，现代媒体，比如电视、报纸和因特网报道了太多城市里的犯罪，比如偷盗、抢劫、杀人等。长期浸润在这种城市生活负面报道中的人，也许会产生这种想法，即没有人是可信的，包括邻居。

另一方面，人们不再感到有必要与邻居交流或者成为团体的一部分。总之，他们不像以前那样需要邻居了。他们工作，挣钱，然后回家。当他们想交谈时，只需拿起手机就可以同世界上任何人通话；当他们有了好想法想交流，只需上网简单点击几下，就可以发布自己的观点。

但是我们都知道这种封闭不好，无论在网上有多少朋友或者粉丝。为了解决这个问题，我建议每个人都有一个"无网时刻"。简单地说，我们可以每天拿出一个小时，在这一小时里，我们试着直接与邻居交往。一旦我们开始关心周围的真人，我们会突然发现自己生活在一个同样关心我们的社区里。这种经历远比拥有成千上万但并不真正了解我们的网友更有价值。同时，所有新闻媒体也应该充分认识到自己在这个问题中的责任，努力多报道城市生活的积极面。

7.6 青少年犯罪增加的原因？该如何惩罚他们？

题目

In many parts of the world children and teenagers are committing more crimes. What are the causes? How should these young criminals be punished?

解析

年轻人犯罪越来越多，原因何在？这里应结合当代社会给年轻人造成的影响来分析。比如，贫富差距的扩大，单亲家庭的增多，吸毒者越来越多，这些无疑都会导致年轻人犯罪率上升。至于解决办法，无非是教育改造和监狱两种方法，可以认为应该结合这两种办法，或者取一种立场，认为教育比监狱更有效。

范文讲解

Many countries are **currently witnessing** a rising criminal rate among people under the age of 18. There may be three reasons for this case, and the methods to punish children and teenagers should focus more on **rehabilitation** than prison.

本段首先改写题目，然后表明即将分析三个原因，并提出自己关于如何惩罚青少年罪犯的观点。

（1）**currently** 目前

（2）**witness** 见证；目睹

（3）**rehabilitation** 恢复；教化

Firstly, poverty could **turn** an **immature** child **into** a criminal. As **the gap between the poor and the rich** widens, young people may start looking for wrong ways to **bridge the gap** when they find their friends are richer. Secondly, with the number of broken families going up, more and more neglected children **have trouble with the law**, as the lack of love and affection from the family makes them angry and violent. As a result, their negative energy might **find an outlet in** committing crimes of all types. Finally, not only taking drugs is itself a crime but it may also lead to various other crimes that young people never intended to commit **in the first place**.

本段具体讨论青少年犯罪率增加的三个**原因**，即贫困、家庭破裂和毒品。

（1）**immature** 不成熟的

（2）**turn... into...** 将……变成……

（3）**the gap between the poor and the rich** 贫富差距

（4）**bridge the gap** 弥补差距

（5）**have trouble with the law** 触犯法律

（6）**find an outlet in...** 在……找到出口

（7）**in the first place** 首先；一开始

How should society punish young lawbreakers in order to prevent or reduce their criminal activity? On the one hand, severe punishment like **locking up** children in adult jails could have a **deterrence effect** by discouraging young criminals from committing new crimes. On the other hand, harsh punishments may have a negative impact on young offenders if they are **incarcerated** in the same way as adults. This could weaken young criminals' already **fragile** links with society, **nourish** their negative **interpersonal networking**, and increase their **likelihood** of future criminal activity.

本段讨论**如何**惩罚青少年罪犯。首先提出监狱的作用，随后提出监狱可能造成的负面影响。

（1）**lock up** 关起来

（2）**deterrence effect** 威慑作用

（3）**incarcerate** 关押

（4）**fragile** 脆弱的

（5）**nourish** 滋养

（6）**interpersonal networking** 人际网络

（7）**likelihood** 可能性

Therefore, rehabilitation is probably a better answer than prison because it provides an environment that **is more conducive to** education.

本段最后提出自己的观点：教育教化比监狱更好。

（1）**be (more) conducive to...** 对……（更）有益

参考译文

许多国家目前都出现了 18 岁以下人口犯罪率增加的情况。造成这种情况的原因可能有三个，而惩罚儿童和青少年的方法更多关注的应该是教化而不是监禁。

首先，贫困会把一个不成熟的孩子变成罪犯。随着贫富差距的增大，当年轻人发现他们的朋友更富有时，就可能会开始寻找错误的方法来弥补这一差距。其次，随着破碎家庭数量的增加，越来越多被忽视的孩子触犯法律，因为缺乏家庭的疼爱和关怀使他们变得愤怒、暴力。因此，他们的消极精力可能会在各种犯罪中找到出路。最后，吸毒本身不仅是一种犯罪，而且还可能导致年轻人本来并没有打算犯的各种其他罪行。

社会应如何惩罚年轻的违法者，以防止或减少他们的犯罪活动？一方面，严厉的惩罚，如将孩子关进成人监狱，可以阻止他们犯下新的罪行，从而产生威慑作用。另一方面，如果青少年罪犯与成年人一样被监禁，严厉的惩罚可能会对他们产生负面影响。这可能削弱青少年罪犯与社会本已脆弱的联系，助长他们消极的人际网络，增加他们今后犯罪的可能性。

因此，教化可能是一个比监禁更好的答案，因为它提供了一个更有利于教育的环境。

7.7 不同文化对老年人和青年人的重视程度不同

题目

In some cultures the old age is highly valued, while in some cultures youth is highly valued. Discuss both views and give your own opinion.

解析

本题是典型的双边讨论题目，因为我们很难锚定一边进行讨论。无论我们论证应该更看重老年人还是青年人，都无法完全自圆其说，因为很明显，老年人和青年人各有价值，都应该被看重。因此，**这样的题目，适合采用双边讨论结构**。

双边讨论结构的作文中，考生在讨论完双方观点后，有必要给出自己的观点。本题分别讨论完老年人和青年人的价值后，如果简单说"老年人和青年人都有价值"，则不足以在审题方面让作文得到高分，原因很简单，这样写没有体现考生自己的观点。

那么，在本题中，我们如何来构建自己的观点呢？回到题目，我们发现题目是这样说的：在有些文化中，更看重老年，而在另外一些文化中，更看重青年。请注意，这里**要求你论证的是"更看重"**（more valued），**也就是要求你讨论为什么在不同文化里，对老年或青年的重视程度不同**。笔者认为原因是传统和现实需求。不同文化对待老年和青年的传统不同；不同文化的现实情况不同，也需要对老年和青年区别对待。于是，本范文的结构如下：

首先，引入话题；

其次，讨论老年人和青年人各自的价值；

再次，说明区别对待的原因一：传统影响；

接着，说明区别对待的原因二：现实考量；

最后，给出结论。

范文讲解

When the 32-year-old Emmanuel Macron and the 72-year-old Donald Trump were elected President of France and the U.S. **respectively**, we can feel the difference in **attitude** of the two countries towards the age: young people are probably more valued in France than in the U.S.

本段通过事例引入拟讨论的话题：不同文化对待年龄有不同的态度。通过事例引入话题是英语文章常用手段。

（1）**respectively** 各自（地）

（2）**attitude** 态度

Of course, the youth **have every reason to** be valued in any culture. They are the most **creative** and energetic population. **It is no exaggeration to say** that young people are what keeps the world going. Yet, with their experience and knowledge, old people are also a valuable **asset** to any nation. If young people keep the world going, then it is the old who keep the young people going.

本段讨论青年人和老年人**各自的优势**：青年人有创造力和活力，老年人有经验和知识。

（1）**have every reason to do...** 有充足的理由做……

（2）**creative** 有创造力的

（3）**it is no exaggeration to say...** 毫不夸张地说……

（4）**asset** 财富

However, it is often found that, in some cultures, the youth are more valued, while in others, the old are more respected. The difference, I believe, mainly **arises from** the traditional values of a given culture. In East Asian countries such as China, Japan, and Korea, for example, people of old age are often **looked up to** and **have the final say over** many important issues, while in many European countries such as France, Germany, and Sweden, the important government positions are often held by young people, because people in these countries traditionally trust young people more than they do the old.

本段讨论不同文化区别对待不同年龄的**原因之一**：传统影响。

（1）**arise from** 来自于，产生于

（2）**look up to** 尊敬

（3）**have the final say over...** 对……有最终发言权

The difference in attitudes towards the old age and the youth also **reflects** the immediate needs of a **particular** culture. If a community suffers from the serious **aging problem**, young people will be more valued to keep the community competitive. By contrast, in a community **overwhelmed with** young people, the old age will be more valued to keep the community **harmonious**.

本段讨论区别对待年龄的**另一个原因**：现实需求。

（1）**reflect** 反映；映射

（2）**particular** 特定的

（3）**aging problem** 人口老化问题

（4）**be overwhelmed with...** 充满了……

（5）**harmonious** 和谐的

To sum up, both the old age and the youth should be valued, yet whether any one of them is more valued **depends upon** the traditional values and the immediate **status quo** of the culture **under discussion**.

本段为**结论**，总结前文讨论的所有观点。

（1）**depend upon** 取决于

（2）**status quo** 现状

（3）**under discussion** 讨论中的

参考译文

当 32 岁的埃玛纽尔·马克龙和 72 岁的唐纳德·特朗普分别当选为法国总统和美国总统时，我们可以感受到两国对待年龄态度上的差异：年轻人在

法国可能比在美国更受重视。

当然，年轻人在任何文化中都有被重视的理由。他们是最有创造力和活力的群体。毫不夸张地说，年轻人是维持世界运转的力量。然而，以老年人的经验和知识，他们也是任何国家的宝贵财富。如果年轻人让世界运转，那么正是老年人让年轻人向前。

然而，人们常常发现，虽然在一些文化中，年轻人更受重视，但在另一些文化中，老年人则更受尊重。我相信，这种差异主要来自特定文化里的传统价值观。例如，在中国、日本和韩国等东亚国家，老年人往往受到尊敬并在许多重要问题上拥有最终发言权，而在许多欧洲国家，如法国、德国和瑞典，重要的政府职位往往由年轻人担任，因为这些国家的人传统上对年轻人的信任多于对老年人的信任。

对老年和青年的态度不同，也反映了一种特定文化的直接需要。如果一个群体遭遇严重的老龄化问题，就会更重视年轻人以保持群体的竞争力。相反，在一个充斥着年轻人的群体里，老年人则会被更看重以保持群体的和谐。

总之，老年和青年都应该受到重视，但是他们中到底谁更受重视，取决于特定文化的传统价值观和眼下的现状。

7.8 闲读比看电视更有利于培养想象力和语言能力吗?

题目

It is believed by many that those people who read for pleasure are better in imagination and language skills than those who prefer to watch TV. To what extent do you agree or disagree?

解析

本题关键词为 reading for pleasure、watching TV、imagination and language skills。因此要比较闲读和看电视，尤其是要在想象力和语言能力培养方面比较两者。

本题可以采取一边倒的方式，即认为闲读／看电视有利于培养想象力和语言能力，这就需要找到2—3个赞同一方的理由，同时驳斥另一方；也可以双边讨论，即说清楚在哪些情况下闲读比看电视好，而在另外的情况下看电视比闲读更好。

本范文采取一边倒结构，完全同意题目给出的观点，即就培养想象力和语言能力而言，闲读远比看电视更好。

范文讲解

People can **entertain** themselves in **multiple** ways. They can read books, surf the Internet, listen to music or watch TV. Many consider that individuals who often read are better in language skills and creative **capabilities** like imagination than those who prefer to watch TV. To a large extent, I am **in favour of** this argument.

本段为开头段，四句话分别完成**三个功能**。第一句和第二句交代背景，第三句改写题目观点，第四句表达自己的观点。这是典型的开头段。

（1）**entertain** 使……娱乐；招待

（2）**multiple** 多样的；多种的（= many）

（3）**capability** 能力

（4）**in favour of** 赞同

Obviously, when one is reading, he may **come across** thousands of words and hundreds of grammar points in a very short time. Then he will be required to **comprehend** the meaning of the words, collocations and sentence structures. Sometimes when he **is faced with** some unknown words or has no idea about what a paragraph is about, he will be forced to take a guess, which is necessary for language learning and use. By contrast, when a person watches TV, what attract him are just the changing pictures presented on the screen and he is less likely to pay enough attention to the **subtitles** or the background voices. As a consequence, he can hardly improve his language skills. When he has something to say, he may feel the idea is just **at the tip of his tongue**, but he can barely describe his mind in his own words.

本段论述在**语言能力**培养方面，阅读比看电视更有优势。阅读要求读者去理解语言，猜测语义，而看电视则只看图像，对语言不太关注。这样，阅读势必更能培养语言能力。当然，如果换个角度，我们也完全可以认为，看电视可能更有利于培养听说能力。

（1）**come across** 遇到

（2）**comprehend** 理解

（3）**be faced with** 面临

（4）**subtitle** 字幕

（5）**at the tip of one's tongue** 在嘴边

In addition, those who read for pleasure often have to imagine in order to understand the world the words **create**, especially when there are no **illustrations**. Therefore, the more they read, the better their imagination becomes and the sharper their mind gets. Those who sit in front of TV all day, however, do not have to imagine as often as those who read for pleasure because the pictures on the screen tell them everything they want to know.

本段论述在**想象力**培养方面，阅读也同样具有优势。

（1）**create** 创造

（2）**illustration** （书中的）插图

In conclusion, TV can **undoubtedly present** knowledge in a much vivid way, but reading is more beneficial. If you want to improve your language skills and imagination, doing more reading is a much better choice.

本段为结尾段，**重申自己的观点**：阅读是提高想象力和语言能力的更好办法。值得注意的是，在提出结论之前，本文先提出了看电视的优势，这是雅思作文中常见的先扬后抑的写法。

（1）**undoubtedly** 毫无疑问地

（2）**present** 呈现

参考译文

人们可以通过多种方式娱乐自己，他们可以读书、上网、听音乐或看电视。许多人认为，在语言技能和创造能力（如想象力）方面，经常阅读的人比那些喜欢看电视的人更好。在很大程度上，我赞成这个论点。

很明显，当一个人阅读的时候，他可以在很短的时间内遇到数千个单词和数百个语法点。然后，他需要理解词语、搭配和句子结构。有时，当他面对一些不明白的词或不知道某段话是什么意思时，他会被迫去猜测，而猜测是语言学习和应用所必需的。相反，当一个人看电视时，吸引他的只是屏幕上变化的图像，他不太可能对字幕或背景声音给予足够的关注，因此，他很难提高语言技能。当他有话要说的时候，他可能会觉得这个想法就在嘴边却很难用自己的语言描述思想。

此外，那些闲读的人往往必须通过想象去了解文字创造的世界，尤其是在没有插图的情况下。因此，读得越多，他们的想象力就越好，头脑就越敏锐。然而，那些整天坐在电视前的人，不必像闲读的人那样经常想象，因为屏幕上的图像告诉了他们想知道的一切。

总之，电视无疑可以以更加生动的方式呈现知识，但阅读更有益处。如果你想提高语言技能和想象力，多阅读是好得多的选择。

7.9 年轻人经常换工作的原因及利弊

题目

Many young people in the workforce today change their jobs or careers every few years. What do you think are the reasons for this? Do the advantages of this outweigh its disadvantages?

解析

本题关键词是 young people 和 change jobs，因此要围绕年轻人换工作这件事来讨论。过去，更换一次工作是很难的，多数人都是在一个岗位上工作到退休，但现在刚毕业几年的年轻人如果没有换几次工作都会觉得自己吃亏了。那么，这到底是什么原因造成的呢？对于这种原因分析的题目，笔者建议大家从三个层次（即物质层次、心理层次和社会层次）去思考，就容易把思路梳理得比较有条理。就年轻人更换工作而言，首先肯定是为了挣更高的工资，获得更好的发展机会；其次，从心理上讲，很多年轻人愿意去尝试新工作，认为这样可以结识不同领域的朋友，增加人生体验；最后，从社会角度看，由于技术的日新月异，工作本身也在不停变化，因此年轻人不得不换工作。那么，频繁更换工作对年轻人来说是好还是坏呢？从好处上讲，这的确可以增加年轻人的工作经历，从而提高他们未来在就业市场上的竞争力，但也有坏处，比如无法在某个领域成为顶级的专家，从而失去更多发展机会。

范文讲解

Not long ago, most people would choose to **stay on the same job** for the entire life, but today young people prefer to try different things and **hop from one job to another**. In my view, there mainly are three reasons why young people are doing so.

本段**直接进入话题**，用过去和现在的对比来提出下文讨论的现象：年轻人不停更换工作。然后提出有三个理由。

（1）**stay on the same job** 坚持做同一份工作

（2）**hop from one job to another** 从一份工作跳到另一份工作

At the most basic level, young people find that frequent job changing can often bring them the pay rise they expect. My friend Edward is a perfect example. As a program designer, he has worked for three different companies in the past five years, and now he earns almost five times as much as he did in the first company. This would not have been possible if he had not been **mobile** enough. The second reason is that by doing different jobs or careers, young people can increase their work experience and **eventually** become more **versatile**. This may **give them a competitive edge**, especially in today's job market where an **all-round employee** is always preferred. Finally, in a world that change takes place almost **on a daily basis**, doing the same job for ever is simply **out of the question**.

本段论述年轻人不停更换工作的**三个原因**，分别为物质原因（能挣更高工资，此处用举例论证）、心理原因（增加工作经验，此处用结果分析）及社会原因（工作一直在变化）。

（1）**at the most basic level** 在最基本的层面上

（2）**mobile** 移动的；流动的

（3）**eventually** 最后

（4）**versatile** 全能的

（5）**give sb a competitive edge** 给某人竞争优势

（6）**all-round employee** 全面的员工

（7）**on a daily basis** 每天

（8）**out of the question** 不可能的

Needless to say, job-hopping may be a bad thing if it is not well-considered. Shifting from job to job may prove to be a waste of time and opportunity since this may easily make a person **Jack of all trades and master of none**. As we know, the person who can provide the most professional service for the company enjoys the best opportunity of promotion. However, if a person does not find the job he is doing interesting or **fulfilling**, then changing job could be a win-win strategy both for the companies and employees. For the companies, "new blood" often means stronger labour force and vitality of the staff. For the employees, a new job means a new opportunity.

本段讨论换工作的**坏处**（无法专门做好一件事情），但接下来又反过来肯定换工作的**好处**（摆脱自己不喜欢的工作）。这样，在结论段作者就需要整体上肯定换工作是一件好的事情。

（1）**Jack of all trades and master of none** 什么都会但什么都不专的人

（2）**fulfilling** 有成就感的

In light of the above discussion, I would conclude that no change of jobs is wasteful as long as it is carefully considered. **Holding on to** a job that we do not like is a crime against our precious life.

本段是**结论**，明确提出自己的观点。

（1）**in light of** 依据

（2）**hold on to** 牢牢抱住；坚持

参考译文

不久以前，大多数人都会选择终身从事同一份工作，但今天的年轻人更喜欢尝试不同的事情，从一份工作跳到另一份工作。在我看来，年轻人之所以这样做，主要有三个原因。

在最基本的层面上，年轻人发现频繁换工作往往会给他们带来期望的加薪。我的朋友爱德华就是个最好的例子。作为一名程序设计师，他在过去五年里为三家不同的公司工作过，现在他的收入几乎是在第一家公司时的五倍。如果他不是如此频繁地变动，是不可能有那样的成就的。第二个原因是，通过从事不同的工作或职业，年轻人可以增加他们的工作经验，并最终变得更多才多艺。这能给他们带来竞争优势，特别是在当今的就业市场上，一个全面的员工总是被青睐的。最后，在一个日新月异的世界里，永远做同样的工作根本是不可能的。

不用说，如果没有好好考虑的话，跳槽可能是一件坏事。从一份工作转到另一份工作可能是浪费时间和机会，因为这可能很容易使一个人成为"万金油"，但一无所专。我们知道，能够为公司提供最专业服务的人享有最佳的晋升机会。但是，如果一个人发现他所从事的工作没有意思或没有成就感，那么换工作对公司和员工来说都是双赢的策略。对公司来说，"新鲜血液"通常意味着更强大的劳动力和活力。对员工来说，新的工作意味着新的机会。

根据以上的讨论，我认为只要仔细考虑，换工作是不会浪费什么的。坚持一份不喜欢的工作是对我们宝贵生命的一种犯罪。

7.10 私家车对个人和环境的利弊

题目

More and more people buy and use their own cars. Do you think the advantages of this trend for individuals outweigh its disadvantages for environment?

解析

本题关键词是 buy and use their own car、individuals、environment，要求比较汽车对个人的好处及对环境的坏处。

汽车的确能够给人们带来很多方便。在拥挤的都市里，虽然有发达的公交系统和地铁系统，但都非常拥挤，有时候还赶不上，严重耽误上班时间，即使挤上去，帅哥美女挤在熙熙攘攘的各色人群中，的确时有尊严不足之感。开私家车让自己出行更方便，更有自由和舒适感，这些是买私家车的好处。但是，那么多人开私家车，就不得不考虑它们对环境的消极影响。这个不难理解。很多专家都指出，北京的雾霾很大程度上就是这个城市的车太多引起的。车一发动，灰尘扬起，尾气外喷，的确容易污染空气。讨论完私家车对个人的好处以及对环境的坏处后，我们的观点应该是什么呢？这里就没有所谓正确答案了。你可以说自由和方便高于一切，可以开发新的科技来解决由此引起的环境问题；你也可以说环境高于一切，出行的方便可以通过改进公交系统来解决；你还可以说，自由方便和环境都很重要，但呼吁尽量减少用车时间，共同维护美好环境，等等。

提醒大家，本题隐藏了一个陷阱。很多同学一看到"汽车"话题过于开心，于是忘记了仔细审题。本题要求比较的是汽车对个人的好处以及对环境的坏处。因此，在讨论汽车的好处时一定要聚焦"汽车对个人的好处"，比如汽车给出行带来的便捷，如果讨论汽车如何增加政府的收入，则属于偏题。在讨论汽车的坏处时一定要聚焦"汽车给环境带来的压力"，比如空气污染、噪音污染等，如果讨论开车耗费人们很多金钱，则属于偏题。因此，建议考生在考场上一定要静下心来，仔细审题后再作答。

范文讲解

Just 50 years ago, to own a car was quite a **luxury**, but today, cars have **found their way into** many households. Statistics show **in China alone**, there are over 140 million cars running on road every day. While cars have brought about conveniences to their users, they have **imposed great pressure on** the environment.

本段用比较和引用数据的方法来改写题目中提出的现象，使其具体化，这种做法可以让第一段显得更生动活泼。如果千篇一律地使用如下开头，则会使文章没有生机：

① With the development of society, more and more people buy and use their own car.

② When it comes to the car ownership and use, many people think they are good to the individuals but very bad to the environment.

这两种典型的作文开头法虽然万能，但正因为其万能，就显得没有任何个性而缺乏吸引力。用数据或者通过比较来引入话题，就显得更为独特。

（1）**luxury** 奢华

（2）**find one's way to/into...** 进入……（比简单的 enter 显得更为地道、生动！）

（3）**in China alone** 仅仅在中国

（4）**impose (great) pressure on...** 给……施加（巨大）压力

Modern city life has made the car an **indispensable means of transport**. Though most cities today have fairly advanced transportation systems like the bus and metro, they tend to be extremely crowded, especially in **rush hours**. This means you might come to your office late or miss some important appointments. If you drive your own car, these problems may well be avoided. At the same time, when you plan to take your family for a trip out of town, you may also enjoy the **flexibility** of when to start off and when to return, rather than having to wait for the bus to arrive.

本段论证**汽车给人们生活带来的便利**：一是避免因乘坐太拥挤的公交或地铁而上班迟到，二是全家出去旅游时更灵活。

（1）**indispensable** 不可或缺的

（2）**means of transport/transportation** 交通运输工具

（3）**rush hour** （上下班）高峰期

（4）**flexibility** 灵活性

However, the increased use of cars has serious **consequences** for our environment. Many experts, for instance, **attribute** the worsening air quality in big cities **to** the cars' **exhaust gas emission** and the dust that rises after them. This accusation is perhaps **well-grounded** if you make a little comparison between the air quality 50 years ago and that of now. In addition to the waste gas and dust, cars also make unbearable noises, which are a headache to all **city dwellers**. Just imagine a time you are shocked awake from your cozy dream by the sharp braking **screech** of a car passing by your house!

本段讨论**汽车对环境的影响**：一是造成了空气质量下降，二是造成了很多噪音。本段最后一句也是一个个性表达的范例，让作文显得更加灵活。

（1）**consequence** 后果

（2）**attribute... to...** 将……归因于……

（3）**exhaust gas emission** 尾气排放

（4）**well-grounded** 有依据的

（5）**city dweller** 城市居民

（6）**screech** 尖叫声

In my view, it is **unrealistic** for the government to put a ban on the car ownership or use since the cars have been so important in our daily life, yet we cannot **overlook** the negative effects they have on the environment. To get out of this **dilemma**, to my mind, there are two **options**, **the first being to develop car technology** and produce cars that burn less fuel and the second, encourage the car owners to use public transportation whenever possible.

本段**表达自己的观点**，提出汽车和环境都重要，并据此提出了两个选择方案：一是设计耗油少的汽车，二是鼓励大家尽量选坐公共交通。其中，"... there are two options, the first being to develop car technology..." 一句后半部分是独立主格结构，因此用 being，而不能用 is。在有把握的前提下，偶尔使用这种"高端"句型，有可能给考官留下好印象。如果没有把握，就要老老实实地写：... there are two options. The first one is to develop car technology...

（1）**unrealistic** 不现实的

（2）**overlook** 忽视

（3）**dilemma** 困境

（4）**option** 选择

参考译文

仅仅在 50 年前，拥有一辆汽车还是一件相当奢华的事情，但今天，汽车已经走进很多家庭了。数据显示，仅在中国，每天就有超过 1.4 亿辆车在路上奔跑。虽然汽车给使用者带来了诸多便利，但它们也给环境造成了巨大压力。

现代城市生活已经使汽车成为一种不可或缺的交通工具。虽然现在大多数城市都有相当发达的交通系统，比如公共汽车和地铁，但它们也容易变得非常拥挤，尤其是在上下班高峰期。这就意味着你可能上班迟到，或者错过一些重要的约会。如果你开自己的车，这些问题完全可以避免。同时，当你计划带家人出城游玩时，你也享有何时出发何时回来的灵活性，而不必等待公交车到来。

然而，汽车使用越来越多，已经给环境带来了严重的后果。比如，许多专家将大城市日益恶化的空气质量归咎于汽车的尾气排放以及汽车后面扬起的尘土。如果稍微比较 50 年前的空气质量和现在的空气质量，（你会发现）这种指责也许是有依据的。除了尾气和尘土外，汽车还制造令人难以忍受的噪音，这令所有城市居民感到头疼。想一想吧，你被经过你家房子的汽车尖厉的刹车声从美梦中惊醒的情形！

我认为，政府禁止拥有或使用汽车是不现实的，因为汽车在我们的日常生活中已经非常重要，但是我们也不能忽视汽车给环境带来的负面影响。我觉得，为了走出这个困境，我们有两个选择：其一，发展汽车科技，制造出耗费燃料较少的汽车；其二，鼓励汽车拥有者尽可能使用公共交通。

7.11 越来越多的人喜欢名牌的原因及利弊

题目

More and more people want to buy famous brands with clothes, cars and other items. What are the reasons behind this? Do you think it is a positive or negative development?

解析

本题关键词为 famous brands。

喜欢名牌衣服、名牌汽车和其他名牌产品，这已经成为越来越多人的习惯。那么，到底是什么原因让人们如此喜欢名牌呢？我们可以从物质、心理和社会三个层面来加以考察。**物质方面**，知名品牌的质量一般说来更好，更值得信赖；**心理方面**，知名品牌能给人带来自我满足感；**社会方面**，使用知名品牌容易获得别人的信任。

至于这种趋势是好还是坏，大家可以根据自己的理解进行选择论述。比如，我们可以认为这是一种坏的趋势：**首先**，追求名牌会让我们花掉更多钱，而这些钱完全可以用来更好地保护身体或者投资教育；**其次**，追求名牌会让我们变成心理扭曲的消费者；**再次**，如果人人都看重品牌，那么这个社会就会变得很势利，买不起名牌产品的人难以得到社会的尊重，从而让社会变得不公正。

范文讲解

Is a famous brand a matter of **identity** or **vanity**? There are reasons to explain why more and more people want to buy brand names. However, **to my mind**, this is a negative trend.

本段直接**进入话题**，同时明确给出自己的观点。

（1）**identity** 身份

（2）**vanity** 虚荣

（3）**to my mind** 在我看来

Although people who are not vanity-conscious generally buy **off-brands** for price benefits, many consumers buy brand names for **a variety of** reasons: quality confidence, social acceptance, and customer **loyalty**. Firstly, recognised brand names usually have shown a **consistency** in product quality that has contributed to the **evolution** of the brand, and for this reason consumers rely on **prior** experience or public word-of-mouth when selecting famous brands of clothes, cars and other items. Secondly, people have a desire to fit in, whether at work or in social circles, so people want to buy famous brands as they believe that the brands will contribute to greater **social acceptance**. Thirdly, consumers develop loyalty to particular brands that provide a consistent, high-quality experience, and that loyalty is essentially an emotional attachment to a brand.

本段论述人们购买名牌的**三个理由**：质量信赖、社会接受度和品牌忠诚度。

（1）**off-brand** 杂牌货

（2）**a variety of** 多种多样的

（3）**loyalty** 忠诚

（4）**consistency** 一致性

（5）**evolution** 进化

（6）**prior** 先前的

（7）**social acceptance** 社会接受度

Although buying famous names is necessary for some special purposes, I believe it is generally a negative development. We all know that the product with a famous name is usually a lot more expensive than its less known **counterpart**, which means we have to pay much more for it. Besides, the strong desire for famous brands may turn us into **irrational** consumers and **prompt** us to try all, even illegal, means to buy them. Finally, if everybody in society **worships** the famous brands, then the world may become an unjust place to live in because people will develop a **biased** attitude to those who cannot afford these brands.

本段讨论为什么热衷品牌**这个趋势是负面的**：付出更多金钱，非理性消费，导致不公平的社会。

（1）**counterpart** 对等的人或物

（2）**irrational** 不理性的

（3）**prompt** 促使

（4）**worship** 崇拜

（5）**biased** 有偏见的

In conclusion, though more and more people prefer famous brands for one reason or another, personally I do not think much of this trend. The **craze** for famous brands, in my view, is harmful to both individuals and society **as a whole**.

本段是**结论**，总结前文的观点。

（1）**craze** 疯狂

（2）**as a whole** 作为整体

参考译文

名牌是身份问题还是虚荣心问题？我们有多个理由解释为什么越来越多的人想买名牌。然而，在我看来，这个趋势是不利的。

虽然没有虚荣心的人通常为了价格优惠而购买非名牌，但许多消费者购买名牌，原因有很多：质量信赖、社会接受度和顾客忠诚度。首先，公认的名牌通常表现出产品质量的一致性，而这一致性促成了品牌的发展，因此消费者依靠以前的经验或者口碑来选择名牌服装、汽车和其他商品。其次，无论是在工作场合，还是在社交圈，人们都渴望融入，所以人们想买名牌是因为他们相信，品牌将有助于他们更好地被社会接受。再次，消费者对那些提供一贯高质量体验的特定品牌有忠诚度，而这份忠诚度本质上是一种对品牌的情感依恋。

虽然为了某些特殊目的购买名牌是必要的，但我认为这个趋势从总体上看是负面的。我们都知道名牌产品比其不知名的同类产品通常要昂贵得多，这意味着我们得为此付出更多的钱。此外，对名牌的强烈渴望可能会使我们变成非理性的消费者，促使我们去尝试所有的，甚至是非法的手段来买下它们。最后，如果社会上的每个人都崇拜名牌，那么世界就可能成为一个不公平的地方，因为人们会对那些买不起名牌的人产生偏见。

总之，虽然越来越多的人因为某种原因而更喜欢名牌，但我个人并不是很看好这一趋势。在我看来，对名牌的狂热于个人和整个社会都是有害的。

7.12 网上商店取代实体商店的利弊

题目

Online shopping is now replacing shopping in store. Do you think it is a positive or negative development?

解析

本题关键词是 online shopping、shopping in store。本题问的是大家对网上购物的态度。由于互联网的发展，现在很多人都不去商店而选择在网上购物。那么，这个趋势是好还是坏呢？

网上购物已经成为多数人的购物习惯，相信大家对本题都不缺观点。网上购物的好处当然很多，比如便捷、节约时间、价格便宜，但坏处也是显而易见的，比如看不见实物而可能买到不适合自己的东西，没有了一家人去商店购物的那种乐趣以及网络欺诈等。总体来说，虽然我们不一定要依赖网上购物，但网上购物的确给我们提供了一种可以选择的购物方式。

范文讲解

Shopping from home used to be a dream of ours, but now it has become a **reality** in our life thanks to the rapid development of the Internet. Many people today **prefer** online shopping **rather than** going to stores.

本段为**引入段**，先提出背景，然后改写题目中提到的现象：网上购物正在取代实体商店购物。

（1）**reality** 现实

（2）**prefer... rather than...** 宁愿……而不是……

Online shopping has many advantages, especially when it is compared with the store shopping. Sitting comfortably at home, no matter how terrible the weather outside might be, and with a few simple **clicks** on our computer or smartphone screen, we can order almost everything we need from clothes to books and from electric **appliances** to air tickets. Then what we have to do is wait one or two days for the **delivery** of our order. The whole **process** is really easy and simple and thus can save us a lot of time, **not to mention** the reduced prices we often enjoy when we shop online.

本段论述**网上购物的好处**，主要包括简单便捷、节约时间。

（1）**click** 点击

（2）**appliance** 器具（尤其是家用电器）

（3）**delivery** 交付，发送

（4）**process** 过程

（5）**not to mention...** 更不用提……

Yet online shopping may **involve** problems, too. First, as we cannot see the **transaction** going on with our own eyes, we may likely buy something that does not really suit us. We often hear our friends complain that they have to **alter** their expensive clothes bought online because it is too long or too short. To make it worse, to return what we have bought and get a different one is always a long and complicated process, which means we may lose the time we have saved from online shopping. Secondly, unlike the store shopping, online shopping **deprives us of** the opportunities to spend quality time together with our family members. I can still remember the excitement when my parents decided to take me to the supermarket to do the weekend shopping.

本段论述**网上购物可能带来的坏处**。首先是可能买到不喜欢的商品，退货又特别复杂，其次是网络购物让我们享受不到一家人外出购物的乐趣。

（1）**involve** 包含；涉及

（2）**transaction** 交易

（3）**alter** 改变

（4）**deprive sb of...** 剥夺某人……

To sum up, the Internet does **provide** us with a new and convenient way of shopping, but we should not completely rely on it. We may **opt for** online shopping when it is necessary, yet I believe the **brick and mortar stores** will never be replaced completely because of the **unique** shopping experience they offer us.

本段为结尾段，**提出自己的观点**：网上购物是一种新的选择，但实体商店购物可能永远也不会消失。

（1）**provide** 提供

（2）**opt for** 选择

（3）**brick and mortar store** 实体商店

（4）**unique** 独特的

参考译文

在家购物曾经是我们的梦想，而由于互联网的迅速发展，现在它已经成为我们生活中的现实。今天许多人喜欢网上购物，而不是去实体商店。

网上购物有许多优点，尤其是当它与实体商店购物相比较时。舒舒服服地坐在家里，不管外面的天气有多糟糕，只要简单地在电脑或智能手机屏幕上点几下，我们几乎可以买到所需的任何东西，从衣服到书籍，从家用电器到机票，然后我们要做的就是等一两天后订单交付。整个过程非常简单容易，因此可以节省很多时间，更不用说我们网上购物时还经常享受到降价优惠。

然而网上购物也可能有问题。首先，由于不能亲眼看到交易的进行，我们可能会买一些并不真正适合自己的东西。我们经常听到朋友抱怨他们不得不把自己在网上购买的昂贵衣服送去裁改，因为它们过长或过短。更糟糕的是，退货换货一直是一个漫长而复杂的过程，这意味着我们可能失去因网上购物节约下来的时间。其次，与实体商店购物不同的是，网上购物剥夺了我们与家人共度一段美好时光的机会。我还记得以前父母决定带我去超市进行周末购物时的兴奋心情。

总之，互联网确实给我们提供了一种新的、便捷的购物方式，但我们不应该完全依赖它。如果有必要，我们可以选择网上购物，但我相信实体商店能够给我们提供独特的购物体验，因此永远不会被彻底取代。

7.13 艺术课应该成为高中必修课吗？

题目

Art classes like painting and drawing are important to students' development and should be made compulsory in high school. To what extent do you agree or disagree?

解析

本题关键词为 art classes、compulsory、high school，需要围绕艺术课在高中是否应该成为必修课这个观点进行讨论。

艺术课程（比如绘画）对学生的发展非常重要，那么是否应该在高中成为必修课？这个问题可能真的见仁见智。赞同者会认为，艺术课程可以帮助高中生走出自我天地，交到更多朋友，帮助他们锻炼智力从而提高其学业成绩，甚至还可以帮助学生锻炼性格等；反对者则会认为，艺术课程不能帮助学生找工作，因此是浪费时间，而且很多学生不喜欢艺术，强迫他们学习不会有任何好处。那么，就这个问题，我们的观点似乎可以采取折中路线：艺术课程应该成为高中必修课，但应该限制课时数，同时大力发展艺术方面的俱乐部，让那些对艺术真正感兴趣的学生能够得到发展，同时又不过多浪费那些的确没有艺术天分的学生的时间和精力。

范文讲解

When the news came that art classes such as music, painting and drawing would be made **mandatory** in my high school, it was met with both **approvals** and **objections**. This mixed responses reflect the different attitudes towards the role of art in the education of high school students.

本开头段使用一个具体事件来引入话题。这种写法在英语作文中还是很常见的，但考生需要注意，这个具体事件必须非常简短，点到为止，引出话题即可。

本文的"必修课"是一个关键词，英语里有三个词可以表达这个意思：mandatory、required、compulsory。

（1）**approval** 赞同

（2）**objection** 反对

Those who **stand up for** art classes argue that art is so important to the students' development that it should be made compulsory. By taking art classes, students may come out of their own world and make friends with those with similar interests. Furthermore, rather than a waste of time, taking art classes can actually help students with other subjects such as maths and physics. The theory is that art can help exercise our **mental power** (imagination, for example) and make us smarter. More importantly, art **calls for persistent** practice and **unyielding stamina**, which are also important qualities that we expect our students to possess.

本段论述艺术课应该**成为必修课的理由**。请注意观察范文如何排列这三个理由的顺序，以及对每一个理由的简要论述。

（1）**stand up for** 赞同；支持

（2）**mental power** 脑力

（3）**call for** 要求

（4）**persistent** 坚持不懈的

（5）**unyielding** 不放弃的

（6）**stamina** 耐力

Objections to art classes as required mainly come from those who think art classes are a waste of time because they are not useful to students. **Except for** the very few who may take art as their lifelong career, the great majority of students will not get a job **in relation to** art when they finish their high school. Besides, what is the point of **compelling** a student who has no interest in art to spend many hours **restlessly** in the art classes?

本段提出相反的观点，即艺术课程**不能作为必修课**：首先，艺术课对大多数同学没有实际用处；其次，很多同学对艺术不感兴趣。

（1）**except for** 除了……之外

（2）**in relation to** 与……相关

（3）**compel** 强迫；迫使

（4）**restlessly** 心神不安地

To my mind, art classes should become compulsory in high school. The objective of education is not just to give students the basic practical **survival skills**, but to prepare them for the future life, both physically and mentally. With this in mind, we can safely conclude that the time spent on art will be **rewarding in the long run**. Of course, schools should be very careful when deciding on the required hours that should be spent on art classes.

本段在前面两段双边讨论后，**提出自己的观点**：支持将艺术课作为必修课，但同时也指出应该小心考虑必修课的课时长度。

（1）**to my mind** 在我看来

（2）**survival skills** 求生技能；生活技能

（3）**rewarding** 有回报的

（4）**in the long run** 从长远看

参考译文

有消息称，诸如音乐、绘画等艺术课程将被我所在的高中列为必修课，赞同和反对皆有。这种不同的反应表明，关于高中教育中艺术的作用，人们的态度不一致。

赞同艺术课程的人认为，艺术对学生的成长非常重要，因此应该成为必修课。通过学习艺术课，学生可以走出自我世界，与具有相同兴趣的人交朋友。而且，上艺术课不是浪费时间，反而能真正帮助学生学习数学和物理等其他课程。赞同者认为艺术能帮助我们锻炼脑力（比如想象力），让我们变得更聪明。更重要的是，艺术需要坚持不懈的练习和永不放弃的耐力，而这些也是我们期待学生拥有的重要素质。

反对将艺术课程列为必修的声音主要来自认为艺术课程对学生没有用处从而是浪费时间的人。除了极少数学生会将艺术作为终身事业，绝大多数学生高中毕业后都不会从事与艺术相关的工作。此外，强迫一个对艺术不感兴趣的学生在艺术课上心神不宁地耗费时间有什么意义？

在我看来，艺术课应该成为高中的必修课。教育的目的不仅是教会学生实用的基本生活技能，还是从身体上和精神上为他们的未来生活做好准备。理解这一点后，我们就可有把握地得出结论：花在艺术上的时间从长远看会有回报的。当然，要求学生在艺术上花多少时间，学校在做这个决定时应该非常小心。

7.14 用社交媒体联络和看新闻的利弊

题目

Nowadays many people use social media every day to keep in touch with others and news events. Do you think the advantages outweigh the disadvantages?

解析

本题关键词为 social media、to keep in touch with others and news events，要求讨论：作为联络他人和看新闻的工具，社交媒体有哪些利弊。

首先，要弄清楚什么是"社交媒体"。社交媒体就是互联网上的平台，在这些平台上大家可以生产并交换信息，比如微博、微信、论坛、播客、博客、网站等，都属于社交媒体。这是相对于传统媒体而言的，比如报纸、收音机、电视、电话、信件等。

在社交媒体上，我们可以与其他人联络，也可以看各种时事新闻。**与传统媒体相比，社交媒体的优势很明显**，如方便、快捷、便宜。这个很好论证。我们在社交媒体上发一条信息，所有朋友都能马上收到并及时回复，而且几乎没有成本；我们可以在社交媒体上一次性发大量信息，包括图文等，这在传统媒体中不可想象。时事新闻传递也更快捷、多样，世界各地发生的任何事情，都能很快看到。

但是，社交媒体也存在问题。比如，在联系别人的时候，你无法确信对方是否已经看到信息；由于可以批量发送，个人隐私无法得到有效保护，有些人甚至利用社交媒体来诬陷别人或从事诈骗，从而造成极坏的影响；此外，社交媒体上的时事新闻传播往往不准确、不全面，读者容易被误导。

总体来说，社交媒体的好处大于坏处。现在是信息时代，越快捷、方便、低成本的信息传递方式越容易受到欢迎。社交媒体的问题可以通过教育、立法等措施得到有效改善。当然，人们也应该学会分辨社交媒体上信息的真伪，从而让社交媒体发挥更大的正面效应。

范文讲解

More and more people today **give up** newspapers, TV, radios and **turn to** various social media for news about the world and communication with others. I think this trend is both positive and negative.

本段开门见山，直接改写题目，然后提出自己的观点。

（1）**give up** 放弃

（2）**turn to** 转向

On the one hand, compared with traditional media, social media can help us reach the world news and other people conveniently and quickly. With social media, people from any corner of the world can **have quick access to** what is going on in all places, **ranging from** big cities such as New York and Shanghai, **to** some **remote** villages in Africa. With a few simple clicks, they can send news about themselves to all their friends around the globe instantly instead of having had to wait a few days when they wrote letters. This is an advantage that traditional media such as newspapers and even phone calls do not enjoy.

本段讨论社交媒体的**好处**：方便快捷。

（1）**have quick access to** 快速获得

（2）**range from... to...** 范围从……到……

（3）**remote** 偏远的

On the other hand, as many of us may have experienced, news given to us through social media is often **inaccurate**, sometimes even **misleading**. Many times we have found that the different versions of the same event on social media are **contradicting** each other and do not know what to believe. Then we have to spend a lot of time **confirming** the truth of the news, which to some extent **offsets** the advantage of reading news online. Besides, the wide use of social media also **gives rise to** crimes such as **fraud** and **blackmail**.

本段讨论社交媒体的**坏处**：虚假新闻多，欺诈多。

（1）**inaccurate** 不准确的

（2）**misleading** 误导的

（3）**contradict** 自相矛盾

（4）**confirm** 确认

（5）**offset** 抵消

（6）**give rise to** 使发生（或存在）

（7）**fraud** 欺诈

（8）**blackmail** 勒索

In my view, though reaching news and others through social media may **involve** certain problems, it is perhaps an **irreversible** trend and a positive development today in a society that places so much emphasis on speed. **That said**, the government should try its best to make social media a better place for us to obtain news and make friends, and we should also **sharpen our eyes** and learn to **discern** real news from fake news, and good people from bad people.

本段给出**自己的观点**：虽然存在问题，但社交媒体利大于弊，不过需要政府加强管理和用户自己小心。

（1）**involve** 包含；涉及

（2）**irreversible** 不可逆转的

（3）**that said** 话虽如此

（4）**sharpen the eyes** 擦亮眼睛

（5）**discern** 分辨

参考译文

　　如今，越来越多的人放弃报纸、电视、无线广播，转向各种社交媒体，以获取世界新闻和与他人的交流。我认为这种趋势既是积极的，也是消极的。

　　一方面，与传统媒体相比，社交媒体可以帮助我们方便、快速地接触世界新闻和他人。有了社交媒体，来自世界任何一个角落的人都可以快速获知各个地方正在发生的事情，从纽约和上海等大城市到非洲的一些偏远村庄。简单地点击几下，他们就可以立即把自己的消息发送给世界各地的朋友，而不必像以往写信那样等上几天。这是报纸甚至电话等传统媒体不具备的优势。

　　另一方面，正如我们很多人可能已经经历的那样，社交媒体提供给我们的新闻往往是不准确的，有时甚至具有误导性。很多时候，我们发现社交媒体上同一事件的不同版本相互矛盾，不知道该相信什么。然后我们必须花很多时间来确认新闻的真实性，这在某种程度上抵消了在线读新闻的优势。此外，社交媒体的广泛使用也引发了欺诈、勒索等犯罪行为。

在我看来，尽管通过社交媒体接触新闻和其他信息可能存在某些问题，但在当今这个如此强调速度的社会中，这可能是一种不可逆转的趋势和积极的发展方向。也就是说，政府应该尽最大努力让社交媒体成为我们获取新闻和交朋友的更好场所，我们也应该擦亮眼睛，学会辨别真实新闻和假新闻，学会辨别好人和坏人。

7.15 生活在大城市不利于身体健康吗？

题目

Some people think living in big cities is bad for people's health. To what extent do you agree or disagree?

解析

本题的关键词是 big cities、bad for health，需要围绕大城市和健康来讨论。

这个话题比较容易构思，也容易写，因为类似的讨论在我们的日常生活中经常发生。记得很早以前，我们就在讨论住在乡下还是城市好，论据无非就是乡下空气好，人际关系亲近，但医疗条件和文化生活相对差一些；而大城市则是空气污浊，噪音很大，而且人际关系冷漠，但可以享受较好的医疗教育机会，可以参与更多的文化活动，等等。本题重点放在身体健康方面。稍微想一下，我们就可以提炼一些观点出来。比如，大城市的空气和噪音污染的确不利于身体健康，大城市复杂的人际关系和剧烈的竞争也不利于心理健康，但是大城市良好的医疗条件有利于我们的身体。因此，结论是，就环境来说，大城市的确不利于身体健康，但大城市的医疗条件对身体康复是有利的。

范文讲解

While enjoying all the **conveniences** such as supermarkets, shopping malls, and public transport, many people complain that living in big cities is harmful for their health. This opinion certainly carries a lot of truth, yet it should also be **treated with a grain of salt**.

开头段**重述题目观点**，同时给出自己的立场。

（1）**convenience** 方便；便利；便利的事物（或设施）

（2）**take/treat sth with a grain of salt** 认为某事被夸大了，只相信其中的一部分

Compared with the rural areas which are usually more peaceful and quiet, big cities are often extremely noisy. The forever crowded streets are full of people rushing back and forth, vehicles **hustling** along, and stores **vying for** attention. Besides, with factories producing wastes and vehicles **emitting** exhaust gas, the air in big cities is often so heavily polluted that many people have to wear a mask when walking outside in the street.

本段讨论大城市危害人们身体健康的**第一个层面**：噪声和污染。

（1）**hustle** 拥挤

（2）**vie for** 争夺

（3）**emit** 散发

Then, the busy city life is also negative for our mental health. The **fierce** competition that exists everywhere in big cities is destructive to our relationship with our colleagues, neighbours, and even friends, **resulting in** our **isolation** and loneliness. In order to **catch up with the Joneses**, we often have to make more money by **working extra hours** which will **eventually** affect our health.

本段论证大城市的繁忙生活影响人们健康的**第二个层面**：激烈竞争和压力。

（1）**fierce** 激烈的

（2）**result in** 导致

（3）**isolation** 孤立

（4）**catch up with the Joneses** 与他人攀比

（5）**work extra hours** 加班工作

（6）**eventually** 最终

Yet big cities do offer many things that can benefit our health. Big cities, for instance, have better sports **facilities** and better equipped gyms and stadiums. They also have more parks and gardens. So we can see many city dwellers enjoy themselves by doing sports in gyms or walking in parks on weekends while in the countryside people can only stay at home. More importantly, in big cities, people enjoy better medical services because the best hospitals and **medical**

professionals are often found in big cities rather than rural countryside.

本段转换角度，论述大城市对人们身体健康有好处的原因：拥有更好的体育设施、公园、医疗服务。

（1）**facilities** 设施

（2）**medical professional** 医护专业人员

So it is hard to decide **with certainty** whether living in big cities is bad or good for our health. Life in big cities does bring about many negative effects on our health (both physical and mental), but it also has much to offer which actually helps us **stay healthy**.

本段是**结论段**，再次表达自己的观点：大城市对我们的健康有利也有弊。

（1）**with certainty** 确定地

（2）**stay healthy** 保持健康

参考译文

在享受大城市的所有便利设施（如超市、购物中心、公共交通等）时，很多人抱怨住在大城市对健康有害。这个观点当然很对，但也需要打个折扣。

与通常说来更平和安静的乡村地区相比，大城市往往非常吵闹。永远拥挤的大街上充满了匆忙来往的人群、熙熙攘攘的车辆、想方设法吸引注意力的商店。此外，城市里有排放废物的工厂，散发尾气的车辆，因此空气经常污染严重，许多人出门上街时不得不戴上口罩。

其次，繁忙的城市生活也不利于我们的心理健康。大城市里无处不在的激烈竞争破坏我们与同事、邻居乃至朋友的关系，导致我们孤独寂寞。为了与他人攀比，我们不得不经常加班加点地挣更多钱，这最终会影响身体健康。

然而，大城市的确提供了很多有利于我们健康的东西。比如，大城市有更好的体育设施和更完善的体育场馆。大城市也有更多公园。因此，我们可以看到，很多城市居民周末会去体育馆运动或者去公园散步，乡村居民则只能待在家里。更重要的是，大城市里的人拥有更好的医疗服务，因为最好的医院和医护人员往往都在大城市而不是在乡村。

因此，很难确定住在大城市对我们的健康是好还是坏。大城市的生活的确给我们的身体（无论是生理还是心理）健康带来很多消极的影响，但实际上也提供了很多东西帮我们保持健康。

7.16 在大城市重修老建筑不如建新房子和新道路吗？

题目

The restoration of old buildings in major cities in the world costs numerous governments' expenditure. This money should be used in new housing and road development. To what extent do you agree or disagree?

解析

本题关键词有 old buildings、major cities、new housing、road development，问题是，大城市里重修老建筑的钱是否应该用于新房子和新道路？

本题其实也是要求"烤鸭"们论证，到底该不该对老建筑进行重修。因为重修老建筑需要花费很多钱，那么到底值不值得呢？这些钱是不是该用于建新的住房，或者新的道路呢？因此，这里还涉及一个小小的比较，即到底老建筑重要还是新的住房和道路更重要？

我们当然可以这样来论证本题：很多老的建筑物既危险，也影响城市面貌，因此完全没有必要重修，可以拆除它们，而节约下来的钱可用于改善现实的住房和道路条件；但也有很多建筑物具有历史文化价值，是民族记忆的一部分，因此应该保留，花再多钱修缮都是值得的。这是双边讨论的思路。

我们也可以这样来论证：老建筑物虽然有价值，但毕竟只是与生活无关的价值；现实生活中需要更好的住房条件和道路条件，这样才能使城市居民生活更幸福、更和谐；因此，用于修缮老建筑物的钱完全应该用于改善住房和道路条件。这是一边倒论证的思路。

本范文采取双边讨论的结构。

范文讲解

Every city has its old buildings. Every year the governments spend large sums of money **restoring** them. Some people consider this **a huge waste of money**, believing the governments' **budget** should go to building new houses and roads, while others insist that the restoration of old buildings in cities **is well worth** the money.

本段为开头段，**直接引入旧建筑的话题**，然后提出两类观点。这里的核心问题是，修缮这些旧建筑需要投入巨资，这是否值得？因此在引入话题时一定要提出"巨资"的问题。

（1）**restore** 修复；恢复

（2）**a huge waste of money** 金钱的极大浪费

（3）**budget** 预算

（4）**be well worth** 完全值得

There are many reasons why some urban old buildings should not be restored. To start with, the old buildings are no longer suitable for people to live in, therefore they should be destroyed and **give way to** new buildings so that people, especially young people in the cities have more living spaces. Secondly, the old buildings can cause inconvenience for the **city dwellers**. Since there is no direct route through the old buildings, people sometimes have to go to and off work by **making a long detour** around them, and in this way much of their time is wasted. Finally, the old buildings may **give rise to** safety problems. More than 100 people, for example, are killed or injured each year in my city, just because of the **collapse** of some ancient buildings.

本段论述**老建筑引起的问题**，主要提出三个问题：空间问题、交通问题、安全问题。当然，也可以论述市容市貌问题。

（1）**give way to** 让位于

（2）**city dweller** 城市居民

（3）**make a long detour** 绕远道

（4）**give rise to** 产生，引起

（5）**collapse** 倒塌

Yet old buildings—at least some of them—are **significant** historically and culturally, and hence should be restored for that reason. They carry some important messages about the city or even the whole nation. The Summer Palace, for instance, is a perfect **reminder** of how the **imperial** family in the Qing Dynasty in feudal China were living and so has great cultural significance. Such old buildings, if well preserved, can become tourist spots and attract thousands of visitors from all **around the globe**.

本段论述**老建筑的价值**，主要从文化角度讲，顺便提及旅游价值。本段使用了举例的论述方法。

（1）**significant** 重要的

（2）**reminder** 提醒物

（3）**imperial** 帝王的

（4）**around the globe** 全球

We all need a **memory** of our past. Many old buildings do have historical and cultural **value** which tells us who we were. We need to take good care of these buildings and keep them as long as possible, however much money it may **involve**, so that they can tell the stories of the city or the nation to our future **generations**. Of course, the money **squandered** on those old buildings with little value should be used to solve more **practical** problems such as housing and traffic.

结尾段，**提出自己的观点**：应该修缮有历史文化价值的老建筑，同时不应在没有价值的老建筑物上花钱。

（1）**memory** 记忆

（2）**value** 价值

（3）**involve** 涉及；包含

（4）**generation** 代；辈

（5）**squander** 浪费

（6）**practical** 实际的

参考译文

每个城市都有旧建筑。每年各国政府都花大笔的钱来修缮它们。有些人认为这是对金钱的极大浪费，他们认为政府的预算应该投去建造新的房子和道路，而其他人则坚持认为修缮城市的旧建筑是值得花钱的。

有些市区旧楼不应修复，原因很多。首先，这些旧建筑物不再适合人们居住，因此它们应该被摧毁，让位给新的建筑，这样人们，特别是城市的年轻人有更多的居住空间。其次，旧建筑物会给城市居民带来不便。因为没有直接穿过旧建筑的道路，人们有时不得不绕远道上下班，这样就浪费了很多时间。最后，这些老建筑会引起安全问题。例如，每年有 100 多人在我住的城市丧生或受伤，就是因为一些古老建筑倒塌。

然而，旧建筑——至少其中一些——在历史上和文化上都具重要性，因此应该予以修复。它们传递一些关于这个城市，甚至整个国家的重要信息。例如颐和园就很好地提醒我们，封建中国的清朝皇族是如何生活的，因此有重要的文化意义。这些古老的建筑，如果保存完好，可以成为旅游景点，吸引成千上万来自世界各地的游客。

我们都需要过去的记忆。许多老建筑确实具有历史和文化价值，告诉我们自己是谁。我们需要照顾好这些建筑物，并尽可能长时间地保存它们，不管这会涉及多少金钱，这样它们就可以向我们的后代讲述城市或国家的故事。当然，浪费在那些价值不大的旧建筑物上的钱应该用于解决更实际的问题，如住房和交通。

7.17 年轻人离开乡村到城市去工作和学习的原因及利弊

题目

Young people are leaving their homes from rural areas to study or work in the cities. What are the reasons? Do advantages of this development outweigh its disadvantages?

解析

本题关键词有 young people、rural areas、cities，要求分析年轻人离开农村到城市工作或学习的原因，并讨论利弊，是一个综合类题目。

就原因而言，观点容易想到，比如农村没有好的工作和学习机会，而这些机会在城市里更容易找到。至于这是好事还是坏事，可以一分为二地讨论。坏处包括城市会越来越拥挤，农村则会越来越萧条；农村人到城市不容易找到工作，从而可能引发很多社会问题。好处当然也有，比如给城市发展提供了人力资源等。综合分析利弊后，可以认为利大于弊。

范文讲解

Nowadays **a growing number of young people** are leaving rural areas in order to **become successful economically or academically** in urban areas.

本段**开门见山**，引出下文即将讨论的现象。注意本段对原文词句进行了较大幅度的改写。

（1）**a growing number of young people** 越来越多的年轻人

（2）**become successful economically or academically** 取得经济上或学业上的成功（这是对题目原文 to study or work 进行的改写）

It is a well-known fact that rural areas do not offer as many economic and academic opportunities as urban areas. Usually, **a variety of** serious issues **confront** young people in villages such as the high unemployment rate and low educational level. So, it is only logical that young people are being pushed away from rural areas and being pulled to urban areas **in search of** better-paid jobs or better-managed schools. In this push-and-pull situation, many families might encourage their children to move to cities to work or study for more economic or academic opportunities.

　　本段讨论**乡村年轻人去城市发展的原因**。首先是乡村缺少机会，然后是这些年轻人也会得到鼓励去城市工作或求学。

　　（1）**a variety of** 各种各样的

　　（2）**confront** 面临

　　（3）**in search of** 寻找

This **one-way traffic** of human resources may have **crucial effects** on both rural and urban areas. To begin with, it may **result in** the imbalance of population between the already intensely populated urban areas and the rural areas that young people **leave behind**. While the cities get increasingly over-crowded, villages will suffer from the **shortage** of manpower. Another possible **downside** of this rural-urban mobility is that, without proper training, the young rural people moving into cities may not be able to find a job, which, then, will bring about a series of social problems. It is **self-evident** that, however, the **migration** of young people from the countryside to cities will provide sufficient human resources necessary for the urban development.

　　本段论述**乡村年轻人进入城市的好处和坏处**，好处包括为城市发展提供劳动力，坏处包括人口拥挤和相关社会问题。

　　（1）**one-way traffic** 单向流动

　　（2）**crucial effect** 至关重要的影响

　　（3）**result in** 导致

　　（4）**leave behind** 留在身后；抛开

　　（5）**shortage** 短缺

　　（6）**downside** 不利之处

　　（7）**self-evident** 明显的；不言而喻的

（8）**migration** 迁移（本文替换使用了几个单词表达同样意思：mobility、movement、traffic、exodus）

To sum up, looking for greater academic and professional opportunities is the major cause of the rural **exodus**. Whether this will **lead to** positive or negative effects, we still have to **wait and see**.

本段**总结**已经论述的原因以及可能带来的影响，但对其最终的影响表示还说不准。

（1）**exodus**（大规模）出走；离开

（2）**lead to** 导致

（3）**wait and see** 拭目以待

参考译文

如今，越来越多的年轻人离开农村，以便在城市取得经济上或学业上的成功。

与城市地区相比，农村地区缺乏经济和求学机会，这是众所周知的事实。通常，农村的年轻人面临着各种各样的严重问题，比如就业率低、教育水平低。因此，年轻人被推着离开农村，并被吸引到城市去寻找薪水更高的工作或上管理更好的学校，这是合乎逻辑的。在这种"你推我拉"的情形中，许多家庭可能会鼓励孩子搬到城市工作或学习，寻求更多经济和学习机会。

这种单向的人力资源流动可能会对农村和城市地区产生至关重要的影响。首先，它可能会导致人口已经密集的城市和年轻人离开的乡村地区之间人口不平衡。当城市变得越来越拥挤时，村庄却将受到劳动力短缺的影响。这种从农村到城市的流动还会有一个缺点：没有受过适当的培训，移居城市的农村青年可能找不到工作，这将带来一系列社会问题。然而，不言而喻，年轻人从农村迁移到城市将为城市发展提供足够的必要人力资源。

总之，寻找更多的学习和职业机会是农村人口外流的主要原因。这会带来正面还是负面的影响，我们仍需拭目以待。

7.18 电视播放审判现场的利弊

题目

In some countries, the criminal trials are shown on TV and the general public can watch them. Do the advantages outweigh the disadvantages?

解析

犯罪题材一般问犯罪的原因、罪犯的惩罚方式、避免犯罪的方法等，但此题要求讨论的话题稍微转换了方式，问的是电视播放犯罪审判这个做法到底是好还是坏。可见雅思作文命题非常灵活，备考雅思时适当了解各类题材的基本写法和基本词汇当然非常必要，但若不提高自己的写作实力或者规范自己的写作思维方式，一味抱着背到现题的心态，是很难在雅思写作中奏效的。

在本作文的审题中，我们发现两个关键词，一是 criminal trials（犯罪审判），二是 shown on TV（电视播放）。关于"电视播放广告的利弊"这样的题目我们不会陌生，但电视里播放犯罪审判又是一种什么样的情形呢？关键是，**讨论这样的题目，我们应该从哪里着手呢？** 如果将本书多次提出的三层次策略，即物质层次、心理层次和社会层次用于"电视播放犯罪审判"这个话题，我们就可得到如下一些可用的观点。

赞同：看电视审判犯人，我们可以学到很多关于法律的知识（物质层面）；电视审判犯人，可以让观众内心感到震慑，从而不敢犯罪（心理层面）；电视审判的关注面大，从而使审判显得更加公正（社会层面）。

反对：电视审判犯人，必定将犯罪细节公之于众，这在某种程度上是在宣传暴力（物质层面）；因为知道要电视播放，法官和律师的注意力往往会从案件审理转移到电视作秀，不利于法律的正常实施（心理层面和社会层面）。

我的观点：作为公民，我们有权利知道犯人是如何得到审判的，因此我赞同电视审判犯人，但是电视审判中也要注意控制那些不宜播放的犯罪细节，并降低电视媒介对审判过程的不良影响。

范文讲解

Whether criminal trials should be shown on TV or not has always been a **controversial** issue. After discussing the advantages of this practice and its disadvantages, I come to believe televising criminal trials is a good thing as long as its negative effects are **brought well under control**.

本段**提出拟讨论的问题，并明确给出自己的观点**。

（1）**controversial** 有争议的

（2）**bring... (well) under control** 让……得到（很好的）控制

Showing criminal trials on TV can serve **multiple** purposes such as educational, **deterrent** and regulatory. When watching how criminals are tried and sentenced, TV viewers will learn a great deal about the law and the legal system. In fact, **it was** from a televised trial **that** I finally understood it is a **violation** of law if you do not stop your car when you see a stop sign. Meanwhile, TV trials can help **bring down** the **crime rate**. People are fearful of their faces shown on TV after they commit crimes because it is generally considered to be a **disgrace** to the family. Finally, aware that they are watched by the general public, the lawyers and judges will have to make sure that the law is followed strictly and the justice is done to the highest standards.

　　本段论证**电视播放犯罪审判的好处**：学到法律知识，产生威慑作用，监督法官审判。请注意，本段开头使用了三个词（即 educational、deterrent、regulatory）高度概括本段的主要内容，使之成为一个标准的主题句（topic sentence）。

　　（1）**multiple** 多样的

　　（2）**deterrent** 威慑的

　　（3）**it is... that...** 正是……（强调句）

　　（4）**violation** 违反

　　（5）**bring down** 降低

　　（6）**crime rate** 犯罪率

　　（7）**disgrace** 侮辱；丢脸

Admittedly, TV trials, particularly the live shows, may bring about negative effects as well. Often the TV trials will present a lot of details of the **criminal offences** such as killing, embezzling, cheating, so much so that they become a promotion of these crimes. As a matter of fact, many **juvenile offenders** admit they have been under great influence of TV criminal shows. More importantly, in TV criminal trials, lawyers and judges may often pay more attention to their own personal images to the TV viewers, thus forgetting the real purpose of the trial, which is to find if a person is guilty or **innocent** and in this way, the justice may be sacrificed.

　　本段讨论**电视播放犯罪审判可能带来的不良影响**：宣扬犯罪细节，干扰法官判案。

（1）**criminal offence** 犯罪行为

（2）**juvenile offender** 青少年罪犯

（3）**innocent** 无罪的；无辜的

However, I personally do like the idea of putting criminal trials on TV. Besides telling us right from wrong in a more **vivid** way and preventing us from committing crimes, TV trials will let us know how the punishment is **meted out** and how justice is done. This, I believe, is what our basic civil right is all about.

本段**总结**，并**明确自己的观点**。

（1）**vivid** 生动的

（2）**mete out (a punishment)** 给予惩罚

参考译文

罪犯审判是否应该在电视上播放一直是一个有争议的问题。在讨论了这种做法的优点和缺点之后，我认为，只要负面影响得到很好的控制，电视转播罪犯审判就是一件好事。

在电视上播放罪犯审判可以达到教育、威慑和监管等多种目的。当看到罪犯如何被审判和判刑时，电视观众会学到关于法律和法律制度的很多知识。事实上，正是从一次电视转播的审判中，我终于明白，看到停车标志如果你不停车，那就是违法行为。同时，电视审判有助降低犯罪率。人们害怕犯罪后在电视上露脸，因为这通常被认为是家庭的耻辱。最后，意识到自己受到公众的关注，律师和法官必将确保严格遵守法律，并以最高标准伸张正义。

诚然，电视审判，特别是直播，也可能带来负面影响。电视审判往往会提供许多犯罪的细节，如杀人、贪污、欺骗，以至于反而宣扬了这些罪行。事实上，许多少年犯承认他们受到了电视刑事节目的巨大影响。更重要的是，在电视上审判罪犯，律师和法官往往会更多地关注自己在电视观众面前的个人形象，从而忘记审判的真正目的，即判断一个人是否有罪，这样，正义就可能被牺牲。

然而，就个人而言，我喜欢电视播放罪犯审判这个想法。除了用更生动的方式告诉我们对错，防止我们犯罪外，电视审判还会让我们知道如何量刑，如何实现公正。我认为，这就是基本民事权利的全部内涵所在。

7.19 解决交通堵塞问题的最好办法是政府免费提供全天候公交服务吗？

题目

The best way for the government to solve the traffic congestion is to provide free public transport 24 hours a day, 7 days a week. To what extent do you agree or disagree?

解析

交通堵塞是个大问题，这在国外中小城市感受不深，但在国内任何一个城市（包括小城市）都已经到了令人崩溃的边缘。怎么办呢？大家想了各种各样的办法，包括限制买车（摇号），限制用车（单双出行），增加用车成本（提高油价，收拥堵费），但始终效果不好。于是又有人提出，那免费提供公共交通，公交免费，地铁免费，这下人们不愿意花钱开自己的车了吧？那么，你觉得这个"免费方案"是否可行呢？它能否解决交通堵塞问题？笔者读过一篇作文范文，大意说同意这个免费方案，但不同意全天候免费，认为全天候没有必要，只需在交通高峰时期免费提供公交服务就可以了。这个思路看起来很巧妙，实际上逻辑一塌糊涂。高峰时期是什么人在出行？其实主要是那些工薪阶层，在他们上下班的时间免费提供公交与否，都会比平时堵塞。从某种意义上，免费有可能加剧这种堵塞。很多在高峰时期本不想出行的人，看到免费也会赶在这个时间出行，其结果是公共交通压力不降反增，而那些有经济实力开自己车出行的，根本就不会在乎这点免费，该开车还开车，这样交通堵塞不是会变得更加严重了吗？另外，免费公交无疑会给政府增加额外的经济压力（政府投资类题目差不多都要考虑到这一点），有那些钱还不如用来多修几条道路更管用。因此，笔者的基本观点是，免费公交虽然可能有助于缓解交通压力，让更少的人自己开车，但从根本上来讲无法解决交通堵塞问题；解决这个问题需要多种合力，包括政府投入多修道路，驾驶员遵守交通法规，限制私车出行等。

本题是"手段–目的"类作文，一般先承认提出的手段有一定效果，然后分析该手段会产生的问题，最后提出更好的办法。

范文讲解

Most of us must have experienced the anger, **frustration** and even despair when we **got stuck in** the long unmovable **procession** of vehicles. Actually, the government has tried **numerous** ways to bring down the traffic, but mostly **in vain**. Recently, it is proposed that 24/7 free public transport be provided to solve the traffic congestion. While I think this proposal may be helpful, it is **far from** the best solution.

本段为**引入段**。笔者建议在引入段尽量杜绝模板写法，比如"when it comes to the issue of how to solve traffic congestion..."或者"nowadays, the problem of traffic congestion has become a heated topic of discussion..."，这种句子虽然随手可写，但已经被用得太多，容易给考官留下模板化印象。那么，怎么才能避免模板化呢？笔者认为，在雅思作文开头段，考生可以去**描写一个问题，而不是简单地提出一个问题**。这里的范文就是在**描写**堵车现象，而不是简单**提出**堵车现象。

（1）**frustration** 沮丧

（2）**get stuck in...** 被陷在……；被困在……

（3）**procession** 队列

（4）**numerous** 许多的

（5）**in vain** 徒劳地

（6）**far from** 远不是；远非

Undoubtedly, with the introduction of free public transport, some people may choose to drive less of their own cars, and this will be helpful to **ease** the traffic, though I doubt the **extent** to which this can help the traffic. When public transport goes free, many people who **otherwise** would stay at home may choose to go out by taking the free transport. This will greatly **undo** the benefits brought by the reduced number of private cars on road and may even **paralyse** the public transport system, especially during the rush hours. Beijing, for instance, found itself in great traffic trouble when the city announced to provide free metro service for its citizens during the Asian Games in 1990. Then in 2008 when Beijing was hosting the Olympic Games, the city never made the similar attempt.

本段首先简要讨论免费公共交通有助于缓解交通，但更可能**带来问题**，采取了例证法。

（1）**ease** 缓解

（2）**extent** 程度

（3）**otherwise** 否则

（4）**undo** 抵消

（5）**paralyse** 使……瘫痪

Therefore, to **combat** the traffic problem, providing free public transport alone is not enough. Instead, we should **assemble** efforts from various sides such as the government, the drivers as well as the **pedestrians**. **On the part of** the government, rather than providing funds for the free public transport, it should make more **investments** on the construction of roads, and introduce stricter traffic laws, rules and regulations. And, if the drivers and pedestrians were more careful in **abiding by** the traffic rules, the traffic problem could also be effectively **alleviated**.

本段提出比提供免费交通**更有效的办法**。

（1）**combat** 对付；解决（= solve; deal with）

（2）**assemble** 汇集；汇聚

（3）**pedestrian** 行人

（4）**on the part of...** 在……方面；对……而言

（5）**investment** 投资

（6）**abide by** 遵守

（7）**alleviate** 减轻

参考译文

当困在长长的、一动不动的车流中，我们多数人一定都经历过愤怒、沮丧，甚至绝望。事实上，政府已经尝试过无数办法来缓解交通堵塞，但多数都没有效果。最近，有人提出，免费提供全天候公共交通服务来解决交通堵塞问题。我认为此举可能有些帮助，但绝非最好的解决办法。

毫无疑问，施行免费公共交通后，有些人会选择少开自己的车，这样会有助于缓解交通，但是我不确定这种做法对交通帮助有多大。当公共交通免费后，许多本来会留在家里的人，也会选择乘坐免费的交通工具出门。这就会在很大程度上抵消路上私家车减少带来的益处，甚至可能使公共交通系统瘫痪，尤其是在交通高峰期。比如，1990 年北京亚运会期间，当该城市宣布为市民提供免费地铁服务后，遇到了巨大的交通麻烦。然后，在 2008 年，当北京举办奥运会时，就没有再做类似的尝试了。

因此，为对付交通问题，仅仅免费提供公共交通服务是不够的。相反，我们应该汇集来自政府、驾驶员、行人等各方力量。政府方面，要做的不是为免费公共交通提供资金，而是要投入更多来修建道路，并且制定更严格的交通法规。同时，如果驾驶员和行人更小心地遵守交通规则，也能有效缓解交通堵塞问题。

7.20 将文化传统用于赚钱会毁掉这些传统还是挽救它们？

题目

Some people think that cultural traditions will be destroyed when they are used as money-making machines aiming at tourists, other people believe that it is the only way to save such traditions in the world today. Discuss both sides and give your own opinion.

解析

本题的核心是，一些文化传统是不是该开放给旅游者来挣钱？有人认为这样会破坏文化传统，有人则认为这是保护文化传统的手段。很明显，把一些具有文化价值的东西作旅游之用，有可能破坏它们，但挣来的钱可以作为这些文化传统的维护之用。因此，本作文要求考生讨论清楚旅游到底如何破坏文化传统，同时又如何筹到资金来保护文化传统，最后给出自己的观点。

范文讲解

As tourism develops, we can see many cultural traditions open to tourists. Some people are deeply worried, thinking this money-making act will destroy these cultural traditions, but others **hold the belief** that **in contemporary world**, putting such traditions into tourism market is the only way to save them.

本段**引出话题**。文化传统随旅游业的发展而开放。有人担忧营利行为会破坏这些文化传统，有人认为这是保留文化传统的唯一方法。请注意范文对题目中语言的重新表述方法。

（1）**hold the belief/view/opinion** 坚持某种看法 / 观点 / 意见

（2）**in contemporary world** 在当今世界

On the one hand, **over-exploitation** of cultural traditions for money may really destroy them. As tourists come from different parts of the world, they have various kinds of tastes, so they may want the cultural traditions to be adapted to their tastes. For instance, a Chinese visitor to Stratford-on-Avon may expect Shakespeare's plays to be performed in a style **similar to** Chinese plays so that he can understand them. **By the same token**, a Chinese local cultural performance also has to be altered in order to **cater to the need of** American tourists in China. These alterations may of course, add some special flavour to the original traditions, but **more often than not**, they will ruin these traditions.

本段论述过度商业开发的**害处**。游客们有不同品味，文化表演也必须有相应的改变来吸引游客（为本土的传统增添特别的风韵，但也时常会破坏这些传统）。本段使用例证法。

（1）**over-exploitation** 过度开发

（2）**similar to** 与……相似

（3）**by the same token** 类似地（= similarly）

（4）**cater to the need of sb** 迎合某人的需求

（5）**more often than not** 经常（= often; frequently）

On the other hand, however, merchandising the cultural traditions may help save them. As we know, preserving cultural traditions **calls for** heavy govern-ment budget, which is not always available. As far as I know, except for the few traditions which appear on the list of "must preserve", many traditions are dis-appearing for financial reasons. By opening them to tourists, they can **generate** income, which, **in turn**, can be used for their preservation and development.

本段论述文化传统商业化的**好处**：其利润可用于文化传统的延续和发展。

（1）**call for** 需要

（2）**generate** 带来，产生

（3）**in turn** 反过来

While as money-making machines, some traditional cultures may suffer, **I firmly believe** opening them to tourists is a better choice. Firstly, cultural tradi-tions, **however ancient and classical**, must change with time. Tourists from the world may bring new perspectives and inspirations, and thus new life to these traditions. At the same time, opening-to-tourism can also bring about money which can effectively relieve government of the financial burden.

本段提出自己的观点，即文化传统商业化是更好的选择，并简要陈述了两个原因：对外开放文化传统可能会带来新的灵感，与时俱进；收益用于维护文化传统，减轻政府财政负担。

（1）**I firmly believe** 我坚信（= I am strongly convinced）

（2）**however ancient and classical** 无论多么古老和经典（= no matter how ancient and classical they are）

参考译文

随着旅游业的发展，我们可以看到许多文化传统都在向游客开放。一些人为此深深地担忧，认为营利行为会破坏这些文化传统，但其他人则相信在当今世界，将这些传统融入旅游业才是保存它们的唯一方式。

一方面，对文化传统的过度商业开发可能会破坏它们。游客们来自世界各地，他们有不同的品味，因此他们可能会要求文化传统适应他们的口味。比如，一个中国游客在参观埃文河畔斯特拉特福时，可能期望莎士比亚的戏剧以一种和中国戏曲相似的风格呈现，以便他能理解它们。同样地，一项中国地方文化表演也必须有相应的改变来迎合来中国游玩的美国游客。这些改动当然会为本土的传统增添特别的风韵，但也时常会破坏这些传统。

然而，从另一方面来说，文化传统商业化也许对其流传有益。正如我们知道的，保存文化传统需要政府大量的预算投入，但政府支持并非总是可以获得的。就我所知，除了那些极少数被列为"必须保护"的传统，许多传统由于财政上的原因正在消失。对游客开放文化传统能带来利润，所产生的利润反过来可用于它们的传承和发展。

尽管作为营利机器，有些传统可能会被破坏，但我坚信对游客开放它们是更好的选择。首先，不管多么古老、多么经典的文化传统都必须与时俱进。来自世界各地的游客可能会为之带来新的视角和灵感，从而增添新的生命力。同时，旅游开放带来的收益可以有效地减轻政府的财政负担。

第八章　雅思习作评改实例

在多年的雅思写作教学过程中，笔者发现众多"烤鸭"面临一个难解的尴尬局面：自己练习写了很多作文，写作水平却不见实质性提升，最后考试成绩依然维持在以前的档次。这其实就涉及作文修改的问题。笔者的基本观点是，"烤鸭"写完习作后，一定要请行家修改自己的作文，指出问题及改进的办法。在这里，"行家"就显得尤其重要。如果修改仅仅发生在语言表达层面，而没有涉及思维层面，那么学生从修改里收获的进步就一定是非常有限的。为此，本书专辟"雅思习作评改实例"一章，详细修改点评学生习作 6 篇，希望读者能从这些修改中得到有益的启发。

8.1 基本语言错误毁掉一篇作文

题目

Do the dangers derived from the use of chemicals in food production and preservation outweigh the advantages? 化学物质用于食品生产和保存的利弊

学生习作

It has been claimed that people use several chemicals in the process of production and preservation. My view is that the disadvantages of using chemicals far outweigh the advantages.

It cannot be denied that people are more likely to use chemicals as a way to extend the time of food preservation, because it can help businessman gain more profits. For example, some agricultural products like vegetables and fruits are easily to become stale when they experience long-term transportation. If not adding some chemicals ingredients to protect food, merchants will suffer great economic damages.

However, there are several disadvantages of over-use chemicals. One the one hand, some of the chemicals ingredients cannot be resoled by digest system, which could effects human health. If chemicals remain in people body for a long time, it may cause diseases like cardiovascular, stomachache or lung disease etc. One the other hand, remain chemicals' elements also damage natural environment. Some farmers use pesticides to protect agricultural products from destroying by harmful insects. However, the remains that cannot resole by ecosystem may pollute surrounding water and soil. To a large extent, if animal drink the water or eat the food, the may died by those poison food. What's more, in the process of producing food, the contaminants that are made by factories directly pour into rivers, also cause habitat destruction, in this way, it account for the loss of biodiversity.

In conclusion, my view is that the disadvantages of this trend far outweigh advantages. If people control the use of chemicals, we will become healthier and also can enhance the human condition.

评分：5.5

总评：内容没有很大问题，相当通顺，逻辑和观点都比较清楚，但出现了一些基本的语法错误和用词错误，拉低了得分，相当遗憾！

逐句修改

第一段：It has been claimed that <u>people use several chemicals in the process of production and preservation</u>. My view is that the disadvantages of using chemicals far outweigh the advantages.

【修改】It has been claimed by many that there is nothing wrong using chemicals in food production and preservation. My view, however, is that the disadvantages of using chemicals far outweigh its advantages.

【点评】it has been claimed that 后面应该接一个观点，但原文不是一个观点，只是一种现象。

第二段：It cannot be denied that people are more likely to use chemicals as a way to extend the time of food preservation, because it can help <u>businessman</u> gain more profits. For example, some agricultural products like vegetables and fruits are <u>easily</u> to become stale when they experience long-term transportation.

If not adding some chemicals ingredients to protect food, merchants will suffer great economic damages.

【修改】It cannot be denied that people are more likely to use chemicals as a way to extend the time of food preservation, because it can help businessmen gain more profits. For example, some agricultural products like vegetables and fruits are easy to become stale when they experience long-term transportation. Without some chemical ingredients to protect them, merchants will suffer heavy economic losses.

【点评】本段错误不多，稍微改正，感觉可以冲7分了。（1）businessman 是单数，此处宜用复数。（2）vegetables and fruits are easily to become stale 中的 easily 是副词，这里宜用形容词 easy 或者 vegetables and fruits easily become stale。（3）if not adding some chemical ingredients 是非常典型的中式表达，相当于"假如不添加一些化学成分"，但其实最合适的英文表达是 without some chemical ingredients（如果没有一些化学成分）。（4）economic damages 表达不合适，宜为 economic losses。

第三段：However, there are several disadvantages of over-use chemicals. One the one hand, some of the chemicals ingredients cannot be resoled by digest system, which could effects human health. If chemicals remain in people body for a long time, it may cause diseases like cardiovascular, stomachache or lung disease. One the other hand, remain chemicals' elements also damage natural environment. Some farmers use pesticides to protect agricultural products from destroying by harmful insects. However, the remains that cannot resolve by eco-system may pollute surrounding water and soil. To a large extent, if animal drink the water or eat the food, they may died by those poison food. What's more, in the process of producing food, the contaminants that are made by factories directly pour into rivers, also cause habitat destruction, in this way, it account for the loss of biodiversity.

【修改】However, there are several disadvantages of over using chemicals. On the one hand, some chemicals cannot be resolved by digestive system, and cause harmful effects on human health. If chemicals remain in our body for a long time, they may lead to diseases like stomachache, cardiovascular or lung diseases. On the other hand, chemicals also damage the natural environment. For instance, some farmers use pesticides to protect agricultural products from harmful insects. However, the residues that cannot be resolved by ecosystem may pollute surrounding water and soil. If animals drink the water or eat the food, they may be poisoned. What's more, in the process of producing food, the contaminants made by factories are directly poured into rivers, causing habitat destruction, which accounts for the loss of biodiversity.

【点评】这个段落原文共 143 个单词，8 个句子，却出现了多达 12 个基本语言错误！这样的作文，就算思想再深刻，得分也不可能高于 6 分。

（1）over-use chemicals 应为 over using chemicals，或者 chemical over-use（把 over-use 当作名词使用）。（2）some of the chemicals ingredients 应为 some chemicals。"some of the..." 指某一范围内的 "一些"，"some..." 则没有限定范围。（3）digest system 应为 digestive system（消化系统）。（4）effects 应为 affect（影响）。（5）people body 应为 our body。（6）it 应为 they，这里代词指代的是前文的复数 chemicals。代词使用是中国英语学习者的一个很大的难题，经常出现错误。（7）remain chemicals' elements 似乎想表达 "残留的化学成分"，但完全不符合规范，不如直接说 "化学物质"（chemicals），考试中不要试图去表达不会用英文规范表达的内容。（8）protect agricultural products from destroying by harmful insects 应为 protect agricultural products from being destroyed by harmful insects，或者更简洁的 protect agricultural products from harmful insects。（9）cannot resolve 应为被动语态 cannot be resolved。（10）they may died by those poison food 应为 they may die from those poisoned food，但前文提及 water 和 food，因而这里仅说 poisoned food 不合适，因此宜改为 they may be poisoned。（11）the contaminants that are made by factories directly pour into rivers 中，主语是 the contaminants，谓语是 pour into rivers，两者是被动关系，因此应该是 the contaminants made by factories are directly poured into rivers。（12）"in this way, it account for the loss of biodiversity" 中 it 指代不明。

第四段：In conclusion, my view is that the disadvantages of this trend far outweigh advantages. If <u>people</u> control the use of chemicals, <u>we</u> will become healthier and also can enhance <u>the human condition</u>.

【修改】In conclusion, the disadvantages of chemical use in food production and preservation far outweigh the advantages. **Though it helps increase profits for businesses, it may cause great dangers to our life as well as the environment**. If we control the use of chemicals, we will become healthier and our living conditions will also be improved.

【点评】结尾没有总结出全文观点，修改文黑体字增加了一句总结观点。原文最后一句中，people、we、the human condition 不停转换，代词游离不定，让人着急，可以统一为第一人称。

8.2 增加句型多样性有助于考试提分

在第一篇习作评改中，笔者指出，一些无心的语言错误可能在很大程度上拉低作文的分数，这点尤其表现在一些低分段的作文中。毫不夸张地说，很多"烤鸭"的作文，即使保持作文原有的思想逻辑和句型表达，只要修改其中明显的语言错误，分数也可以直接提升 0.5—1 分。对那些一写就错的"烤鸭"，笔者的建议很直接，不要好高骛远去追求什么新颖立意和高分词汇/句型，把基本的句子写好才是上策。

然而，基本的句子写作这一关闯过之后，若想进一步提分，"烤鸭"就要注意增加句型的多样性了。首先需要说明的是，句型多样性并不意味着满篇都写长句或从句。恰恰相反，句型多样性要求长短句有机结合，实现文章的节奏感。总体来说，实现句型多样性的方法，有副词句首、介词短语句首、分词短语句首、插入语、从句、后置分词短语、强调句、倒装句等，这些方法可以打破单调的"主＋谓＋宾"结构，让句子写作显示出多样性来。此外，笔者还有个建议：在表达段落主题句或结论时，一般使用短句（或常规句型）以突显明确的观点，在论证主题句或举例的时候，一般使用长句（或更丰富的句型变化）以体现论证的深度和层次感。

题目

Schooling is no longer necessary, since more and more information is accessible on the Internet, and students can study just as well at home. To what extent do you agree or disagree? 网络时代，学生是否不需要去学校了？

学生习作

The boost of information on the Internet enables students to absorb information at home. Some think traditional schooling will disappear in the future. Generally, I believe in the necessity of schooling, although study online do have benefits.

It is true that acquiring knowledge online is an accessible way for students to be well-informed about the world. Simply clicking the mouse, various information will be displayed to students immediately. It is easy for them to know the most advanced technology, the culture of a foreign country, etc. However, education is not only about absorbing useful information, but also educate students to be good members in society. To achieve this end, the school system should continue to be the mainstream way of education.

Schooling is a desirable way to improve students' soft skills. As the world becoming increasingly competitive, no one will excel if he is knowledgeable but lack of teamwork spirit. This can be made up by attending traditional classes and do collaborative assignments with classmates. By communicating with each other and expressing themselves, students have the opportunity to realise the importance of cooperation, and thus better themselves comprehensively.

Learning at home from Internet can not raise students' awareness of being a moral person, which may bring about indifference to society. This is less possible to happen in a traditional school, where there are all kinds of extra-curricular activity, volunteer work, for instance, to help build up their sense of responsibility to society and sympathy to others.

In general, although the Internet is convenient to acquire knowledge, I do not think schooling will disappear because of the meaning of education. Learning online can only be a complement rather than a substitute.

评分：6.5

总评：具备比较好的词汇量和用英语表达思想的能力。思维逻辑清楚，连贯性较好。

逐句修改

第一段：The boost of information on the Internet enables students to absorb information at home. Some think traditional schooling will disappear in the future. Generally, I believe in the necessity of schooling, although study online do have benefits.

【修改】As vast amount of information is now available on the Internet, some people think traditional schooling will disappear in the near future because students can study at home. Generally, I believe in the necessity of schools, although online learning does have benefits.

【点评】（1）the boost of information 搭配不太地道。（2）schooling 是"教育"，在学校的教育和在家里的教育都可称 schooling，但这里要表达的是"学校的必要性"，而不是"教育的必要性"，因此 schooling 宜改作 schools。（3）study online do have benefits 是一处比较大的语法错误，至少应该是 studying online does have benefits。对 7 分作文而言，类似错误一定要避免。（4）本段前两句使用了两个短句，这固然没有什么语法问题，但如果将这两句合成一句，可以增加句型的多样性。

第二段：It is true that acquiring knowledge online is an accessible way for students to be well-informed about the world. Simply clicking the mouse, various information will be displayed to students immediately. It is easy for them to know the most advanced technology, the culture of a foreign country, etc. However, education is not only about absorbing useful information, but also educate students to be good members in society. To achieve this end, the school system should continue to be the mainstream way of education.

【修改】It is true that learning online is an ideal way for students to be well-informed about the world. A few simple clicks can immediately bring various information to the students such as the most advanced technology and the culture of a foreign country. However, education is not just about giving students useful information, but about telling them how to become good members of society as well. To achieve this end, the traditional school system should remain the major way of education.

【点评】（1）Simply clicking the mouse, various information will be displayed to students immediately. 本句有较严重的语法错误。现在分词短语放在句首的句子，可以增加句式的丰富性，值得鼓励，但一定要注意，这个现在分词的逻辑主语一定要与主句的主语一致。在这里，clicking the mouse 的逻辑主语应该是 students，但后面句子的主语是 various information，这就造成了语法错误。有以下三种修改方式：

① Just clicking the mouse, the students can immediately access various information.

② Just click the mouse, and various information will be displayed on the screen.

③ A few simple clicks of the mouse can bring various information to the students.

（2）"education is not only about absorbing useful information, but also educate students to be good members in society" 这句也有比较严重的语法错误，主要是 absorb information 和 educate students 两个动词词组的逻辑主语不同，前者的主语是 students，后者的主语是 education，这样就前后不一致了。可以修改为 "education is not only about absorbing useful information, but also trying to be good members of society"（两个动词词组的逻辑主语统一为 students）或 "education is not only about giving useful information to students, but also telling them to be good members of society"（两个动词词组的逻辑主语统一为 education）。

（3）原文中的第二和第三句可以合并成为一句，请参看修改文是如何合并的。

第三段：Schooling is a desirable way to improve students' soft skills. <u>As the world becoming increasingly competitive</u>, no one will excel if he is knowledgeable but <u>lack of</u> teamwork spirit. This can be made up by attending traditional classes and <u>do</u> collaborative assignments with classmates. By communicating with each other and expressing themselves, students have the opportunity to realise the importance of cooperation, and <u>thus better themselves comprehensively</u>.

【修改】School is a more desirable place for students to improve their soft skills. As the world is becoming increasingly competitive, no one without the teamwork spirit can succeed no matter how knowledgeable he may be. This important sense of cooperation can be developed by attending traditional classes where students can do collaborative assignments with their classmates. By communicating with each other and expressing themselves, students have the opportunity to understand the importance of cooperation, and learn how to work together with others.

【点评】（1）as the world becoming increasingly competitive 是较严重的语法错误，应该是 as the world is becoming increasingly competitive。（2）no one will excel if he is knowledgeable but lack of teamwork spirit 中，lack 一词的用法出现错误，lack of 应该是 lacks。注意 lack 是及物动词，只有作名词的时候才用"for lack of..."（因为缺少……）。（3）This can be made up by attending traditional classes and do collaborative assignments with classmates. 这句严格讲是病句，do 应该为 doing，与 attending 并列。（4）thus better themselves comprehensively 属于中式思维，意思表达不太清楚。

第四段：Learning at home from Internet can not raise students' awareness of being a moral person, which may bring about indifference to society. This is less <u>possible</u> to happen in a traditional school, where there are all kinds of extra-curricular activity, volunteer work, <u>for instance</u>, to help build up their sense of responsibility to society and sympathy to others.

【修改】Learning alone at home from the Internet is not a good way of fostering students' sense of morality, which may bring about their indifference to others. However, this is less likely to happen in the traditional school, where there are all kinds of extra-curricular activities, volunteer work, among others, to help students build up their sense of responsibility for society and sympathy to others.

【点评】本段错误不多。（1）增加了 however，使两句之间的转折关系更清楚。（2）possible 改为 likely，搭配为 it is less likely to happen。（3）for instance 改为 among others，表示列举。

第五段：In general, <u>although the Internet is convenient to acquire knowledge</u>, I do not think schooling will disappear <u>because of the meaning of education</u>. Learning online can only be a complement rather than a substitute.

【修改】To conclude, although the Internet provides a more convenient way of learning things, I do not think schools will disappear because they do have a role to play in education. Learning online can only be a complement rather than a substitute.

【点评】（1）although the Internet is convenient to acquire knowledge 表达不清楚，主语和谓语的搭配不太合适。此处是说 the Internet 学习知识更方便？这显然不合逻辑。应该是 the Internet 提供了一个更方便的学习方式。（2）because of the meaning of education 表达也不太清楚。（学校不会消失）是因为教育的意义？应该是说，（学校不会消失）是因为学校在教育中有自己的功能。原文的表达过于中式思维，看起来好像是那么回事，但写成英语就不清楚了。

8.3 简洁明快是好作文的标志

莎士比亚曾经说过，brevity is the soul of wit，也就是说，最大的智慧就在于简洁明快。诚然，现代英语早已摆脱了维多利亚时代英语的矫揉造作，力求思维的直接和表达的简洁。然而，由于受汉语的影响，很多同学在写英语的时候往往难以做到直接和简明，思想兜来兜去，语言翻来覆去，读起来很不顺，从而导致失分。

题目

In a number of cities, some people think it is necessary to spend large sums of money on constructing new railway lines for very fast trains between cities. Others believe the money should be spent on improving existing public transport. 修建新铁路好还是改善现有交通好？

学生习作

The public transport, doubtlessly, is indispensable to connect each other from various places. To make the cross-city journey more time-saving and convenient, some people argue that the government spending in infrastructure investment should emphasize on building new lines for high-speed trains. Others believe that it's acceptable to improve the current public transport. From my point of view, actually, it's a more attractive option to construct new railway lines for express trains.

The first obvious benefit for the second option is that it takes less money to improve the existing public transport system than to establish completely new lines for more advanced trains. To construct new lines, the government has to spend a large amount of money from the very first beginning. Such investment is not needed to improve the current public transport system. However, I think the first option is still a desirable choice. Even though it's definitely more expensive to build new lines and purchase high-speed trains. The money is worthwhile when the citizens can be more satisfied about the trains with latest technology, when the citizens do not have to spend that much precious time on the commuting. As an old saying goes, time is money. They earn more time thanks to government's generous investment on public transport. Instead of wasting their time on the road, they can have more freedom in time management.

The second obvious benefit for the second option is that it takes less time to improve the existing public transport system than to establish completely new lines for faster trains. It's no easy thing to design and construct new lines and it's quite reasonable to assume that it might take years to work on the project. However, in spite of the advantages of the second option, the first option is still a more considerate one. We have to admit that improvement is less time-consuming than construction but it's hard to identify how to improve the current system, would the improvement an effective one, can the improvement solve the emerging demand for people going out. With a through consideration of the above factors, we'd rather design new lines and buy qualifying trains at first.

To spend large sums of money on constructing new railway lines for very fast trains between cities is the most effective solution which enables citizens to have more freedom when they go out.

评分：6

总评：结构清楚，切题有逻辑，能用英语表达思想，词汇基本正确，语法基本正确。但是，语言使用不够灵活，显得比较呆板，重复表达现象不少，几个地方有较大语法错误和词汇使用不当之处。另外，文章写得过长，有些地方行文啰唆。

逐句修改

第一段：The public transport, doubtlessly, is indispensable to connect each other from various places. To make the cross-city journey more time-saving and convenient, some people argue that <u>the government spending in infrastructure</u>

investment should emphasize on building new lines for high-speed trains. Others believe that <u>it's acceptable to improve</u> the current public transport. From my point of view, actually, <u>it's a more attractive option to construct</u> new railway lines for express trains.

【修改】The public transport is doubtlessly very important in our life. To make the inter-city journey more time-saving and convenient, some people argue that the government should spend as much as it can building new lines for fast trains, while others believe it is better to improve the current transport system. In my view, constructing new high-speed railway lines is the more attractive option.

【点评】（1）作为开头段，原文太长了。（2）画线的几个句子虽然从语法上讲基本正确，但写得非常啰唆，不简练。（3）"it's acceptable to improve…"中的acceptable使用并不准确，advisable更准确，或者用更简单准确的better。（4）"it's a more attractive option to construct…"这个句型与前面一个句型完全相同，一般不将两个完全相同的句型放在一起，读起来显得很呆板。

第二段：The first obvious benefit for the second option is that it takes less money to improve the existing public transport system than to establish completely new lines for more advanced trains. To construct new lines, the government has to spend a large amount of money from the very first beginning. Such investment is not needed to improve the current public transport system. However, I think the first option is still a desirable choice. <u>Even though it's definitely more expensive to build new lines and purchase high-speed trains.</u> <u>The money is worthwhile when the citizens can be more satisfied about the trains with latest technology, when the citizens do not have to spend that much precious time on the commuting.</u> As an old saying goes, time is money. They earn more time thanks to government's generous investment on public transport. Instead of wasting their time on the road, they can have more freedom in time management.

【修改】Obviously, improving the existing transport system is much cheaper than constructing new railway lines, which will cost a large sum of the government budget. But I believe the money spent here is worthwhile because the fast train system will save the citizens much precious time. For instance, travelling from Guangzhou to Beijing by the fast train takes less than seven hours in contrast to more than 20 hours by the traditional train. So, instead of wasting their time on the road, people can enjoy more freedom in their time management.

【点评】本段重点讲高速铁路可以节约人们很多宝贵时间。（1）原文显得过于重复啰唆，思维不直接。应该学会直接思维，这样才能使文章显得更加轻快、通顺。（2）Even though it's definitely more expensive to build new lines and purchase high-speed trains. 这是一个破碎句，句号应该改为逗号。（3）The money is worthwhile when the citizens can be more satisfied about the trains with latest technology, when the citizens do not have to spend that much precious time on the commuting. 本句中，第二个 when 前应该加 and。（4）笔者在修改文中增加了一个例子来具体证明 fast train 是如何节约人们时间的。在写作中适当增加此类例子可以增加说服力，也可以让行文显得更加灵活、生动、具体。

第三段：The second obvious benefit for the second option is that <u>it takes less time to</u> improve the existing public transport system than to establish completely new lines for faster trains. <u>It's no easy thing to</u> design and construct new lines and <u>it's quite reasonable to</u> assume that it might take years to work on the project. However, in spite of the advantages of the second option, the first option is still a more considerate one. We have to admit that improvement is less time-consuming than construction but <u>it's hard to</u> identify how to improve the current system, would the improvement an effective one, can the improvement solve the emerging demand for people going out. With a <u>through</u> consideration of the above factors, we'd rather design new lines and buy qualifying trains at first.

【修改】Another reason why people support the improvement option is that it is less time-consuming. Designing and constructing new lines is never easy, which may take years to complete. However, how to improve the current system and make it effective to meet the ever increasing demand of people for travelling is perhaps a more difficult issue. The re-planning and re-construction usually involve more complicated factors than building something that is completely new.

【点评】本段论述改进现有交通系统其实也很难，虽然可能更节约时间。（1）原文啰唆，重复表述多，不简洁。（2）原文句式重复太多，"it is... to..."句型反复使用到令人无聊的地步，考生在写作训练中要找到办法改变这一写作习惯。（3）through 应该是 thorough。

第四段：To spend large sums of money on constructing new railway lines for very fast trains between cities is the most effective solution which enables citizens to have more freedom when they go out.

【修改】To conclude, constructing new railway lines for very fast trains is a much preferable solution to the transport problem between cities. Though it may be more money and time costly, a new fast train railway will give people more freedom and convenience when they travel.

【点评】总结段应该对原文进行恰当总结。

8.4 准确把握题目要求是好作文的前提

笔者一直都在强调，写好雅思作文要做到思路清晰，语言流畅。很多同学的语言基础很好，往往在阅读和听力中取得高分，但写作老是"败走麦城"。发生这种情况的原因可能是多种多样的，其中有一个原因可能被很多同学忽略，那就是没有准确把握题目要求。本书多次提醒考生，要完整理解雅思考试作文题目中的要求，并对其中所有观点给予回应（同意还是不同意）。

题目

Some countries achieve international sporting success by building specialized facilities to train top athletes instead of providing sports facilities that everyone can use. Do you think it is a positive or negative development? 专业体育还是大众体育？

学生习作

In order to achieve success in international sports games, some countries put great investment for the top athletes rather than the individuals. However, whether this policy can bring optimistic effects to people has been a controversial issue. In my view, specialized facilities for excellent athletes can have positive impacts on sports industry.

To begin with, focusing on specialized facilities can be beneficial to sports development of many nations. This is because international sporting success always mainly relies on the top athletes, and only professional training and specialized facilities can inspire potential abilities, helping them perform well in the global competitions. Meanwhile, it will attract public's attention correspondingly, and then encourage them to participate in the sports. For example, Yao Ming achieved great success in National Basketball Association, which stimulated massive interest in playing basketball for most ages people in China. According to official statistics, there are approximately two million basketball player. As a result, this kind of sports has been the most popular activity in this country. Therefore, personal success can facilitate the sports development of a country.

In contrast, it is also true that government should provide ordinary people with access to sports facilities. Basically, with the improvement of living standard nowadays, individuals lay more emphasis on outdoor sports rather than work only. Hence, the administration should not neglect the needs of citizens, and build more public facilities for them because countries offer specialized facilities with public money.

In conclusion, specialized facilities are essential for top athletes to fight for honor in the international events. In addition, the nations should also not ignore the demands of individuals for sports.

评分：6

总评：具有用英语来表达思想的能力，也具有一定的逻辑思考能力。文章有连贯性，词汇不错，语法也比较正确（尽管有相当多的小错误）。本文的最大问题是结构不够合理，段落长短分配不合理，对题目中观点的回应不够准确完整，尤其是没有充分回应"不为大众提供体育设施"这个部分（没有针对这个部分表达自己的观点和进行论证）。

逐句修改

第一段：In order to achieve success in international sports games, some countries <u>put great investment for</u> the top athletes rather than the individuals. <u>However, whether this policy can bring optimistic effects to people has been a</u>

controversial issue. In my view, specialized facilities for excellent athletes can have positive impacts on sports industry.

【修改】In order to achieve success in international sports games, some countries spend a great deal of budget on specialized facilities for top athletes rather than on the sports facilities for the general public. In my view, while this practice will bring some short-term positive benefits to the sports industry, it will also cause many problems.

【点评】（1）"put great investment for..."是不准确的表达法。（2）However, whether this policy can bring optimistic effects to people has been a controversial issue. 这句话是典型的模板，对上下文没有任何贡献，反而可能被考官认定为模板而导致丢分，建议删除。（3）从作文后面的讨论来看，本文并不是完全赞同题目中的观点，而是一个双边讨论的结构，因此，在第一段的结尾不宜如此明确地支持一方观点。修改文用 while 来引导双方观点。

第二段：To begin with, focusing on specialized facilities can be beneficial to sports development of many nations. This is because international sporting success always mainly relies on the top athletes, and only professional training and specialized facilities can inspire potential abilities, helping them perform well in the global competitions. Meanwhile, it will attract public's attention correspondingly, and then encourage them to participate in the sports. For example, Yao Ming achieved great success in National Basketball Association, which stimulated massive interest in playing basketball for most ages people in China. According to official statistics, there are approximately two million basketball player. As a result, this kind of sports has been the most popular activity in this country. Therefore, personal success can facilitate the sports development of a country.

【修改】To begin with, providing specialized facilities for top athletes can be beneficial to the overall sports development of a nation. This is because international sporting success always relies on the top athletes, and the professional training and specialized facilities can help them perform well in the global competitions. The gold medals they win, in turn, will attract the attention of the general public, especially the young people, and encourage them to participate in sports. For example, Yao Ming's great success in the National Basketball Association has stimulated massive interest in basketball in China and according to official statistics, has drawn approximately two million Chinese people to the basketball court, making basketball the most popular sports in this country.

【点评】（1）本段论证思路问题不大，先给出主题句，然后解释主题句，最后提供一个恰当的例子。修改文仅仅调整了一些语句，使行文更加简洁、流畅、准确。（2）focusing on specialized facilities 不准确，应该是 providing specialized facilities。（3）inspire potential abilities 搭配不恰当，对这类没有把握的表达，建议谨慎使用，或者放弃不用。（4）meanwhile 这个连接词使用不恰当。这里的逻辑是，specialized facilities 可以帮助 top athletes 在全球比赛成功，而这**反过来**会促进一个国家的体育产业，而不是这**同时**会促进一个国家的体育产业。也就是说，运动员的成功与国家体育产业的发展不是并列关系，而是因果关系，因此连接词应该是 in turn，不是 meanwhile。（5）本段用姚明的例子来证明一个运动员的成功可以带动整个体育产业，这是很恰当的。但习作中，这个举例共占用了 3 句话，显得比较零碎。**雅思高分作文的举例一般用高度浓缩的 1—2 句**。（6）本段已经很长，最后一句段落总结可以删除。

第三段：In contrast, it is also true that government should provide ordinary people with access to sports facilities. Basically, with the improvement of living standard nowadays, individuals lay more emphasis on outdoor sports rather than work only. Hence, the <u>administration</u> should not neglect the needs of citizens, and build more public facilities for them because <u>countries offer specialized facilities with public money</u>.

【修改】However, the benefits gained from the success of top athletes may be reduced if there are not enough sports facilities for the general public. Take Yao Ming again for example. When thousands of youngsters are inspired by his success and feel the need to play basketball, only to find that they do not have a basketball court, then, what is the use of Yao Ming's success? Meanwhile, without millions of people playing basketball, the chances of a country finding a basketball star like Yao Ming would be very small. For these reasons, the government should try to provide adequate sports facilities for the public, not just for the few top players.

【点评】（1）本段应该对题目中的"不给大众提供足够的运动设施"进行回应。如果大众没有运动设施，即使受到顶级运动员的鼓舞，也没有办法参加运动；同时，没有大众参与运动，出现顶级运动员的机会也很小。因此，给大众提供运动设施非常重要。遗憾的是，习作仅仅提出"政府应该给大众提供运动设施，因为随着生活水平的提高，人们更强调户外运动了"。这个回应没有准确抓住题目的要求，没有分析"不给大众提供足够的运动设施"可能带来的问题。（2）administration 的意思是"当局"，比如 Obama administration、Trump administration，是一个政治学概念，用在这里不合适。（3）countries offer specialized facilities with public money 表达不清，是雅思写作中应该极力避免的大错误。

第四段：In conclusion, specialized facilities are essential for top athletes to fight for honor in the international events. In addition, the nations should also not ignore the demands of individuals for sports.

【修改】In conclusion, providing specialized facilities for top players enables them to win honour in international events and promote a country's sports industry, but enough sports facilities for all people are also important. After all, what really matters is the health of all people, rather than the success of a few top athletes.

【点评】习作结尾相当weak。首先，这个结尾没有突出"体育产业"，而"体育产业"恰恰是习作第二段的核心词汇。其次，习作采取的是双边讨论结构，应该在结尾体现出自己的观点或倾向，但本习作仅仅指出提供专业设施和满足大众需求都重要，而没有自己明确的观点。修改文则突出了为大众提供运动设施的重要性，因为"最重要的是所有人的健康，而不是个别顶级运动员的成功"。

8.5 注意标点符号

在雅思写作考官给定的评分细则里，经常出现"本作文的标点符号使用有不少问题"的评语。很多同学不太明白这个标点符号问题究竟指的是什么。其实，对中国学生而言，标点符号问题往往出现在该用句号的时候却用逗号，从而造成所谓的流水句（run-on sentence）。流水句写得多了，分数也会无可奈何随之流走，非常可惜。

很麻烦的是，中国学生中英语流水句现象非常普遍，而且难以根除。笔者曾经在某个作文班一开始时就与学生打赌：课程结束之后，如果学生的英语作文完全根除了流水句，那笔者就请全班吃饭！学生们都发誓不犯这个错误。但到最后，笔者还是在学生的作文中发现了两例十分典型的流水句。这两句让全班其他同学的努力付之东流。那么，为什么中国学生非常容易写出英语流水句来呢？究其原因，还是因为中文语法的影响。中文里使用流水句完全是自然、合理的！随便摘录一句中文，"我们要保护环境，这很重要"。我们一般在这句中使用逗号，而不会使用句号。但若按照中文将这句转化为英语 "We should protect the environment, this is important." 那就是标准的流水句了，因为 We should protect the environment 已经是一个完整的句子，而 this is important 也是一个完整的句子，两个完整的句子之间必须要有连接词来表达它们之间的关系，这才符合英语语法要求。因此，这个句子可以按照以下方式修改：

① We should protect the environment. This is important.

② We should protect the environment, and this is important.

③ We should protect the environment, which is important.

题目

Some people think that a sense of competition in children should be encouraged. Others believe that children who are taught to co-operate rather than compete become more useful adults. Discuss both these views and give your own opinion. 竞争还是合作？

学生习作

With the development of interaction between human beings, sense to deal with fierce competitions have become the most important thing for education in many schools. However there are still some of people insisting that cooperating with others can makes children more useful when they grow up. In the following essay, both of views of education would be discussed and my own opinion would be given.

Students in schools are suffering under lager pressure of competition, from this, teachers and parents are all encouraging students to develop their sense of competition. As a result, children could realize that they have to study very well in order to get to a famous university and finally be employed by a well paid company. And this realization might encourage teenagers to be diligent and work hard on study. Besides, developing children's competition sense provides a "warm up" for their future job, when they get to work, competitions are more intense and unavoidable. The earlier children develop the sense of competition the better they can fit in the working environment.

By contrast, only competition is not enough to train a children into useful adults when they grow up, corporation is also extremely important. First, corporation can insure the quality of the product they made which the diversity of students could provide better and all-round ideas. As a result, the decision made by a team is more reliable and more feasible. Second, working as a team can also help children develop their skills of communication and they can understand other better. This could foster children into a useful person when they start to work the society.

Conclusively, although competition sense is very necessary, the usage of corporation cannot be ignore. So teachers should improving the sense of competition of students while developing their skills to corporate.

评分：5.5

总评：具有一定的英语表达能力，能用英语表达观点并对其进行一定程度的论证，逻辑基本清楚（个别地方模糊），词汇能达意（有不少错误），句型能传达思想（有较多错误，个别地方影响读者理解）。需要在语言表达准确度上进一步努力。

逐句修改

第一段：<u>With the development of interaction between human beings</u>, sense to deal with fierce competitions have become the most important thing for education in many schools. However there are still some of people insisting that cooperating with others <u>can makes</u> children more useful when they grow up. <u>In the following essay</u>, both of views of education would be discussed and my own opinion would be given.

【修改】As the interaction among people increases day by day, many schools have regarded it as the most important thing to develop children's sense of competition. However, some people still insist that cooperation with others makes children more useful when they grow up. In my view, sense of competition and cooperation are equally significant for children's growth.

【点评】（1）作为开头段，基本合格，笔者仅仅做了部分语言调整。（2）with the development of interaction between human beings 这个表达是很奇怪的，interaction 怎么会发展？显然，这里想说的是人类之间的交往越来越多，可改为 as the interaction among people increases。（3）can makes 是一个绝对的语法错误。（4）in the following essay 是个套路化表达，请尽量避免。应该直接表达观点。

第二段：<u>Students in schools are suffering under lager pressure of competition, from this, teachers and parents are all encouraging students to develop their sense of competition.</u> As a result, children could realize that they have to study very well in order to get to a famous university and finally be employed by a well paid company. And this realization might encourage teenagers to be diligent and work hard on study. <u>Besides, developing children's competition sense provides a "warm up" for their future job, when they get to work, competitions are more intense and unavoidable.</u> The earlier children develop the sense of competition the better they can fit in the working environment.

【修改】As students in school are suffering from huge pressure, teachers and parents are all encouraging students to develop their sense of competition. As a result, children realize that they have to study very well in order to get to a famous university and finally be employed by a well-paying company. And this realization might give impetus to teenagers to be diligent and work hard. Besides, developing children's sense of competition provides a "warm up" for their future job, since competitions will become more intense when they get to the job market. The earlier children develop the sense of competition the better they can fit in the working environment.

【点评】（1）本段写培养竞争意识的好处，原文基本意思表达清楚。（2）原文有一个不太好的倾向，在两个意思有关联的句子之间，不用连接词，从而让句子成为流水句。比如：

① Students in schools are suffering under lager pressure of competition, from this, teachers and parents are all encouraging students to develop their sense of competition.

前后两个独立句子之间用 from this 相连接，而且都是逗号，这是受汉语语法影响的结果。英语中，需要把两个句子用句号分开，或者把其中一个句子变成从句，可修改为：As students in school are suffering from huge pressure, teachers and parents are all encouraging students to develop their sense of competition.（把前面一句变成原因状语从句）

② Besides, developing children's competition sense provides a "warm up" for their future job, when they get to work, competitions are more intense and unavoidable.

这同样是个流水句，因为前面是一个独立句子，后面又是一个独立句子，两者用逗号连接，而且没有任何连接词。修改为：Besides, developing children's sense of competition provides a "warm up" for their future job, since competitions will become more intense when they get to the job market.（把后面一句变成原因状语从句）

第三段：By contrast, only competition is not enough to train a children into useful adults when they grow up, corporation is also extremely important. First, corporation can insure the quality of the product they made which the diversity of students could provide better and all-round ideas. As a result, the decision made by a team is more reliable and more feasible. Second, working as a team can also help children develop their skills of communication and they can understand other better. This could foster children into a useful person when they start to work the society.

【修改】However, only competition is not enough to train children into useful adults when they grow up, for cooperation is also extremely important. First, as the decisions made by a team are always more reliable and feasible, the products a team makes can be ensured in quality because together, they can provide better and all-round ideas. Second, working as a team can also help children develop their skills of communication and they can understand each other better. This could foster children into a useful person when they start to work.

【点评】（1）本段讲合作的好处。论述显得比较薄弱，而且有些句子无法读懂，逻辑也比较混乱，是本习作中最糟糕的一个段落。可以这样论证：合作可以让学生学会如何与人打交道，如何沟通协调，为了一个共同的目标做出自己的努力；将来学生在工作中往往不需要单打独斗，而是需要与人合作，因此合作尤其重要。（2）by contrast 不太合适，此处是转折，应该用 however。（3）第一句还是流水句，修改文中添加了 for 就规避了这个错误！（4）本段最大问题是这两句：First, cooperation can insure the quality of the product they made which the diversity of students could provide better and all-round ideas. As a result, the decision made by a team is more reliable and more feasible. 这里要讲的原因到底是什么？是说合作能够带来更可靠的决定，还是合作能够带来更好的产品？笔者的理解是合作首先带来更可靠的决定，然后才是带来更好的产品。写作中一定要理顺思想之间的关系，颠倒后就让人无法读懂。

第四段：Conclusively, although competition sense is very necessary, the usage of corporation cannot be ignore. So teachers should improving the sense of competition of students while developing their skills to corporate.

【修改】In conclusion, although the sense of competition is very necessary, the ability to cooperate with others cannot be ignored. So teachers should cultivate children's sense of competition and develop their skills to cooperate.

【点评】（1）结论段意思上没有大问题，但语法上错误不少。（2）conclusively 不常用，还是 in conclusion 更常见。（3）the usage of cooperation 这个表达非常奇怪，是"合作的用法"之义吗？（4）cannot be ignore 应该是 cannot be ignored。（5）should improving 应该是 should improve。

8.6 段落内逻辑须清晰明了

在英语写作课上，相信很多同学都听老师说过要给段落写主题句，也就是 topic sentence，然后整个段落再围绕这个主题句展开（当然展开的方式是多种多样的）。为什么要写主题句呢？是不是所有段落都必须要写主题句？笔者认为，主题句很重要，尤其对初学者而言，老师规定必须写主题句也是合理的，因为这样可以确保每个段落只表达一个明确的观点。如果没有主题句，很多学生就可能在一个段落里写出两个或两个以上观点来，从而破坏段落观点的唯一性原则。当然，对于写作老手来说，不写主题句，他一样能够让读者轻松 get（明白）他在段落中表达的唯一观点，但对多数以 6、7 分为目标的"烤鸭"而言，笔者强烈建议大家养成写段落主题句的习惯。

主题句出来之后，后面的句子就需要对主题句进行适度展开。这里需要注意两个问题：一是不能在同一段引入与主题句不同的新观点，二是句子之间要保持恰当的逻辑关系，共同为主题句服务。但恰恰在这个方面，很多同学都不太注意。写下主题句后，在后面的论证过程中似乎忘记了主题句，散漫随意地论证，结果造成段落内逻辑松散，甚至前后矛盾。这样的作文势必给考官造成极大的阅读困难，分数拉低就在所难免了。

题目

Many museums charge for admission while others are free. Do you think the advantages of charging people for admission to museums outweigh the disadvantages? 博物馆应该收门票吗？

学生习作

There is a widespread public interest in visiting museums. Some museums charge for entrance while some are free. This raises questions about whether the advantages outweigh the disadvantages. Considering the museums' cultural and educational importance, I strongly argue that it is quite fair for visitors to pay the admission fee.

Museums serve us differently for city leaders, museum professionals and the general public. It could be great places to spend out on weekends with family members and friends. It could be fun and enlightening for a family to look for entertainment on a Sunday afternoon. To city leaders, museums can be seen as way to increase sophistication of its inhabitants. To a museum professional, a museum might be seen as a way to educate the public about the museum's mission, such as civil rights or environmentalism. Museums are, above all, storehouse of knowledge. Admissions contribute to the normal running of museums and the funds of the frequent exhibits for the public. Some staffs are hired to manage the museums and maintain its daily clearness and tidiness.

Admissions may become the barrier to stop people from entering. Conversely, it encourages people to be better prepared before they get inside for a deep visit. Imagine that you are entering the Picasso Museum without knowing anything about him, what kind of impact could this museum have on you? You will definitely walk out of it with regret and wish you could have known him more. Such rare opportunity could be missed when the live history is brought out in front of you and you could benefit a lot by asking a lot of questions and exchanging ideas with the people around. Museums were initially established for the increase and diffusion of knowledge. In such sense, Museums' initial purpose is perfectly fulfilled.

Museums should be made accessible to the masses with entry charged in their affordable range in order to maintain the healthy running of the museums and we are contributing to the preservation of the human kind's valuable assets which stand up until now.

评分：6

总评：结构清晰，能围绕主题展开讨论，能用英语比较正确地表达自己的思想，词汇幅度不错，明显语法错误较少，标点符号方面没有什么错误。但是，段落内论证方式需要更加清晰，逻辑需要更加合理，句与句之间的关联需要更加紧密。从本篇习作看，稍加改进，作文得分还有较大提升空间。

逐句修改

第一段：There is a widespread public interest in visiting museums. Some museums charge for entrance while some are free. This raises questions about whether the advantages outweigh the disadvantages. Considering the museums' cultural and educational importance, I strongly argue that it is quite fair for visitors to pay the admission fee.

【修改】There is a huge public interest in visiting museums. Some museums charge for entrance while some are free. This raises questions about whether the advantages of charging an admission fee outweigh its disadvantages. Considering the museums' cultural and educational importance, I would argue that it is quite fair for visitors to pay the admission fee.

【点评】开头段引出话题，表明观点，中规中矩。修改不多。若要进一步提高得分，需要考虑在作文开头凸显个性化。比如，本题可考虑使用一个知名事件来引入话题：Just a few years ago, the Metropolitan Museum of Art in New York City went into a lawsuit because of the admission fee it charged. This raises questions among the public about whether museums should charge for entrance and if they should, how much the fee should be. Considering the museums' cultural and educational importance, I would argue that it is quite fair for visitors to pay the admission fee.

第二段：Museums serve us differently for city leaders, museum professionals and the general public. It could be great places to spend out on weekends with family members and friends. It could be fun and enlightening for a family to look for entertainment on a Sunday afternoon. To city leaders, museums can be seen as way to increase sophistication of its inhabitants. To a museum professional, a museum might be seen as a way to educate the public about the museum's mission, such as civil rights or environmentalism. Museums are, above all, storehouse of knowledge. Admissions contribute to the normal running of museums and the funds of the frequent exhibits for the public. Some staffs are hired to manage the museums and maintain its daily clearness and tidiness.

【修改】Museums serve multiple functions and for every one of them the visitors should pay. Spending out on weekends with family members or friends in a museum is enjoyable as well as enlightening. A history museum narrates stories about a nation's past, and an art museum brings the original drawings of many famous artists like Da Vinci to the visitors. So, for the thrilling experience and the precious knowledge, the visitors have every reason to support the museum by paying the admission fee. As we know, the day-to-day running and maintenance of a museum are rather costly, and the government budget is not always available, so the entrance fee from the visitors is sometimes extremely important for the survival of a museum.

【点评】本段讲人们为什么需要支付博物馆门票的第一个理由。原文区分博物馆对三种人的不同功能，却没有说清楚人们为什么要为这三种功能支付门票。作者似乎忘记了，本文要论证的是人们为什么需要买门票，而不是博物馆的功能。因此，本段的主题句就不合适，因为它突出的是博物馆的不同功能，而不是为什么人们应该买门票。接下来本段重点也不是在论证买门票的重要性，只是到了最后两句才回到段落的主题。这样，本段就显得脱离了本文的主题，使文章读起来缺乏逻辑，这个问题在下一段也同样存在。笔者在修改的时候，在第一句（也就是段落主题句）就点出 visitors should pay for the multiple functions of museums，这就扣到主题了。接下来主要从 enjoyable 和 enlightening 两个方面说明博物馆能够带给 visitors 什么（举历史博物馆和艺术博物馆为例）。最后再补充一句，说明游客的这些钱对博物馆的日常运营非常重要。

第三段：Admissions may become the barrier to stop people from entering. Conversely, it encourages people to be better prepared before they get inside for a deep visit. Imagine that you are entering the Picasso Museum without knowing anything about him, what kind of impact could this museum have on you? You will definitely walk out of it with regret and wish you could have known him more. Such rare opportunity could be missed when the live history is brought out in front of you and you could benefit a lot by asking a lot of questions and exchanging ideas with the people around. Museums were initially established for the increase and diffusion of knowledge. In such sense, Museums' initial purpose is perfectly fulfilled.

【修改】Admittedly, admission fee may become the barrier to keep people from entering the museum. Yet, quite paradoxically, the money visitors pay can actually improve their experience in the museum because they will make more preparations before their visit. If the visitors do not have to spend a penny, they will more often than not enter the Picasso Museum and then walk out of it without learning anything. This is, of course, a great shame because the visitors take the free admission for granted and have not checked for more information about Picasso and when they do get in, they cannot benefit from exchanging ideas with people around.

【点评】与第二段一样，本段大部分篇幅在讲去博物馆之前没做准备的情况，但没有联系为什么游客应该买门票，读起来感觉有些偏题了。其实，作者想表达的逻辑是清楚的。游客付钱后，就会认真准备。但是如果免费，他们就不准备，这样进去博物馆什么都学不到，因此，支付门票是好的。但这个逻辑是暗含的，没有明确出来。而修改文则把这个逻辑说得更清晰直接。

第四段：Museums should be made accessible to the masses with entry charged in their affordable range in order to maintain the healthy running of the museums and <u>we are contributing to</u> the preservation of the human kind's valuable assets which stand up until now.

【修改】Museums should be made accessible to the masses with entry charged in their affordable range in order to maintain the healthy running of the museums. By paying the entrance fee, we are contributing to the preservation of the humankind's most valuable assets.

【点评】最后结论段写得很精彩，但是在 "we are contributing to..." 前面应该加上 by paying the entrance fee。

下 篇
雅思写作
Task 1

第一章 图表题

1.1 概述

图表题是雅思作文 Task 1 中最常考的题型，其中最为常见的有饼状图、线型图、柱状图、表格，或者这些图表的混合。以有无时间推移变化为标准，我们可以把图表题分为**静态图**和**动态图**。那么，雅思考试为什么要设置图表写作题型呢？大家知道，欧美国家比较讲究用数据说话，很多文章中都有各种数据表格，这个题型就是促使大家学会看懂表格，并用冷静客观的语言来描绘表格中的数据。

因此，这个题型首先要求大家看懂图表，包括图表的起点、终点、上升或下降的趋势、显著的特征等，然后要求大家能够客观地描绘图表。有些同学画蛇添足，硬要给自己看出的趋势来个原因分析，甚至表达自己的价值和情感判断，这都是没有必要的，弄不好会被扣分。

1.2 静态图

静态图，即无时间推移变化的图表题，常见类型有饼状图、柱状图和表格。静态图的写作重点在比较关系上，包括最高点、最低点、平均值等，要掌握常见的比较句式和排序句式。

比如，2022 年 7 月 23 日雅思写作的 Task 1 涉及的是在 2012 年这个静态时间段里，美国各年龄段打游戏使用的设备情况。

This chart below shows percentage of people playing games with different types of electronic devices in the USA in 2012.

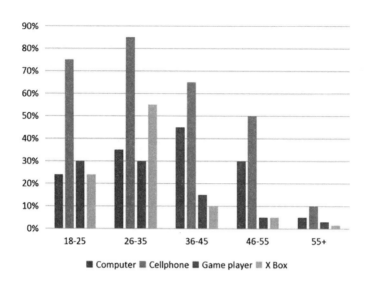

再如，2016 年 6 月 16 日雅思写作的 Task 1 涉及的是在 2009 年这个静态的时间段里，某欧洲国家移民的情况。

The following pie chart shows the reasons why people migrated from/to a European country in 2009.

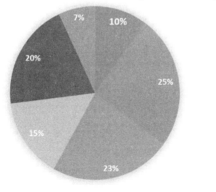

Reasons for immigrants to a European country in 2009

1.2.1 静态图作文必备表达

（1）最高值 / 最低值

数字 + of + 整体 + was / went on…

the figure for… was + 数字

the proportion of… was + 数字

the figure for… was the highest/lowest, at + 数字

A accounted for + 数字 + of + 整体

A accounted for the highest/smallest proportion of + 整体

国家 + has the highest/lowest figure for…, at + 数字

（2）其次

A is the second most popular, and it makes/takes up 26% of the total survey.

The proportion of foreign students from Asia was the highest, followed by that of Europe.

Asian students contributed the maximum proportion, and Europe ranked second.

Japan led other countries in life expectancy (81.2 years); Australia and Canada followed behind, 80.55 years and 80.2 years respectively.

（3）罗列（三个数据以内）

The figures for A, B, and C were similar, + 数字 1, + 数字 2 + and + 数字 3, respectively.

1.2.2 范文解析

题目 1

The table below gives information about the underground railway systems in six cities.

Summarise the information by selecting and reporting the main features, and make comparisons where relevant. Write at least 150 words.（《剑桥雅思 5》, Test 4）

Underground Railway Systems

City	Date opened	Kilometres of route	Passengers per year (in millions)
London	1863	394	775
Paris	1900	199	1,191
Tokyo	1927	155	1,927
Washington DC	1976	126	144
Kyoto	1981	11	45
Los Angeles	2001	28	50

解析

本题是关于六大城市的地铁情况，表格中的数据包括城市、开通时间、里程以及每年客流量。从开通时间看，比较重要的信息有，London 地铁于 1863 年（距今已经 160 年）最早开通，最晚的 Los Angeles 地铁 2001 年才开通，两者相距近 140 年。从里程看，比较重要的信息有，最长的 London 地铁 394 公里，而最短的 Kyoto 地铁仅仅 11 公里。而从客流量看，Tokyo 居首，达到 1.93 billion，其次是 Paris，再其次是 London，而其他几个城市的地铁流量较小，最小的是 Kyoto，仅为 45 million。

很明显，考生可以分三段，分别描写这三个维度的内部信息，揭示出最大值、最小值或平均数等相关信息。与此同时，考生还应对维度之间的显著信息加以比较。本题中，里程不是最长的 Tokyo 地铁每年的客流量远远超过其他地铁，这个维度之间的比较信息就非常显著，需要考生去描写。总之，图表类题目就是要找准描写的维度，然后**描写维度内和维度间的显著信息**。

范文讲解

The table shows the details **regarding** the underground railway systems in six cities.

图表作文的第一段通常从总体上说明图表的主要内容。该内容在题目中可以找到，但考生需要对题目表述进行改写。

几个主要词汇：表格 table，饼图 pie chart，柱状图 bar chart。无论表格、饼图还是柱状图，都可用 diagram 或 graph 来统称。

"本图显示 / 展示 / 说明 / 解释……"中，动词一般用 show 就可以了。其他可替换的动词包括 illustrate（图解）、provide data about sth（提供关于……的数据）、describe（描写）、reveal（显示，揭示）等。

regarding 相当于 about，是"关于"的意思。

London has the oldest underground railway system among the six cities. It was opened in the year 1863, and **it is already 160 years old. Paris is the second oldest**, which was opened in the year 1900. **This was then followed by** the railway systems in Tokyo, Washington DC and Kyoto. **Los Angeles has the newest underground railway system**, and was only opened in the year 2001.

本段从开通时间的维度描写图表，突出最早和最晚。

描述图表时，重要的一点是不能简单描写，而是要进行一定程度的归纳和比较。黑体字部分都是从表格中归纳出来的内容，比如"在这 6 个城市中，伦敦拥有最古老的地铁系统""它已经有 160 年了""洛杉矶的地铁系统最新"等。

语言上，要注意避免单调的重复。克服重复的办法包括词汇替换和句型转换。比如，London underground railway system was opened in the year 1863，接下来说巴黎地铁在 1900 年开通就不能再简单地重复写成 Paris underground railway system was opened in the year 1900，可通过句型转换来避免重复，如"Paris is the second oldest, which was opened in the year 1900"。当然，"开通"一词还可替换，比如"投入使用"（put into use），这样上句还可改成"Paris is the second oldest, which was put into use in the year 1900"。这样就在句型和词汇两个层面上实现了灵活替换。

In terms of the length, London, **for certain**, has the longest underground railway system. It **boasts** 394 kilometres of route in total, **which is nearly twice as long as the system in Paris**. Kyoto, **in contrast**, has the shortest metro system. It only has 11 kilometres of route, which is less than 1/30 that of London.

本段从里程维度来比较 6 条地铁，依然突出最长和最短。

本段使用了几个连接词组：in terms of 在……方面，for certain 无疑地，in contrast 与此相反。

boast 本来是"吹牛"的意思，但可用作及物动词，表示"拥有"，可用来替换 have 这样的动词。比如：Our school library boasts 3 million copies of books.

这里的难点仍然是要对表格中数据进行归纳分析。比如，说完伦敦地铁长 394 公里，就不能再说巴黎地铁长 199 公里了，而是要对这种关系进行分析重新表述，如"伦敦地铁长 394 公里，几乎是巴黎地铁的 2 倍长"，英语就是：London underground railways system boasts 394 kilometres of route in total, which is nearly twice as long as the Paris system.

Interestingly, Tokyo, **which only has 155 kilometers of route, serves the greatest number of passengers**, at nearly 2 billion passengers per year. The system in Paris has the second greatest number of passengers, at more than 1 billion passengers per year. The smallest underground railway system, Kyoto, serves the smallest number of passengers per year **as predicted**.

本段从客流量维度来比较 6 条地铁。在比较客流量时，范文在地铁长度和客流量之间进行了一个横向比较：Tokyo 地铁只有 155 公里长，但运送了最大量的乘客。这种维度之间的比较也是需要的，考生要找出维度之间的显著信息加以比较。本题中，不是最长的 Tokyo 地铁其乘客运送量却最大，这个信息就很显著，应该被考生描写出来。

interestingly（有趣的是……）这类副词很有效，表明学生理解数据之间的关系。

as predicted（和预计的一样）这个表达也很好表明了学生对数据的理解。

参考译文

表格显示了六大城市的地铁系统的详细情况。

在这六大城市中，伦敦的地铁系统是最古老的。它在 1863 年开通，已经有 160 年历史。巴黎其次，在 1900 年开通。接下来分别是东京、华盛顿和京都地铁系统。洛杉矶的地铁系统最新，在 2001 年才开通。

在长度方面，伦敦地铁系统无疑是最长的，它共有 394 公里里程，几乎是巴黎的 2 倍。与此相对照，京都地铁系统最短，只有 11 公里里程，仅不到伦敦的 1/30。

有趣的是，东京地铁系统虽然只有 155 公里里程，每年却服务了最多乘客，几乎达到 20 亿人次。巴黎地铁系统的流量居次，每年达到 10 亿人次以上。最短的京都地铁系统每年的客流量最小，这不出意外。

题目 2

The charts below show the main reasons for study among students of different age groups and amount of support they received from employers.

Summarise the information by selecting and reporting the main features, and make comparisons where relevant. Write at least 150 words. (《剑桥雅思 5》，Test 2）

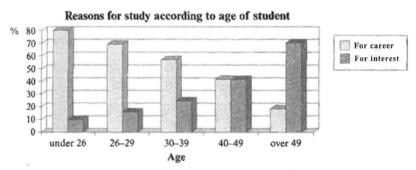

Employer support, by age group
(Time off and help with fees)

解析

本题由两个柱状图构成，前一个是关于不同年龄段的人学习的原因，后一个是关于雇主对不同年龄段的人学习的支持率。所以，这个题目的主体部分需要分两段来描写。就学习原因而言，一个明显的趋势就是，随着年龄逐渐增大，为了工作（career）而学习的人越来越少，而为了兴趣（interest）而学的人越来越多。具体来讲，26 岁以下，80% 的人都是为了工作而学，仅有 10% 是为兴趣而学的。此后随着年龄的增长，虽然为兴趣而学的人越来越多，为工作而学的越来越少，但直到 40—49 这个年龄段，为兴趣而学的人才赶上为工作而学的人，而超过 49 岁后，情况几乎发生了逆转，为兴趣而学的人达到 70%，为工作而学的人则降到不足 20%。在雇主对学习的支持方面，雇主对 26 岁以下的人给予的支持最多，近 70%，对 30—39 岁的人支持最少，仅 30% 出头。有趣的是，雇主对 49 岁以上的人学习也给予了较多支持，达到 40% 以上，高于他们对 30—49 岁年龄段的人的支持。

范文讲解

The first graph shows that there is a gradual decrease in study for career reasons as age increases. Nearly 80% of students under 26 years study for their career. This percentage gradually **declines** by 10%–20% every **decade**. Only 40% of 40–49 yr olds and 18% of over 49 yr olds are studying for career reasons **in late adulthood**.

本段直接描写第一幅图中为工作而学的情况。第一句指出总体趋势，后面给出具体数据：最高点（26 岁以下），最低点（49 岁以上），中间则每 10 年下降 10%—20%。注意，本段中的 "This percentage gradually declines by 10%–20% every decade." 不是原图给定的，而是从图表中分析出来的。

（1）**decline** 下降

（2）**decade** 10 年

（3）**in late adulthood** 壮年晚期

Conversely, the first graph also shows that study **stemming from** interest increases with age. There are only 10% of under 26 yr olds studying out of interest. The percentage increases slowly till the beginning of the fourth decade, and dramatically in late adulthood. Nearly same number of 40—49 yr olds study for career and interest. However 70% of over 49 yr olds study for interest in comparison to 18% studying for career in that age group.

本段描写为兴趣而学习的情况。最低点和最高点直接给出具体数据，其他给出趋势。注意，本段中 "The percentage increases slowly till the beginning of the fourth decade, and dramatically in late adulthood." 也是观察出来的趋势，最后一句则横向比较了 49 岁以上年龄段 study for interest 和 study for career 的数据。

（1）**conversely** 相反地

（2）**stem from** 来自……

The second graph shows that employer support is **maximum (approximately 60%)** for the under 26 yr students. It **drops** rapidly to 32% up to the third decade of life, and then increases in late adulthood up to about 44%. It is unclear whether employer support is only for career-focused study, but the highest level is for those students who mainly study for career purposes.

本段描写第二个柱状图，即雇主对不同年龄段学习的支持情况。雇主支持率有一个波动的趋势，对 26 岁以下的支持最大，接下来快速下降，然后又有所回升。描写完雇主支持率后，本段试图揭示本题中两个图之间的关系，即横向比较：雇主最支持的年龄段是为工作学习比例最高的年龄段（即 26 岁以下）。在有两幅图的题目中，考生在分别描述之后，最好能找到一个角度，揭示出两幅图之间的联系。

（1）**maximum** 最大的；最大值

（2）**approximately** 大约

（3）**drop** 下降

参考译文

第一幅图显示，随着年龄增长，为工作而学者逐渐减少。26 岁以下的学生中接近80%为工作而学。但此后每10年，这个比例就逐渐下降10%—20%。40—49岁为工作而学的只有40%，49岁以上只有18%是为工作而学习。

相反，第一幅图也显示，随着年龄增长，为兴趣而学的人逐渐增加。26岁以下，仅有10%是为兴趣而学。40岁之前，这个比例缓慢增长，但在壮年晚期大幅增长。40—49岁为工作和兴趣而学的人基本持平。然而，49岁以上为兴趣而学的人有70%，相较之下，那个年龄段为工作而学习的只有18%。

第二幅图显示，雇主对26岁以下学生的支持最大（大约60%）。在30—39岁，这个比例快速下降至32%，然后在壮年晚期又增长到约44%。雇主是否只支持基于工作的学习尚未可知，但他们支持程度最高的是那些主要为工作而学习的学生。

题目3

The pie chart below shows the main reasons why agricultural land becomes less productive. The table shows how these causes affected three regions of the world during the 1990s.

Summarise the information by selecting and reporting the main features, and make comparisons where relevant. Write at least 150 words. （《剑桥雅思5》，Test 1）

Causes of worldwide land degradation

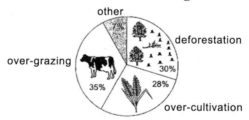

Causes of land degradation by region

Region	% land degraded by...			
	deforestation	over-cultivation	over-grazing	Total land degraded
North America	0.2	3.3	1.5	5%
Europe	9.8	7.7	5.5	23%
Oceania*	1.7	0	11.3	13%

* A large group of islands in the South Pacific including Australia and New Zealand

解析

本题由饼图和表格构成。饼图涉及全球土地退化的三大原因，包括过度放牧、砍伐树木和过度开垦。表格则涉及三大洲（北美、欧洲、大洋洲）土地退化的原因分布。可以看出，在全球范围内，造成土地退化的三大原因所占比例接近，比例最大的过度放牧占35%，过度开发最小，但也占28%。但是具体到每个洲，情况则有比较大的变化。比如，在北美，砍伐树木所占比例很小，只有0.2%，而在欧洲这个数据为9.8%。在大洋洲，过度开垦造成土地退化的比例几乎为零，但过度放牧则是主要原因。从土地退化总体情况看，北美只有5%，而欧洲则有23%，是北美的4倍以上。

范文讲解

The pie chart shows how farmland is degraded **globally**. According to the chart, overgrazing was **the leading cause** of land degradation worldwide, **accounting for** 35%. This is followed by deforestation, at 30%. Another important reason why land becomes less productive is over-cultivation, which **is responsible for** 28% of the total degraded land. The remainder (7%) is caused by other reasons.

本段描写饼图，说明造成全球土地退化的原因。写作中注意词汇替换和句型变化。这里讲土地退化的两个原因时，第一句用 overgrazing 作主语，句子为 overgrazing was the leading cause of land degradation worldwide，第二句用 another reason 作主语，句子为 "another important reason... is over-cultivation"，两个句子的主语发生了变化，句型也就跟着改变。

（1）**globally** 全球范围内

（2）**the leading cause** 首要原因

（3）**account for** 占……比例（= be responsible for）

The table compares the percentage of land degraded and the **various** reasons for degradation in three regions, namely North America, Europe and Oceania, during the 1990s. Of the three regions, Europe was the most seriously **affected**, with 23% of its agricultural land being degraded. This figure was higher than the percentages for North America and Oceania **combined**. In Europe, forest land clearance accounted for 9.8% of total degradation, whereas this only affected 0.2% of land in North America and 1.7% in Oceania. Europe also suffered from over-cultivation and overgrazing, at 7.7% and 5.5%, **respectively**. In contrast, Oceania has 13% of degraded land, and this was mainly caused by over-grazing (11.3%). The least affected region was North America, where only 5% of land was degraded, mainly **due to** over-cultivation (3.3%) and overgrazing (1.5%).

本段描写表格。首先将表格内容总结出来，表格比较了三个地区土地退化比例及其原因分布。接着具体描写这两个方面的内容。在比较三个地区土地退化情况时，范文写了这么两句：Of the three regions, Europe was the most seriously affected, with 23% of its agricultural land being degraded. This figure was higher than the percentages for North America and Oceania combined. 这是对表格中数据进行分析的结果。

（1）**various** 各种各样的

（2）**affected** 受影响的

（3）**combine** 联合起来

（4）**respectively** 各自（地）

（5）**due to** 因为，由于

In summary, overgrazing is the most serious threat to farmland worldwide and Europe was the biggest victim of land degradation in the 1990s.

本段将饼图和表格中最显著的两个特征揭示出来。

参考译文

饼图显示了全球范围内耕地退化的原因。如图所示，过度放牧是全球土地退化的首要原因，占 35%。接下来是砍伐树木，占 30%。另外一个降低土地生产力的重要原因是过度开垦，造成了 28% 的土地退化。其他原因占 7%。

表格比较了 1990 年代期间三个地区（即北美、欧洲和大洋洲）土地退化的比例及各种原因。在这三个地区中，欧洲受到的影响最为严重，23% 的农业土地都退化了。这个数据比北美和大洋洲比例之和还高。在欧洲，砍伐造成 9.8% 土地退化，而在北美，砍伐只占 0.2%，在大洋洲，占 1.7%。欧洲也深受过度开垦和过度放牧所害，分别占 7.7% 和 5.5%。与此相对，大洋洲有 13% 土地退化，主要是过度放牧所致（11.3%）。受影响最小的地区是北美，只有 5% 土地退化，主要是因为过度开垦（3.3%）和过度放牧（1.5%）。

总之，全球范围内，过度放牧是对耕地的最严重威胁，而在 1990 年代，欧洲是土地退化最大的受害地区。

1.3 动态图

动态图，即有时间推移变化的图表题，常见类型有线型图、饼状图、柱状图和表格。动态图重点是读懂图表中的动态变化关系和规律，包括趋势、最高点、最低点等，并用恰当的语言表达出来。

比如，2022 年 9 月 3 日的图表是关于 2011 年到 2015 年澳大利亚人均年消耗奶制品量及其变化的百分比情况。

The table below shows the consumption of four kinds of dairy products per person per year and their changes in percentage in Australia from 2011 to 2015.（220903）

	Milk (litre)	Cheese (kg)	Butter (kg)	Yogurt (kg)
2011	104	13.6	3.6	7.4
2012	106	13.4	3.7	7.4
2013	107	13.5	3.8	7.4
2014	106	13.5	3.9	7.4
2015	105	13.6	4	7.2
% Change	1%	0	8%	-3%

再如，2015 年 12 月 31 日的线型图是关于 1985 年到 2010 年间某两个国家用于生产有机食品的土地变化情况。

The line graph below shows the land used for organic crops in two countries between 1985 and 2010.

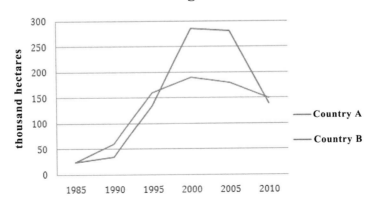

land for organic food

1.3.1 动态图作文必备表达

（1）趋势词汇

上升类动词：increase, rise, grow, jump, surge, shoot up, soar

下降类动词：decrease, decline, fall down, drop, sink, dip

波动类动词：fluctuate

持平类动词：remain the same, stabilize, remain stable, remain constant

修饰动词的副词：slightly 轻微地，slowly 缓慢地，gradually 逐渐地，steadily 稳定地，rapidly 迅速地，moderately 温和地/轻微地，significantly 明显地，sharply 明显地，dramatically 急剧地，drastically 急剧地

上升类名词：increase, rise, growth, jump, surge

下降类名词：decrease, decline, fall, reduction, drop

波动类名词：fluctuation

修饰名词的形容词：slight, slow, gradual, steady, rapid, moderate, significant, sharp, dramatic, drastic

（2）极值类词汇和表达

最高点：reach the peak/top/highest point, increase to the peak/top/highest point（所有上升类的动词都可以用来替换 increase）

最低点：reach the bottom/lowest point, drop to the bottom/lowest point（所有下降类的动词都可以用来替换 drop）

占了……比例：occupy, make up, take up, account for, represent, be responsible for

（3）倍数的表达方式

double 是两倍/大一倍

increase/decrease three times 增长到三倍/减少到 1/3

（4）大约的表达方式

approximately/about/around + 数字

（5）趋势的表达句式

变化主体/图画中主体 + 趋势动词 + 副词 + 数值 + 时间区间

The number of aged people over 65 increased significantly from 1 million in 1940 to 1.2 million in 2000.

there be + 形容词 + 表示趋势的名词 + in + 变化的主体 + 时间区间

There was a significant increase in the number of aged people over 65 from 1 million in 1940 to 1.2 million in 2000.

时间 + see/experience/witness + 表示趋势的名词 + in + 变化的主体 + 数值

The period from 1940 to 2000 saw an upward trend in the number of aged people over 65 from 1 million to 1.2 million.

表示趋势的名词 + be + seen/experienced/witnessed + in + 变化的主体 + 时间

An upward trend was seen in the number of aged people over 65 from 1 million in 1940 to 1.2 million in 2000.

1.3.2 范文解析

题目 1

The graph and table below give information about water use worldwide and water consumption in two different countries.

Summarise the information by selecting and reporting the main features, and make comparisons where relevant. Write at least 150 words. (211016)

Global water use by sector

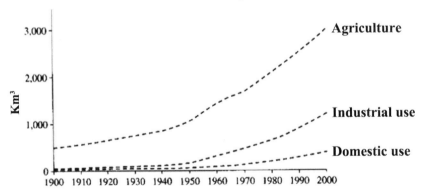

Water consumption in Brazil and Congo (Kinshasa) in 2000

Country	Population	Irrigated land	Water consumption per person
Brazil	176 million	26,500 km^2	359 m^3
Democratic Republic of the Congo	5.2 million	100 km^2	8 m^3

解析

本题是动态图和静态图的混合题。前面的线型图是 1900—2000 年间全球范围内农业、工业和家用三个领域用水变化状况；后面的静态表格是 2000 年巴西和刚果（金）两个国家的农业用水量。

线型图中，三个领域的用水普遍呈上升趋势，其中农业用水基数最高，上升也最快，工业用水和家庭用水在 1940 年前相差无几，但从 1950 年开始，工业用水明显开始高于家庭用水。表格比较了巴西和刚果（金）的农业用水情况，可以看出，无论是总用水量、耕地面积，还是人均农业用水，巴西都远远高于刚果（金）。

范文讲解

The graph shows how the amount of water used worldwide changed between 1900 and 2000. **Throughout the century**, the largest quantity of water was used for agricultural purposes, and this **increased dramatically from** about 500 km^3 **to** around 3,000 km^3 in the year 2000. Water used in the industrial and domestic sectors also increased, but consumption was **minimal** until mid-century. From 1950 onwards, industrial use grew steadily to just over 1,000 km^3, while domestic use rose more slowly to only 300 km^3, both far below the levels of consumption by agriculture.

本段描写动态线型图，重点是从 1900—2000 年三个领域的用水情况，首先是三个领域各自的变化情况，其次是三个领域的比较。

（1）**throughout the century**（在整个世纪中），这是用来替换 from 1900 to 2000 的。

（2）**increase dramatically from... to...** 从……激增到……

（3）**minimal** 极少的

The table illustrates the differences in agricultural consumption of water in some areas of the world **by contrasting** the amount of irrigated land in Brazil (26,500 km^2) with that in the DRC (100 km^2). **This means** that a huge amount of water is used in agriculture in Brazil, and **this is reflected** in the figures for water consumption per person: 359 m^3 compared with only 8 m^3 in the Congo (Kinshasa). With a population of 176 million, the figures for Brazil indicate how high agricultural water consumption can be in some countries.

本段描写表格，句式灵活，使用了"by doing..."（通过做……），"this means..."（这意味着……），"this is reflected in..."（这反映在……）等连接句型。

参考译文

上图显示了全球用水量在 1900—2000 年间的变化情况。在这个世纪，农业用水量最大，从 500 km³ 激增到 2000 年的 3,000 km³。工业用水和家庭用水也增长了，但是直到世纪中叶，这两个领域的用水量都非常少。从 1950 年开始，工业用水稳定增长到略高于 1,000 km³，而家庭用水增长更为缓慢，仅仅到 300 km³，两者均远低于农业用水水平。

表格对比了巴西（26,500 km²）和刚果民主共和国（100 km²）的耕地面积，并以此表明世界某些地区的农业用水差异。这意味着，巴西有大量水用于农业，反映在人均用水数据上，巴西为 359 m³，而刚果（金）仅为 8 m³。巴西人口 1.76 亿，这些数据说明，在某些国家农业用水量是多么巨大。

题目 2

The three pie charts below show the changes in annual spending by a particular UK school in 1981, 1991 and 2001.

Summarise the information by selecting and reporting the main features, and make comparisons where relevant. Write at least 150 words. （《剑桥雅思 8》，Test 2）［图见下页］

解析

本题有三幅饼图，分别描述一所英国学校在 1981 年、1991 年、2001 年的各项支出百分比。很显然，这里既需要静态描写各个年份的情况，又要动态描写趋势和变化。比如，保险支出一路飙高，教师工资起起伏伏，但都是学校支出的最大部分，而其他工作人员工资比例则一直下降，从 1981 年的 28% 降到了 2001 年 15%，几乎降了一半，2001 年设备支出大大高于 1991 年。

范文讲解

The pie charts show **expenditure** on **running costs** by a British school in 1981, 1991 and 2001.

本段以常规方式开头，从总体上描述三幅图的内容。

（1）**expenditure** 花费；消耗；费用；支出

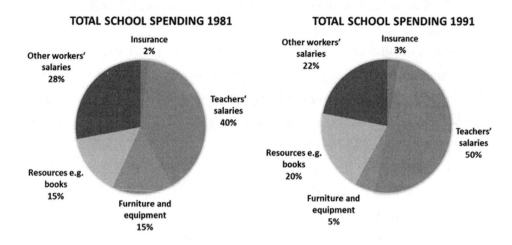

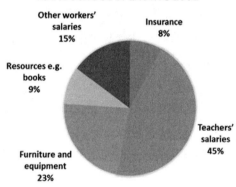

（2）**running cost** 运营成本

In all three years, the greatest expenditure was on teachers' salaries, which rose from 40% in 1981 to 45% **twenty years later**. **The period had also seen a significant increase in** spending on furniture and equipment, from 15% to 23%, despite a fall in 1991. Insurance, which only accounted for 2% in 1981, rose **fourfold** to reach 8% by 2001.

本段主要描写增长的部分。这也是此类图表作文解题技巧之一：可以先写增长的内容，再写减少的内容，这样文章会显得更有逻辑性和条理性。**越复杂的图表，越需要考生拟定一个清晰的描写顺序**。

（1）**twenty years later**（20年后），是用来替换 in 2001 的。

（2）**The period has also seen a significant increase in...**（这个阶段，……也大幅增长），这个句式值得模仿。

（3）**fourfold** 4 倍

On the other hand, other workers' pay fell from 28% to 15% of total spending in the same **time frame**. Although there was an increase in expenditure on resources such as books, which grew from 15% to 20% between 1981 and 1991, this figure dropped **steeply** to 9% by 2001.

本段讲下降的部分。

（1）**time frame** 一段时间

（2）**steeply** 大幅度地

Overall, during the period shown, there were increases in spending for staff salaries, equipment and insurance, but mostly **at the expense of** resources and other workers' salaries.

本段将增长的部分和下降的部分结合起来论述。

（1）**at the expense of...** 以……为代价

参考译文

这些饼图显示了1981年、1991年和2001年英国一所学校的运营成本花销。

在这3年中，最大的花销是教师工资，从1981年的40%涨到20年后的45%。这个阶段，在家具和设备上的花费也有大幅增加，从15%增加到23%，虽然1991年有所下降。保险方面，1981年只占2%，2001年增长到原来的4倍，为8%。

另一方面，在同一时期内，其他员工的工资在总体花费中从28%下降到了15%。虽然花在书籍这类资源方面的经费有所增长，在1981年和1991年期间从15%上涨到20%，但到2001年，这个数字急剧下滑至9%。

总体来说，在图中的时期内，花在教师、设备和保险上的经费都有所增加，但这些增加主要是建立在减少资源经费和其他员工工资基础上的。

题目 3

The table below shows the consumption of four kinds of dairy products per person per year and their changes in percentage in Australia from 2011 to 2015.

（220903）

	Milk (litre)	Cheese (kg)	Butter (kg)	Yogurt (kg)
2011	104	13.6	3.6	7.4
2012	106	13.4	3.7	7.4
2013	107	13.5	3.8	7.4
2014	106	13.5	3.9	7.4
2015	105	13.6	4	7.2
% Change	1%	0	8%	-3%

解析

这个图表显示的是从 2011 年到 2015 年这 5 年间，澳大利亚人均年消耗的乳制品量（包括牛奶、奶酪、黄油和酸奶）的变化情况。按照前面所说的写作原则，**需要先确定描写顺序**，那么这里应该遵从什么顺序呢？我们可以将 milk 和 butter 归为一类，因为它们都在增加，然后将 cheese 和 yogurt 归为一类，因为它们都没有增加，甚至在下降。一旦确定了写作顺序，接下来就能避免流水账式的写作，显示出考生对数据的理解和分析。

范文讲解

The table reveals how dairy products were **consumed annually** by every Australia in the five years from 2011 to 2015.

本段从总体上描写图表，难点是对题目语言的改写。题目中使用了 consumption，本段则将 consumption 引导的名词短语改换成以 consume 为谓语的从句，使句型发生变化。

（1）**consume** 消耗；吃掉

（2）**annually** 每年

The biggest change happened to the consumption of butter. In 2011, the **average** Australian consumed 3.6 kg butter per year, and this figure increased by 0.1 kg every year, reaching 4 kg in 2015. In other words, 8% more butter was consumed in 2015 than five years before. Milk also showed **an upward tendency**, although the increase, from 104 litre in 2011 to 105 litre in 2015, was much more **moderate** than butter.

本段描写 butter 和 milk 两种显示出增加态势的产品。首先说明 butter 的增加最快，然后具体描写 butter 如何增加，其中 this figure increased by 0.1 kg very year 是对图表数据进行分析后的结果。milk 也在增加，但横向比较，其增加幅度远不如 butter。

（1）**average** 普通的；平均的

（2）**an upward tendency** 上升的趋势

（3）**moderate** 温和的，适中的

On the other hand, the **consumption level** of cheese **in the given period** remained almost unchanged. It started with 13.6 kg in 2011, but dropped to 13.4 kg in 2012, but in the following three years, the figure returned to 13.6 kg. **In terms of** yogurt, the consumption even decreased from 7.4 kg in 2011 to 7.2 kg five years later, though the change took place only in 2015. **From 2011 all the way through 2014**, the amount of yogurt consumed was exactly the same, at 7.4 kg per person per year.

本段描写 cheese 和 yogurt。虽然在 2011 年和 2015 年，cheese 的消耗完全相同，但在 5 年间还是有明显变化的，2012 年下降，然后又上升。yogurt 则是保持了 4 年相同的消耗水平后，突然在 2015 年下降。

（1）**consumption level** 消耗水平

（2）**in the given period** 在给定的时间内

（3）**in terms of** 在……方面

（4）**from 2011 all the way through 2014** 从 2011 年一直到 2014 年

参考译文

该表格显示了从 2011 年到 2015 年的 5 年中，澳大利亚人均年消耗乳制品的情况。

最大的变化发生在黄油的消耗上。2011 年，澳大利亚人平均每年消耗 3.6 公斤黄油，这一数字每年增加 0.1 公斤，在 2015 年达到 4 公斤。换句话说，2015 年的黄油消耗量比 5 年前增加了 8%。牛奶也显示出了上升的趋势，从 2011 年的 104 升增加到 2015 年的 105 升，但这个增长比黄油要缓和得多。

另一方面，在这段时期内奶酪的消耗水平几乎保持不变。2011 年为 13.6 公斤，2012 年下降到 13.4 公斤，但在随后的 3 年中，这一数字又回到了 13.6 公斤。就酸奶而言，消耗量甚至从 2011 年的 7.4 公斤下降到了 5 年后的 7.2 公斤，不过这一变化仅仅发生在 2015 年。从 2011 年一直到 2014 年，酸奶的消耗量完全相同，为每人每年 7.4 公斤。

1.4 图表题练习

练习 1

The table below shows the total population and the proportion of males and females aged 15 and aged 75 in the UK from 1911 to 2011.

Summarise the information by selecting and reporting the main features, and make comparisons where relevant. （220820）

	1991	2001	2011
Total Population (million)	36.1	46.1	56.1
% of people aged 15	1.86%	1.48%	1.23%
Males	334,200	349,400	354,400
Females	335,700	333,900	333,700
% of people aged 75	0.23%	0.55%	0.70%
Males	34,100	160,200	181,300
Females	47,400	254,900	210,100

练习 2

The line graph shows the percentage of workforce in five different industries in Australia during 40 years between 1962 and 2002.

Summarise the information by selecting and reporting the main features, and make comparisons where relevant. （220806）

The percentage of workforce in five industries in Australia from 1962 to 2002

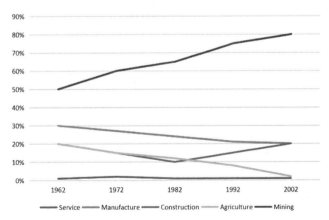

练习 3

This chart below shows percentage of people playing games with different types of electronic devices in the USA in 2012.

Summarize the information by selecting and reporting the main features and make comparisons where relevant.（220723）

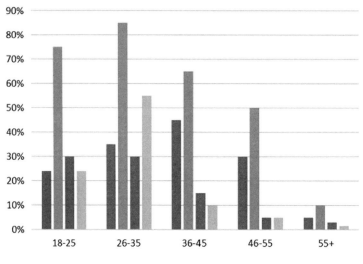

第二章　地图题

2.1 概述

地图题是雅思写作中比较少见的题型，一般 1 年能碰到 3—4 次，概率为 6%—8%。虽然地图题不是复习的重点，但考生还是应该充分掌握地图题的基本命题方式和解题技巧。雅思考试中的地图题大体分两种，一种为地理变迁题，一种为选址题。所谓地理变迁题，就是要求考生描述某个地理位置在某个时段的变化情况；所谓选址题，则是给出 2—3 个地址，让考生描述选择。无论是地理变迁题还是选址题，都要求考生掌握描写方位的基本技能。此外，考生还要注意以下几个方面：

首先，明确文章使用的时态，描写过去的地图要使用过去时，描写现在的地图要用现在时，描写未来规划的地图要用将来时。这个一定要十分清楚。

其次，有条理地组织主体段的内容。一般是先静态描写第一个地图，然后在描写第二个地图时要对比不同之处，并将差异描写出来。

最后，掌握本题型的重点词汇和句型，有效地把每个方位、每个地址描述清楚。

2.2 表示方位的必备表达

（1）A 在 B 的东方 / 西方 / 南方 / 北方

A is / lies / is located / is situated in/on/to the east/west/south/north of B. in 表 A 在 B 内部，on 表 A 和 B 接壤，to 表 A 和 B 分开。

比如：

A lies 120 km to the northwest of B.

A 在 B 西北部的 120 千米处。

A is in the south-eastern corner of B.

A 在 B 东南角。

（2）在河流或道路的南边 / 北边等

on the south/southern side of the river

在河流的南面

on both sides of the road

在道路两边

at the southern end of the river

在河流的最南边

（3）A 在 B 的对面

A is on the opposite side of B.

A 在 B 的对面。

A is opposite to B.

A 和 B 相对。

2.3 表示变化的必备表达

（1）原有事物

the original/previous/former garden

原来的 / 之前的 / 以前的花园

（2）原有事物尺寸上变大 / 变小，数量增多 / 减少，或者消失了

The size of the library has been enlarged/extended/halved/reduced by half.

图书馆的规模扩大了 / 延伸了 / 减半了 / 压缩了一半。

The number of homes has increased/risen/grown/reduced/decreased/ dropped/fallen/doubled/tripled to 500.

家庭的数量增加了 / 上升了 / 上涨了 / 压缩了 / 减少了 / 下降了 / 下跌了 / 增加了一倍 / 增加了两倍，达到了 500。

The farms completely disappeared / were removed.

农场完全消失了 / 给清除了。

（3）原有事物的形态发生了变化

A becomes B.

A 变成了 B。

A is transformed/reconstructed/redeveloped/converted/changed into B.

A 被转型 / 重建 / 重新开发 / 转变 / 改变成 B。

A is replaced/substituted by B. = A gives way to B.

A 被 B 给替换了。

（4）图形上新添事物

a newly-built road

一条新建的道路

A new car park was built / established / set up / constructed / completed and opened in the middle of B.

在 B 的中间，新建了 / 建起了 / 修建了 / 完成了 / 建完并开放了一个新的停车场。

A new IT centre has been added to the library.

图书馆增加了一个新的 IT 中心。

The year 2000 saw two additions to the land: a pond in the northern part and a vegetable garden on the opposite side.

2000 年，这块地新增了两个事物：北边的池塘，以及池塘对面的蔬菜园。

2.4 范文解析

题目 1

The diagram below shows the development of the village of Kelsby between 1780 and 2000.

Summarise the information by selecting and reporting the main features, and make comparisons where relevant.（060916）［图见下页］

解析

这里共有三幅图，涉及某个村庄在 1780 年、1860 年、2000 年的地理变化情况，题目要求考生描写其中包含的重要信息。可以看到，农田（farmland）和森林（woods）逐渐减少，到 2000 年时已经全部消失，但体育场地（sports

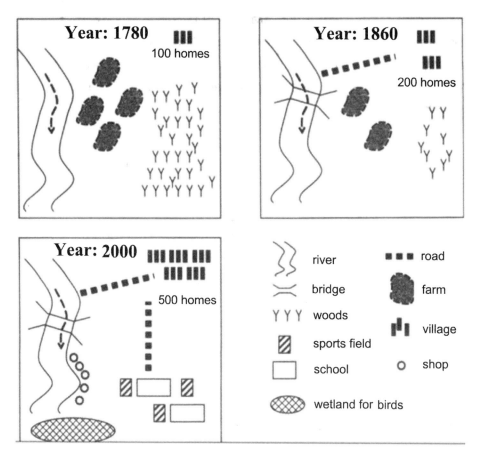

field）和商店（shop）则从无到有。在某种意义上，这种题与之前讲过的动态图表作文比较类似，都要求描写图形里面所包含的变化趋势，但动态图表多是数字，需要掌握数字上升下降这样的描写方法，而地图变迁题则要求描绘地理位置及其变化情况。

范文讲解

The three maps illustrate how the village of Kelsby changed from1780 through 1860 to 2000.

本段为引入段，对三幅地图所示内容进行总体概括。本段与图表题写作方法没有区别。

In 1780, Kelsby had only 100 homes. There was **a large expanse of woods** in the eastern part of the village and **four plots of farmland** in the centre. In the west was a river flowing from north to south.

本段静态描写 1780 年村庄的状况，应该掌握方位的表达，比如这里的 in the eastern part of the village（在村庄的东部）、in the centre（在中央）、in the west（在西部）、from north to south（从北向南）。同时注意，不能全部使用"there was... in..."这样的句型，应适当替换。比如本段中最后一句就不宜写：There was a river in the west flowing from north to south.

（1）**a large expanse of woods** 一大片森林

（2）**four plots of farmland** 四块农田

The year 1860 saw a doubling of the number of homes, but the size of farmland and woods was **halved**. In the same year, a bridge was **constructed** over the river and a road was paved linking the river to the **residences**.

本段描写 1860 年村庄的情况，注意比较 1860 年与 1780 年的差异。重要的差异是农田和森林减少了，同时有了一座桥，还有一条路连通河与住宅区。

"the year... saw..."是一个比较地道的表达法。比如：The 21st century saw the rise of China.（21 世纪见证了中国的崛起。）

（1）**half** 减半

（2）**construct** 修建

（3）**residence** 住宅

140 years later, the number of homes more than doubled to 500, but farms and woods completely disappeared. In their places, several school buildings and sports facilities were constructed at the south-eastern corner of the village, which were connected with the residential areas in the north **via** a newly-built road. Some shops opened up along the **river bank** and **a large stretch of wetland** for birds was established at the southern end of the river.

本段写 2000 年村庄的情况，尤其要注意与之前的情况进行比较。住户增加，农田和森林消失，有了学校和体育设施，还有了商店。140 years later 是用来替换 in 2000 的。

（1）**via** 通过

（2）**river bank** 河岸

（3）**a large stretch of wetland** 一大片湿地

参考译文

三幅地图显示了科尔斯比村庄从 1780 年到 1860 年，再到 2000 年的变化情况。

在 1780 年，科尔斯比只有 100 户人家。在村庄的东部有一大片森林，在中间有四块农田。西面有一条从北向南的河流。

1860 年，村里的住户增加了一倍，但是农田和森林的面积缩小了一半。在同一年，河上架起了桥，河流与住户之间铺了一条道路。

140 年后，住户增加了一倍多，达到 500，但是农田和森林完全消失了，取而代之的是几座学校大楼和体育设施，建立在村庄的东南角，通过一条新修的道路与北面的住宅区相连。沿河岸开张了一些商店，在河流的南端，建了一大片鸟类湿地。

题目 2

The maps show the changes of a small village from 1995 to present.

Summarise the information by selecting and reporting the main features, and make comparisons where relevant.（140405）

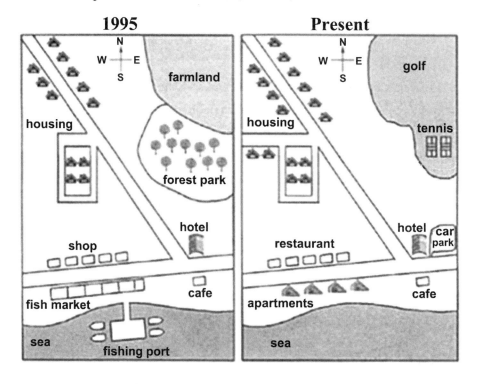

解析

本题同样要求描写一个村庄在不同时间的变化情况。首先应该静态描写该村庄在 1995 年的情况，然后描写现在发生了哪些变化。比如，1995 年的森林公园和农场现在已经消失，变成了高尔夫球场和网球场；1995 年的商店现在变成了餐馆；1995 年的海滨渔港和鱼市场已经不见，取而代之的是海边公寓，等等。

范文讲解

The maps reveal the changes of the village over the period from 1995 to present.

开头同数据型图表文章一样，对地图做概括性的描写。

In the first picture, the village was divided into three parts by two major roads. In the southern part, there was a fishing port on the sea, and a fish market, which was near the port, **was just located at** the south side of the major road. **Opposite to** the market, there was a block of shops sitting on the other side of the road. East of the shops, a hotel and a cafe were built at the **joint** of the two major roads. The northwest part was basically a residential area, and some of the houses were surrounded by a **rectangular** road. In addition, a farmland of great acreage occupied the northeast corner, while a forest park of similar size was established on the south of the farmland.

本段描写第一幅地图。首先说这幅地图被两条主路分成了三个部分，然后从南到北分别开始描述各个部分。这样写会比较有条理，但要注意避免文字和句型的重复。

（1）**be located at/in...** 位于……

（2）**opposite to...** 在……对面

（3）**joint** 交叉处

（4）**rectangular** 长方形的

In the second picture, the village has changed a lot. The fishing port has gone and the fish market is **replaced** by a block of apartments. Several restaurants also **take up the place of** the shops on the road side. Moreover, a car park is newly built to the east of the hotel. In addition, the housing area becomes larger and a branch road is built from the rectangular road to the west. Finally, a sports field for tennis and golf **occupy the place of previous** farmland and the forest park.

本段写村庄目前的情况，尤其要比较两幅图的不同之处，指出村庄所发生的变化，包括消失的建筑物、被替代的建筑物、新建的建筑物等。

表示"A被B替代"的表达法有 A is replaced by B、B takes up the place of A、B occupies the place of A、B is built in the place of A。

To conclude, these years have witnessed rapid development in the village.

结尾段，考生仅需重申村庄有变化的事实即可。

参考译文

两幅地图显示了村庄从 1995 年到现在的变化情况。

在第一幅图中，村庄被两条主路分割成了三个部分。在南边，有一个海滨渔港和一个靠近港口的鱼市场，市场的位置在主路的南面。市场对面是林立于道路另一侧的商铺。商铺的东面，两条主路的交叉处，建有一家旅店和一家咖啡店。西北边主要是住宅区，有些房子被长方形的道路包围。此外，一大片耕地占据了东北角，而在耕地以南则是一个面积与之相似的森林公园。

第二幅图中，村庄发生了很大变化。渔港已经消失，鱼市场也被公寓楼取代。几家餐馆取代了路边商店的位置。而且，在酒店东面，新建了一个停车场。此外，住宅区扩大了，从长方形道路朝西新建了一条支路。最后，一个网球和高尔夫运动场占据了以前耕地和森林公园的位置。

总之，这些年来，村庄取得了快速发展。

2.5 地图题练习

练习 1

The map below is of the town of Garlsdon. A new supermarket (S) is planned for the town. The map shows two possible sites for the supermarket.

Summarise the information by selecting and reporting the main features, and make comparisons where relevant. (《剑桥雅思 5》，Test 3)

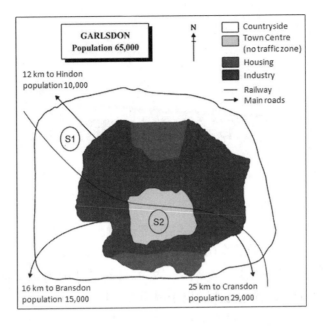

练习 2

The two maps below show an island, before and after the construction of some tourist facilities.

Summarise the information by selecting and reporting the main features, and make comparisons where relevant.（《剑桥雅思 9》，Test 1）

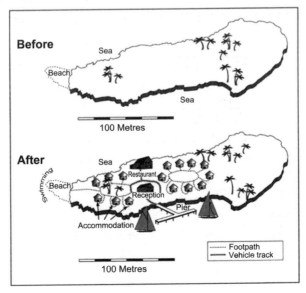

第三章 流程图

3.1 概述

雅思写作流程图属于冷门题型，一年大约能考 3—5 次，概率为 6%—8%。一旦考到，一些考生较为头疼，因为流程图跟其他数据图差距较大。流程图是纯文字的，以描述为主，属于说明文。相比之下，柱状图、饼状图、表格等数据图有数据可以进行分析和比较。同时，流程图所考内容往往也是各位"烤鸭"不太熟悉的内容，比如红砖的生产过程、蝴蝶的演变过程等。

比如，2016 年 5 月 28 日就考了流程图写作，是关于可可豆的加工过程。如果考生不太熟悉 press（压）、grind（磨）、refine（提炼）这些词汇，的确会有比较大的难度。

The diagram below shows the steps of processing cocoa beans.

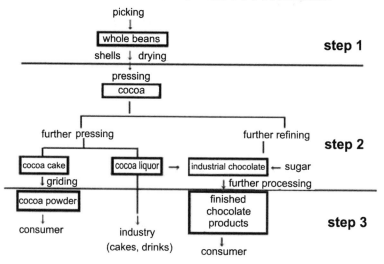

STEPS IN PROCESSING THE COCOA BEANS

写好流程图作文，需要注意以下几点：

按顺序描述，用好表示顺序的连接词。流程图不可避免地要说明过程的各个步骤和先后顺序。表示过程通常用 process 或 procedure，过程的各个阶段和步骤用 stage 或 step。在谈到第一个步骤时可以用连接词 in the first place、to begin with、in the first stage 等引出。进入中间的步骤时可以用 then、next、after this/that 等。最后一个步骤可以用 finally 或 lastly。当然，如果有一些平行的步骤也可以用 at the same time、meanwhile 等。

学会灵活使用被动语态。流程图表现的是客观的工艺流程或事物发展的过程，因此，要尽量避免用 we should / must / need to do sth 的主动语态，改为 sth should / must / needs to be done 这样的被动语态。被动语态和情态动词的恰当搭配，可以使文章显得更具有客观性和学术化色彩。

写好引言段和结尾段。在引言段和结尾段写作中可以适当进行过程的阶段划分和总结，使文章的构思上一个层次，摆脱"流水账"的俗套。

要善于"绕开"专业的概念表达。在流程图中，有时不可避免地会出现一些比较专业的概念，不会的时候要善于利用已知的简单词汇，试着把这些"专业"的概念用简单的方式表达出来。例如，不知道如何表达"房间通风"（ventilation）这个概念，可以用 air moving through the house 来说明，不知道如何说"斧头"（axe）和"锯子"（saw），就用 special tools 来绕过，虽然描述得不是很精确，但总比不写或写错了要好。

3.2 流程图首段必备表达

（1）The diagram shows the structure of...

这幅图显示了……的结构。

（2）The picture illustrates...

这幅图解释了……

（3）The whole procedure can be divided into... stages.

整个步骤可以分为……阶段。

（4）It mainly consists of...

主要包括……

（5）It works as follows.

其原理如下。

（6）It always involves following steps.

它总是涉及如下步骤。

3.3 描述流程 / 过程的必备表达

（1）firstly/secondly/finally 首先 / 其次 / 最后

（2）the first step is... / the next step is... / the final step is... 首先是……/
接下来是……/ 最后是……

（3）simultaneously 同时

（4）subsequently 后来

（5）after this stage 这个阶段 / 步骤之后

（6）in the course of... 在……过程中

3.4 范文解析

题目 1

The recycling process of glass bottles（090926）

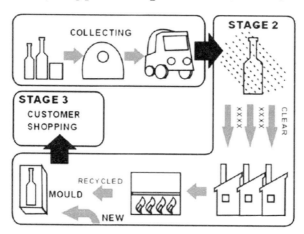

解析

本题是关于玻璃瓶的回收流程。首先要学会看懂流程图。这个玻璃瓶回
收流程的第一步是 collecting，也就是把废旧玻璃瓶收集起来；然后进入 stage

2，清洗后送到熔炉，高温煅烧，再用模具做成新的玻璃瓶；最后进入 stage 3，也就是让新的玻璃瓶重新进入市场流通。这就是玻璃瓶回收的整个流程。

范文讲解

This diagram **illustrates** the recycling process of glass bottles. The whole process is a **cycle** which can be divided into three main stages.

第一段与图表题和地图题没有本质区别，先总体概括图形的基本内容。与图表题和地图题不一样的是，流程图往往需要在这里概括出整个流程需要多少步骤。

（1）**illustrate** 说明，解释

（2）**cycle** 循环

In the first stage, used bottles are collected at a recycling point ready to be transported by a truck. **The second stage starts** in a cleaning plant, where these recycled bottles are sorted by colour into green, brown and clear ones and washed by high-pressurized water. **When the cleaning is done**, the bottles are conveyed to a glass factory where they are cut into glass pieces which are then poured into a furnace. **After being heated in the furnace**, the broken glasses are melted into liquid, which flows into a glass mould. Here glass liquid from other sources is added and **the moulding process takes place**. **In the final stage**, new, empty bottles are filled with liquid, then packed and dispatched to the supermarket ready to be picked by consumers. **At this point**, **a cycle has been completed** and **a new cycle will begin**.

本段详细描述玻璃瓶的回收过程。注意描写过程中连接词的使用。本段中出现的连接词有 in the first stage、the second stage starts、when the cleaning is done、after being heated in the furnace、the moulding process takes place、in the final stage、at this point、a cycle has been completed、a new cycle will begin。

注意被动语态的使用。本段多次使用被动语态，几乎每句都有。

参考译文

本图显示玻璃瓶的回收流程。整个流程是一个循环，主要分三个阶段。

在第一阶段，将旧玻璃瓶在回收点收集起来，以便用卡车运走。第二阶段开始于清洗车间，回收的玻璃瓶按颜色分拣成绿色、褐色和透明色，并用高压水清洗。清洗完毕之后，这些玻璃瓶被送至玻璃厂破碎成碎片，然后倒

进熔炉。在熔炉中加热之后，这些碎片玻璃被熔成液体，流进玻璃模具。这时倒入其他玻璃溶液，模铸流程开始。最后阶段，新的空瓶被装入液体，并打包派送到超市，供用户选购。至此，一个循环宣告结束，新的循环即将开始。

题目 2

The life cycle of silkworm and the procedure of silk cloth making（《剑桥雅思 6》，Test 3）

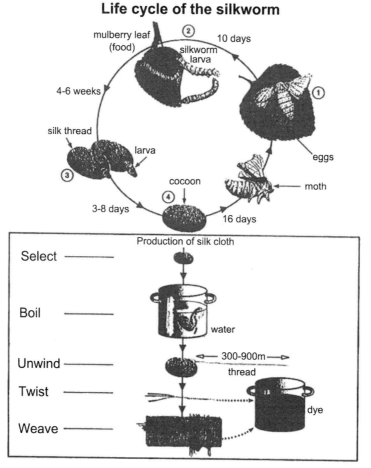

解析

本题由两幅图构成。上图是关于蚕茧的形成过程，下图则是关于蚕茧如何变成丝绸的过程。整个过程比较复杂，不可能每个步骤都非常完整地描述，因此，选择哪些关键步骤，如何将次要步骤一笔带过，就是本题的关键所在。

范文讲解

The diagrams illustrate the main stages in the life cycle of silkworms and the **procedure** of silk cloth making. From the diagrams it can be seen that the cocoons are necessary **raw materials** used for silk cloth production.

首先概述两幅图的主要内容，并阐明两幅图之间的联系，即蚕茧是生产丝绸所必需的原材料。当然，不是必须要写两幅图之间的关系。

（1）**procedure** 步骤

（2）**raw material** 原材料

In the first stage, eggs are produced by the moth and it takes ten days for each egg to become a silkworm larva that feeds on mulberry leaves. **This stage lasts** for up to six weeks until the larva produces a cocoon of silk thread around itself. **After a period of about three weeks**, the adult moths **eventually emerge** from these cocoons and the life cycle begins again.

本段描写第一幅图，即蚕茧的生产过程。注意图中的几个步骤如何被融入一个句子中表达。比如，本段第一句话就包含了三个步骤：蛾子产卵，十天后卵变成幼蚕，幼蚕吃桑叶。

（1）**in the first stage** 在第一个阶段

（2）**this stage lasts for...** 这个步骤持续……

（4）**after a period of about three weeks** 大约三周后

（5）**eventually** 最终；最后

（6）**emerge** 出现

When it comes to the production of silk cloth, once the cocoons are selected, they are boiled in water and the **threads** can be separated in the unwinding stage. Each thread is between 300 and 900 metres long, which means they can be twisted together, **dyed** and then used to produce cloth in the weaving stage.

本段描述蚕茧如何做成丝绸。众多步骤被融进两个句子中，每个句子中均有被动语态句。

（1）**thread** 蚕丝

（2）**dye** 染色

Overall, the diagrams show that the cocoon stage of the silkworm can be used to produce silk cloth through a very simple process.

本段为总结，并点明两幅图之间的关系。

参考译文

这两幅图解释了蚕生命周期中的主要阶段，以及丝绸的制作步骤。从图中可以看到，蚕茧是丝绸制作的必要原材料。

在第一个阶段，蛾子产卵，十天后，卵变成幼蚕，幼蚕吃桑叶。这个阶段可持续长达六周，直到幼蚕吐出蚕丝茧将自己包裹住。大约三周后，成熟的蚕蛾最终破茧而出，生命周期重又开始。

至于丝绸生产，一旦选出蚕茧，就将其置入水中煮沸，然后在抽丝阶段将蚕丝分离出来。每根蚕丝的长度在 300 米到 900 米之间，这意味着它们可以被拧在一起进行染色，然后在纺织阶段用来生产丝绸。

总体来看，这两幅图显示，通过非常简单的步骤，蚕在蚕茧阶段可以被用来生产丝绸。

3.5 流程图练习

练习 1

The diagram below shows the process of producing olive oil.

Summarise the information by selecting and reporting the main features, and make comparisons where relevant. （210116）

How to produce olive oil

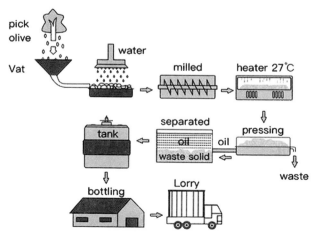

练习2

The diagram below shows the process for recycling plastic bottles.

Summarise the information by selecting and reporting the main features, and make comparisons where relevant. (《剑桥雅思 16》，Test4)

How plastic bottles are recycled

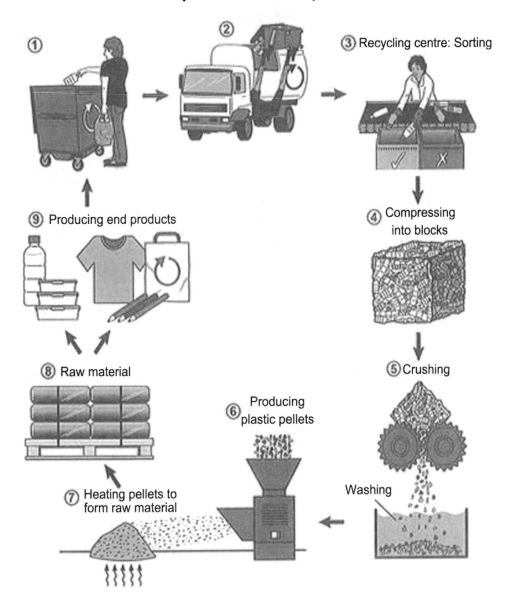

练习 3

The diagram below shows how electricity is generated in a hydroelectric power station.

Summarise the information by selecting and reporting the main features, and make comparisons where relevant. (《剑桥雅思 14》，Test 3）

Hydroelectric power station

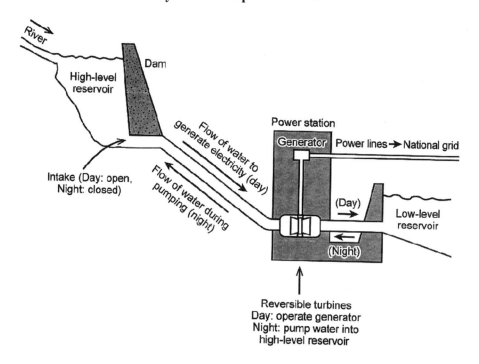